The Backwoods Preacher

Barlow

THE BACKWOODS PREACHER:

AN

AUTOBIOGRAPHY

OF

PETER CARTWRIGHT,

FOR MORE THAN FIFTY YEARS A PREACHER IN THE BACKWOODS
AND WESTERN WILDS OF AMERICA.

EDITED BY W. P. STRICKLAND.

REPRINTED FROM THE THIRTY-FIRST AMERICAN EDITION
WITH AN INTRODUCTORY PREFACE AND NOTES.

LONDON:

ALEXANDER HEYLIN, 28, PATERNOSTER ROW.

1858.

LONDON:

PRINTED BY WILLIAM NICHOLS,

32, LONDON WALL.

U

INTRODUCTORY PREFACE.

ENGLISH literature is rich in the department of autobiography, if the value rather than the number of its treasures be considered. France, indeed, has memoirs innumerable; but the great majority of them are tedious from their undue length, and worthless from their egregious trifling, while the few exceptions to this rule have a historical rather than a personal interest,—are strongly marked with the national character, but only slightly distinguished by individual traits. It is far otherwise with those charming productions of the English press in which we are accustomed to find the amusement of romance blended with the simpler interest of truth. Some few of the heroes of these narratives are typical of large and ordinary classes; but the most part are full of character, racy, humourous, and original;—and the memoirs of religious worthies are certainly not the most deficient in individuality and power.

Into this interesting class of English books we welcome the Autobiography of Peter Cartwright. To that position it has many high and some peculiar claims. The character of the author is so strongly marked, his will and courage so indomitable, that he would probably have attained distinction in any sphere; but it pleased Divine Providence to place him in that for which by nature he was best adapted, and to furnish him still more richly with those gracious aids which were equally necessary to direct and qualify his natural gifts. No man after reading this volume can hold a light or contemptuous opinion of Peter Cartwright. There is something in his character which extorts admiration, even when it repels sympathy; but there is much in common betwixt him and all his readers in this country. He speaks our Saxon language, maintains our Protestant faith, is bone of our English bone, and warm with the blood, not only of a man, but a brother. He is one of those brave men who have taken the traditions of Alfred into the wilderness of the Far West, and sown the seeds of our civil and religious freedom in a wider

A 2

area and under a broader sky. If we regard him merely as a pioneer of civilization, and estimate the strictly secular results of his career, we must form the highest opinion both of the man and his works. The Backwoods Preacher of America appears before us in a new and striking figure. Single in purpose, intent only on gathering lost sheep into the fold of Christ, he brings an ameliorating agency of the most various kind to soften the asperities of a semi-barbarous life, and to develope virtues and charities long deadened by hardship, isolation, and disgust. Hospitality is one of the first-fruits of this influence, an earnest and promise of all the rest. Where the preacher comes, all rudeness and opposition seem to melt before him. With a mixture of simplicity and boldness, very suitable to the messenger of God who seeks no interests of his own, he enters the house with a salutation of peace, and invokes upon its inmates the unwonted blessings of prayer. It is not often that the friendly advances of the itinerant preacher are resisted and repelled. He is mostly welcome as a man, even when little regarded as an Evangelist. His *bonhommie* is generally remarkable; for with all his labours he is a happy man, and religion has cherished rather than depressed the kindlier feelings of his nature. But he is not wholly discouraged even by a sullen and reluctant reception. Some member of the household may be ready and eager to profit by his visit; some word of comfort may drop like balm into the heart of an anxious wife; some word of prayer may touch the conscience of an intemperate and wicked husband. At all times he is ready with counsel, reproof, encouragement, and teaching. After more or less success he pursues his journey; and perhaps on a future round he finds a heartier welcome, sees with delight that his instructions have availed, and learns that a number of the neighbouring families have gathered to profit by his ministry. Thus he forms a church in the wilderness; and children that would have lacked such inestimable advantages may now hear the Gospel in their youth, and have their characters formed upon the basis of its Divine morality. Could society in the rude Western settlements start under fairer auspices than these? or is any agency of civilization comparable to that which is supplied by the teaching and example of this humble band of itinerating Preachers?

The present narrative is occupied with the details of such a course as we have briefly sketched. Peter Cartwright may be taken as an eminent example of the class to which he belongs. There is no reason to doubt that his pious and devoted labours present a faithful picture of many a Backwoods Preacher's life, sometimes almost scene for scene, and always in respect of the same marvellous and beneficial result. When we think of the deeds to which a religious sense of duty actuates these devoted persons, and others whose motives or actions are allied to theirs, we remember that the poetic moralist has said,—

"The world knows nothing of its greatest men;"

and seem to 'find in their obscure but noble annals a just interpretation of the saying. But Providence gives, ever and anon, a glimpse of their existence to the world at large, and mankind is called to admire in one veteran survivor the virtues which hallowed every member of this heroic Legion of the Cross. It is this reflection which makes the Autobiography of Peter Cartwright so suggestive and significant. He is only one among many brethren. It would be a depressing thought, indeed, that he had sallied forth alone into the uncultivated wilds. What is a single pioneer in the great and stubborn forest, though his arm be of the stoutest and his axe of the keenest sort? It is encouraging to know that a thousand others have gone forth in every direction, and that the sun looks every day upon another clearance.

But it is time to speak of characteristics more personal to our author. We may fairly say that he is a bold man even for a Backwoods Preacher. His sound intrepid heart evidently beats in a vigorous and elastic body. He is not more surely called to preach the Gospel than he is exactly fitted to lead an itinerant Preacher's life. Not cumbered with learning, not checked by timidity, not too sensitive, nor yet fastidious, he has energy, endurance, good humour, and a ready wit. In his scrip is a hymn-book, and a Bible, perhaps a few tracts, a couple of dollars, and a dozen cents. With these good qualities and this small property, he mounts upon his cob and rides cheerfully away. We have no fear for Peter Cartwright as he disappears behind the wood. His object is to do good to others; but he is able and prepared to have justice for himself. He is no fanatic in his reading of Scripture; and no man need attempt to rob him of his cloak under the expectation of receiving his coat also. Still Peter is essentially a man of peace. When he does exercise his belligerent faculties, it is generally in a *rencontre* with some bigoted opponent, whether Baptist or Socinian, or with some dandified disturber of the peace in Christian meetings; and it must be allowed that he routs the enemy very quickly and completely. Some of these discomfitures, recorded in Peter's narrative with vigorous brevity, are among the raciest anecdotes of their class; and a few of them, it must be owned, are more in keeping with the pugnacious character of the man than with the peaceful office of the Christian Preacher.

Few readers of this memoir will find any difficulty in imagining the author's figure. Yet the following graphic sketch of his appearance in old age will not be the less acceptable:—

"The next in advance of years is Dr. Peter Cartwright, a large, square-built man, with some native ruggedness, mingled with a good deal of humour, both in his looks and in his speeches. There is a granite-like texture in his flesh, and a knotted roughness in his features, that stamp him as one who is hardy and enduring. And yet it would be a great omission in the slightest sketch of his appearance to represent him as lacking in geniality and good nature; for both his mouth and eyes, as well as the radiant play of the upper part of his cheeks, tell of a kindly and sociable nature. His head is large, and firmly supported between ample and compact shoulders. His brow is broad, and overhung with a mass of iron-grey hair. His eyes are intensely deep in colour, and shine like dark fires beneath his shaggy eye-brows, while crow's-feet wrinkles mark their corners, and add to the peculiar expression of his countenance. His complexion, never fair, is deeply tanned by the sun. His voice, when he begins to speak, is tremulous, but, as he proceeds, its old power returns, its rich natural organ tones are recovered, and he swells and rolls its deep diapasons most manfully. At times, to give point and wing to his side-shot arrows, he assumes a mock tragic tone and look, and then, after relating some backwood anecdote which convulses the assembly with irresistible laughter while he himself is solemnly grave, he falls upon his antagonist with overwhelming power, and leaves the victim prostrate under sarcasms. When roused by combined opposition, he launches in swift succession keen-edged sentences, and thoughts vivid and scathing as lightning, and then, with a voice roaring like a forest hurricane, he pours out his condemnations and warnings, with a force that crushes his foe, and fills others that hear with a sensation approaching to awe. Indeed, to hunt down and put to the cover of shame those whom he regards as dangerous to constitutional Methodism seems to be regarded by him as his proper vocation. He plainly performs this work with all the zest of a backwoodsman hunter, and, to accomplish it, he spares neither bishops, deputations, presiding elders, ministers, nor people. On some occasions he is absolutely terrible in execution, and seems to stand on the floor of the Conference as fearless and as irresistible as the lion in his domain."*

From this sketch it would seem that the marked features of Mr. Cartwright's character are little altered or subdued by age. The instincts of the old lion yet remain. Of course, it is a strong unreasoning prejudice which induces him to "roar" against the "downy doctors" of his latter days; but it is also a very natural one under the circumstances, and quite pardonable in the rugged hero, whose whole life has been engrossed by self-denying labours.

This book may fall into the hands of literary purist or religious precisian; and in either case the reader will be shocked. We leave the former to accommodate his taste or throw the book aside, as his humour dictates; but we should be sorry to leave the latter under the influence of a serious if not fatal prejudice.

Sudden conversions, amid scenes of overwhelming religious excitement, are the characteristic results of the labours of this itinerant Evangelist. Mr. Cartwright's evident delight is in a camp-meeting, mustering from three to five hundred strong. There, from a central platform, this Son of Thunder deals out the awful truths of revelation, and preaches at the top of his voice "of righteousness, temperance, and judgment to come." Sinners of every stamp are smitten by these appeals: they "drop right and left," like beasts of slaughter; the wail of repentance is followed by the prayer of faith, and many are "powerfully converted." Now it is this feature of the Backwoods life, and the Preacher's ministry, which the quiet Parish Priest of England will find it difficult to understand or to approve, and which many a formalist will not scruple to denounce and even vilify with opprobrious names. The question will be asked, Are these con-

* Jobson's "America and American Methodism," pp 207, 209.

versions genuine? is this, indeed, the work of God?—or does that mocking spirit, the Enemy of souls, and the Prince of the power of the air, take advantage of the mixed mysterious elements of human nature, and increase his own influence by a bold travesty of the Saviour's work of grace? Indeed, this may be very possible; and it would be rash to deny that Satan has at some times, and to some degree, thus profited by his spiritual cunning, and thus perverted and alloyed the means of grace devised for holy ends: but if more than this be asserted, the answer is still as in our Saviour's day: "If Satan cast out Satan, how can his kingdom stand?" For it must be remembered that the subsequent lives of these converts, for the most part, are the abiding proof of their conversion. And as for the tumultuous feelings, the strange excitement, the bodily prostration, the loud and indecorous shoutings, which attended upon the new birth of these souls, when the place, the circumstances, the preacher, and the sinner, are all taken into account, we might almost call these consequences natural,—not, however, as excluding the silent and profound operation of the Holy Ghost, but as representing the mere external and inevitable signs of the strife which takes place when the devil of sin is suddenly cast out of a human heart. Surely it would be matter of more surprise, and cause of more distrust, if less outward commotion attended upon the conversion of souls in such a promiscuous assemblage, where the ignorant and careless are startled by sudden light, and the vicious, hardened, and depraved break down under the influence of sudden fear. When the strongest passions of the soul are aroused, and a moment of time seems pressed with the awful interests of eternity, it is surely no cause for wonder that the pleading voice still rises into higher and harsher notes, or that the body trembles with an excitement so unusual and so fierce. These movements of sudden upheaval and confusion mark only an early stage of the new creation. There is every reason to believe that the scenes of turbulent emotion recorded in this volume were followed by long periods of individual calm, by a deep and settled peace, and by an assiduous cultivation of all the fruits and graces of the Spirit. God Himself may have looked with satisfaction on the result, and pronounced it "very good."

LONDON, *September*, 1858.

AUTHOR'S PREFACE.

For many years past, and especially during the last ten or twelve, I have been almost unceasingly importuned to write out a history of my life, as one among the oldest Methodist travelling preachers west of the mountains This would necessarily connect with it a history of the rise and progress of the Methodist Episcopal Church in the great valley of the Mississippi. And surely a work of this kind, written by a competent historiographer, who had kept himself posted, or had kept a journal of his life, and the many thrilling incidents connected with the history of the Church, or the life of a pioneer travelling preacher, could not fail to interest the Church and many of her friends, and would rescue from oblivion many, very many incidents that are now lost, and gone for ever beyond the reach of the historian's pen.

I have regretted through life that some of my cotemporaries, who were much better qualified for the task than I am, did not write out such a work as is contemplated in this imperfect sketch. Had I seriously thought of sending such a work into the world, I should have tried hard to have been better prepared. But it must be remembered that many of us early travelling preachers, who entered the vast wilderness of the West at an early day, had little or no education; no books, and no time to read or study them if we could have had them. We ,had no colleges, nor even a respectable common school, within hundreds of miles of us. Old *Dyke* or *Dilworth* was our spelling-book; and what little we did learn, as we grew up, and the means of education increased among us, we found, to our hearts' content, that we had to unlearn, and this was the hardest work of all

And now that I am old and well stricken in years, it has been, and is, my abiding conviction, that I cannot write a book that will be respectable, or one that will be worth reading , but l have reluctantly yielded to the many solicitations of my friends, and I am conscious that there must be many imperfections and inaccuracies in the work.. I have no books to guide me , my memory is greatly at fault; ten thousand interesting facts have escaped my recollection ; names and places have passed from me which cannot be recalled; and I fear that many scenes and incidents, as they now occur to my recollection, will be added to, or diminished from.

Moreover, as I well understand that I have been considered constitutionally an eccentric minister, thousands of the thrilling incidents that have gained publicity, and have been attributed to me, when they are not found in my book, will create disappointment. But I trust their place will be supplied by a true version, and though some of them may not be as marvellous, they may nevertheless be quite as interesting. I have many to record that have not seen the light, which will be quite as thrilling as any that have been narrated, and their truthfulness will make them more so.

Some of our beloved bishops, book agents, editors, and old men, preachers and private members, as well as a host of our young, strong men and ministers, who are now actively engaged in building up the Church, have urged me to undertake this sketch of my life; and I have not felt at liberty to decline, but send it out with all its imperfections, hoping that it may in some way, and to some extent, conduce to the interests of the Redeemer's kingdom, and do more than merely gratify an idle curiosity, or offend the fastidious taste of some of our present more highly favoured and better educated ministers, who enjoy the many glorious advantages of books, a better education, and improved state of society, from which we as early pioneers were almost wholly excluded.

Right here I wish to say, (I hope without the charge of egotism,) when I consider the insurmountable disadvantages and difficulties that the early pioneer Methodist preachers laboured under in spreading the Gospel in these Western wilds in the great valley of the Mississippi, and contrast the disabilities which surrounded them on every hand, with the glorious human advantages that are enjoyed by their present successors, it is confoundingly miraculous to me that our modern preachers cannot preach better and do more good than they do. Many nights, in early times, the itinerant had to camp out, without fire or food for man or beast. Our pocket Bible, Hymn Book, and Discipline constituted our library. It is true we could not, many of us, conjugate a verb or parse a sentence, and murdered the king's English almost every lick. But there was a Divine unction attended the word preached; and thousands fell under the mighty power of God, and thus the Methodist Episcopal Church was planted firmly in this Western wilderness, and many glorious signs have followed, and will follow, to the end of time.

I will here state, that, at an early period of my ministry, I commenced keeping a journal, and kept it up for several years, till at length several of our early missionaries to the Natchez country returned, and many of them, I found, were keeping a journal of their lives and labours, and it seemed to me we were outdoing the thing;

and under this conviction I threw my manuscript journals to the moles and bats. This act of my life I have deeply regretted; for if I had persisted in journalizing, I could now avail myself of many interesting facts, dates, names, and circumstances, that would greatly aid me in my sketch.

I know it is impossible for my friends to realize the embarrassments I labour under, for the want of some safe guide to my failing and 'treacherous memory. I therefore ask great indulgence from any and all who may chance to read this imperfect sketch, and pray that our kind Saviour may forgive any inaccuracies or errors that it may contain. If I had my ministerial life to live over again, my present conviction is that I would scrupulously keep a journal. But this cannot be; therefore I must submit.

And now, in the conclusion of this Introduction, I will say, I ask forgiveness of God for all the errors of this work, and all the errors of my whole life, especially of my ministerial life. I also ask for the forgiveness of the Methodist Episcopal Church, as one of her unworthy ministers, for any wrongs I may have done to her, or to the world. I also most sincerely ask the prayers of the Church, that while my sun is fast declining, and must soon set to rise on earth no more, I may have a peaceful and happy end, and that I may meet any that I may have been the instrument of doing good to, with all my dear brethren, safe in heaven, to praise God together for ever. Amen.

PETER CARTWRIGHT.

Pleasant Plains, Ill.

CONTENTS.

a *

THE BACKWOODS PREACHER.

AUTOBIOGRAPHY

OF

PETER CARTWRIGHT.

CHAPTER I.

PARENTAGE.

I was born September 1st, 1785, in Amherst County, on James River, in the State of Virginia. My parents were poor. My father was a soldier in the great struggle for liberty in the Revolutionary war with Great Britain He served over two years. My mother was an orphan. Shortly after the United Colonies gained their independence, my parents moved to Kentucky, which was a new country. It was an almost unbroken wilderness from Virginia to Kentucky at that early day, and this wilderness was filled with thousands of hostile Indians, and many thousands of the emigrants to Kentucky lost their lives by these savages. There were no roads for carriages at that time, and although the emigrants moved by thousands, they had to move on pack-horses. Many adventurous young men went to this new country. The fall my father moved, there were a great many families who joined together for mutual safety, and started for Kentucky. Besides the two hundred families thus united, there were one hundred young men, well armed, who agreed to guard these families through, and, as a compensation, they were to be supported for their services. After we struck the wilderness, we rarely travelled a day but we passed some white persons, murdered and scalped by the Indians while going to or returning from Kentucky. We travelled on till Sunday, and, instead of resting that day, the voice of the company was to move on.

It was a dark, cloudy day, misty with rain. Many Indians were seen through the day skulking round by our guards. Late in the evening we came to what was called "Camp Defeat," where a number of emigrant families had been all murdered by the savages a short time

B

before.   Here the company called a halt to camp for the night.   It was a solemn, gloomy time; every heart quaked with fear.

Soon the captain of our young men's company placed his men as sentinels all round the encampment.   The stock and the women and children were placed in the centre of the encampment.   Most of the men that were heads of families were placed around outside of the women and children.   Those who were not placed in this position, were ordered to take their stand outside still, in the edge of the brush. It was a dark, dismal night, and all expected an attack from the Indians.

That night my father was placed as a sentinel, with a good rifle, in the edge of the brush.   Shortly after he took his stand, and all was quiet in the camp, he thought he heard something moving toward him, and grunting like a swine.   He knew there was no swine with the moving company; but it was so dark he could not see what it was. Presently he perceived a dark object in the distance, but nearer him than at first, and believing it to be an Indian, aiming to spring upon him and murder him in the dark, he levelled his rifle, and aimed at the dark lump as well as he could, and fired.   He soon found he had hit the object, for it flounced about at a terrible rate; and my father gathered himself up, and ran into camp.

When his gun fired, there was an awful screaming throughout the encampment by the women and children.   My father was soon inquired of as to what was the matter.   He told them the circumstances of the case, but some said he was scared and wanted an excuse to come in; but he affirmed that there was no mistake, that there was something, and he had shot it; and if they would get a light and go with him, if he did not show them something, then they might call him a coward for ever.   They got a light, and went to the place, and there they found an Indian, with a rifle in one hand and a tomahawk in the other, dead. My father's rifle-ball had struck the Indian nearly central in the head.

There was but little sleeping in the camp that night.   However, the night passed away without any further alarms, and many glad hearts hailed the dawn of a new day.   The next morning, as soon as the company could pack up, they started on their journey.

In a few days after this, we met a lone man, who said his name was Baker, with his mouth bleeding at a desperate rate, having been shot by an Indian.   Several of his teeth and his jaw-bone were broken by a ball from the Indian's gun.   His account of a battle with the Indians was substantially as follows :—

There were seven young white men returning to Virginia from Kentucky, all well armed; one of them, a Frenchman, had a considerable sum of money with him.   All seven were mounted on fine horses, and they were waylaid by seven Indians.   When the white men approached near the ambush, they were fired on by the Indians, and three shot down; the other four dismounted and shot down three of the Indians. At the second fire of the Indians two more of the white men fell, and at the second fire of the white men two more of the Indians fell. Then there were two and two. At the third fire of the Indians, Baker's only remaining companion fell, and he received the wound in the mouth. Thinking his chance a bad one, he wheeled and ran, loading his gun as he went. Finding a large hollow tree, he crept into it, feet foremost, holding his rifle ready cocked, expecting them to look in, when he intended to fire. He heard the Indians cross and recross the log twice, but they did not look in. At this perilous moment, he heard the large cow-bell that was on one of the drove of cattle of our company, and shortly after he crawled out of the log, and made his way to us, the happiest man I think I ever saw. Our company of young men rushed to the battle-ground, and found the dead white men and Indians, and dug two separate graves, and buried them where they fell. They got all the horses and clothes of the white men slain, and the Frenchman's money, for the surviving Indians had not time to scalp or strip them.

When we came within seven miles of the Crab Orchard, where there were a fort and the first white settlement, it was nearly night. We halted, and a vote was taken whether we should go on to the fort, or camp there for the night. Indians had been seen in our rear through the day. All wanted to go through, except seven families, who refused to go any further that night. The main body went on, but they, the seven families, carelessly stripped off their clothes, lay down without any guards, and went to sleep.

Some time in the night, about twenty-five Indians rushed on them, and every one—men, women, and children—was slain, except one man, who sprang from his bed, and ran into the fort, barefooted and in his night clothes. He brought the melancholy news of the slaughter.

The captain of the fort was an old experienced ranger and Indian warrior. These murderous bands of savages lived north of the Ohio River, and would cross over into Kentucky, kill and steal, and then recross the Ohio into their own country. The old captain knew the country well, and the places of their crossing the river. Early next morning he called for volunteers, mounted men, and said he could get ahead of them. A goodly company turned out, and, sure enough, they got ahead of the Indians, and formed an ambush for them. Soon they saw the Indians coming, and, at a given signal, the whites fired on them. At the first shot all were killed but three; these were pursued, two of them killed, and but one made his escape to tell the sad news. All the plunder of the murdered families was retaken.

Thus you see what perilous times the first settlers had to reach that new and beautiful country of " *canes and turkeys.*"

Kentucky was claimed by no particular tribe of Indians, but was regarded as a common hunting-ground by the various tribes, east, west, north, and south. It abounded in various valuable game, such as buffalo, elk, bear, deer, turkeys, and many other smaller game; and hence the Indians struggled hard to keep the white people from taking possession of it. Many hard and bloody battles were fought, and thousands killed on both sides; and rightly was it named the "land of blood." * But finally the Indians were overpowered and driven off, and the white man obtained a peaceable and quiet possession.

It was chiefly settled by Virginians, as noble and brave a race of men and women as ever drew the breath of life. But Kentucky was far in the interior, and very distant from the Atlantic shores; and though a part of the great Mississippi Valley, the mouth of the Mississippi and thousands of miles up this "father of waters" belonged to foreign and, in some sense, hostile nations, that were not very friendly to the new republic.

The Kentuckians laboured under many, very many, disadvantages and privations; and had it not been for the fertility of the soil, and the abundance of wild meat, they must have suffered beyond endurance. But the country soon filled up, and entered into the enjoyment of improved and civilized life.†

CHAPTER II.

EARLY LIFE.

AFTER my father reached Kentucky, he rented a farm for two years in Lincoln County, on what was called the "hanging.fork of Dicks River," near Lancaster, the county seat.

My mother, being a member of the Methodist Episcopal Church, sought and obtained an acquaintance with two Methodist travelling preachers, namely, John Page and Benjamin Northcut, men of precious memory,—men that are to be numbered as early pioneers in the West, who laboured hard and suffered much to build up the infant Methodist Church in the wilderness.

In the fall of 1793 my father determined to move to what was then called the Green River country, in the southern part of the State of Kentucky. He did so, and settled in Logan County, nine miles

----

* The word *Kentucky* signifies, "*the dark and bloody ground.*"

† Ken... ... ... State ad... ... the count... ... after the Union. In 1790, the p... ...lation was 73,677; in 1850, it had increased to 982,405.

south of Russellville, the county seat, and within one mile of the state line of Tennessee.

Shortly after our removal from Lincoln to Logan County, my father's family was visited by Jacob Lurton, a travelling preacher of the Methodist Episcopal Church. Though my father was not a professor of religion, yet he was not an opposer of it; and when Jacob Lurton asked the liberty of preaching in his cabin, he readily assented.

I was then in my ninth year, and was sent out to invite the neighbours to come and hear preaching. Accordingly they crowded out, and filled the cabin to overflowing. Jacob Lurton was a real son of thunder. He preached with tremendous power, and the congregation were almost all melted to tears; some cried aloud for mercy, and my mother shouted aloud for joy.

Jacob Lurton travelled several years, married, and located in Kentucky, from whence he removed to Illinois, and settled near Alton, where he died many years ago. His end was peaceful and happy.

Shortly after Jacob Lurton preached at my father's cabin, he or his successor organized a small class, about four miles from my father's, where my mother attached herself again to the Church. I think there were thirteen members, one local preacher, one exhorter, and a class-leader. Here my mother regularly walked every Sabbath to class-meeting for a number of years, and seldom missed this means of grace. This little society ebbed and flowed for years, until about 1799, when a mighty revival of religion broke out, and scores joined the society. We built a little church, and called it _Ebenezer_. This was in what was then called Cumberland Circuit, and Kentucky District, in the Western Conference, the seventh Conference in the United States.*

Logan County, when my father moved to it, was called "Rogues' Harbour." Here many refugees, from almost all parts of the Union, fled to escape justice or punishment; for although there was law, yet it could not be executed, and it was a desperate state of society. Murderers, horse thieves, highway robbers, and counterfeiters fled here, until they combined, and actually formed a majority. The honest and civil part of the citizens would prosecute these wretched banditti, but they would swear each other clear; and they really put all law at defiance, and carried on such desperate violence and outrage, that the honest part of the citizens seemed to be driven to the necessity of uniting together, and taking the law into their own hands under the name of Regulators. This was a very desperate state of things.

Shortly after the Regulators had formed themselves into a society,

* The Methodist Episcopal Church _North_, is now divided into forty-seven Conferences. The Methodist Episcopal Church _South_, into twenty-three.

and established their code of bye-laws, on a court day at Russellville, the two bands met in town. Soon a quarrel commenced, and a general battle ensued between the rogues and Regulators, and they fought with guns, pistols, dirks, knives, and clubs. Some were actually killed, many wounded; the rogues proved victors, kept the ground, and drove the Regulators out of town. The Regulators rallied again, hunted, killed, and lynched many of the rogues, until several of them fled, and left for parts unknown. Many lives were lost on both sides, to the great scandal of civilized people. This is but one view of frontier life.

When my father settled in Logan County, there was not a news-paper printed south of Green River, no mill short of forty miles, and no schools worth the name. Sunday was a day set apart for hunting, fishing, horse-racing, card-playing, balls, dances, and all kinds of jollity and mirth. We killed our meat out of the woods, wild; and beat our meal and hominy with a pestle and mortar. We stretched a deer-skin over a hoop, burned holes in it with the prongs of a fork, sifted our meal, baked our bread, ate it, and it was first-rate eating too. We raised, or gathered out of the woods, our own tea. We had sage, bohea, cross-vine, spice, and sassafras teas, in abundance. As for coffee, I am not sure that I ever smelled it for ten years. We made our sugar out of the water of the maple-tree, and our molasses too. These were great luxuries in those days.

We raised our own cotton and flax. We water-rotted our flax, broke it by hand, scutched it; picked the seed out of the cotton with our fingers; our mothers and sisters carded, spun, and wove it into cloth, and they cut and made our garments and bed clothes, &c. And when we got on a new suit thus manufactured, and sallied out into company, we thought ourselves "*as big as anybody.*"

There were two large caves on my father's farm, and another about half a mile off, where was a great quantity of material for making saltpetre. We soon learned the art of making it, and our class-leader was a great powder maker.

Let it be remembered, these were days when we had no stores of dry goods or groceries; but the United States had a military post at Fort Messick, on the north bank of the Ohio River, and south end of the State of Illinois. Here the government kept stores of these things. After we had made a great quantity of saltpetre, and had manufactured it into powder really number one, strange to say, it came into the mind of our class-leader to go to Fort Messick on a trading expedition. Then the question arose, what sort of a vessel should be made ready for the voyage. This difficulty was soon solved; for he cut down a large poplar tree, and dug out a large and neat canoe, and launched it into Red River, to go out into Cumberland River, and at the mouth of said river to ascend the Ohio River to the fort.

Then proclamation was made to the neighbourhood to come in with their money or marketing; but powder was the staple of the trading voyage. They were also notified to bring in their bills, duly signed, stating the articles they wanted. Some sent for a quarter of a pound of coffee, some one yard of ribbon, some a butcher knife, some for a tin cup, &c., &c. I really wish I had the bill; I would give it as a literary curiosity of early days.

Our leader went and returned, safe and sound,'made a good exchange, to the satisfaction of nearly all concerned; and for weeks it was a great time of rejoicing, that we, even in Kentucky, had found out the glorious advantages of navigation.

I was naturally a wild, wicked boy, and delighted in horse-racing, card-playing, and dancing. My father restrained me but little, though my mother often talked to me, wept over me, and prayed for me, and often drew tears from my eyes; and though I often wept under preaching, and resolved to do better and seek religion, yet I broke my vows, went into young company, rode races, played cards, and danced.

At length my father gave me a young race-horse, which well-nigh proved my everlasting ruin; and he bought me a pack of cards, and I was a very successful young gambler; and though I was not initiated into the tricks of regular gamblers, yet I was very successful in winning money. This practice was very fascinating, and became a special besetting sin to me; so that, for a boy, I was very much captivated by it. My mother remonstrated almost daily with me, and I had to keep my cards hid from her; for if she could have found them, she would have burned them, or destroyed them in some way. O, the sad delusions of gambling! How fascinating, and how hard to reclaim a practised gambler! Nothing but the power of Divine grace saved me from this wretched sin.

My father sent me to school, boarding me at Dr. Beverly Allen's; but my teacher was not well qualified to teach correctly, and I made but small progress. I, however, learned to read, write, and cipher a little, but very imperfectly. Dr. Allen, with whom I boarded, had, in an early day, been a travelling preacher in the Methodist Episcopal Church. He was sent south to Georgia, as a very gentlemanly and popular preacher, and did much good. He married in that country a fine, pious woman, a member of the Church; but he, like David, in an evil hour, fell into sin, violated the laws of the country, and a writ was issued for his apprehension. He warned the sheriff not to enter his room, and assured him if he did he would kill him. The sheriff rushed upon him, and Allen shot him dead. He fled from that country to escape justice, and settled in Logan County, then called

" Rogues' Harbour." His family followed him, and here he practised medicine. To ease a troubled conscience he drank in the doctrine of Universalism; * but he lived and died a great friend to the Methodist Church.

It fell to my lot, after I had been a preacher several years, to visit the doctor on his dying bed. I talked and prayed with him. Just before he died, I asked him if he was willing to die and meet his final Judge with his Universalist sentiments. He frankly said he was not. He said he could make the mercy of God cover every case in his mind but his own, but he thought there was no mercy for him; and in this state of mind he left the world, bidding his family and friends an eternal farewell, warning them not to come to that place of torment to which he felt himself eternally doomed

CHAPTER III.

CANE RIDGE CAMP-MEETING.

TIME rolled on, population increased fast around us, the country improved, horse thieves and murderers were driven away, and civiliza-tion advanced considerably. Ministers of different denominations came in, and preached through the country; but the Methodist preachers were the pioneer messengers of salvation in these ends of the earth. In Rogues' Harbour there was a Baptist church, a few miles west of my father's, and a Presbyterian congregation a few miles north, and the Methodist *Ebenezer*, a few miles south.

There were two Baptist ministers, one an old man of strong mind and *good*, very *good*, natural abilities, having been brought up a rigid Calvinist, and having been taught to preach the doctrine of particular election and reprobation. At length his good sense revolted at the *horrid idea*, and, having no correct books on theology, he plunged into the opposite extreme, namely, universal redemption. He lived in a very wicked settlement. He appointed a day to publish his recanta-tion of his old Calvinism and his views on universal and unconditional salvation to all mankind. The whole country, for many miles around, crowded to hear the *joyful news*. When he had finished his discourse, the vilest of the vile multitude raised the shout, expressing great joy that there was no hell or eternal punishment.

I will here state a circumstance that occurred to the old gentleman and myself. He was a great smoker, and as he passed my father's one

* The Universalists teach that all mankind will finally be holy and happy in heaven. In 1850 they had, in the United States, 494 churches, having accommo-dation for 205,462 persons.

day, to marry a couple, he came to the fence, and called to me, and said, "Peter, if you will bring me a coal of fire to light my pipe, I will tell you how to get out of hell, if you ever get there." Although I was very wicked, the expression exceedingly shocked me, and neither the devil nor any of his preachers have ever been able, from that day to this, seriously to tempt me to believe the *blasphemous doctrine*.

The other Baptist minister soon took to open drunkenness, and with him his salvation by *water* expired; but if ever there was a jubilee in hell, it was then and there held over these apostate and fallen ministers, B. A. and Dr. Allen.

Somewhere between 1800 and 1801, in the upper part of Kentucky, at a memorable place called "Cane Ridge," there was appointed a sacramental meeting by some of the Presbyterian ministers; at which meeting, seemingly unexpected by ministers or people, the mighty power of God was displayed in a very extraordinary manner; many were moved to tears and cried aloud for mercy. The meeting was protracted for weeks. Ministers of almost all denominations flocked in from far and near. The meeting was kept up by night and day. Thousands heard of the mighty work, and came on foot, on horseback, in carriages and waggons. It is supposed that there were in attendance at times during the meeting from twelve to twenty-five thousand people. Hundreds fell prostrate under the mighty power of God, as men slain in battle. Stands were erected in the woods, from which preachers of different Churches proclaimed repentance toward God and faith in our Lord Jesus Christ; and it was supposed by eye and ear witnesses that between one and two thousand souls were happily and powerfully converted to God during the meeting. It was not unusual for one, two, three, and four to seven preachers to be addressing the listening thousands at the same time from the different stands erected for the purpose. The heavenly fire spread in almost every direction. It was said by truthful witnesses, that at times more than one thousand persons broke out into loud shouting all at once, and that the shouts could be heard for miles around.

From this camp-meeting, for so it ought to be called, the news spread through all the Churches, and through all the land, and it excited great wonder and surprise; but it kindled a religious flame that spread all over Kentucky, and through many other States. And I may here be permitted to say, that this was the first camp-meeting ever held in the United States, and here our camp-meetings took their rise.

As Presbyterian, Methodist, and Baptist ministers all united in the blessed work at this meeting, when they returned home to their different congregations, and carried the news of this mighty work, the revival spread rapidly throughout the land; but many of the ministers and members of the synod of Kentucky thought it all disorder, and tried to stop the work. They called their preachers who were engaged in the revival to account, and censured and silenced them. These ministers then rose up and unitedly renounced the jurisdiction of the Presbyterian Church, organized a Church of their own, and dubbed it with the name of *Christian.** Here was the origin of what was called the *New Lights.* They renounced the Westminster Confession of Faith, and all Church discipline, and professed to take the New Testament for their Church discipline. They established no standard of doctrine; every one was to take the New Testament, read it, and abide by his own construction of it. Marshall, M'Namar, Dunlevy, Stone, Huston, and others, were the chief leaders in this *trash trap.* Soon a diversity of opinion sprang up, and they got into a Babel confusion. Some preached Arian, some Socinian, and some Universalist doctrines; so that in a few years you could not tell what was *harped* or what was *danced.* They adopted the mode of immersion, the water-god of all exclusive errorists; and directly there was a mighty controversy about the way to heaven, whether it was by water or by dry land.

In the meantime a remnant of preachers that broke off from the Methodist Episcopal Church in 1792, headed by James O'Kelly, who had formed a party because he could not be a bishop in the said Church, which party he called the Republican Methodist Church, came out to Kentucky, and formed a union with these New Lights. Then the Methodist Episcopal Church had war, and rumours of war, almost on every side. The dreadful diversity of opinion among these New Lights, their want of any standard of doctrines, or regular Church discipline, made them an easy prey to prowling wolves of any description.

Soon the Shaker† priests came along, and off went M'Namar, Dunlevy, and Huston into that foolish error. Marshall and others retraced their steps. B. W. Stone stuck to his New Lightism, and fought many bloodless battles, till he grew old and feeble, and the mighty Alexander Campbell, the *great,* arose, and poured such floods of regenerating water about the old man's cranium, that he formed a union with this giant errorist, and finally died, not much lamented out of the circle of a few friends.

This Christian, or New Light, Church is a feeble and scattered people, though there are some good Christians among them. I

---

* In 1850 this sect had, in the United States, 812 churches, with accommodation for 296,050 persons. Their Church system is "*liberal*" in the extreme. Every member being free to determine for himself in matters of faith and practice what the Scriptures enjoin. Immoral and disorderly conduct alone unfitting for Church membership.

† See Appendix A.—*The Shakers.*

suppose, since the day of Pentecost, there was hardly ever a greater revival of religion than at Cane Ridge ; and if there had been steady, Christian ministers, settled in Gospel doctrine and Church discipline, thousands might have been saved to the Church that wandered off in the mazes of vain speculative divinity, and finally made shipwreck of the faith, fell back, turned infidel, and lost their religion and their souls for ever. But evidently a new impetus was given to the work of God, and many, very many, will have cause to bless God for ever for this revival of religion throughout the length and breadth of our Zion.

CHAPTER IV.

CONVERSION.

IN 1801, when I was in my sixteenth year, my father, my eldest half-brother, and myself, attended a wedding about five miles from home, where there was a great deal of drinking and dancing, which was very common at marriages in those days. I drank little or nothing ; my delight was in dancing. After a late hour in the night, we mounted our horses and started for home. I was riding my race-horse.

A few minutes after we had put up the horses, and were sitting by the fire, I began to reflect on the manner in which I had spent the day and evening. I felt guilty and condemned. I rose and walked the floor. My mother was in bed. It seemed to me, all of a sudden, my blood rushed to my head, my heart palpitated, in a few minutes I turned blind ; an awful impression rested on my mind that death had come, and I was unprepared to die. I fell on my knees, and began to ask God to have mercy on me.

My mother sprang from her bed, and was soon on her knees by my side, praying for me, and exhorting me to look to Christ for mercy ; and then and there I promised the Lord that if He would spare me, I would seek and serve Him ; and I never fully broke that promise. My mother prayed for me a long time. At length we lay down, but there was little sleep for me. Next morning I rose, feeling wretched beyond expression. I tried to read in the Testament, and retired many times to secret prayer through the day, but found no relief. I gave up my race-horse to my father, and requested him to sell him. I went and brought my pack of cards, and gave them to mother, who threw them into the fire, and they were consumed. I fasted, watched, and prayed, and engaged in regular reading of the Testament. I was so distressed and miserable, that I was incapable of any regular business.

My father was greatly distressed on my account, thinking I must die, and he would lose his only son. He bade me retire altogether from business, and take care of myself.

Soon it was noised abroad that I was distracted, and many of my associates in wickedness came to see me, to try and divert my mind from those gloomy thoughts of my wretchedness; but all in vain. I exhorted them to desist from the course of wickedness which we had been guilty of together. The class-leader and local preacher were sent for. They tried to point me to the bleeding Lamb; they prayed for me most fervently. Still I found no comfort, and although I had never believed in the doctrine of unconditional election and reprobation, I was sorely tempted to believe I was a reprobate, and doomed, and lost eternally, without any chance of salvation.

At length one day I retired to the horse-lot, and was walking and wringing my hands in great anguish, trying to pray, on the borders of utter despair. It appeared to me that I heard a voice from heaven, saying, "Peter, look at Me." A feeling of relief flashed over me as quick as an electric shock. It gave me hopeful feelings, and some encouragement to seek mercy; but still my load of guilt remained. I repaired to the house, and told my mother what had happened to me in the horse-lot. Instantly she seemed to understand it; and told me the Lord had done this to encourage me to hope for mercy, and exhorted me to take encouragement, and seek on, and God would bless me with the pardon of my sins at another time.

Some days after this, I retired to a cave on my father's farm, to pray in secret. My soul was in an agony; I wept, I prayed, and said, "Now, Lord, if there is mercy for me, let me find it ," and it really seemed to me that I could almost lay hold of the Saviour, and realize a reconciled God. All of a sudden, such a fear of the devil fell upon me, that it really appeared to me that he was surely personally there, to seize and drag me down to hell, soul and body, and such a horror fell on me, that I sprang to my feet and ran to my mother at the house. My mother told me this was a device of Satan to prevent me from finding the blessing then. Three months rolled away, and still I did not find the blessing of the pardon of my sins.

This year, 1801, the Western Conference of the Methodist Episcopal Church existed, and I think there was but one presiding elder's district in it, called the Kentucky District. William M'Kendree* (afterward bishop) was appointed to the Kentucky District. Cumberland Circuit, which, perhaps, was six hundred miles round, and lying partly in Kentucky and partly in Tennessee, was one of the Circuits of this District. John Page and Thomas Wilkerson were appointed to this Circuit.

* See Appendix B.—*Bishop M'K'nd, ee.*

In the spring of this year, Mr. M'Grady, a minister of the Presbyterian Church, who had a congregation and meeting-house, as we then called them, about three miles north of my father's house, appointed a sacramental meeting in this congregation, and invited the Methodist preachers to attend with them, and especially John Page, who was a powerful Gospel minister, and was very popular among the Presbyterians. Accordingly he came, and preached with great power and success.

There were no camp-meetings in regular form at this time; but as there was a great waking up among the Churches, from the revival that had broken out at Cane Ridge, before mentioned, many flocked to those sacramental meetings. The church would not hold the tenth part of the congregation. Accordingly, the officers of the church erected a stand in a contiguous shady grove, and prepared seats for a large congregation.

The people crowded to this meeting from far and near. They came in their large waggons, with victuals mostly prepared. The women slept in the waggons, and the men under them. Many stayed on the ground night and day for a number of nights and days together. Others were provided for among the neighbours around. The power of God was wonderfully displayed; scores of sinners fell under the preaching, like men slain in a mighty battle; Christians shouted aloud for joy.

To this meeting I repaired, a guilty, wretched sinner. On the Saturday evening of said meeting, I went, with weeping multitudes, and bowed before the stand, and earnestly prayed for mercy In the midst of a solemn struggle of soul, an impression was made on my mind, as though a voice said to me, "Thy sins are all forgiven thee." Divine light flashed all round me, unspeakable joy sprung up in my soul. I rose to my feet, opened my eyes, and it really seemed as if I was in heaven; the trees, the leaves on them, and everything seemed, and I really thought were, praising God. My mother raised the shout, my Christian friends crowded around me, and joined me in praising God, and though I have been since then, in many instances, unfaithful, yet I have never, for one moment, doubted that the Lord did, then and there, forgive my sins, and give me religion.

Our meeting lasted without intermission all night; and it was believed by those who had a very good right to know, that over eighty souls were converted to God during its continuance. I went on my way rejoicing for many days. This meeting was in the month of May. In June our preacher, John Page, attended at our little church, *Ebenezer;* and there, in June, 1801, I joined the Methodist Episcopal Church, which I have never for one moment regretted. I have never for a moment been tempted to leave the Methodist Episcopal Church, and if they were to turn me out, I would knock at the door till taken in again. I suppose, from the year 1786 Methodist preachers had been sent to the West; and we find among these very early pioneers, F. Poythress, presiding elder, T. Williamson, I. Brooks, Wilson Lee, James Haw, P. Massie, B. M'Henry, B. Snelling, J. Hartly, J. Talman, J. Lillard, Kobler, and others.

Perhaps the first Conference holden in the West was held in Kentucky, in April, 1789, and then at different points till 1800, when the Western Conference was regularly organized, and reached from Redstone and Greenbrier to Natchez, covering almost the entire Mississippi valley. I can find at this time a record of but 90 members in 1787, and 5 travelling preachers. From 1787 up to 1800, Bishop Asbury* visited the Western world, called together the preachers in Conferences, changed them from time to time, and regulated the affairs of the infant Church in the wilderness as best he could.

Several times the Western preachers had to arm themselves in crossing the mountains to the East, and guard Bishop Asbury through the wilderness, which was infested with bloody, hostile savages, at the imminent risk of all their lives. Notwithstanding the great hazard of life, that eminent apostle of American Methodism, Bishop Asbury, showed that he did not count his life dear, so that he could provide for the sheep in the wilderness of the West.

At the time I joined the Church in 1801, according to the best accounts that I can gather, there were in the entire bounds of the Western Conference, of members, probationers, coloured and all, 2,484, and about 15 travelling preachers. In the United States and territories, East and West, North and South, and Canada, 72,874. Total in Europe and America, 196,502. The number of travelling preachers this year, for all America and Canada, was 307; and during the same year there were 8,000 members added to the Methodist Episcopal Church.

I believe, to say nothing of some local preachers who emigrated to the West at a very early day, that James Haw and Benjamin Ogden were the first two regular itinerant preachers sent out in 1786. After travelling and preaching for several years, they both became disaffected to the Methodist Episcopal Church, and withdrew, with the secession of James O'Kelly, elsewhere named in my sketches. O'Kelly left the Church in 1792. He was a popular and powerful preacher, and drew off many preachers and thousands of members with him. He formed what he called the Republican Methodist Church, flourished for a few years, and then divisions and subdivisions entered among his followers.

* See Appendix C.—*Bishop Asbury*.

Some of his preachers turned Arians, some Universalists, and some joined the so-called New Lights, and some returned to the Methodist Episcopal Church; and the last authentic account I had of O'Kelly he was left alone in his old age, and desired to return to the Methodist Episcopal Church again; but whether he was ever received I am not informed. And here was an end of the first grand secession from our beloved Church.

James Haw and Benjamin Ogden, we have said, became disaffected, and left the Church with O'Kelly's party. They soon found that they could not succeed to any considerable extent in these Western wilds. Haw veered about and joined the Presbyterians, became a pastor in one of their congregations with a fixed salary, but lived and died in comparative obscurity.

Ogden backslid, quit preaching, kept a groggery, and became wicked, and raised his family to hate the Methodists. In the year 1813, when I was on the Wabash District, Tennessee Conference, Breckenridge Circuit, at a camp-meeting in said Circuit, Benjamin Ogden attended. There was a glorious revival of religion, and Ogden got under strong conviction, and professed to be reclaimed, joined the Church again, was licensed to preach, was soon recommended and received into the travelling connexion again, and lived and died a good Methodist preacher. He was saved by mercy, as all seceders from the Methodist Episcopal Church will be, if saved at all

To show the ignorance the early Methodist preachers had to contend with in the Western wilds, I will relate an incident or two that occurred to Wilson Lee in Kentucky He was one of the early pioneer Methodist preachers sent to the West. He was a very solemn and grave minister. At one of his appointments, at a private house on a certain day, they had a motherless pet lamb. The boys of the family had mischievously learned this lamb to butt. They would go near it, and make motions with their heads, and the lamb would back and then dart forward at them, and they would jump out of the way, so that the sheep would miss them.

A man came into the congregation who had been drinking and frolicking all the night before. He came in late, and took his seat on the end of a bench nearly in the door, and, having slept none the night before, presently he began to nod; and as he nodded and bent forward, the pet lamb came along by the door, and seeing this man nodding and bending forward, he took it as a banter, and straightway backed and then sprang forward, and gave the sleeper a severe jolt right on the head, and over he tilted him, to the no small amusement of the congregation, who all burst out into laughter; and grave as the preacher, Mr. Lee, was, it so excited his risibilities that he almost lost his balance. But recovering himself a little, he went on in a most solemn and impressive strain. His subject was the words of our Lord · " Except a man deny himself, and take up his cross, he cannot be My disciple." He urged on his congregation, with melting voice and tearful eyes, to take up the cross,—no matter what it was, take it up.

· There were in the congregation a very wicked Dutchman and his wife, both of whom were profoundly ignorant of the Scriptures and the plan of salvation. His wife was a notorious scold, and so much was she given to this practice, that she made her husband unhappy, and kept him almost always in·a perfect fret, so that he led a most miserable and uncomfortable life. It pleased God that day to cause the preaching of Mr. Lee to reach their guilty souls, and break up the great deep of·their hearts. They wept aloud, seeing their lost condition; and they then and there resolved to do better, and from that time forward to take up the cross and bear it, be it what it might.

The congregation were generally deeply affected. M. _ :e exhorted them and prayed for them as long as he consistently could, and, having another appointment some distance off that evening, he dismissed the congregation, got a little refreshment, saddled his horse, mounted, and started for his evening appointment. After riding some distance, he saw a little ahead of him a man trudging along, carrying a woman on his back. This greatly surprised Mr. Lee. He very naturally supposed that the woman was a cripple, or had hurt herself in some way, so that she could not walk. The traveller was a small man, and the woman large and heavy.

Before he overtook them, Mr. Lee began to cast about in his mind how he could render them assistance. When he came up to them, lo and behold, who should it be but the Dutchman and his wife that had been so affected under his sermon at meeting! Mr. Lee rode up and spoke to them, and inquired of the man what had happened, or what was the matter, that he was carrying his wife.

The Dutchman turned to Mr. Lee, and said, "Besure you did tell us in your sarmon dat we must take up de cross and follow de Saviour, or dat we could not be saved or go to heaven; and I does desire to go to heaven so much as any pody; and dish vife is so pad, she scold and scold all de time, and dish woman is de createst cross I have in de whole world, and I does take her up and pare her; for I must save my soul."

You may be sure that Mr. Lee was posed for once; but after a few moments' reflection he told the Dutchman to put his wife down, and he dismounted from his horse. He directed them to sit down on a log by the road side. He held the reins of his horse's bri le, and sat down by them, took out his Bible, read to them several passages of Scripture, and explained and expounded to them the way of the Lord more perfectly. He opened to them the nature of the cross of Christ, what it is, how it is to be taken up, and how they were to bear that cross; and after teaching and advising them some time, he prayed for them by the road side, left them deeply affected, mounted his horse, and rode on to his evening appointment.

Long before Mr. Lee came around his Circuit to his next appointment, the Dutchman and his scolding wife were both powerfully converted to God; and when he came round, he took them into the Church. The Dutchman's wife was cured of her scolding. Of course, he got clear of this cross. They lived together long and happily, adorning their profession, and giving ample evidence that religion could cure a scolding wife, and that God could and did convert poor ignorant Dutch people.

This Dutchman often told his experience in lovefeasts with thrilling effect, and hardly ever failed to melt the whole congregation into a flood of tears; and on one particular occasion, which is vividly printed on my recollection, I believe the whole congregation in the love-feast, which lasted beyond the time allotted for such meetings, broke out into a loud shout.

Thus Brother Lee was the honoured instrument in the hand of God of planting Methodism, amid clouds of ignorance and opposition, among the early settlers of the far West. Brother Lee witnessed a good confession to the end. At an early period of his ministry he fell from the walls of Zion, with the trump of God in his hand, and has gone to his reward in heaven. Peace to his memory.

CHAPTER V.

THE GREAT REVIVAL.

FROM 1801, for years, a blessed revival of religion spread through almost the entire inhabited parts of the West, Kentucky, Tennessee, the Carolinas, and many other parts, especially through the Cumberland country, which was so called from the Cumberland River, which headed and mouthed in Kentucky, but in its great bend circled south through Tennessee, near Nashville. The Presbyterians and Methodists in a great measure united in this work, met together, prayed together, and preached together.

In this revival originated our camp-meetings, and in both these denominations they were held every year, and, indeed, have been ever since, more or less. They would erect their camps with logs, or frame them, and cover them with clapboards or shingles. They would also erect a shed, sufficiently large to protect five thousand people from wind and rain, and cover it with boards or shingles; build a large stand, seat the shed; and here they would collect together from forty to fifty miles around, sometimes further than that. Ten, twenty, and sometimes thirty ministers, of different denominations, would come together and preach night and day, four or five days together; and, indeed, I have known these camp-meeting to last three or four weeks, and great good resulted from them. I have seen more than a hundred sinners fall like dead men under one powerful sermon, and I have seen and heard more than five hundred Christians all shouting aloud the high praises of God at once; and I will venture to assert that many happy thousands were awakened and converted to God at these camp-meetings. Some sinners mocked, some of the old dry professors opposed, some of the old starched Presbyterian preachers preached against these exercises; but still the work went on and spread almost in every direction, gathering additional force, until our country seemed all coming home to God.

In this great revival the Methodists kept moderately balanced; for we had excellent preachers to steer the ship, or guide the flock. But some of our members ran wild, and indulged in some extravagances that were hard to control.

The Presbyterian preachers and members, not being accustomed to much noise or shouting, when they yielded to it went into great extremes and downright wildness, to the great injury of the cause of God. Their old preachers licensed a great many young men to preach, contrary to their confession of faith. That confession of faith required their ministers to believe in unconditional election and reprobation, and the unconditional and final perseverance of the saints. But in this revival they, almost to a man, gave up these points of high Calvinism, and preached a free salvation to all mankind. The Westminster Confession required every man, before he could be licensed to preach, to have a liberal education; but this qualification was dispensed with, and a great many fine men were licensed to preach without this literary qualification, or subscribing to those high-toned doctrines of Calvinism.

This state of things produced great dissatisfaction in the Synod of Kentucky, and messenger after messenger was sent to wait on the Presbytery, to get them to desist from their erratic course, but without success. Finally they were cited to trial before the constituted authorities of the Church. Some were censured, some were suspended, some retraced their steps, while others surrendered their credentials of ordination, and the rest were cut off from the Church.

While in this amputated condition, they called a general meeting of all their licentiates. They met our presiding elder, J. Page, and a number of Methodist ministers, at a quarterly-meeting in Logan County, and proposed to join the Methodist Episcopal Church as a body; but our aged minister declined this offer, and persuaded them to rise up and embody themselves together, and constitute a Church. They reluctantly yielded to this advice, and, in due time and form, constituted what they denominated the "Cumberland Presbyterian Church;"* and in their confession of faith split, as they supposed, the difference between the Predestinarians and the Methodists, rejecting a partial atonement or special election and reprobation, but retaining the doctrine of the final unconditional perseverance of the saints.

What an absurdity! While a man remains a sinner, he may come, as a free agent, to Christ, if he will; and if he does not come, his damnation will be just, because he refused offered mercy; but as soon as he gets converted, his free agency is destroyed, the best boon of heaven is then lost; and although he may backslide, wander away from Christ, yet he *shall* be brought in. He cannot finally be lost if he has ever been really converted to God.

They make a very sorry show in their attempt to support this left foot of Calvinism. But, be it spoken to their credit, they do not often preach this doctrine. They generally preach Methodist doctrine, and have been the means of doing a great deal of good, and would have done much more if they had left this relic of John Calvin behind.

In this revival, usually termed in the West the "Cumberland Revival," many joined the different Churches, especially the Methodist and Cumberland Presbyterians. The Baptists also came in for a share of the converts, but not to any great extent. Infidelity quailed before the mighty power of God, which was displayed among the people. Universalism was almost driven from the land. The Predestinarians of almost all sorts put forth a mighty effort to stop the work of God.

Just in the midst of our controversies on the subject of the powerful exercises among the people under preaching, a new exercise broke out amongst us, called the *jerks*, which was overwhelming in its effects upon the bodies and minds of the people No matter whether they were saints or sinners, they would be taken under a warm song or sermon, and seized with a convulsive jerking all over, which they could not by any possibility avoid, and the more they resisted the

---

* This Church, in addition to the peculiarities of doctrine here specified, is also peculiar in its ecclesiastical polity, having grafted on the Presbyterian polity the *itinerating* system of the Methodists. It numbers about 50,000 communicants.

more they jerked. If they would not strive against it, and would pray in good earnest, the jerking would usually abate. I have seen more than five hundred persons jerking at one time in my large congregations. Most usually persons taken with the jerks, to obtain relief, as they said, would rise up and dance. Some would run, but could not get away. Some would resist; on such the jerks were generally very severe.

To see those proud young gentlemen and young ladies, dressed in their silks, jewellery, and prunella, from top to toe, take the *jerks*, would often excite my risibilities. The first jerk or so, you would see their fine bonnets, caps, and combs fly; and so sudden would be the jerking of the head, that their long loose hair would crack almost as loud as a waggoner's whip.

At one of my appointments in 1804, there was a very large congregation turned out to hear the Kentucky boy, as they called me. Among the rest there were two very finely dressed, fashionable young ladies, attended by two brothers with loaded horsewhips. Although the house was large, it was crowded. The two young ladies, coming in late, took their seats near where I stood, and their two brothers stood in the door. I was a little unwell, and I had a phial of peppermint in my pocket. Before I commenced preaching I took out my phial and swallowed a little of the peppermint. While I was preaching, the congregation was melted into tears. The two young gentlemen moved off to the yard fence, and both the young ladies took the jerks, and they were greatly mortified about it. There was a great stir in the congregation. Some wept, some shouted, and before our meeting closed several were converted.

As I dismissed the assembly, a man stepped up to me, and warned me to be on my guard; for he had heard the two brothers swear they would horsewhip me when meeting was out, for giving their sisters the jerks. "Well," said I, "I'll see to that."

I went out and said to the young men that I understood they intended to horsewhip me for giving their sisters the jerks. One replied that he did. I undertook to expostulate with him on the absurdity of the charge against me, but he swore I need not deny it; for he had seen me take out a phial, in which I carried some truck that gave his sisters the jerks. As quick as thought it came into my mind how I would get clear of my whipping, and, jerking out the peppermint phial, said I, "Yes; if I gave your sisters the jerks, I'll give them to you." In a moment I saw he was scared. I moved toward him, he backed; I advanced, and he wheeled and ran, warning me not to come near him, or he would kill me. It raised the laugh on him, and I escaped my whipping. I had the pleasure, before the year was out, of seeing all four soundly converted to God, and I took them into the Church.

While I am on this subject, I will relate a very serious circumstance which I knew to take place with a man who had the jerks at a camp-meeting, on what was called the Ridge, in William Magee's congregation. There was a great work of religion in the encampment. The jerks were very prevalent. There was a company of drunken rowdies who came to interrupt the meeting. These rowdies were headed by a very large drinking man. They came with their bottles of whiskey in their pockets. This large man cursed the jerks, and all religion. Shortly afterward he took the jerks, and he started to run, but he jerked so powerfully he could not get away. He halted among some saplings, and, although he was violently agitated, he took out his bottle of whiskey, and swore he would drink the damned jerks to death; but he jerked at such a rate he could not get the bottle to his mouth, though he tried hard. At length he fetched a sudden jerk, and the bottle struck a sapling and was broken to pieces, and spilled his whiskey on the ground. There was a great crowd gathered round him, and when he lost his whiskey he became very much enraged, and cursed and swore very profanely, his jerks still increasing. At length he fetched a very violent jerk, snapped his neck, fell, and soon expired, with his mouth full of cursing and bitterness.

I always looked upon the jerks* as a judgment sent from God, first, to bring sinners to repentance, and, secondly, to show professors that God could work with or without means, and that He could work over and above means, and do whatsoever seemeth Him good, to the glory of His grace and the salvation of the world.

There is no doubt in my mind that, with weak-minded, ignorant, and superstitious persons, there was a great deal of sympathetic feeling with many that claimed to be under the influence of this jerking exercise; and yet, with many, it was perfectly involuntary. It was, on all occasions, my practice to recommend fervent prayer as a remedy, and it almost universally proved an effectual antidote.

There were many other strange and wild exercises into which the subjects of this revival fell; such, for instance, as what was called the running, jumping, barking exercise. The Methodist preachers generally preached against this extravagant wildness. I did it uniformly in my little ministrations, and sometimes gave great offence; but I feared no consequences when I felt my awful responsibilities to God. From these wild exercises, another great evil arose from the heated and wild imaginations of some. They professed to fall into trances and see visions; they would fall at meetings and sometimes at home, and lay apparently powerless and motionless for days, sometimes for a week at a time, without food or drink; and when they came to, they professed to have seen heaven and hell, to have seen

* See Appendix D.—*The Jerks and Revival Extravagances.*

God, angels, the devil, and the damned; they would prophesy, and, under the pretence of Divine inspiration, predict the time of the end of the world, and the ushering in of the great millennium.

This was the most troublesome delusion of all; it made such an appeal to the ignorance, superstition, and credulity of the people, even saint as well as sinner. I watched this matter with a vigilant eye. If I opposed it, I should have to meet the clamour of the multitude; and if any one opposed it, these very visionists would single him out, and denounce the dreadful judgments of God against him. They would even set the very day that God was to burn the world, like the self-deceived modern Millerites. They would prophesy, that if any one did oppose them, God would send fire down from heaven and consume him, like the blasphemous Shakers. They would proclaim that they could heal all manner of diseases, and raise the dead, just like the diabolical Mormons. They professed to have converse with spirits of the dead in heaven and hell, like the modern spirit-rappers. Such a state of things I never saw before, and I hope in God I shall never see again.

I pondered well the whole matter in view of my responsibilities, searched the Bible for the true fulfilment of promise and prophecy, prayed to God for light and Divine aid, and proclaimed open war against these delusions. In the midst of them along came the Shakers, and Mr. Rankin, one of the Presbyterian revival preachers, joined them; Mr. G. Wall, a visionary local preacher among the Methodists, joined them; all the country was in commotion.

I made public appointments and drew multitudes together, and openly showed from the Scriptures that the delusions were false. Some of these visionary men and women prophesied that God would kill me. The Shakers soon pretended to seal my damnation. But nothing daunted,—for I knew Him in whom I had believed,—I threw my appointments in the midst of them, and proclaimed to listening thousands the more sure word of prophecy. This mode of attack threw a damper on these visionary, self-deluded, false prophets, sobered some, reclaimed others, and stayed the fearful tide of delusion that was sweeping over the country.

I will here state a case which occurred at an early day in the State of Indiana, in a settlement called Busroe. Many of the early emigrants to that settlement were Methodists, Baptists, and Cumberland Presbyterians. The Shaker priests, all apostates from the Baptist and the Cumberland Presbyterians, went over among them. Many of them I was personally acquainted with, and had given them letters when they moved from Kentucky to that new country. There were then no Methodist Circuit preachers in that region.

An old local preacher, Brother Collins, withstood these Shakers, and in private combat was a full match for any of them; but he was not eloquent in public debate, and hence the Shaker priests overcame my old brother, and by scores swept members of different Churches away from their steadfastness into the muddy pool of Shakerism.

The few who remained steadfast sent to Kentucky for me, praying me to come and help them. I sent an appointment, with an invitation to meet any or all of the Shaker priests in public debate; but instead of meeting me, they appointed a meeting in opposition, and warned the believers, as they called them, to keep away from my meeting; but, from our former acquaintance and intimate friendship, many of them came to hear me. I preached to a vast crowd for about three hours, and I verily believe God helped me. The very foundations of every Shaker present were shaken from under him. They then besought me to go to the Shaker meeting that night. I went, and when I got there we had a great crowd. I proposed to them to have a debate, and they dared not refuse. The terms were these: A local preacher I had with me was to open the debate; then one or all of their preachers, if they chose, were to follow, and I was to bring up the rear. My preacher opened the debate by merely stating the points of difference. Mr. Brayelton followed, and, instead of argument, he turned everything into abuse and insulting slander. Then he closed, and Mr. Gill rose, but, instead of argument, he uttered a few words of personal abuse, and then called on all the Shakers to meet him a few minutes in the yard, talk a little, and then disperse.

Our debate was out in the open air, at the end of a cabin. I rose, called them to order, and stated that it was fairly agreed by these Shaker priests that I should bring up the rear, or close the argument. I stated that it was cowardly to run, that if I was the devil himself, and they were right, I could not hurt them. I got the most of them to take their seats and hear me. Mr. Gill gathered a little band, and he and they left. They had told the people in the day that if I continued to oppose them, God would make an example of me, and send fire from heaven and consume me. When I rose to reply, I felt a Divine sense of the approbation of God, and that He would give me success.

I addressed the multitude about three hours, and when I closed my argument I opened the door of the Church, and invited all that would renounce Shakerism to come and give me their hand. Forty-seven came forward, and then and there openly renounced the dreadful delusion. The next day I followed those that fled; and the next day I went from cabin to cabin, taking the names of those that returned to the solid foundation of truth; and my number rose to eighty-seven. I then organized them into a regular society, and the next fall had a preacher sent to them. And perhaps this victory may be considered among the first-fruits of Methodism in that part of this new country. This was in 1808.

At this meeting I collected, as well as I could, the names and places where it was supposed they wanted Methodist preaching. I made out and returned a kind of plan for a Circuit, carried it to Conference, and they were temporarily supplied by the presiding elder in 1809 and 1810. In 1811 the Circuit was called St. Vincennes, and was attached to the Cumberland District, and Thomas Stillwell appointed the preacher in charge.

CHAPTER VI.

EXHORTING AND FIRST PREACHING.

I WILL now resume my personal narrative. I went on enjoying great comfort and peace. I attended several camp-meetings among the Methodists and Presbyterians. At all of them there were many souls converted to God. At one of these camp-meetings something like the following incident occurred :—

There was a great stir of religion in the crowded congregation that attended. Many opposed the work, and among the rest a Mr. D——, who called himself a Jew. He was tolerably smart, and seemed to take great delight in opposing the Christian religion. In the intermissions, the young men and boys of us, who professed religion, would retire to the woods and hold prayer-meetings; and if we knew of any boys that were seeking religion, we would take them along and pray for them. Many of them obtained religion in these praying circles, and raised loud shouts of praise to God, in which those of us that were religious would join.

One evening a large company of us retired for prayer. In the midst of our little meeting this Jew appeared, and he desired to know what we were about. Well, I told him. He said it was all wrong, that it was idolatry to pray to Jesus Christ, and that God did not, nor would He, answer such prayers. I soon saw his object was to get us into debate and break up our prayer-meeting. I asked him, "Do you really believe there is a God?"

"Yes, I do," said he.

"Do you believe that God will hear your prayers?"

"Yes," said he.

"Do you really believe that this work among us is wrong?"

He answered, "Yes."

"Well now, my dear sir," said I, "let us test this matter. If you are in earnest, get down here and pray to God to stop this work; and if it is wrong, He will answer your petition and stop it; if it is not wrong, all hell cannot stop it."

The rest of our company, seeing me so bold, took courage. The Jew hesitated. I said, "Get down instantly and pray; for, if we are wrong, we want to know it." After still lingering and showing unmistakeable signs of his unwillingness, I rallied him again. Slowly he kneeled, cleared his throat, and coughed. I said, "Now, boys, pray with all your might that God may answer by fire."

Our Jew began and said, tremblingly, "O Lord God Almighty," and coughed again, cleared his throat, and started again, repeating the same words. We saw his evident confusion, and we simultaneously prayed out aloud at the top of our voices. The Jew leaped up and started off, and we raised the shout and had a glorious time. Several of our mourners were converted, and we all rose and started into camp at the top of our speed, shouting, having, as we firmly believed, obtained a signal victory over the devil and the Jew.

In 1802 William M'Kendree was presiding elder of Kentucky District. John Page and Thomas Wilkerson were appointed to the Cumberland Circuit. The Conference this fall was held at Strother's Meeting-house, Tennessee. This was the first time I saw Bishop Asbury, that great, devoted man of God. Here the Cumberland District was formed, and John Page appointed presiding elder. The name of Cumberland Circuit was changed into Red River Circuit, and Jesse Walker was appointed to ride it. This was the Circuit on which I lived.

The membership of the Western Conference this year numbered 7,201; the travelling preachers numbered 27, probationers and all.

At a quarterly-meeting held in the spring of this year, 1802, Jesse Walker, our preacher in charge, came to me and handed me a small slip of paper, with these words written on it:—

"PETER CARTWRIGHT is hereby permitted to exercise his gifts as an exhorter in the Methodist Episcopal Church, so long as his practice is agreeable to the Gospel. Signed in behalf of the society at Ebenezer.
                                                "JESSE WALKER, A. P."
"May, 1802."

I was very much surprised I had not been talked to by the preacher, nor had I formally attempted to exhort. It is true, in class and other meetings, when my soul was filled with the love of God, I would mount a bench and exhort with all the power I had, and it is also true that my mind had been deeply exercised about exhorting and preaching too. I told Brother Walker I did not want licence to exhort; that if I did not feel happy I could not exhort, but if my soul got happy I felt that I had licence enough. He urged me to keep the licence, alleging that it was the more orderly way, and I yielded to his advice.

To show how matters were done up in those early days of Methodism, I will here state that this permit to exhort was all the licence I ever received from the Church to preach until I received my parchment of ordination.

The fall of this year my father moved from Logan County down toward the mouth of the Cumberland River, into what was called Lewiston County. This was a new country, and, at least, eighty miles from any Circuit. There was no regular Circuit, and no organized classes; but there were a good many scattered members of the Methodist Episcopal Church through that region of country. I applied to Brother Page, our presiding elder, for a letter for myself, my mother, and one sister, which he gave us. On examination, I found that mine contained a "Benjamin's mess." It not only stated my membership and authority to exhort, but it gave me authority to travel through all that destitute region, hold meetings, organize classes, and, in a word, to form a Circuit, and meet him at the next fall at the fourth quarterly-meeting of the Red River Circuit, with a plan of a new Circuit, number of members, names of preachers, if any, exhorters, class-leaders, &c., &c., &c. I am sorry I did not preserve the document; for, surely, all things considered, it would be a curiosity to educated and refined Methodists at this day.

I felt bad on the reception of this paper, and told Brother Page I did not want to take it, for I saw through the solemn responsibilities it rolled upon me. I told him just to give me a simple letter of membership; that, although I did think at times that it was my duty to preach, I had little education, and that it was my intention to go to school the next year. He then told me that this was the very best school or college that I could find between heaven and earth; but advised me, when my father got settled down there, if I could find a good moral school with a good teacher, to go to it through the winter; then, in the spring and summer, form the Circuit, and do the best I could

Shortly after my father settled himself, I inquired for a good teacher and school, and found that there was one a few miles off, taught by a well-educated teacher, a seceder minister, who had finished his education in Lexington, Ky., under a Mr. Rankin. I went and entered as a scholar, and boarded with a fine old Methodist man, close by. This school was called Brown's Academy. He taught all the branches of a common English education, also the dead languages. I now thought Providence had opened my way to obtain a good education, which I had so long desired, and of which I had been deprived without remedy. I entered the school and was making very rapid progress.

The brother with whom I boarded, being a zealous man of God, insisted that we should hold meetings on Sundays and in the evenings. To this I consented. We held prayer-meetings on evenings, and Sundays I attempted to exhort the large congregations that attended. We soon collected a small class from the scattered Methodists around, had a few conversions, and I began to think that God had wonderfully opened my way before me. But soon a storm of persecution arose. My teacher was a very bigoted seceder, and I believe he hated the Methodists more than he hated the devil. I know he hated them worse than the bottle; for he would get drunk at times.

There was a large class of young men in school about my age, and they were very wicked and profane. I saw my perilous condition, and put myself under strong restraints, so that I should give no one any just offence. My teacher would try to draw me into debate, but this I avoided. The young men set themselves to play tricks and start false reports on me, by way of diversion calling me the Methodist preacher. Teacher and all would do this. I told Mr. Brown and all the rest that I was no preacher, but that I wished I was a good one. At length two of these young students fixed a plan to duck me in the creek that ran hard by. There was a very beautiful grassy plat of ground right on the bank of the creek, in a retired spot. The bank was about seven feet perpendicular, and there was a deep hole of water right opposite, in which the water was ten feet deep. They decoyed me to this place under the pretence that they wanted me to pray for them, pretending to be in great distress on account of their sins. I was suspicious, but thought if they were sincere it would be wrong to refuse them. So, putting myself on my guard as best I could, I went with them, not knowing their plan. When we came to the bank of the creek, they both seized me, intending to throw me over the perpendicular bank into the deep water. As quick as thought, I jerked loose from one, and gave the other a sudden flirt over the bank into the stream. The other and I clinched, and, being nearly equal in strength, a hard tussle ensued. In the scuffle we fell to the ground, and I rolled over toward the precipice, holding him fast, until, at length, into the deep hole we both went, and then had to swim out.

Although this, to me, was an unpleasant affair, yet there was no shouting over me ; for if I had got wet, I had ducked both of them. I bore all these things for some time patiently; but, my difficulties increasing, I complained to Mr. Brown, the teacher. He would do nothing to bring things right. I then left the school, deeply regretting that I was thereby deprived of the privilege of finishing my education. I then prepared myself, and started out to form a kind of Circuit, and gather up scattered members and organize classes. I had much opposition in some places, but in others was kindly received. We had some very powerful displays of Divine grace, a goodly number obtained religion, and I received about seventy into society, appointed leaders, met classes, sung, prayed, and exhorted, and, under the circumstances, did the best I knew how.

Here I found the celebrated James Axley, and took him into the Church. Peace to his memory. He was in after years favourably known as a powerful and successful travelling preacher. He was a great and good man of God. He married, located, and long since went to his reward.

In the fall of this year, 1803, I met Brothers Page and Walker, reported my success and the plan of the Circuit. It was called Livingston Circuit, and Jesse Walker was appointed to it, and travelled it in 1804 and 1805. The increase of members this year was over 9,000 throughout the Connexion. In the Western Conference the increase was 1,500. The number of travelling preachers was about 35. There were four presiding-elder Districts in the Western Conference· Holston, Cumberland, Kentucky, and Ohio. Brother Page located, and Lewis Garrett succeeded him on the Cumberland District. The Red River Circuit, in this District, was a very large one. It had but one preacher appointed to it, namely, Ralph Lotspeich.

Brother Garrett, the new elder, called on me at my father's, and urged me to go on this Circuit with Brother Lotspeich. My father was unwilling, but my mother urged me to go, and finally prevailed. This was in October, 1803, when I was a little over eighteen years of age. I had a hard struggle to give my consent, and although I thought it my duty to preach, yet I thought I could do this, and not throw myself into the ranks as a Circuit preacher, when I was liable to be sent from Greenbrier to Natchez; no members hardly to support a preacher, the Discipline only allowing a single man eighty dollars, and in nine cases out of ten he could not get half of that amount. These were times that tried men's souls and bodies too.

At last I literally gave up the world, and started, bidding farewell to father and mother, brothers and sisters, and met Brother Lotspeich at an appointment in Logan County. He told me I must preach that night. This I had never done; mine was an exhorter's dispensation. I tried to beg off, but he urged me to make the effort. I went out and prayed fervently for aid from heaven. All at once it seemed to me as if I could never preach at all, but I struggled in prayer. At length I asked God, if He had called me to preach, to give me aid that night, and give me one soul, that is, convert one soul under my preaching, as evidence that I was called to this work.

I went into the house, took my stand, gave out a hymn, sang, and prayed. I then rose, gave them for a text Isaiah xxvi. 4: "Trust ye in the Lord for ever: for in the Lord Jehovah is everlasting strength." The Lord gave light, liberty, and power; the congregation was melted into tears. There was present a professed infidel. The word reached his heart by the Eternal Spirit. He was powerfully convicted, and, as I believe, soundly converted to God that night, and joined the Church, and afterward became a useful member of the same.

I travelled on this Circuit one quarter, took twenty-five into the Church, and at the end of three months received six dollars. The health of Brother Crutchfield, who was on the Waynesville Circuit, having failed, he retired from labour, and Brother Garrett placed me on that Circuit in his place, and put on the Circuit with me Thomas Lasley, a fine young man, the son of an old local preacher who lived in Green County.

Our Circuit was very large, reaching from the north of Green River to the Cumberland River, and south of said river into the State of Tennessee. Here was a vast field to work in; our rides were long, our appointments few and far between. There were a great many Baptists in the bounds of the Circuit, and among them were over thirty preachers, some of whom were said to be very talented. In the four weeks that it took us to go round the Circuit, we had but two days' rest, and often we preached every day and every night; and although in my nineteenth year, I was nearly beardless, and cut two of my back jaw teeth this year. Hence they called me the "boy preacher," and a great many flocked out to hear the boy. A revival broke out in many neighbourhoods, and scores of souls were converted to God and joined the Methodist Episcopal Church; but there was also considerable persecution.

We had a preaching place in what, at that early day, was called Stockton Valley. There were several of the members of the Methodist Episcopal Church scattered around in the neighbourhood, but no organized class. The Baptists, some years before, had a society here, and had built a log meeting-house, which was very common at an early day in the West. It was covered with boards. The Baptists flourished here for a considerable time, and they had enjoyed regular monthly preaching; but the society had nearly died out, and the preaching had been withdrawn for several years. The house was old and out of repair. As I passed round my Circuit, I was requested to preach a funeral sermon at this old church. Accordingly, I left an appointment on a Sabbath. When I came, there was a very large congregation. While I was preaching, the power of God fell on the assembly, and there was an awful shaking among the dry bones. Several fell to the floor and cried for mercy.

The people besought me to preach again at night. I gave out an appointment accordingly, and, having several days' rest, owing to a new arrangement in the Circuit, I kept up the meeting night and day for some time, and at every coming together we had a gracious work. Many obtained religion, and great was the joy of the people. There were twenty-three very clear and sound conversions. As a matter of course they felt a great love to me, whom they all claimed as the instrument, in the hand of God, of their conversion. I was young and inexperienced in doctrine, and especially was I unacquainted with the proselyting tricks of those that held to exclusive immersion as the mode, and the only mode, of baptism. I believe if I had opened the doors of the Church then, all of them would have joined the Methodist Church; but I thought I would give them time to inform themselves. Accordingly, I told them that when I came again, I would explain our rules and open the doors of the Church, and then they could join us if they liked our rules and doctrines. In the mean time I left them some copies of our Discipline to read.

After doing this I started on my Circuit round, and although the Baptist preachers had left this place, without preaching in it for years, yet, in a few days after I was gone, there were sent on appointments for the next Sabbath three of the Baptist preachers, and they came on, and all three preached as their custom was, and they all opened with the cry of, " Water, water! You must follow your Lord down into the water." They then appointed what they called a union meeting there, to commence the next Friday and hold over Sabbath; and although I have lived long and studied hard, I have never to this day found out what a Baptist means by a union meeting. But to return. The few scattered Methodists in the neighbourhood took the alarm, for fear these preachers would run my converts into the water before I would come round, and they dispatched an old exhorter after me, saying I must come immediately, or my converts would all be ducked. I had appointments out a-head, and I told the old exhorter, if I went, he must go on and fill my appointments, to which he readily agreed. So back I came on Friday to the commencement of their union meeting. Two of them preached, but they paid no attention to me at all.

As they had no meeting at night, I gave out an appointment for night at S——'s, Esq. He and his wife were two of my converts, and kind of leaders in the neighbourhood. The people flocked out, and we had a good meeting and two conversions

Next day we repaired to the old log meeting-house, and heard two more water sermons. When they were done preaching, they opened the way for persons to join the Church by giving in their experience. One old lady arose, and gave in something for an experience that had happened about ten years before. Then an old man rose, and told a remarkable dream he had in North Carolina twenty years before. They were both accordingly received by giving them the right hand of fellowship. There was then a seeming pause The preachers urged the people to come forward and give in their experience. O, how I felt! I was afraid that some one of my young converts would break the way, and the rest would then follow, and so I would lose all my converts. At length one of those young converts rose, and gave in his experience, claiming me, under God, as the instrument of his conviction and conversion; then another and another, till twenty-three of them told their experience; every one of them claiming me, under God, as the instrument of their salvation.

Their experiences were pronounced good, and the right hand of fellowship was freely given, and there was great joy in the camp, but it was death in the pot to me. I thought I could not bear up under it. I was sitting thinking what I would do. "I am bereft of my children, and what have I left?" Just behind me sat a very intelligent lady, who had long been a member of the Methodist Episcopal Church. About the time they were done giving the right hand of fellowship and rejoicing over my stolen children, a thought struck my mind very forcibly to give in my experience, and act as though I intended to join the Baptist Church. "It may be that I can yet save them." I rose up, and gave in my experience; they gave me the right hand of fellowship, and then there was great rejoicing over the Methodist preaching boy.

Just as I sat down I felt some one touch me on the shoulder. I turned, and, as I looked round, I met the eyes of my intelligent Methodist sister, and the large tears were coursing down her cheeks and dropping off her chin.

"O, brother," said she, in a subdued tone, "are you going to leave us?"

I replied to her, "Dear sister, fear not; I know what I am about. Pray hard. I hope to retake my children yet." And though she did not understand my plan, yet my reply seemed to quiet her fears.

There was a fine creek running near the old church. The preachers directed us all to appear next morning at nine o'clock, with a change of apparel, to be baptized.

I held meeting again that night, and had a good time. My situation was a critical one. I had no one to advise with. I dared not tell any one what I was going to do, for fear my plan would out and my object be defeated. I rose early next morning, retired to the woods, and if ever I asked God in good earnest for help, it was then.

Brother and Sister S——, with whom I stayed, prepared a change of apparel, in order to baptism. At the appointed hour we all met at the creek, but I took no change of apparel. I had been baptized, and I did not intend to abjure my baptism. But I kept this all to myself. There was a great crowd out to see us immersed. My twenty-three young converts, and the two old, dry dreamers that first gave in their experience, were all dressed and ready for the performance of what they considered to be their Christian duty. The preachers appeared. One of them sang and prayed, then gave us an exhortation, and bade us come forward. I knew all the time that it was all-important to my success that I should present myself first. Accordingly I stepped forward, and said, "Brother M——," who was the preacher and administrator, "I wish to join the Baptist Church, if I can come in with a good conscience. I have been baptized, and my conscience is perfectly satisfied with it, and I cannot submit to be re-baptized. Can I come into your Church on these terms?"

The position I occupied startled the preacher.

"When were you baptized?" he asked.

"Years gone by," I replied.

"But how was it done? Who baptized you?" was the next inquiry.

"One of the best preachers the Lord ever made."

"Was it done by sprinkling?"

"Yes, sir."

"That is no baptism at all."

I replied, "The Scriptures say that baptism is not the putting away the filth of the flesh, but the answer of a good conscience; and my conscience is perfectly satisfied with my baptism, and your conscience has nothing to do with it."

"Well," said he, "it is contrary to our faith and order to let you come into the Baptist Church in that way. We cannot do it."

"Brother M——," said I, "your faith and order must be wrong. The Church has heard my experience, and pronounced it good; and you believe that I am a Christian, and cannot fall away so as to be finally lost. What am I to do? Are you going to keep me out of the Church, bleating round the walls like a lost sheep in a gang by myself? Brother M——, you must receive me into the Church. I have fully made up my mind to join you on these terms; now, will you let me into the Church?"

Our preacher by this time had evidently lost his patience, and he very sharply bid me stand away, and not detain others. It was an intensely thrilling moment with me. I cast a look around on the crowd, and saw they were enlisted in my favour. I cast a wistful eye on the young converts; their eyes met mine most sympathetically, and many of them were weeping, they were so deeply affected. They all involuntarily seemed to move toward me, and their looks plainly spoke in my favour. It was an awful moment. O, how I felt! Who can describe my feelings?

I stepped aside. Brother S—— stood next to the preacher, dressed ready for baptism; his wife was also dressed, and leaning on her husband's arm. Brother S—— said:—

"Brother M——, are you going to reject Brother Cartwright, and not receive him into the Church?"

"I cannot receive him," said Brother M——.

"Well," said Brother S——, "if Brother Cartwright, who has been the means, in the hand of God, of my conversion, and the saving of so many precious souls, cannot come into the Church, I cannot and will not join it." "Nor I," said his wife; "Nor I," "Nor I;" and thus it went round, until every one of my twenty-three young converts filed off, and gathered around me. "That's right, brethren," said I; "stand by me, and don't leave me; the Lord will bring all right!"

Well, the two old dreamers were baptized, and then the preachers urged the rest to come; but all in vain. Now, my dear reader, just imagine, if you can, how I felt. I had a great mind to shout right out, and should have done so, but forbearance, at that time at least, was a virtue.

From the creek we repaired to the old log-church. Three of their ministers preached; and you may depend on it, I got a large share of abuse. They compared me to the Pharisees of old; for they said I would not go in myself, and those that would go in I had prevented; but I bore it as best I could. They stated that in all probability these souls that I had hindered would be lost; and if so, their damnation would be laid to me! But this did not alarm me much; for they had pronounced us all Christians good and true, and had often in their sermons there said that if a person were really converted, he never could lose his religion. How, then, could we be lost? and what was there to alarm us? The congregation saw the absurdity, and more and more were interested in my favour.

Next came on their communion. There were some loose planks laid across the benches, and all the members of their particular faith, that

D

had been immersed, were invited to seat themselves on these planks. I was determined to give them another downward tilt; so I took my seat with the communicants; and some of the young converts, seeing me do so, seated themselves there also. But when the deacons came with the bread and wine, they passed us by. When they had got round, I rose and asked for the bread and wine for myself and the young converts. This threw a difficulty in the way of the deacons; however, they asked the preachers if they might give us the elements. The preachers peremptorily forbade it.

I then said, "My brethren, you, after hearing our experience, pronounced us Christians; and you say a Christian never can be lost; and our Saviour pronounced a solemn woe on those that offend one of His little ones : now do, therefore, give us the bread and wine!"

One of the preachers gave me a sharp reproof, and told me to be silent. This treatment enlisted the sympathies of almost the entire assembly, and they cried out, "Shame! shame!" Just as the preacher was about to dismiss the congregation, I rose, and asked of them the privilege of speaking to the people fifteen or twenty minutes, to explain myself. This they refused. I said, "Very well; I am in a free country, and know my rights." He then dismissed them, and I sprang on a bench, and said to the people that if they would meet me a few rods from the church, and hear me, I would make my defence.

The people flocked out; I mounted an old log, and the crowd gathered around me. I showed them the inconsistency of the Baptist preachers, and laid it to them as well as my inexperience would permit; and closed by saying that, as I and my children in the Gospel could not, in any consistent way, be admitted into the Baptist Church, I was now determined to organize a Methodist Church. I explained our rules, and invited all that were willing to join us, to come forward, and give me their hands and names. Twenty-seven came forward, —all of my twenty-three young converts, and four others; and before the year ended, we took into the Church there seventy-seven members, but my Baptist friends blowed almost entirely out. I was greatly encouraged to go on, and do the best I could.

This year, (1804,) in the Western Conference there were 9,600 members; our increase was 2,400   The number of travelling preachers was 36.   Our Annual Conference this fall was held in October, at Mount Gerizim, in Kentucky. Our Annual Conferences in those days were universally held with closed doors, none but members of the Conference, or visiting members from other Annual Conferences, being permitted to occupy seats in the body. At this Conference Bishop Asbury presided.

At the close of my labours on Waynesville Circuit, I was recommended to the Annual Conference by the quarterly meeting as a proper person to be received into the travelling connexion. There were eighteen preachers recommended and received at this Conference, and, perhaps, of this number, I am the only surviving one left. One by one, these early pioneers in the travelling ranks have fallen victims to death; most of them, as far as I am informed, witnessed a good confession, and have gone to heaven to swell the triumphant shouts of the redeemed, and meet their spiritual children in a better country than the "far West." There was one of this number that made shipwreck, and proved the truth of God's word, which says, " One -sinner destroyeth much good."

CHAPTER VII.

PRIMITIVE METHODISM.

At this Conference, in October, 1804, I was sent as the junior preacher to Salt River and Shelbyville Circuits, which were joined together, Benjamin Lakin in charge, and William M'Kendree presiding elder.

The Circuit was in the Kentucky District. It was a large six weeks' Circuit, and extended from the rolling fork of Green River south, to the Ohio River north, and even crossed the Ohio into what was then called Clark's, or the Illinois Grant, now in the eastern portion of Indiana State. We had a little Book Concern then in its infancy, struggling hard for existence. We had no Missionary Society; no Sunday-school Society; no Church papers; no Bible or Tract Societies; no colleges, seminaries, academies, or univers.ties , all the efforts to get up colleges under the patronage of the Methodist Episcopal Church in these United States and territories, were signal failures. We had no pewed churches, no choirs, no organs; in a word, we had no instrumental music in our churches anywhere. The Methodists in that early day dressed plain; attended their meetings faithfully, especially preaching, prayer and class-meetings; they wore no jewellery, no ruffles , they would frequently walk three or four miles to class-meetings and home again, on Sundays; they would go thirty or forty miles to their quarterly meetings, and think it a glorious privilege to meet their presiding elder and the rest of the preachers. They could, nearly every soul of them, sing our hymns and spiritual songs. They religiously kept the Sabbath day; many of them abstained from dram-drinking, not because the temperance reformation was ever heard of in that day, but because it was interdicted in the General Rules of our Discipline. The Methodists of that day stood up and faced their preacher when they sung; they kneeled down in the public congregation as elsewhere, when the preacher said, "Let us pray." There was no standing among the members in time of prayer; especially the abominable practice of sitting down during that exercise was unknown among early Methodists. Parents did not allow their children to go to balls or plays; they did not send them' to dancing schools; they generally fasted once a week, and almost universally on the Friday before each quarterly-meeting. If the Methodists had dressed in the same "superfluity of naughtiness" then as they do now, there were very few even out of the Church that would have any confidence in their religion. But O, how have things changed for the worse in this educational age of the world! I do declare there was little or no necessity for preachers to say anything against fashionable and superfluous dressing in those primitive times of early Methodism; the very wicked themselves knew it was wrong, and spoke out against it in the members of the Church. The moment we saw members begin to trim in dress after the fashionable world, we all knew they would not hold out. Permit me here to give a few cases in confirmation of some things I have said

This year, in my Circuit, there lived a very wealthy, fashionable family. The good lady governess of this family attended a two days' meeting I held in the neighbourhood. On Saturday, under preaching, the Lord reached her proud heart, and although, perhaps, she was the finest dressed lady in the congregation, when I invited mourners, she was the first that came and fell on her knees, praying aloud for mercy. It pleased God, before our meeting closed, to bless her with a sense of pardoning mercy, and she rose and shouted aloud for joy; she also joined the Church. When we closed the meeting, I gave out our love-feast for next morning at eight o'clock; not a word was said about dress. She went home, intending to come to lovefeast next morning, but it occurred to her that all her superfluities ought to be laid aside now, and that she, as a Christian, for example's sake, ought to go in plain attire; but, alas for her! she had not a plain dress in the world. Said she to herself, "What shall I do?" She immediately hunted up the plainest and most easily altered dress she had. To work at it she went; trimmed it and fixed it tolerably plain. To lovefeast she came; and when she rose to speak, she told all about her trouble to get plainly attired to appear in lovefeast as she thought she ought to. Take another case :—

I travelled in the State of Ohio in 1806, and at a largely attended camp-meeting near New Lancaster, there was a great work of God going on; many were pleading for mercy; many were getting religion;

and the wicked looked solemn and awful. The pulpit in the woods
was a large stand; it would hold a dozen people, and I would not let
the lookers-on crowd into it, but kept it clear that at any time I might
occupy it for the purpose of giving directions to the congregation.

There were two young ladies, sisters, lately from Baltimore, or
somewhere down east. They had been provided for on the ground in
the tent of a very religious sister of theirs. They were very fashion-
ably dressed; I think they must have had, in rings, earrings, bracelets,
gold chains, lockets, &c., at least one or two hundred dollars' worth of
jewellery about their persons. The altar was crowded to overflowing
with mourners; and these young ladies were very solemn. They met
me at the stand, and asked permission to sit down inside it. I told
them that if they would promise me to pray to God for religion, they
might take a seat there. They were too deeply affected to be idle
lookers-on; and when I got them seated in the stand, I called them,
and urged them to pray; and I called others to my aid. They became
deeply engaged; and about midnight they were both powerfully converted. They rose to their feet, and gave some very triumphant
shouts; and then very deliberately took off their gold chains, earrings,
lockets, &c., and handed them to me, saying, "We have no more use
for these idols. If religion is the glorious, good thing you have
represented it to be, it throws these idols into eternal shade."

Take still another case in point. In 1810, when I was travelling in
West Tennessee, at a camp-meeting I was holding there was a great
revival in progress. At that time, it was customary for gentlemen of
fashion to wear ruffled shirts. There was a wealthy gentleman thus
attired at our meeting, and he was brought under strong conviction.
I led him to the altar with the mourners; and he was much engaged.
But it seemed there was something he would not give up. I was
praying by his side, and talking to him, when all on a sudden he stood
erect on his knees, and with his hands he deliberately opened his shirt
bosom, took hold of his ruffles, tore them off, and threw them down
in the straw; and in less than two minutes God blessed his soul,
and he sprang to his feet, loudly praising God.

I state these cases to show that unless the heart is desperately
hardened through the deceitfulness of sin, there is a solemn conviction on all minds that fashionable frivolities are all contrary to the
humble spirit of our Saviour; but idolatry is dreadfully deceptive,
and we must remember that no idolater hath any inheritance in the
kingdom of God. Let the Methodists take care.

We had at this early day no course of study prescribed, as at
present; but William M'Kendree, afterward bishop, but then my presiding elder, directed me to a proper course of reading and study. He

selected books for me, both literary and theological; and every quarterly visit he made, he examined into my progress, and corrected my errors, if I had fallen into any. He delighted to instruct me in English grammar.

Brother Lakin had charge of the Circuit. My business was to preach, meet the classes, visit the society and the sick, and then to my books and study; and I say that I am more indebted to Bishop M'Kendree for my little attainments in literature and divinity, than to any other man on earth. And I believe that if presiding elders would do their duty by young men in this way, it would be more advantageous than all the colleges and biblical institutes in the land; for they then could learn and practise every day.

Suppose, now, Mr. Wesley had been obliged to wait for a literary and theologically trained band of preachers before he moved in the glorious work of his day, what would Methodism have been in the Wesleyan Connexion to-day? Suppose the Methodist Episcopal Church in these United States had been under the necessity of waiting for men thus qualified, what would her condition have been at this time? In despite of all John Wesley's prejudices, he providentially saw that, to accomplish the glorious work for which God had raised him up, he must yield to the superior wisdom of Jehovah, and send out his "lay preachers" to wake up a slumbering world. If Bishop Asbury had waited for this choice literary band of preachers, infidelity would have swept these United States from one end to the other.

Methodism in Europe this day would have been as a thousand to one, if the Wesleyans had stood by the old land-marks of John Wesley: but no; they must introduce pews, literary institutions, and theological institutes, till a plain, old-fashioned preacher, such as one of Mr. Wesley's "lay preachers," would be scouted, and not allowed to occupy one of their pulpits. Some of the best and most useful men that were ever called of God to plant Methodism in this happy republic, were among the early pioneer preachers, east, west, north, and south; and especially in our mighty West. We have no such preachers now as some of the first ones, who were sent out to Kentucky and Tennessee.

The Presbyterians and other Calvinistic branches of the Protestant Church, used to contend for an educated ministry, for pews, for instrumental music, for a congregational or stated salaried ministry. The Methodists universally opposed these ideas, and the illiterate Methodist preachers actually set the world on fire, (the American world at least,) while they were lighting their matches!

Methodist preachers were called by literary gentlemen, illiterate, ignorant babblers. I recollect once to have come across one of these

Latin and Greek scholars, a regular graduate in theology. In order to bring me into contempt in a public company, he addressed me in Greek. In my younger days I had learned ¡considerable of German. I listened to him as if I understood it all, and then replied in Dutch. This he knew nothing about, neither did he understand Hebrew. He concluded that I had answered him in Hebrew, and immediately caved in, and stated to the company that I was the first educated Methodist preacher he ever saw.

I do not wish to undervalue education, but really I have seen so many of these educated preachers who forcibly reminded me of lettuce growing under the shade of a peach-tree, or like a gosling that had got the straddles by wading in the dew, that I turn away sick and faint. Now this educated ministry and theological training are no longer an experiment. Other denominations have tried them, and they have proved a perfect failure; and is it not strange that Methodist preachers will try to gather up these antiquated systems, when enlightened Presbyterians and Congregationalists have acknowledged that the Methodist plan is the best in the world, and try to improve, as they say, our system, alleging that our educational institutions have created a necessity for theological institutes? Verily we have fallen on evil times. Is it possible that now, when we abound in education, we need biblical instruction more than when we had no education, or very little? Surely, if we ever needed Bible instruction, it was when we could derive no benefit from literary institutions. This is my common-sense view of the subject.

I awfully fear for our beloved Methodism. Multiply colleges, universities, seminaries, and academies; multiply our agencies, and editorships, and fill them all with our best and most efficient preachers, and you localize the ministry and secularize them too; then farewell to itinerancy; and when this fails we plunge right into Congregationalism, and stop precisely where all other denominations started. I greatly desire to see all the interests of the Methodist Church promoted, and when all our presidents, professors, editors, and agents shall be laymen, and our ministers follow their appropriate calling, namely, preach the Gospel to a dying world; and if they will not fall into the travelling ranks and be men of one work, let them locate; for it is certain, as long as they fill these offices and agencies, it is like a man undertaking to ride a race with the reins of his horse's bridle tied to a stump. Every man who fills these offices and agencies, and retains a membership in the travelling connexion, is a clog to the itinerant wheels, and must, ere long, stop the travelling car; and when that takes place, farewell to Methodism.

Is it not manifest that the employing so many of our preachers in these agencies and professorships is one of the great causes why we have such a scarcity of preachers to fill the regular work ? More-over, these presidents, professors, agents, and editors, get a greater amount of pay, and get it more certainly too, than a travelling preacher, who has to breast every storm, and often falls very far short of his disciplinary allowance. Here is a great temptation to those who are qualified to fill those high offices to seek them, and give up the regular work of preaching and trying to save souls. And is it not manifest to every candid observer that very few of those young men who believe they are called of God to preach the Gospel, and are persuaded to go to a college or a biblical institute, the better to qualify them for the great work of the ministry, ever go into the regular travelling ministry ? The reason is plainly this : having quieted their consciences with the flattering unction of obtaining a sanctified education, while they have neglected the duty of regularly preaching Jesus to dying sinners, their moral sensibilities are blunted, and they see an opening prospect of getting better pay as teachers in high schools or other institutions of learning, and from the prospect of gain they are easily persuaded that they can meet their moral obligations in disseminating sanctified learning. Thus, as sure as a leaden ball tends to the earth in obedience to the laws of gravity, just so sure our present *modus operandi* tends to a congregational ministry. And if this course is pursued a little longer, the Methodist Church will bid a long, long farewell to her beloved itinerancy, to which we, under God, owe almost everything that is intrinsically valuable in Methodism.

It is said that the young men who are studying in the Biblical Institute at Concord, which is patronized by all the New-England Con-ferences, spend their evenings, and especially their Sabbaths, in the surrounding villages, lecturing and preaching, to the great satisfaction and edification of the Churches, and their brethren give them some-thing to aid in their support while they are prosecuting their studies. But who is so hoodwinked or cable-towed by prejudice, as not to see that this very course is well calculated to sap the foundation of the itinerancy, and supplant the regularly appointed pastor, or supersede his labours, and will finally end in a settled ministry ? But I must resume the narrative.

Our Conference this fall, 1805, was held at Cole's Meeting-house, Scott County, Kentucky. Bishop Asbury, in consequence of affliction, failed to be with us, and the Conference elected William M'Kendree president. Six more preachers were admitted on trial. The number of travelling preachers was 38. Our membership numbered 11,877 ; and our increase in members was 2,277.

CHAPTER VIII.

SCIOTO CIRCUIT.

My appointment, during 1805–6, was on the Scioto Circuit, Ohio State and District. John Sale was presiding elder, and James Quinn* was senior preacher, or preacher in charge. The reader will see how greatly I was favoured the first two years of my regular itinerant life, to be placed under two such men as Benjamin Lakin and James Quinn, and more, two such presiding elders as William M'Kendree and John Sale. These four men were able ministers of Jesus Christ, lived long, did much good, witnessed a good confession, died happy, and are 'all now safely housed in heaven. Peace to their memory for ever !

Scioto Circuit extended from the Ohio River to Chillcothe, situated on that river; and crossed it near the mouth, at what is now called Portsmouth. It was a four-weeks' Circuit, and there were 474 members on it. Dr. Tiffin, who was governor of the State, was a local preacher; and both he and his wife were worthy members of our Church. He lived at Chillicothe, then the seat of government for the State.

There were two incidents happened while I was on the east end of this Circuit, which I will relate.

We had an appointment near Eagle Creek. Here the Shakers broke in Mr. Dunlevy, whom we have mentioned elsewhere as having been a regular Presbyterian minister, who had left that Church and joined the New Lights. His New Light increased so fast, that he lost what little sense he had, and was now a ranting Shaker. He came up here, and roared and fulminated a while, led many astray, flourished for some time, and then his influence died away, and he left for parts unknown.

On the south-eastern part of the Circuit, we took in a new preaching place, at a Mr. Moor's. We gave them Sunday preaching. Mr. Moor had built a large hewn log-house, two stories high There was no partition in the second story ; but it was seated, and he gave it to us to preach in. Not far from this place lived a regularly educated Presbyterian preacher, who had a fine family, and was in many respects a fine man, but, unhappily, he had contracted a love for strong drink. He had preached in this neighbourhood, and was much beloved, for he was withal a very good preacher.

In making my way on one occasion to Mr. Moor's, to my Sunday appointment, I got lost and was belated, and when I arrived, there

* See Appendix E.—*James Quinn.*

was a large assembly collected, and this minister was preaching to them, and he preached well, and I was quite pleased with the sermon so far as I heard it. When he was done, he undertook to make a public apology for a drunken spree he had got into a few days before. " Well," thought I, " *this* is right; all right, I suppose !" But to excuse himself for his unaccountable love of whiskey, he stated that he had been informed by his mother that before he was born she longed for whiskey; and he supposed that this was the cause of his appetite for strong drink, for he had loved it from his earliest recollection. This was the substance of his apology.

I felt somewhat indignant at this; and when I rose to close after him, I stated to the congregation that I thought the preacher's apology for drunkenness was infinitely worse than the act of drunkenness itself; that I looked upon it as a lie, and a downright slander on his mother; and that I believed his love of whiskey was the result of the intemperate use of it, in which he had indulged until he formed the habit; and that I, for one, was not willing to accept or believe the truth of his apology; that I feared the preacher would live and die a drunkard, and be damned at last; and that I hoped the people there would not receive him as a preacher until he gave ample evidence that he was entirely cured of drunkenness.

After I made these statements, I felt that God was willing to bless the people there and then; and, raising my voice, gave them as warm an exhortation as I could command. Suddenly an awful power fell on the congregation, and they instantly fell right and left, and cried aloud for mercy. I suppose there were not less than thirty persons smitten down; the young, the old, and middle-aged, indiscriminately, were operated on in this way. My voice at that day was strong and clear; and I could sing, exhort, pray, and preach almost all the time, day and night. I went through the assembly, singing, exhorting, praying, and directing poor sinners to Christ. While I was thus engaged, the Presbyterian minister left.

There were a few scattered members of the Church around this place, who got happy and shouted aloud for joy, and joined in and exhorted sinners, and they helped me very much. Indeed, our meeting lasted all night, and the greater part of next day. Between twenty and thirty professed religion, and joined the Church; and fully as many more went home under strong conviction and in deep distress. Many of them afterward obtained religion, and joined the Church.

There was a very remarkable case that I will mention here. There was one lady about forty-five years old, who was a member of the Presbyterian Church, and a very rigid predestinarian. Her husband was a Methodist, and several of their children had obtained religion among the young converts. This lady got powerfully convicted, and concluded that she never had any religion. She had fallen to the floor under the mighty power of God. She prayed and agonized hard for days. At length the devil tempted her to believe that she was a reprobate, and that there was no mercy for her. She went into black despair under this temptation of the devil, and such was the desperate state of her mind, that at length she conceived that she was Jesus Christ, and took it upon her, in this assumed character, to bless and curse any and all that came to see her.

The family were, of course, greatly afflicted, and the whole neighbourhood were in great trouble at this afflictive dispensation. Her friends and all of us used every argument in our power, but all in vain. She at length utterly refused to eat, or drink, or sleep. In this condition she lingered for thirteen days and nights, and then died without ever returning to her right mind. A few persecutors and opposers of the Methodists tried to make a great fuss about this affair, but they were afraid to go far with it, for fear the Lord would send the same affliction on them.

The Hockhocking River lay immediately north of us, the Scioto River between us. John Meek and James Axley were appointed to that Circuit. The Circuit reached from the Scioto to Zanesville, on the Muskingum River. It was a hard and laborious Circuit. Brother Meek's health failed, and Brother Sale, our presiding elder, moved me me from Scioto, and placed me on this Circuit with Brother Axley. I was sorry to leave the brethren in Scioto Circuit, and especially Brother Quinn, whom I dearly loved, but Brother Sale was still my presiding elder, and Brother Quinn's family lived in Hockhocking Circuit, and a precious family it was.

I got to see Brother Quinn every round. Brother Axley and myself were like Jonathan and David There were no parsonages in those days, and Brother Quinn lived in a little cabin on his father-in-law's land. He had several children, and his cabin was small. When the preachers would come to see him, they would eat and converse with Brother Quinn and family, but would sleep at old Father Teel's, Brother Quinn's father-in-law. The first time I came round, I spent the afternoon with Brother Quinn. He made some apologies, and told me I could sleep better at Father Teel's. "But," said he, " I will tell you how you must do. You will sleep, at Father Teel's, in one part of his double cabin; he and his family will sleep in the other. His custom is to rise early. As soon as ever he dresses himself he commences giving out a hymn, sings, and then goes to prayer; he does not even wait for his family to get up. He serves the preachers the same way.

He never was known to wait a minute for any preacher except Bishop Asbury. You must rise early, dress quickly, and go right into the other room, if you want to be at morning prayer. I thought I would tell you beforehand, that you might not be taken by surprise."

I thanked him. "But," said I, "why don't the preachers cure the old man of this disorderly way?"

"O, he is old and set in his way," said Brother Quinn.

"You may rest assured I will cure him," said I.

"O, no," said he, "you cannot."

So I retired to old Father Teel's to sleep. We had family prayer, and I retired to rest. I had no fear about the matter, for I was a constant early riser, and always thought it very wrong for preachers to sleep late and keep the families waiting on them. Just as day broke I awoke, rose up, and began to dress; but had not nigh accomplished it when I distinctly heard Teel give out his hymn and commence singing, and about the time I had got dressed I heard him commence praying. He gave thanks to God that they had been spared through the night, and were all permitted to see the light of a new day, and at the same time I suppose every one of his family was fast asleep. I deliberately opened the door and walked out to the well, washed myself, and then walked back to my cabin. Just as I got to the door, the old brother opened his door, and, seeing me, said :—

"Good morning, sir. Why, I did not know you were up."

"Yes," said I; "I have been up some time."

"Well, brother," said he, "why did you not come in to prayers?"

"Because," said I, "it is wrong to pray of a morning in the family before we wash."

The old brother passed on, and no more was said at that time. That evening, just before we were about to retire to rest, the old brother set out the book and said to me :—

"Brother, hold prayers with us."

"No, sir," said I.

Said he. "Come, brother, take the book and pray with us."

"No, sir," said I; "you love to pray so well you may do it yourself."

He insisted, but I persistently refused, saying,—

"You are so fond of praying yourself, that you even thanked God this morning that He had spared you all to see the light of a new day, when your family had not yet opened their eyes, but were all fast asleep. And you have such an absurd way of holding prayers in your family, that I do not wish to have anything to do with it."

He then took up the book, read, and said prayers, but you may rely on it the next morning things were much changed. He waited for me, and had all his family up in order. He acknowledged his error, and told me it was one of the best reproofs he ever got. I then prayed with the family, and after that all went on well.

Our last quarterly-meeting was a camp-meeting. We had a great many tents, and a large turn-out for a new country, and, perhaps, there never was a greater collection of rabble and rowdies. They came drunk, and armed with dirks, clubs, knives, and horse-whips, and swore they would break up the meeting. After interrupting us very much on Saturday night, they collected early on Sunday morning, determined on a general riot. At eight o'clock I was appointed to preach. About the time I was half through my discourse, two very fine-dressed young men marched into the congregation with loaded whips, and hats on, and rose up and stood in the midst of the ladies, and began to laugh and talk. They were near the stand, and I requested them to desist and get off the seats; but they cursed me, and told me to mind my own business, and said they would not get down. I stopped trying to preach, and called for a magistrate. There were two at hand, but I 'saw they were both afraid. I ordered them to take these men into custody, but they said they could not do it. I told them, as I left the stand, to command me to take them, and I would do it at the risk of my life. I advanced toward them. They ordered me to stand off, but I advanced. One of them made a pass at my head with his whip, but I closed in with him, and jerked him off the seat. A regular scuffle ensued. The congregation by this time were all in commotion. I heard the magistrates give general orders, commanding all friends of order to aid in suppressing the riot. In the scuffle I threw my prisoner down, and held him fast; he tried his best to get loose; I told him to be quiet, or I would pound his chest well. The mob rose, and rushed to the rescue of the two prisoners, for they had taken the other young man also. An old and drunken magistrate. came up to me, and ordered me to let my prisoner go. I told him I should not. He swore if I did not, he would knock me down. I told him to crack away. Then one of my friends, at my request, took hold of my prisoner, and the drunken justice made a pass at me; but I parried the stroke, and seized him by the collar and the hair of the head, and, fetching him a sudden jerk forward, brought him to the ground, and jumped on him. I told him to be quiet, or I would pound him well. The mob then rushed to the scene, they knocked down seven magistrates, and several preachers and others. I gave up my drunken prisoner to another, and threw myself in front of the friends of order. Just at this moment, the ringleader of the mob and I met; he made three passes at me, intending to knock me down. The last time he struck at me, by the force of his own effort, he threw the side of his face toward me. It seemed at that moment I·had not power to resist temptation, and I struck a sudden blow in the burr of the ear and dropped him to the earth. Just at that moment the friends of order rushed by hundreds on the mob, knocking them down in every direction. In a few minutes, the place became too strait for the mob, and they wheeled and fled in every direction; but we secured about thirty prisoners, marched them off to a vacant tent, and put them under guard till Monday morning, when they were tried, and every man was fined to the utmost limits of the law. The aggregate amount of fines and costs was near three hundred dollars. They fined my old drunken magistrate twenty dollars, and returned him to court, and he was cashiered of his office. On Sunday, when we had vanquished the mob, the whole encampment was filled with mourning; and although there was no attempt to resume preaching till evening, yet such was our confused state, that there was not then a single preacher on the ground willing to preach, from the presiding elder, John Sale, down. Seeing we had fallen on evil times, my spirit was stirred within me. I said to the elder, " I feel a clear conscience; for under the necessity of the circumstances we have done right; and now I ask to let me preach."

" Do," said the elder; " for there is no other man on the ground can do it."

The encampment was lighted up, the trumpet blown, I rose in the stand, and required every soul to leave the tents and come into the congregation. There was a general rush to the stand. I requested the brethren, if ever they prayed in all their lives, to pray now. My voice was strong and clear, and my preaching was more of an exhortation and encouragement than anything else. My text was, "The gates of hell shall not prevail." In about thirty minutes the power of God fell on the congregation in such a manner as is seldom seen; the people fell in every direction, right and left, front and rear. It was supposed that not less than three hundred fell like dead men in mighty battle; and there was no need of calling mourners, for they were strewed all over the camp-ground; loud wailings went up to heaven from sinners for mercy, and a general shout from Christians, so that the noise was heard afar off. Our meeting lasted all night, and Monday and Monday night; and when we closed on Tuesday, there were two hundred who had professed religion, and about that number joined the Church.

Brother Axley and myself pulled together like true yoke-fellows. We were both raised in the backwoods, and well understood frontier life. Brother Axley was truly a child of nature; a great deal of sternness and firmness about him as well as oddity. He knew nothing about polished life. I will here relate a little circumstance that took place with him and myself at Governor Tiffin's, in Chillicothe.

This year, Brother Axley, while I was on the Scioto Circuit, came over to see me, and he preached for me in Chillicothe. The governor and his amiable wife were much delighted with Brother Axley. The governor's house was the preacher's home, and we went there. The governor was easily excited, and he had not entire command of his risibilities. Sister Tiffin had great command of herself. She could control the muscles of her face, and look stern, when she pleased. They had no children; but they had a very nice little lap-dog. We were called from the parlour to supper, and, among other eatables, they had fried chicken, and tea and coffee. Sister Tiffin asked Brother Axley if he would have some of the chicken. He said, yes, he was very fond of it. She helped him to some; it was a leg unjointed. Brother Axley never offered to cut the flesh off of it, but took it in his fingers, and ate it in that way; and when he had got the flesh from the bone, he turned round and whistled for the little lap-dog, and threw the bone down on the carpet. I saw the governor was excited to laughter, but he suppressed it. I cast an eye at Sister Tiffin; she frowned, and shook her head at me, as much as to say, "Do not laugh." This passed off tolerably well.

It was the custom in those days to eat a while before the tea and coffee were dished out. Said Sister Tiffin to Brother Axley, "Will you have a cup of tea or coffee?" He asked her if she had any milk. She answered, "Yes." "Well, sister," said he, "give me some milk, for they have nearly scalded my stomach with tea and coffee, and I don't like it." I really thought the governor would burst out into loud laughter, but he suppressed it, and I thought I must leave the table to laugh, but casting my eye again at Sister Tiffin, she frowned, and shook her head at me, which helped me very much.

When we went up to bed, said I: "Brother Axley, you surely are the most uncultivated creature I ever saw. Will you never learn any manners?"

Said he, "What have I done?"

"Done!" said I; "you gnawed the meat off of your chicken, holding it in your fingers; then whistled up the dog, and threw your bone down on the carpet, and more than this, you talked right at the governor's table, and in the presence of Sister Tiffin, about scalding your stomach with tea and coffee." He burst into tears, and said, "Why did you not tell me better? I didn't know any better."

Next morning when we awoke, he looked up and saw the plastering of the room all round. "Well," said he, "when I go home I will tell my people that I slept in the governor's house, and it was a stone house too, and plastered at that."

Having been raised almost in a cane brake, and never been accustomed to see anything but log-cabins, it was a great thing for him to behold a good house and sleep in a plastered room. But I tell you, my readers, he was a great and good minister of Jesus Christ. He often said, a preacher that was good and true, had a trinity of devils to fight; namely, superfluous dress, whiskey, and slavery; and he seldom ever preached but he shared it to all three of these evils like a man.of God.

Brother Axley entered the travelling connexion in 1804, travelled nineteen years, and in 1823 located. He was remarkably useful as a local preacher. He was industrious and economical; lived neat and comfortable, but, by going security for a friend, he lost nearly all his property. The Church helped him; but he never recovered his former easy and comfortable circumstances, and died in comparative poverty.

CHAPTER IX.

ITINERANT LIFE.

At the close of this Conference year, 1806, I met the Kentucky preachers at Lexington, and, headed by William Burke, about twenty of us started for Conference, which was held in East Tennessee, at Ebenezer Church, Nollichuckie, September 15th. Our membership had increased to 12,670; our net increase was about 800.

This year another presiding-elder District was added to the Western Conference, called the Mississippi District. The number of our travelling preachers increased from 38 to 49. Bishop Asbury attended the Conference. There were thirteen of us elected and ordained deacons. Two years before there were eighteen of us admitted on trial; that number, in this short space of time, had fallen to thirteen; the other five were discontinued at their own request, or from sickness, or were reduced to suffering circumstances, and compelled to desist from travelling for want of the means of support.

I think I received about forty dollars this year; but many of our preachers did not receive half that amount. These were hard times in those Western wilds; *many*, very *many*, pious and useful preachers, were literally starved into a location. I do not mean that they were starved for want of food; for although it was rough, yet the preachers generally got enough to eat. But they did not generally receive in a whole year money enough to get them a suit of clothes; and, if people, and preachers too, had not dressed in home-spun clothing, and the good sisters had not made and presented their preachers with clothing, they generally must retire from itinerant life, and go to work and clothe themselves. Money was very scarce in the country at this early day, but some of the best men God ever made breasted the storms, endured poverty, and triumphantly planted Methodism in this Western world.

When we were ordained deacons at this Conference, Bishop Asbury presented me with a parchment certifying my ordination in the following words, namely :—

" KNOW all by these presents, That I, Francis Asbury, *bishop of the Methodist Episcopal Church* in America, under the protection of Almighty God, and with a single eye to His glory, by the imposition of my hands and prayer, have this day set apart Peter Cartwright for the office of a DEACON in the said Methodist Episcopal Church ; a man whom I judge to be well qualified for that work ; and do hereby recommend him to all whom it may concern, as a proper person to administer the ordinances of baptism, marriage, and the burial of the dead, in the absence of an elder, and to feed the flock of Christ, so long as his spirit and practice are such as become the Gospel of Christ, and he continueth to hold fast the form of sound words, according to the established doctrine of the Gospel.

" In testimony whereof, I have hereunto set my hand and seal this sixteenth day of September, in the year of our Lord one thousand eight hundred and six.

" FRANCIS ASBURY."

I had travelled from Zanesville, in Ohio, to East Tennessee, to Conference, a distance of over five hundred miles ; and when our appointments were read out, I was sent to 'Marietta Circuit, almost right back, but still further east. Marietta was at the mouth of the Muskingum River, where it emptied into the Ohio. This Circuit extended along the north bank of the Ohio one hundred and fifty miles, crossed over the Ohio River at the mouth of the Little Kanawha, and up that stream to Hughes River, then 'east to Middle Island. I suppose it was three hundred miles round. I had to cross the Ohio River four times every round.

It was a poor and hard Circuit at that time. Marietta and the country round were settled at an early day by a colony of Yankees. At the time of my appointment I had never seen a Yankee, and I had heard dismal stories about them. It was said they lived almost entirely on pumpkins, molasses, fat meat, and bohea tea ; moreover, that they could not bear loud and zealous sermons, and they had brought on their learned preachers with them, and they read their sermons, and were always criticizing us poor backwoods preachers. When my

E

appointment was read out, it distressed me greatly.   I went to Bishop
Asbury, and begged him to supply my place, and let me go home.   The
old father took me in his arms, and said,—

"O no, my son; go in the name of the Lord.   It will make a man
of you"

Ah, thought I, if this is the way to make men, I do not want to be
a man.   I cried over it bitterly, and prayed too.   But on I started,
cheered by my presiding elder, Brother J. Sale.   If ever I saw hard
times, surely it was this year; yet many of the people were kind, and
treated me friendly.   I had hard work to keep soul and body together.
The first Methodist house I came to, I found the brother a Universalist.
I crossed over the Muskingum River to Marietta.   The first Methodist
family I stopped with there, the lady was a member of the Methodist
Episcopal Church, but a thorough Universalist.   She was a thin-faced,
Roman-nosed, loquacious Yankee, glib on the tongue, and you may
depend on it, I had a hard race to keep up with her, though I found it a
good school, for it set me to reading my Bible.   And here permit me to
say, of all the isms that I ever heard of, they were here.   These descend-
ants of the Puritans were generally educated, but their ancestors were
rigid Predestinarians; and as they were sometimes favoured with a little
light on their moral powers, and could just "see men as trees walking," they jumped into Deism, Universalism, Unitarianism, &c., &c.
I verily believe it was the best school I ever entered   They waked me
up on all sides; Methodism was feeble, and I had to battle or run,
and I resolved on the former.

There was here in Marietta a preacher by the name of A. Sargent;
he had been a Universalist preacher; but finding such a motley gang
as I have above mentioned, he thought (and thought correctly too)
that they were proper subjects for his imposture.   Accordingly, he
assumed the name of Halcyon Church, and proclaimed himself the millennial messenger.   He professed to see visions, fall into trances, and
to converse with angels.   His followers were numerous in the town
and country.   The Presbyterian and Congregational ministers were
afraid of him.   He had men preachers and women preachers.   The
Methodists had no meeting-house in Marietta.   We had to preach in
the court-house when we could get a chance.   We battled pretty
severely.   The Congregationalists opened their Academy for me to
preach in.   I prepared myself, and gave battle to the Halcyons.   This
made a mighty commotion.   In the meantime we had a camp-meeting
in the suburbs of Marietta.   Brother Sale, our presiding elder, was
there   Mr. Sargent came, and hung around, and wanted to preach,
but Brother Sale never noticed him.   I have said before that he professed to go into trances and have visions.   He would swoon away,

fall, and lie a long time; and when he would come too, he would tell what mighty things he had seen and heard.

On Sunday night, at our camp-meeting, Sargent got some powder, and lit a cigar, and then walked down to the bank of the river, one hundred yards, where stood a large stump. He put his powder on the stump, and touched it with his cigar. The flash of the powder was seen by many at the camp; at least the light. When the powder flashed, down fell Sargent; there he lay a good while. In the meantime, the people found him lying there, and gathered around him. At length, he came too, and said he had a message from God to us Methodists. He said God had come down to him in a flash of light, and he fell under the power of God, and thus received his vision.

Seeing so many gathered around him there, I took a light, and went down to see what was going on. As soon as I came near the stump, I smelled the sulphur of the powder; and stepping up to the stump, there was clearly the sign of powder, and hard by lay the cigar with which he had ignited it. He was now busy delivering his message. I stepped up to him, and asked him if an angel had appeared to him in that flash of light.

He said, " Yes."

Said I, " Sargent, did not that angel smell of brimstone ?"

" Why," said he, " do you ask me such a foolish question ?"

" Because," said I, "if an angel has spoken to you at all, he was from the lake that burneth with fire and brimstone!" and raising my voice, I said, "I smell sulphur now!" I walked up to the stump, and called on the people to come and see for themselves. The people rushed up, and soon saw through the trick, and began to abuse Sargent for a vile impostor. He soon left, and we were troubled no more with him or his brimstone angels.

I will beg leave to remark here, that while I was battling successfully against the Halcyons, I was treated with great respect by the Congregational minister and his people, and the Academy was always open for me to preach in; but as soon as I triumphed over and vanquished them, one of the elders of the Congregational Church waited on me, and informed me that it was not convenient for me to preach any more in their Academy. I begged the privilege to make one more appointment in the Academy, till I could get some other place to preach in. This favour, as it was only one more time, was granted.

I then prepared myself, and when my appointed day rolled around, the house was crowded, and I levelled my whole Arminian artillery against their Calvinism; and challenged their minister, who was present, to public debate; but he thought prudence the better part of valour, and declined. This effort secured me many friends, and some persecution; but my way was opened, and we raised a little class, and had a name among the living.

I will here mention a special case of wild fanaticism that took place with one of these Halcyon preachers while'I' was on this Circuit. He worked himself up into the belief that he could live so holy in this life, that his animal nature would become immortal, and that he would never die; and he conceived that he had gained this immortality, and could live without eating In despite of all the arguments and persuasion of his friends, he refused to eat or drink. He stood it sixteen days and nights, and then died a suicidal death. His death put a stop to this foolish delusion, and threw a damper over the whole Halcyon fanaticism.

I will here state something like the circumstances I found myself in at the close of my labours on this hard Circuit. I had been from my father's house about three years; was five hundred miles from home; my horse had gone blind; my saddle was worn out, my bridle reins had been eaten up and replaced (after a sort) at least a dozen times; and my clothes had been patched till it was difficult to detect the original. I had concluded to try to make my way home, and get another outfit. I was in Marietta, and had just seventy-five cents in my pocket. How I would get home and pay my way I could not tell.

But it was of no use to parley about it; go I must, or do worse; so I concluded to go as far as I could, and then stop and work for more means, till I got home. I had some few friends on the way, but not many; so I cast ahead.

My first day's travel was through my Circuit. At about thirty-five miles' distance there lived a brother, with whom I intended to stay all night. I started, and late in the evening, within five miles of my stopping place, fell in with a widow lady, not a member of the Church, who lived several miles off my road. She had attended my appointments in that settlement all the year. After the usual salutations, she asked me if I was leaving the Circuit

I told her I was, and had started for my father's.

" Well," said she, " how are you off for money? I expect you have received but little on this Circuit."

I told her I had but seventy-five cents in the world. She invited me home with her, and told me she would give me a little to help me on. But I told her I had my places fixed to stop every night till I got to Maysville; and if I went home with her, it would derange all my stages, and throw me among strangers. She then handed me a dollar, saying it was all she had with her, but if I would go home with her she would give me more. I declined going with her, thanked her for the dollar, bade her farewell, moved on, and reached my lodging-place.

By the time I reached the Ohio River, opposite Maysville, my money was all gone. I was in trouble about how to get over the river, for I had nothing to pay my ferriage.

I was acquainted with Brother J. Armstrong, a merchant in Maysville, and concluded to tell the ferryman that I had no money; but if he would ferry me over, I could borrow twenty-five cents from Armstrong, and would pay him. Just as I got to the bank of the river he landed, on my side, with a man and a horse; and when the man reached the bank, I saw it was Colonel M. Shelby, brother to Governor Shelby, of Kentucky. He was a lively exhorter in the Methodist Episcopal Church, and an old acquaintance and neighbour of my father's.

When he saw me, he exclaimed :—

" Peter, is that you?"

" Yes, Moses," said I, " what little is left of me."

" Well," said he, " from your appearance you must have seen hard times. Are you trying to get home."

"Yes," I answered.

" How are you off for money, Peter?" said he.

" Well, Moses," said I, " I have not a cent in the world."

" Well," said he, " here are three dollars, and I will give you a bill of the road, and a letter of introduction till you get down into the barrens, at the Pilot Knobb "

You may be sure my spirits greatly rejoiced. So I passed on very well for several days and nights on the colonel's money and credit; but when I came to the first tavern beyond the Pilot Knobb, my money was out. What to do I did not know, but I rode up and asked for quarters. I told the landlord I had no money; had been three years from home, and was trying to get back to my father's. I also told him I had a little old watch, and a few good books in my saddle-bags, and I would compensate him in some way. He bade me alight and be easy.

On inquiry I found this family had lived here from an early day, totally destitute of the Gospel and all religious privileges. There were three rooms in this habitation, below—the dining-room, and a back bed-room, and the kitchen. The kitchen was separated from the other lower rooms by a thin plank partition, set up on an end; and the planks had shrunk and left considerable cracks between them.

When we were about to retire to bed, I asked the landlord if he had any objection to our praying before we lay down. He said, " None at all;" and stepped into the kitchen, as I supposed, to bring in the family. He quickly returned with a candle in his hand, and said, " Follow me." I followed into the back bed-room. Whereupon he set down the candle, and bade me good night, saying, " There, you can pray as much as you please."

I stood, and felt foolish. He had completely ousted me; but it immediately occurred to me that I would kneel down and pray with a full and open voice; so down I knelt, and commenced praying audibly. I soon found, from the commotion created in the kitchen, that they were taken by surprise as much as I had been. I distinctly heard the landlady say, "He is crazy, and will kill us all this night. Go, husband, and see what is the matter." But he was slow to approach; and when I ceased praying, he came in, and asked me what was the cause of my acting in this strange way. I replied, "Sir, did you not give me the privilege to pray as much as I pleased?" "Yes," said he, "but I did not expect you would pray out." I told him I wanted the family to hear prayer; and as he had deprived me of that privilege, I knew of no better way to accomplish my object than to do as I had done, and I hoped he would not be offended.

I found he thought me deranged, but we fell into a free conversation on the subject of religion, and, I think, I fully satisfied him that I was not beside myself, but spoke forth the words of truth with soberness.

Next morning I rose early, intending to go fifteen miles to an acquaintance for breakfast, but as I was getting my horse out of the stable the landlord came out, and insisted that I should not leave till after breakfast. I yielded, but he would not have anything for my fare, and urged me to call on him if ever I travelled that way again. I will just say here, that in less than six months I called on this landlord, and he and his lady were happily converted, dating their conviction from the extraordinary circumstances of the memorable night I spent with them.

I found other friends on my journey till I reached Hopkinsville, Christian County, within thirty miles of my father's, and I had just six and a quarter cents left. This was a new and dreadfully wicked place. I put up at a tavern kept by an old Mr. M'. The landlord knew my father. I told him I had not money to pay my bill, but as soon as I got home I would send it to him. He said, "Very well," and made me welcome. His lady was a sister of the apostate Dr. Allen whom I have elsewhere mentioned.

Shortly after I laid down I fell asleep. Suddenly I was aroused by a piercing scream, or screams, of a female. I supposed that somebody was actually committing murder. I sprung from my bed, and, after getting half dressed, ran into the room from whence issued the piercing screams, and called out, "What's the matter here?" The old gentleman replied, that his wife was subject to spasms, and often had them. I commenced a conversation with her about religion I found she was under deep concern about her soul. I asked if I might pray for her. "O, yes," she replied, "for there is no one in this place that cares for my soul."

I knelt and prayed, and then commenced singing, and directed her to Christ as an all-sufficient Saviour, and prayed again. She suddenly sprung out of the bed and shouted, "Glory to God! He has blessed my soul." It was a happy time indeed. The old gentleman wept like a child. We sung and shouted, prayed and praised, nearly all night. Next morning the old landlord told me my bill was paid tenfold, and that all he charged me was, every time I passed that way, to call and stay with them.

Next day I reached home with the six and a quarter cents unexpended. Thus I have given you a very imperfect little sketch of the early travel of a Methodist preacher in the Western Conference. My parents received me joyfully. I tarried with them several weeks. My father gave me a fresh horse, a bridle and saddle, some new clothes, and forty dollars in cash. Thus equipped, I was ready for another three years' absence.

Our Conference, this year, was held in Chillicothe, September 14th, 1807. Our increase of members was 1,180; increase of travelling preachers, 6. From the Conference in Chillicothe I received my appointment for 1807–8, on Barren Circuit, in Cumberland District, James Ward, presiding elder, who employed Lewis Anderson to travel with me. This brother is now a member of the Illinois Conference. It was a four weeks' Circuit. We had several revivals of religion in different places. The Circuit reached from Barren Creek, north of Green River, to the head of Long Creek, in Tennessee State. I received about forty dollars quarterage. We had an appointment near Glasgow, the county seat of Barren County. A very singular circumstance took place in this Circuit this year, something like the following —

There were two very large Baptist Churches east of Glasgow. These Churches had each very talented and popular preachers for their pastors, by the name of W. and H. The Baptists were numerous and wealthy, and the great majority of the citizens were under Baptist influence. The Methodists had a small class of about thirteen members. There lived in the settlement a gentleman by the name of L., who was raised under the Baptist influence, though not a member of the Church. His lady was a member of one of these large Baptist Churches. Mr. L. was lingering in the last stages of consumption, but without religion. These Baptist ministers visited him often, and advised, and prayed with and for him. Learning that I was in the neighbourhood, he sent for me. I went; he seemed fast approaching his end, wasted away to a mere skeleton; he had to be lifted, like a child, in and out of the bed. I found him penitent, and prayed with him, sat up with him, and in the best way I knew I pointed him to Jesus. It pleased God to own the little effort, and speak peace to his troubled soul; he was very happy after this. He told me the next morning that he wished to be baptized, join the Church, and receive the sacrament. In the mean time, the Baptist ministers came to see him, and, as I knew he was raised under Baptist denominational influences, I was at a loss to know how to act. I took the two Baptist ministers out, and said to them, "This afflicted brother has obtained religion, and he desires to be baptized, join the Church, and receive the sacrament. And," said I, "brethren, you must now take the case into your own hands, and do with it as you think best. He was raised a Baptist, and, as a matter of course, he believes in immersion. And," said I, "my opinion is, if he is immersed, he cannot survive it; and as you are strong in the faith of immersion, you must administer it."

"No, no," said they; "he is your convert, and you must do all he desires. We believe, as well as you, that he cannot be immersed."

"Now," said I, "brethren, he wants not only to be baptized, but wants to join the Church, the Baptist Church of course; and if I baptize him by sprinkling or pouring, you will not receive him into the Baptist Church; or, in other words, if I do, will you receive him into your Church?"

"Well, no," said they; "we cannot do it."

"Now," said I, "brethren, this is a very solemn affair. You will not baptize him and take him into your Church; and if I baptize him, still you will not receive him. There must be something wrong about this very solemn matter."

They then said they would have nothing to do with it; that I must manage it in my own way. I then went and consulted the wife of the sick man. I told her what her ministers had said. "Now," said I, "sister, what must I do?"

Said she, "Go and ask my husband, and do as he wishes, and I will be satisfied."

I went, and said, "Brother L., if I baptize you, it must be by sprinkling or pouring; you cannot be immersed."

Said he, "I know I can't, and I am willing to be baptized in any mode; it is not essential."

As soon as preparation was made, I baptized him by sprinkling, and then proceeded to consecrate the elements and administer the sacrament. I turned and invited both of the Baptist ministers to come and commune with the dying saint, but they refused. Then I turned to his wife, and invited her to come and commemorate the dying sorrows of her Saviour with her dying husband. She paused for a moment, and then, bursting into a flood of tears, said, "I will;" and came forward, and I administered to them both.

After this I said, "Brother L., do you wish to have your name enrolled with the members of the little class of Methodists that worship in the neighbourhood?"

He said, "O, yes," and then added, "Before you get round your Circuit, I shall be no more on earth, and I wish you to preach at my funeral."

After consultation with his wife, I left an appointment for his funeral. In a few days he breathed his last, and went off triumphant.

When I came to the appointment, there was a vast crowd. We had a very solemn time. I stated all the circumstances above narrated, and at the close I opened the door of the Church, and Mrs. L., and six others of her relatives, all members of the Baptist Church, came forward and joined the Methodists This circumstance gave us a standing that enabled us to lift our heads and breathe more freely afterward.

In the course of this year we carried Methodist preaching into a Baptist congregation on Bacon Creek. A great many of their members gave up Calvinism, close communion, and immersion, and joined the Methodist Church; and we took possession of their meeting-house, and raised a large Society there that flourishes to this day. Out of this revival several preachers were raised up that trained and blessed the Methodist Episcopal Church for years afterward.

CHAPTER X.

MEETING IN A WAGGON.

OWING to the newness of the country, the scarcity of money, the fewness of our numbers, and their poverty, it was a very difficult matter for preachers to obtain support, especially married men with families. From this consideration many of our preachers delayed marriage, or, shortly after marriage, located. Indeed, such was our poverty, that the Discipline was a perfectly dead letter on the subject of house rent, table expenses, and a dividend to children; and although I had acted as one of the stewards of the Conference for years, these rules of the Discipline were never acted upon, or any allowance made, till 1813, when Bishop Asbury, knowing our poverty and sufferings in the West, had begged from door to door in the older Conferences, and came on and distributed ten dollars to each child of a travelling preacher under fourteen years of age

After mature deliberation and prayer, toward the close of my labours on the Barren Circuit, I thought it was my duty to marry, and was joined in marriage to Frances Gaines, on the 18th of August, 1808, which was her nineteenth birthday; and we had our infare at my father's, on the 1st of September following, which was my twenty-third birthday.

The Conference, this fall, was held at Liberty Hill, Tennessee, on the 1st of October, 1808. Our increase in members this year was about 1,350; our increase of travelling preachers was 10. We had three new presiding-elder Districts formed this year, namely, Indiana, Miami, and Muskingum, making seven presiding-elder Districts in the Western Conference.

At this Conference I was elected and ordained an elder by Bishop M'Kendree. The parchment reads as follows, viz. —

" KNOW all men by these presents, That I, William M'Kendree, one of the bishops of the Methodist Episcopal Church in America, under the protection of Almighty God, and with a single eye to His glory, by the imposition of my hands and prayer, (being assisted by the elders present,) have this day set apart Peter Cartwright for the office of an elder in the said Methodist Episcopal Church ; a man whom I judge to be well qualified for that work ; and I do hereby recommend him, to all whom it may concern, as a proper person to administer the sacraments and ordinances, and to feed the flock of Christ, so long as his spirit and practice are such as become the Gospel of Christ.

" In testimony whereof, I have hereunto set my hand and seal, this fourth day of October, in the year of our Lord one thousand eight hundred and eight.

" WILLIAM M'KENDREE."

" *Liberty Hill, Tennessee.*"

My appointment, this year, was to Salt River Circuit, Kentucky District, James Ward presiding elder. This was a part of the Circuit I had travelled in the years 1804 and 1805.

In the course of this year my father died, and left me to settle his little estate, which, owing to the forms of law, took me several months, which was the longest time I have ever had from the regular work of a travelling preacher in fifty years ; but upon a proper presentation of the case to my presiding elder, he gave me liberty to go and attend to this business. Giving me this liberty by the presiding elder was then according to Discipline.

At the close of the Conference year 1808–9, I attended Conference at Cincinnati, and there reported myself ready for regular work, and my appointment was to Livingston Circuit. Our increase of membership was 4,051 ; our increase of travelling preachers was 21.

Livingston Circuit was in the Cumberland District, Learner Blackman presiding elder. This was my first field of labour as an exhorter; which Circuit I had formed in the days of my boyhood, and had then returned to J. Page, presiding elder, 70 members. They had increased now to 427 ; a good increase for six years.

We had not a very prosperous year, but we had some gracious outpourings of the Spirit of God. I held a camp-meeting this year, which lasted four days and nights, without any ministerial aid, save one little exhorter and an old drunken Baptist preacher, who preached for me once, on Sunday. He then and there confessed his dissipation, and wept bitterly, and made us all cry. We had about thirty converts at this meeting. At the close of the meeting we had many seekers who had not obtained comfort. Twelve of them got into a two-horse waggon, and myself with them. We had to go about fifteen miles ; but before we reached our home every one of them got powerfully converted, and we sung and shouted aloud along the road, to the very great astonishment of those who lived along the way. That night the whole neighbourhood gathered in, and we had a glorious time. Several more were powerfully converted, and many deeply convicted. The work broke out around the settlement, and scores were brought to a saving knowledge of the truth.

I will here relate an incident that took place this year, concerning one of our Methodist preachers; his name was J D He was raised a very bigoted Dunker, or Seventh-day Baptist. When the Methodist preachers came into his settlement, he violently opposed them, asserting the Dunkers were right and everybody else wrong. After a while, however, he either *really* or *pretendedly* got under deep conviction, and professed religion. (This was when the Methodists had borne down all opposition and become popular.) He joined the Methodists, and they soon licensed him to preach. Now he had found the right way, and all the rest were wrong. He had considerable talent, but was a very lazy man However, the Methodists got him on a Circuit a while, and he was popular, but did not get money enough to support him ; so he located, and went into land speculations, and got under par as a good man. This year he moved into the bounds of my Circuit, and we renewed our former acquaintance, preached together often, and really we were in a fair way of doing much good. We broke into a very large Free-will Baptist settlement, where the preacher was a very weak brother. We rose high in public opinion, and the Baptists offered us a good salary if we would join them and become their pastors. This was a little too much for my Brother D. He came to me one day, and said, "Brother Cartwright, you and I have young and growing families; if we would join these Baptists, they would give us a handsome support, and, as they have no preacher in all this country of any talents, we could sway a mighty influence, getting hundreds into their Church, and secure a good living for our families in all time to come. Don't you think," said he, "it would be best to do it?" I replied, "Brother D , 'get thee behind me, Satan: for thou art an offence to me.' If money, sir, or a good living, had been my prime object in joining a Church, I should never have joined the Methodists , but when I joined them, I joined them from a firm conviction, believing them to be the best people in the world; and the longer I live with them, and the more I understand of their doctrine and system of Church government, the more firmly I am settled in mind to abide my choice; and this world has not treasure enough to allure me from the Methodist Church."

Poor human nature! The temptation was too strong. Brother D. yielded, joined the Free-will Baptists, and was soon installed their pastor. Well, now, he proclaimed, he had certainly found the right way, and all the world was wrong. Well, it was not long before he was caught in a criminal act, which ruined his moral character, and he was dismissed from his pastoral charge. I will here say that this said J. D., was formerly my armour-bearer in the great contest I had with the Shakers at Busroe, in Indiana, mentioned elsewhere in this narrative. What next? Why, J. D. went and joined the Shakers; and now from heaven God had revealed it to him that he was right and everybody else wrong. The Shakers, hearing of his instability of character, had very little confidence in him. They put him to hard labour to try him. This he could not stand; and presently left them, took up with a scattered band of New Lights, moved to Texas, and I expect the devil has got him in safe keeping long before this time.

Our increase for 1809–10 was 1,950. Increase of travelling preachers, 15

At this Conference I was returned to Livingston Circuit, Cumberland District; Learner Blackman presiding elder. At the close of this year, 1810–11, we met at New Chapel, Shelby County, Kentucky, November 1st, 1810 Our increase of members, this Conference year, 4,264 ; increase of travelling preachers, 13.

The Western Conference met the last time as the Western Conference, at Cincinnati, October 1st, 1811, and our increase this year was 3,6 0. Our increase in preachers was 1 . Our strength of membership in the entire Western Conference at its last session as a Western Conference, was 30,741. In 1787, we had but ninety members that were officially reported from the West; and if, as we have elsewhere stated, that at the General Conference of May 1st, 1800, in Baltimore, the Western Conference was regularly organized, with about two thousand members, the reader will plainly see what God wrought in eleven years by the pioneer fathers that planted Methodism in this vast Western wilderness, and of the little band of travelling preachers that then ploughed the wilderness, say twelve men, none are now living save Mr. Henry Smith. In the fall of 1804, when I joined the Conference, there were a little over 9,000 members in the Western Conference, in 1811, 30,741. There were then a little over 40 travelling preachers, and in 1810 over 100; and yet, at this time there are not more than six of us left lingering on the shores of time to look back, look around, and look forward to the future of the Methodist Episcopal Church, for weal or for woe. Lord, save the Church from desiring to have pews, choirs, organs, or instrumental music, and a Congregational ministry, like other heathen Churches around them!

In 1804, the membership of the whole Church was 119,945, travelling preachers 433, throughout the United States', territories and Canada. Their increase this year, throughout the Union, was 6,811. In 1812, when the Western Conference was divided into Ohio and Tennessee Conferences, our entire membership had increased to 184,567; increase of members in eight years, near 65,000. Travelling ministers in 1804, 433; in 1812, 688.

In 1811 we elected our delegates to the first delegated General Conference ever holden by the Methodist Episcopal Church. This General Conference was holden in New York, May 1st, 1812. At this General Conference, the Western Conference, which had existed some twelve years, was divided into two Annual Conferences, called Ohio and Tennessee. The Ohio Conference was composed of the following presiding-elder Districts, namely, Ohio District, Muskingum District, Scioto District, Miami District, Kentucky District, and Salt River District: six. Tennessee Conference was composed of the following Districts, namely, Holston District, Nashville District, Cumberland District, Wabash District, Mississippi District, and Louisiana District: six. It will be seen that the State of Kentucky was divided between the two Conferences. There were members in Ohio Conference, 23,284; in Tennessee Conference, 22,700. There were in Ohio Conference, travelling preachers, 64; in Tennessee, 62. These statistics are for 1812.

I was appointed to Christian Circuit, Wabash District, James

Axley presiding elder. This was a four weeks' Circuit, most of it parts and fragments of other Circuits. I formed it into a four weeks' Circuit. We had some splendid revivals this year, and took in some three hundred members. We had two or three very successful camp-meetings; at one of them I baptized one hundred and twenty-seven adult persons and forty-seven children, all by sprinkling, save seven adults, whom I immersed. One of them was the daughter of a very celebrated Baptist minister.

In the north end of my Circuit there was a District of densely populated country, about thirty-five miles across   A Methodist preacher had seldom, even if ever, preached in this district of country. About midway of it there lived a Baptist minister, with a large society and a large meeting-house. He, at an early day, had settled among them, and prejudiced nearly all the country against the Methodist preachers and people.

I had to make a day's ride through this settlement every round, and thought it singular that no Methodist preacher, as I could learn, had ever made a break in it; and I determined to make one in this region somehow or somewhere. While riding through, I stopped at many houses, and asked for the privilege to preach among them. They looked shy, and denied me. I prayed God to open my way; and at length, through an acquaintance I had made, left an appointment to preach at the Baptist meeting-house on my next round.

The Baptist minister publicly warned the people not to hear me; but somehow the novelty of the thing excited their curiosity, and, though a week-day, a large congregation turned out, and, among the rest, their preacher. He told me he should not hinder me that time from preaching in his meeting-house; "but," said he, "you must leave no more appointments at my church, or if you do, you will find the doors barred against you." Well, I had to submit. I went in, and preached as well as I could, and the congregation were considerably affected, even to weeping. I called on the Baptist minister to conclude, but he refused; so, after closing the services, I told the congregation that I could preach to them every round, but that their minister had forbidden me the use of his meeting-house any more; but if there was any man present that would open his private house for me to preach in, I would leave an appointment. A gentleman rose up, and tendered me the use of his house, and invited me home with him for dinner; so I left an appointment, and went with this man and partook of his hospitalities.

When I came round to my appointment, the house was filled to overflowing, though large. While I was preaching, near the close of the discourse, suddenly the power of God fell on the congregation like a flash of lightning, and the people fell right and left, some screamed aloud for mercy, others fell on their knees and prayed out aloud; several Baptist members fell to the floor under the power of God. There was a Baptist preacher present. After I had talked, and exhorted, and sung a long time, I called on this preacher to pray, but he was so astounded that, he told me, he could not pray. Our meeting lasted nearly all night. About twelve persons were converted in the good old way, and shouted aloud the praises of God. I opened the doors of the Church, and thirteen came forward and joined. From this time the work broke out, and many professed religion, and we succeeded in planting Methodism on a firm footing here. The Baptist minister who was pastor of the congregation that worshipped at the meeting-house where I preached, had a dreadful rude set of children, especially a daughter whom they called Betsy She would stand on the seats, point and laugh, and when any would fall under the power of God, she would say it was nothing but a Methodist fit.

At a camp-meeting this summer, held on the land of R. Dellam, Esq., now of St. Louis, a fine man, old Valentine Cook, of precious memory, attended with me, and laboured like a true minister of Christ. There was a large crowd of people, and mostly raised under old Baptist influence and prejudice, and as ignorant of Methodism and the power of religion as the beasts that perish. There were several preachers to aid Brother Cook and myself, but all our preaching seemed powerless. The meeting dragged heavily till Sunday. Brother Cook and myself walked out to pray: when we rose from our knees, Brother Cook said to me:—

"Brother, have you any faith?"

"A little," I replied.

"I have some," said he.

We were both to preach in succession, commencing at eleven o'clock. He was to preach first, and I to follow. Said he to me:—

"If I strike fire, I will immediately call for mourners, and you must go into the assembly and exhort in every direction, and I will manage the altar. But," said he, "if I fail to strike fire, you must preach, and if you strike fire, call the mourners and manage the altar. I will go through the congregation, and exhort with all the power God gives me"

We repaired to the stand. He preached; it seemed as if every word took effect. There was no outbreak; the vast crowd were melted into silent tears. When he closed, he bade me rise and preach. I did so. Just as I was closing up my sermon, and pressing it with all the force I could command, the power of God suddenly was displayed, and sinners fell by scores through all the assembly. We had no need of a mourners' bench.   It was supposed that several hundred fell in five minutes; sinners turned pale; some ran into the woods, some tried to get away and fell in the attempt; some shouted aloud for joy; among the rest my Baptist preacher's daughter, whom we have called Betsy.   As I went through the assembly, I came across Betsy, who had fallen to the earth, and was praying at a mighty rate.   When I came to her, she said to me :—

"O, do pray for me; I am afraid I am lost and damned for ever!"

I said to her, "Betsy, get up, you have only got a Methodist fit," (using her former language;) but she roared the louder two or three times.   I bid her get up, saying to her, "You are playing the hypocrite, and have only got a Methodist fit; get up, Betsy."   But I assure you she was past getting up.   Just hard by I saw her father, the Baptist preacher.   He was crying, and shaking every joint in him. I went to him, and said, "Brother A., come and pray for Betsy." He replied,—

"Lord, have mercy on me!   I cannot pray."

"Amen," said I.   "Pray on, Brother A., the Lord will have mercy."   I then exhorted Betsy, and prayed for her.   If ever I saw the great deep of a sinner's heart broken up, hers was.   She wrestled and prayed all night.   Next morning, about sunrise, the Lord in a powerful manner converted her.   She rose and went over the camp-ground like a top.   She at length met her father, the preacher, and of all the exhortations that I ever heard fall from the lips of a mortal, hers was the most powerful to her father.   She said to him :—

"You, father, have taught me from my childhood to hate and despise the Methodists, till my soul was well-nigh lost and ruined for ever!"

She then assured him that he had no religion at all, and begged him to repent and get his soul converted.   She made him kneel down, and she engaged for him in mighty prayer.

About eleven o'clock on Monday I opened the doors of the Church, and forty-two joined, and, among the rest, Betsy.   From this meeting a revival spread almost through the entire country round, and great additions were made to the Methodist Church.   The Circuit was large, embracing parts of Logan, Muhlenburgh, Butler, Christian, and Caldwell Counties in Kentucky, and parts of Montgomery, Dixon, and Stewart Counties in Tennessee.

On the west part of Red River there was a Presbyterian settled, who had a large brick church.   He had settled at an early day, and the few scattered Methodists who lived in the bounds of his congregation, having no Methodist preaching, had joined his Church rather than live out of Church altogether.   I was invited to preach about five miles from this minister's church. I sent an appointment. At the time a large congregation turned out; the people were deeply affected. When I closed, I stated to the assembly that I could preach to them every four weeks, if they desired it. They told me they did, and I accordingly left another appointment. When I came, the house was crowded, and the Presbyterian minister came. I preached, and there was a general weeping all through the congregation. The minister concluded for me, and I left another appointment. The minister stayed and dined with me. After dinner he asked me to walk out with him. I did so. When we had seated ourselves, he told me he wanted to talk to me about my preaching in that neighbourhood. He said that this neighbourhood was in the bounds of his congregation; that I was heartily welcome to preach; "but," said he, "you must not attempt to raise any society." I told him that was not our way of doing business; that we seldom ever preached long at any place without trying to raise a society. He said I must not do it. I told him the people were a free people and lived in a free country, and must and ought to be allowed to do as they pleased; that I should never condescend to try to proselyte, but if I continued to preach there, and if any of the people desired to join the Methodist Church, I should surely give them the privilege to do so; and that I understood there were ten or twelve members of the Methodist Church had joined his Church as Methodists, with the fair understanding that if the Methodists ever organized a society convenient to them, they were to have the privilege of joining their own Church without any hard thoughts or censures. He said that was true; but if we raised a society, it would diminish his membership, and cut off his support. "Well," said I, "my dear sir, if the people want me to preach to them, I shall do it, and if they desire to join our Church, I shall take them in; and I intend, when I come next time, to organize a class, for several have desired me to do so." Said he, "I will be here, and will openly oppose you." Said I, "If you think that the best way, do so." While I was absent for three Sabbaths successively, he opened his batteries on me, told them what I had said, and warned them not to attend my meeting. This roused the whole country, and made me many fast friends, even his own members remonstrated against his course, saying to him, nobody was obliged to join the Methodists; and if they preferred the Methodist Church to his, it was their right to join it.

When I came round, we had a vast crowd out, but the minister did not appear. At the close of my sermon I read our General Rules, and explained our economy. I then told them that my father had fought in the Revolution to gain our freedom and liberty of conscience; that I felt that my Presbyterian brother had no bill of sale of the people;

F

that I was no robber of Churches; but if I had any members in my Church that liked the Presbyterians better than the Methodists, I wanted them to go and join them; but if there were any there that day that believed the Methodist doctrine, and were willing to conform to the Discipline of the Methodist Church, and desire to join us, let them come and give me their hand, and I would form them into a Class and appoint them a leader. There were twenty-seven came forward; thirteen of them were members of this minister's Church. I publicly ascertained this fact, and then told the thirteen that I did not want to give any offence, and that I wanted them all to go to their next meeting, and ask a letter, stating their reasons, and I would receive them into full membership at once. One of them, a fine, intelligent man, and an elder, said that he knew they would not give them letters. I remarked, " Go and ask for them; and if they refuse, come back, and I will receive you any how." They went, but the Church would not give them letters, although there was nothing against their moral characters. After that I received them into the Methodist Church. Public opinion was in my favour, and many more of this preacher's members came and joined us, and the minister sold out and moved to Missouri, and before the year was out I had peaceable possession of his brick church.

CHAPTER XI.

SLAVERY IN THE CHURCH.

In the fall of 1812, our Tennessee Conference was holden at Fountain Head, State of Tennessee, on the first of November. At this first session of the Tennessee Conference the Illinois District was organized, and J. Walker appointed presiding elder The Illinois Circuit, as a mission, was formed in 1804, and Benjamin Young appointed to it. It was attached to the Cumberland District, L. Garrett presiding elder. Brother Young returned sixty-seven members.

At this Conference I was appointed by Bishop Asbury to the Wabash District, which was then composed of the following Circuits, namely, Vincennes, in the State of Indiana; and Little Wabash and Fort Massack, in Illinois. These three Circuits were north of the Ohio River; the balance of the District was in Kentucky, namely, Livingston, Christian, Henderson, Hartford, and Breckenridge Circuits. In travelling the District I had to cross the Ohio River sixteen times during the year.

I told Bishop Asbury that I deliberately believed that I ought not to be appointed presiding elder, for I was not qualified for the office ; but he told me there was no appeal from his judgment. At the end of six months I wrote to him, begging a release from the post he had assigned me ; but when he returned an answer, he said I must abide his judgment, and stand in my lot to the end of the time. I continued accordingly in the service, but the most of the year was gloomy to me, feeling that I had not the first qualification for the office of a presiding elder. Perhaps I never spent a more gloomy and sad year than this in all my itinerant life ; and from that day to this I can safely say the presiding elder's office has had no special charms for me ; and I will remark, that I have often wondered at the aspirations of many, very many, Methodist preachers for the office of presiding elder ; and have frequently said, if I were a bishop, that such aspirants should always go without office under my administration. I look upon this disposition as the out-cropping of fallen and unsanctified human nature, and whenever this spirit, in a large degree, gets into a preacher, he seldom ever does much good afterward.

We had through the summer and fall of this Conference year some splendid camp-meetings, many conversions, and many accessions to the Church. In the fall we met at Conference, October 1st, 1813, at Rees's Chapel, Tennessee. The name of Wabash District was changed to Green River District, and Vincennes, Little Wabash, and Fort Massack Circuits, north of the Ohio River, were stricken off and attached to the Illinois District, and Dixon and Dover Circuits, south of the Cumberland River, that had belonged to Nashville District, were attached to Green River District. I was appointed by Bishop Asbury presiding elder of this District, sometime in the course of the summer of this Conference year, 1813. We had a camp-meeting in the Breckenridge Circuit, and a glorious good work of religion was manifest throughout the meeting. It was at this meeting that Benjamin Ogden, one of the early preachers sent to the West, who became disaffected, and left the Methodist Episcopal Church under the secession of J. O'Kelly, and backslid, professed to be reclaimed, and returned to his mother Church.

Slavery had long been agitated in the Methodist Episcopal Church, and our preachers, although they did not feel it to be their duty to meddle with it politically, yet, as Christians and Christian ministers, be it spoken to their eternal credit, they believed it to be their duty to bear their testimony against slavery as a moral evil ; and this is the reason why the General Conference, from time to time, passed rules and regulations to govern preachers and members of the Church in regard to this great evil. The great object of the General Conference was to keep the ministry clear of it, and there can be no doubt that the course pursued by early Methodist preachers was the cause of the emancipation of thousands of this degraded race of human beings; and it is clear to my mind, if Methodist preachers had kept clear of slavery themselves, and gone on bearing honest testimony against it, that thousands upon thousands more would have been emancipated who are now groaning under an oppression almost too intolerable to be borne. Slavery is certainly a domestic, political, and moral evil. Go into a slave community, and you not only see the dreadful evils growing out of the system in the almost universal licentiousness which prevails among the slaves themselves, but their young masters are often tempted and seduced from the paths of virtue, from the associations in which they are placed; and there is an under-current of heart-embittering feeling of many ladies of high and noble virtue, growing out of the want of fidelity of their husbands, and the profligate course of their sons. Let any one travel through slave states, and see the thousands of mixed blood, and then say if I have misrepresented the dreadful causes of domestic disquietude that often falls with mountain weight on honourable wives and mothers. And although, in the infancy of this Republic, it seemed almost impossible to form a strong and democratic confederacy, and maintain their independence without compromising constitutionally this political evil, and thereby fixing a stain on this land of the free and home of the brave, yet it was looked upon as a great national or political evil, and by none more so than General Washington, the father of the Republic. I will not attempt to enumerate the moral evils that have been produced by slavery; their name is Legion. And now, notwithstanding these are my honest views of slavery, I have never seen a rabid abolition or free-soil society that I could join, because they resort to unjustifiable agitation, and the means they employ are generally unchristian. They condemn and confound the innocent with the guilty; the means they employ are not truthful at all times; and I am perfectly satisfied that if force is resorted to, this glorious Union will be dissolved, a civil war will follow, death and carnage will ensue, and the only free nation on the earth will be destroyed. Let moral suasion be used to the last degree for the sake of the salvation of the slaveholders, and the salvation of the slaves. Let us not take a course that will cut off the Gospel from them, and deliver them over to the uncovenanted mercies of God, or the anathemas of the devil. I have had glorious revivals of religion among the slaves, and have seen thousands of them soundly converted to God, and have stood by the bedside of the dying slave, and have heard the swelling shout of Christian victory from the dying Negro as he entered the cold waters of the river of Jordan.

At our Breckenridge Circuit camp-meeting the following incident occurred. There were a Brother S and family, who were the owners of a good many slaves. It was a fine family, and Sister S. was a very intelligent lady, and an exemplary Christian. She had long sought the blessing of perfect love, but she said the idea of holding her fellow-beings in bondage stood out in her way. Many at this meeting sought and obtained the blessing of sanctification; Sister S. said her whole soul was in an agony for that blessing, and it seemed to her at times that she could almost lay hold, and claim the promise, but she said her slaves would seem to step right in between her and her Saviour, and prevent its reception; but while on her knees, and struggling as in an agony for a clean heart, she then and there covenanted with the Lord, if He would give her the blessing, she would give up her slaves and set them fiee She said this covenant had hardly been made one moment when God filled her soul with such an overwhelming sense of Divine love, that she did not really know whether she was in or out of the body. She rose from her knees, and proclaimed to listening hundreds that she had obtained the blessing, and also the terms on which she had obtained it. She went through the vast crowd with holy shouts of joy, and exhorting all to taste and see that the Lord was gracious; and such a power attended her words that hundreds fell to the ground, and scores of souls were happily born into the kingdom of God that afternoon and during the night. Shortly after this they set their slaves free, and the end of that family was peace.

There was another circumstance happened at this camp-meeting that I will substantially relate. It was one of our rules of the camp-meeting that the men were to occupy the seats on one side of the stand, and the ladies the other side, at all hours of public worship. But there was a young man, finely dressed, with his bosom full of ruffles, that would take his seat among the ladies, and if there was any excitement in the congregation, he would rise to his feet, and stand on the seats prepared for the occupancy of the ladies. I reproved him several times; but he would still persist in his disorderly course. At length, I reproved him personally and sharply, and said, "I mean that young man there, standing on the seats of the ladies, with a ruffled shirt on." And added, "I doubt not that ruffled shirt was borrowed."

This brought him off the seats in a mighty rage. He swore he would whip me for insulting him. After a while, 1 was walking round on the outskirts of the congregation; and he had a large company gathered round him, and was swearing at a mighty rate, and saying he would certainly whip me before he left the ground.

I walked up, and said, "Gentlemen, let me in here to this fellow."

They opened the way. I walked up to him, and asked him if it was me he was cursing, and going to whip.

He said it was.

"Well," said I, " we will not disturb the congregation fighting here; but let us go out into the woods, for if I am to be whipped, I want it over, for I do not like to live in dread ".

So we started for the woods, the crowd pressing after us. I stopped, and requested every one of them to go back, and not a man to follow; and assured them if they did not go back, that I would not go another step; they then turned back. The camp-ground was fenced in. When we came to the fence, I put my left hand on the top rail' and leaped over. As I lighted on the other side, one of my feet struck a grub, and I had well-nigh sprained my ankle; it gave me a severe jar; and a pain struck me in the left side from the force of the jar, and involuntarily I put my right hand on my left side, where the pain had struck me. My redoubtable antagonist had got on the fence, and, looking down at me, said,

" Ah! you are feeling for a dirk, are you?"

As quick as thought, it occurred to me, how to get clear of a whipping. " I'll give you the benefit of all the dirks I have ," and advancing rapidly toward him, he sprang back on the other side of the fence from me. I jumped over after him, and a regular foot race followed. I was so diverted at my cowardly bully's rapid retreat, that I could not run fast, so he escaped, and I missed my whipping

There was a large pond not very far from the camp-ground, and what few rowdies were there, concluded they would take my bully and duck him in that pond as a punishment for his bad conduct; so they decoyed him off there, and they got a long pole, and stripped some hickory bark, and securing him on the pole, two of them, one at each end, waded in, and ducked him nearly to death; he begged and prayed them to spare his life; he promised them that he would never misbehave at meeting again, and that he would immediately leave the ground if they would let him go. On these conditions they released him, and I got clear of my ruffle-shirted dandy.

It may be asked what I would have done if this fellow had gone with me to the woods. This is hard to answer, for it was a part of my creed to love everybody, but to fear no one; and I did not permit myself to believe any man could whip me till it was tried; and I did not permit myself to premeditate expedients in such cases. I should no doubt have proposed to him to have prayer first, and then followed the openings of Providence.

This year there was a considerable decrease in membership in the Methodist Episcopal Church, owing chiefly to the war with England; and we felt the sad effects of war throughout the West, perhaps as sensibly as in any part of the Union. A braver set of men never lived than was found in this Western world, and many of them volunteered and helped to achieve another glorious victory over the legions of England and her savage allied thousands. Of course there were many of our members went into the war, and deemed it their duty to defend our common country under General Jackson.

In the fall of 1813, October 1st, our Conference was held at Rees's Chapel, Tennessee, and for 1813–14 our appointments remained pretty much as they were before. I was returned to the Green River District. This year the Missouri District was formed, and admitted as part of the Tennessee Conference. In the course of this year, or about this time, there were new fields of labour entered by our preachers along the Cumberland River, near the line between Tennessee and Kentucky. We preached in new settlements, and the Lord poured out His Spirit, and we had many convictions and many conversions. It was the order of the day, (though I am sorry to say it,) that we were constantly followed by a certain set of proselyting Baptist preachers. These new and wicked settlements were seldom visited by these Baptist preachers until the Methodist preachers entered them; then, when a revival was gotten up, or the work of God revived, these Baptist preachers came rushing in, and they generally sung their sermons; and when they struck the *long roll*, or their sing-song mode of preaching, in substance it was, "Water!" "Water!" "You must follow your blessed Lord down into the water!" I had preached several times in a large, populous, and wicked settlement, and there were serious attention, deep convictions, and a good many conversions; but, between my occasional appointments, these preachers would rush in, and try to take our converts off into the water; and, indeed, they made so much ado about baptism by immersion, that the uninformed would suppose that heaven was an island, and there was no way to get there but by *diving* or *swimming*.

Among the Baptist preachers that rushed in on us in this new settlement there came along a lank, long-legged, and extremely illiterate and ignorant old preacher by the name of H——s, and he was as impudent as a wolf. He sent an appointment, and he was to blow the Methodists sky-high. I had never seen him, nor had he ever seen me. I heard of his appointment, and concluded that I would go; and if he really killed all the Methodists, if I could muster force enough I would bury them out of the way. The time came on, and this mighty Goliath appeared, with two armour-bearers. I stayed out until he commenced the battle, then I moved into the congregation, and took my seat with pen, ink, and paper; thinking if I was to be killed, and he did not dispatch me too suddenly, I would at least try to write my will. He commenced the battle by warning the people to take care of these Methodist preachers that wore black broadcloth coats, silk jackets, and fair-topped boots, and a watch in their pockets ; that rode fine fat horses, &c.   He then said he would tell them how these Methodist preachers got the money to buy all these fine clothes and horses.   He said, that in order to join the Methodist Church, the preachers received twenty-five cents for every one that they took into the Church, and twenty-five cents for every baby they sprinkled, and that these babies were considered members of the Church, and thus that every member, adult or infant, had to pay a dollar a head annually , and that these moneys constituted a large fund, and the Methodist preachers could well afford to dress fine and ride fat horses.   But, said he, here is poor old H——s, (alluding to himself,) if he can get a wool hat and a wallet of dumplings, he is content, and thinks himself well off.   " Now," said he, " my dear brethren, these Methodist preachers often remind me, in the doctrine they preach, of the manner of certain men that catch monkeys in certain countries.   The monkeys are very fond of black haws ; the monkey-catchers go and scatter these black haws around the roots of the trees in which the monkeys are, and then they retire : the monkeys come down and devour the haws.   The next time these monkey-catchers come, they bring sheep-saffron, that very much resembles black haws.   They scatter the sheep-saffron around the roots of the trees and retire, and the poor, simple monkeys eat up the saffron, and it makes them so sick they cannot climb, but lie down, and then these men rush out and catch them.   So it is," said he, " my brethren, with these Methodist preachers.   They preach some truth, which takes with the people , then they come with their sheep-saffron, or rotten doctrine, and the poor, simple people, like the foolish monkeys, swallow down these false doctrines, and it makes them sick, and then these Methodist preachers catch them."   He then compared Methodist preachers to a boy climbing a pole, &c.   You may be sure this was a deadly shot.

As soon as he was done, to keep up appearances, he said, if there was any one present that wanted to reply to him, let him come forward. I arose, and marched up, and took the stand, and in a very little time nailed all his lies to the counter ; and by respectable gentlemen out of any Church proved his statements to be false, and poured round upon round on him so hot and so fast, that he started for the door.   I ordered him to stop, and told him, if he did not, I would shoot him in the back for a Tory; he got out at the door.   He was taken so at surprise, and charged on so suddenly, that he forgot his hat, and he peeped round the door-chink at me.   I blazed away at him till he dodged back and started off, bare-headed, for home, talking to himself by the way.   As he retreated in this situation, he was met by a gentleman, who hailed him, and said, "Mr. H——s, what is the matter? where is your hat?" "O Lord," he exclaimed, "that Methodist bull-dog Cartwright came to my meeting, and opened a fire on me that no mortal man could stand, and I left." "Come," said the gentleman, "go back and get your hat." "No," said he, "I will not go back, if I never see another hat on earth." This encounter blowed this proselyting, sheep-stealing preacher to *never*, where another Baptist preacher that I once heard of would have gone to, if he had jumped off.

Now I must explain this allusion a little. At an early day I heard a Baptist preacher preach, and toward the close he alluded to his own experience. When in a state of conviction, he said he was in great distress; he sought relief on the right and left, but found none, and at length he said he thought he would start off and travel to the ends of the *yearth*, and when he got there that he would jump off; and now stopping suddenly, he asked his congregation, "Where do you think I would have gone to?" and answering for them, said he, "I should have gone to NEVER."

While I am giving a few strictures on the unworthy conduct of a few of the preachers of this denomination, I will state another incident that occurred about this time. I settled on a little new place, near the road leading from Hopkinsville, Christian County, to Russellville, Logan County, Kentucky, and was destitute of stabling. Presently there rode up an old gentleman and a youth he called his son.

He asked me if Peter Cartwright, a Methodist preacher, lived there. I answered he did.

He asked, "Are you the man?"

I answered, "Yes."

"Well," said he, "I am a Baptist preacher, have been to Missouri after this my sick son, and I have called to stay all night with you." I told him to do so, and alight and come in. I disposed of their horses as best I could, supper was prepared, and they partook of our fare. After supper they both stepped into the other room, and when they returned I smelt whiskey very strongly; and although these were not the days of general temperance as now going on, yet I thought it a bad sign for a preacher to smell very strong of whiskey, but said nothing. When we were about to retire to bed, I set out the books and said, "Brother, it is our custom to have family prayer; take the books and lead in family prayer." He began to make excuses, and declined. I urged him strongly, but he refused; so I took the books, read, sung, and prayed; but he would not sing with me, neither did he, nor his son, kneel when we prayed. Next morning the family was called together for family prayer; again I invited him to pray with us, but he would not. As soon as prayer was over, he went into the other room, and brought out his bottle of whiskey; he asked me to take a dram. I told him I did not drink spirits. He offered it to all my family, but they all refused. After breakfast he and his son harnessed up their horses to start on their way home.

"Perhaps, brother," said he, " you charge ? "

"Yes," said I, " all whiskey-drinking preachers, that will not pray with me, I charge."

"Well," said he, " it looks a little hard that one preacher should charge another."

"Sir," said I, "you have given me no evidence that you are a preacher, and I fear you are a vile impostor; and when any man about me drinks whiskey, and will not pray with me, preacher or no preacher, I take a pleasure in charging him full price ; so haul out your cash." He did so, but very reluctantly.

I am glad these unworthy examples of these preachers do not apply to the Baptist ministry generally, but many of them are friends of temperance, and scorn the contemptible business of proselyting members from other Churches. So may they continue, and give up their exclusive baptism by immersion.

CHAPTER XII.

CAMP-MEETING INCIDENTS.

ON the 29th of September, 1814, our Tennessee Conference commenced its session at Kenerley's Chapel, nine miles north of Russellville, Logan County, Kentucky. Bishops Asbury and M'Kendree were both present.

These two venerable bishops of the Methodist Episcopal Church were both single men, and lived and died without ever marrying. There is no doubt but the scanty means of a support, and the vast field of their pastoral labour, induced them to remain unmarried, and devote their whole time to the building up the Church. Their field of ministerial labour was from East to West, from North to South, all over these United States and Territories, and the British Provinces in Canada. The Union itself was in its infancy. When these men bestowed the most of their ministerial labour, we had just thrown off the yoke of the British government, just ended a bloody war; great scarcity of money prevailed ; the Methodist Churches were few, feeble, and poor ; a single man in that early day was only allowed sixty-four, eighty, and never more than one hundred, dollars, and the bishops no more than any other single travelling preacher, and always dependent on the voluntary contributions of the people for this small pittance. Many of our married preachers had been starved into a location, and many more, during their illustrious sacrificing lives, were actually compelled to desist from travelling for want of means of support for their families. From the poverty of the Church, and the vastness of the field of their itinerant life, Mr. Asbury, and Bishop M'Kendree too, advised the travelling preachers to remain single; but a few years proved to these devoted bishops themselves that Methodist preachers were but men, subject to like passions with other men. The various courtships and marriage contracts, to be consummated at some future and distant day, satisfied these devoted men of God that it was better for *even* Methodist preachers to marry than to remain single, after they had formed a ministerial character; and although I had travelled ten years, had a wife and two children, and had acted as steward of the Conference for several years, yet up to this time, as I have elsewhere stated in this narrative, no allowance had been made for me, or any other travelling married preacher, for house rent and table expenses, or for our children.

At this Conference, Bishop Asbury came with ten dollars for every travelling preacher's child or children born in the travelling connexion. This money he had begged from door to door down East, in the older and wealthier Conferences, for the suffering children of the married travelling itinerants in the West. This, indeed, was a fatted calf to many of us, who had received hardly enough to keep soul and body together. At this Conference the stewards were instructed to settle all the claims of the preachers and their families as the Discipline provides.

By an examination of the Minutes for 1814–15, it will be seen that the Ohio Conference still had its six presiding elder Districts, and Tennessee eight Districts. For several years, about this time, our increase of members was small, owing to the war and rumours of war. The travelling preachers in the Ohio Conference had increased to sixty-three, and in the Tennessee Conference to sixty-six.

At a camp-meeting holden this year, in the edge of Tennessee, for the Christian Circuit, there were a great many people attended, and among them a gang of rowdies. The ringleaders of the rowdies went by the names of J. P. and William P, two brothers; their parents were fine members of the Methodist Episcopal Church. I found it would be hard to keep order, and I went to J. P., and told him I wanted him to help me keep order. Said I, " These rowdies are all afraid of you, and if you will help me, you shall be captain, and choose your own men."

He said he did not want to engage in that way; but if I would not bind him up too close, but let him have a little fun, away off, he would then promise me that we should have good order in the encampment through the meeting.

I said, "Very well; keep good order in the congregation, and if you have any little fun, let it be away off, where it will not disturb the worship of God."

There came into the congregation a young, awkward fellow, that would trespass on our rules by seating himself all the time among the ladies. It was very fashionable at that time for the gentlemen to roach their hair; and this young man had a mighty bushy roached head of hair. I took him out several times from among the women, but he would soon be back again.

I told J. P. I wished he would attend to this young man. "Very well," said he; and immediately sent off and got a pair of scissors, and planted his company about half a mile off; then sent for this young fellow, under the pretence of giving him something to drink. When they got him out there, two of them, one on each side, stepped up to him with drawn dirks, and told him they did not mean to hurt him if he would be quiet; but if he resisted or hallooed, he was a dead man. They said they only wanted to roach his hair, and put him in the newest Nashville fashion. The fellow was scared almost to death, but made no resistance whatever. Then one with the scissors commenced cutting his hair, and it was haggled all over at a masterly rate. When they were done shearing him, they let him go; and he came straight to the camp-ground. Just as he entered it, I met him; he was pale as a cloth. He took off his hat, and said, "See here, Mr. Cartwright, what them rowdies have done!" I had very hard work to keep down my risibilities; but I told him he had better say nothing about it; for if he did, they might serve him worse. He soon disappeared, and interrupted us no more during the meeting.

Our camp-ground was right on the bank of a creek. Just behind the preachers' camp, there was about room enough to place two or three carriages; then the bank of the creek, which was about ten feet high. Not far from the shore was a deep hole of water, about six feet deep. William P., the brother of my captain of order, was very rude, and I reproved him sharply. I understood that he swore he would run my carriage (which I had placed behind the preachers' tent, right on the bank) into the creek. There was but one way to pass to my carriage. At night I lay watching, with a good stick in my hand; and presently I saw William take hold of my carriage, and begin to turn it, in order to run it down the bank into the creek. I slipped out, and rushed upon him with my cudgel. I was in the only pathway; and he, fearing a good knock-down, leaped over the bank right into the deep hole of water, and came out on the other side, and ran off.

It made him very angry that he was defeated. He swore that he would have satisfaction out of me before the meeting was over. In the meantime, the power of God fell upon the people gloriously; many hardened sinners were arrested, and a great many were converted; and on Sunday the mighty power of God was felt to the utmost verge of the congregation. On Sunday night, our altar was crowded with weeping penitents. While I was in the altar, labouring with the mourners, I saw William come up and lean on the pale, on the outside of the altar. I kept my eye on him; and suddenly he leaped over into the altar, and fell at full length, and roared like a bull in a net, and cried aloud for mercy. While I was talking to and praying for him and others, I trod on something near where he had been standing that felt soft I stooped down and looked, and lo and behold, what should it be but a string of frogs, strung on a piece of hickory bark! I took them up, and carried them into the tent, not knowing what it meant.

Just about daybreak, Monday morning, William P. raised the shout of victory, after struggling hard all night. Our meeting went on gloriously all that day, and for several days and nights, with very little preaching or intermission; and many were the happy subjects of converting grace. Some time on Monday, my notorious William came to me, and told me that he gathered and strung that batch of frogs, and brought them to the altar, intending, while I was stooping and praying for the mourners, to slip them over my head and round my neck; and while he was seeking an opportunity to do this, the mighty power of God fell on him. He said he never wanted to be any nearer hell than he felt himself to be when the power of God arrested him. Many of the very worst rowdies that attended this meeting were struck down and converted to God, and thus ended the Frog Campaign. About seventy joined the Church.

There was another incident which occurred at this meeting that I will relate. Not very distant from Hopkinsville, near which town I lived, there was a very interesting, fashionable, wealthy family, who were raised with all the diabolical hatred that a rigidly enforced predestinarian education could impart against the Methodists. It had pleased God, at a camp-meeting near them, that I superintended, to arrest the wife and two of the daughters of the gentleman who was the head of this family, and they were powerfully converted, and joined the Methodist Church, and, as is common, they felt greatly attached to me as the instrument, in the hands of God, of their salvation. This enraged the husband and father of these interesting females very much. He not only threatened to whip me, but to kill me. He said I must be a very bad man, for all the women in the country were falling in love with me; and that I moved on their passions, and took them into the Church with bad intentions. His eldest daughter, a fine, beautiful, intelligent young lady, wanted to attend the above-mentioned camp-meeting, and bespoke a seat in my carriage, in company with others going to the same meeting. At first her father swore she should not go; but on second thought he consented, but told his wife and daughter that he would go along, and that he would watch me closely, and that he had no doubt, before he would return, he would catch me at my devilment, and be able to show the world that I was a bad man, and put a stop to the women all running mad after this bad preacher. His daughter made ready, and we all started. We had about twenty-eight miles to go to reach the encampment. His daughter thought it her duty to tell me the designs of her father, and said she hoped I would be on my guard; for she verily thought that her father was so enraged, that if he could not get something to lay to my charge to ruin my character as a preacher, he would kill me from pure malice. I told her, of course, I was wide awake and duly sober, and I had not the least fear but what God would give me her father as a rescued captive from the devil before the camp-meeting closed. Said I, " You must pray hard, and the work will be done." I said to her, " It is not the old big devil that is in your father; it must be a little weakly, sickly, devil that has taken possession of him, and I do not think that it will be a hard job to cast him out. Now," said I, " if God takes hold of your father and shakes him over hell a little while, and he smells brimstone right strong, if there was a ship-load of these little sickly devils in him, they would be driven out just as easy as a tornado would drive the regiments of musquitoes from around and about those stagnant ponds in the country. Cheer up, sister; I believe God will give me your father before we return." Seeing me so bold and confident, she wept, and raised the shout in anticipation of so desirable an event. When we got to the camp-ground, I had the company and their horses all taken care of, and then said to this man, "We have a large preachers' tent, well provided with good beds; come, you must go with me and lodge in the preachers' tent." He seemed taken by surprise, and hesitated, but I took him right into the tent. " Now, sir," said I, " make yourself at home; for I hope to see you soundly converted before this camp-meeting comes to a close." I saw his countenance fall, and perhaps this was the starting-point of his deep and pungent convictions. The trumpet sounded for preaching; I mounted the stand and preached; this man came and heard me. I saw clearly from his looks, that he was convicted, and had a hard struggle in his mind. He said to me, after the meeting was over, that my taking him into the preachers' tent, and treating him so kindly, was the worst whipping he ever got; he could not sleep, he said. Sometimes he thought he was a poor mean devil to treat me as he had done ; and surely I must be a Christian, or I never could treat him so kindly after he had said so many hard and bitter things about me. As the meeting progressed, his convictions increased, till he could neither eat nor sleep.

On Sunday night, when such a tremendous power fell on the congregation, and my gang of rowdies fell by dozens on the right and left, my special persecutor fell suddenly, as if a rifle-ball had been shot through his heart. He lay powerless, and seemed cramped all over, till next morning ; and about sunrise he began to come to. With a smile on his countenance, he then sprang up, and bounded all over the camp-ground, with swelling shouts of glory and victory, that almost seemed to shake the encampment. This was a glorious time for his daughter; she came leaping and skipping to me, and shouted out that those little mean and sickly devils were cast out of her father. He joined the Church, went home, and for days the family did little else but sing, pray, and shout the high praises of God

From this family a blessed revival broke out and spread all round, and many were awakened and converted to God. O, how often the devil overshoots the mark by inducing his subjects to persecute preachers and the Church ! God is above the devil, and the devil can never be cast out until he is first raised, or waked up.

Although I have never laid much stress on dreams, yet on Monday night of this camp-meeting I had a dream that made some impression on my mind. I here relate it and what followed, and let it go for what it is worth ; for " what is the chaff to the wheat ? " In my night visions I thought I went on a fishing expedition. I thought the fish bit well, and I drew up and threw out many excellent, fine fish. At length I felt that a large fish, or something else, had got hold of my hook. I began to draw whatever it was out, but it came slow and pulled heavy. At length I drew it to land, when, behold, it was a large mud turtle. I awoke, and lo, it was a dream ; and I was glad of it.

There had been in attendance on our camp-meeting an old apostate Baptist preacher, who had left his wife, who was yet living, and taken up with a young woman, and they were actually living in open adultery. He had, as he said, been awfully convicted during the meeting. He said he knew he had once enjoyed religion, but had lost it. He knew he had lost it all, and that, therefore, the doctrine of the unconditional perseverance of the saints, which he had preached for many years, was false; but he wanted to be saved, and he desired to join the Methodist Church. He said he belonged to a secret society, and they had not excluded him from that society, and they were honourable, high-minded men.

All this took place in the public congregation. I told him that if we, as a Church, could do him any good on fair scriptural terms, we should be glad to do it. "But," said I, "you cannot be so ignorant as not to know that the word of God condemns your course, and if our sins are as dear to us as a right foot, or hand, or eye, they must be cut off, or plucked out, and cast from us, or we cannot enter heaven. Now, sir, are you willing, and will you give up this course of living, put away the woman with whom you are now living, and go and live with your lawful wife, and will you do it now?"

. He burst into tears, wrung his hands in apparent agony, and said he wanted to be saved. "But will you not take me in on trial six months?"

"No, sir, we will not, unless you sacredly pledge yourself, before God and the Church, that you will, from this moment, abandon your present course of living."

He said he was afraid to promise this.

"Then," said I, "it is altogether useless to say another word on the subject; for we will not, under any consideration, receive you even on trial.

So we parted, and I fear he was eternally lost. Now whether this was my mud turtle or not, about which I dreamed, I cannot say; yet it really looked to me very much like it.

. A few years before this, there had been transferred from the Baltimore Conference a warm-hearted, lively, and zealous preacher by the name of James Ward. His labours were greatly blessed, and some very powerful revivals of religion followed. There was also a tolerably popular Baptist minister, by the name of J V——n, who attended several of Brother Ward's meetings , and whether he was in reality stirred up, or from other considerations, I will not pretend to judge, but so it was; he started out on a large preaching scale. He was a tolerably good preacher, and he was popular, and he soon had a mighty stir in the Baptist Church, and hundreds joined that Church, and he baptized them. He greatly erred on one subject; that was, he took a great deal of pleasure in proselyting from other Churches and making them members of his Church, as he said, by "wetting their jackets," that is, immersing them. He had been very successful in the upper counties of Kentucky.

I had once accidentally fallen in at one of his appointments, and heard him preach, but had no introduction to him; and from this circumstance I knew him, but he did not know me. About this time he sent a train of appointments down in the southern parts of Kentucky and West Tennessee, about Nashville, &c., &c. I had been on to Baltimore, attending General Conference, and was returning home near Hopkinsville, in Southern Kentucky, in the month of June. We travelled in those days mostly on horseback. It was very warm, and dusty riding. When I got to Nashville, I was informed that Mr. V. had just closed a protracted meeting in Nashville, and was to start for Hopkinsville that morning, and that it was probable I would fall in with him; and so it turned out. A few miles from Nashville I fell in with him. It being so warm and dusty, I had pulled off my coat and neckerchief, and tied them on behind me, and of course I was very dirty, and looked, I suppose, very little like a preacher. I rode up and spoke to Mr. V, and he to me. I had, in one respect, the advantage of him. I knew him, but he did not know me, but I studiously avoided calling him by name. He was very familiar and loquacious.

" You are travelling, sir ? "

" Yes, sir," was my reply.

" What parts are you from ? "

" I am directly from the City of Baltimore," said I

" Well, what is the news in that country ? " said he.

" Nothing very strange," said I.

" Well," said he, " what is the most prevalent religion, or most numerous denomination in that city ?"

" Well," said I, " those despicable Methodists are the most numerous of any Protestant Church there," answering him with a view to draw him out.

" Well," said he, " that is a pity, for they are on a very rotten and sandy foundation."

" Yes," said I ; " but perhaps the people might fall into worse hands."

" Hardly," said he. " But, sir, how are the Baptists prospering in and about Baltimore ? "

" Well," said I, " the Baptists are hardly known in that country."

" Are you not mistaken, sir ? "

" No, sir, I am not mistaken "

" Well, what can be the cause of that ? "

" Why, sir, it is not strange at all ; the Baptists are exclusive immersionists, and won't commune with any other Christian denomination ; and they, on these principles, cannot flourish among an enlightened and intelligent religious community."

Just here the battle commenced, and this was what I wanted. He began to eulogize the Baptists, and contended that their mode of baptism was the only one that was scriptural. The battle, or argument, lasted several hours, as we rode on side by side; but at length he showed unmistakeable signs of confusion; for he left the field of argument, and began to boast of the hundreds of Methodists and Presbyterians that he had immersed, and said he was on his way then to Hopkinsville, and expected to immerse many of the Methodists, the converts of Peter Cartwright, a Methodist preacher that lived down there; "and, sir," said he, "there is no Scripture for infant baptism." I then asked the following questions —

"Do you believe that all children are saved, and go to heaven, and that there is not one infant in hell?"

"Certainly, I do," said he.

"Well, if there are no children in hell, and all children dying in minority go to heaven, is not that Church that has no children in it more like hell than heaven?"

This question closed our argument, for he answered not at all. Just then we came to the forks of the road; the right, which he was to go, led to Russellville, and the left, my road, to Hopkinsville. As we shook hands and parted, said I, "Mr. V., I know you, and have the advantage of you; my name is Peter Cartwright; I live two miles from Hopkinsville, where you are going next week to wet so many of the jackets of my Methodist members; call and stay all night with me; I will help you make out your notes, and will see to the wetting of the jackets of my members." He promised to do so, but never came to my house. He attended to his appointments, but wet no Methodist jackets, and never succeeded in winning any great spoils in that region of country. He flourished a while; then joined the Campbellites; then left them, and returned to the Baptist Church, as I am informed; then moved to Missouri, and died. I hope his end was peaceful.

CHAPTER XIII.

BISHOP ASBURY.

IN the fall of 1815 our Conference was holden at Bethlehem Meeting-house, in Wilson County, Tennessee. Bishops Asbury and M'Kendree attended, though they were both in feeble health, and this was the last Conference in the West that we were permitted to see Bishop Asbury. He preached to us with great unction and power, though in extremely feeble health, not able to stand, and had to sit while he spoke to us for the last time. At this Conference we elected our delegates to the General Conference, which was to meet in Baltimore on the first of May, 1816. After: the election was over, Bishop Asbury called us (that is, the delegates elected) to his room, and then and there told us about the dissatisfaction that had made its appearance among some of the preachers with the government of the Methodist Episcopal Church, explained the cause, and advised us to hold fast to the landmarks of discipline with a firm grasp. His whole soul seemed to go out after the unity of Methodism, and to adopt every prudential measure to prevent any schism among us. He was very desirous to reach the General Conference; but the Lord ordered it otherwise; for, after he left Tennessee to go to South Carolina, he was attacked with a complication of diseases; but still slowly moved on north, in hope of meeting the General Conference in Baltimore On the 24th of March he reached Richmond, Virginia, where he preached his last sermon. Being too feeble to walk, he was carried in the arms of his friends to the house of God, and then propped on a table; there, as he sat, he delivered his last message to mortal man, hardly able to do so for want of breath. His sermon had a thrilling effect upon the congregation. After preaching he was borne back to his carriage, and still urged on his way towards Baltimore. But when he arrived at the house of his old friend, Mr. George Arnold, about twenty miles south of Fredericsburgh, Virginia, he could proceed no further.

It was on Friday evening, the 29th of March, when this man of God, who had travelled half a century near three hundred thousand miles, was taken from his carriage the last time. He lingered till Sunday, the 31st of March, in great distress of body On that day, at the usual hour of religious worship, he requested the family to come together. The Rev. John W. Bond, who had been his travelling companion for two years, prayed, and read and expounded the twenty-first chapter of Revelation. During these exercises the dying man of God was calm, and much engaged in prayer. A few minutes after the close of these religious services, as he was sitting in his chair, with his head reclined on the hand of his faithful attendant, without a struggle or a sigh, he fell asleep in death.

He was buried in the family burying-ground of Brother Arnold, at whose house he died; but the General Conference, at its session on the 1st of May, 1816, at the request of the people of Baltimore, ordered his remains to be removed, and deposited in a vault prepared for that purpose beneath the pulpit of Eutaw Street church.

The re-interment of this great and good man presented a scene of the most thrilling interest that I ever beheld. The body, was

followed from the Light Street to the Eutaw Street church by a vast
concourse of people. At the head of the procession marched Bishop
M'Kendree, the faithful colleague of the departed Asbury; next
followed the members of the General Conference, and last came the
people in almost unnumbered thousands.   Bishop M'Kendree pronounced the funeral oration, and many were the tears shed by the
weeping attendants; and the mortal body of the venerable Bishop
Asbury was laid to rest till the general resurrection.
Over the vault is inscribed the following epitaph .—

SACRED
to the Memory of
THE REV. FRANCIS ASBURY,
Bishop of the
Methodist Episcopal Church
He was Born in England, August 20th, 1745,
Entered the Ministry at the Age of Seventeen;
Came a Missionary to America, 1771;
Was ordained Bishop in this City, December 27th, 1784;
Annually visited the Conferences in the United States, with
much Zeal, continued to preach the Word
for more than half a Century,
and literally ended his Labours with his Life,
near Fredericsburgh, Virginia,
in the full Triumph of Faith, on the 31st of March, 1816,
aged 70 years, 7 months, and 11 days.
His Remains were deposited in this Vault, May 10th, 1816,
by the General Conference then sitting in this City.
His Journals will exhibit to Posterity his Labours, his Difficulties,
his Sufferings, his Patience, his Perseverance,
his Love to God and Man.
His Remains were again removed from this Vault, and deposited,
by Order of the General Conference of 1852, in a
Cemetery near Baltimore; and a Monument
is raised to perpetuate his Memory to
future Generations.

I will here state a case, in reference to Bishop Asbury's transcend-
ently superior talent to read men, which occurred at one of our Western
Conferences.   The Conference had been preceded with glorious revivals of religion, and many of the wealthy, and some of the learned,
had joined the Methodist Episcopal Church, among whom were two
very learned young men, one of them the son of a very distinguished,
learned teacher, the other the son of a general,—a distinguished,
wealthy man. Both of these young men professed to have a call to
the ministry, and came with a recommendation to the Conference to
be received on trial in the travelling connexion.   They were both
present, and Bishop Asbury had narrowly observed their conduct and

conversation. At the proper time Brother Learner Blackman, their presiding elder, presented their recommendations. He spoke of them in the highest terms, and considered them a great acquisition to the ministry and the Church. The Conference received them with great unanimity. Bishop Asbury had sat with his eyes nearly shut After they were received, he seemed to wake up. "Yes, yes!" he exclaimed; "in all probability they both will disgrace you and themselves before the year is out." And sure enough, in six months one was riding the Circuit with a loaded pistol and a dirk, threatening to shoot and stab the rowdies; the other was guilty of a misdemeanour, and in less than nine months they were both out of the Church. Bishop Asbury would often say to the preachers, "You read books, but I read men."

We received our appointments for this Conference year, 1815–16, with but little dissatisfaction. I was returned to the Green River District. Our increase of members or preachers, in the Ohio and Tennessee Conferences, was but small this year, though we had some increase.

In the spring of 1816 our General Conference convened, on the 1st of May, in the city of Baltimore. This was the second delegated General Conference of the Methodist Episcopal Church, and the first to which I was elected.

We had no steamboats, railroad cars, or comfortable stages in those days. We had to travel from the extreme West on horseback. It generally took us near a month to go; a month was spent at General Conference, and nearly a month in returning to our fields of labour. How different the facilities of travel then and now!

Bishop Asbury being dead, and Bishop M'Kendree's health being poor, it became necessary to have two more bishops, and, accordingly, we elected Enoch George and R. R. Roberts, two good men, and talented, regularly drilled in the itinerant work, and well prepared, from experience and practice, to sympathize with the seven hundred travelling preachers they had to station every year, suiting their talents to over two hundred and fourteen thousand members in these United States and Territories, and the Provinces of Canada

This was a year of general prosperity throughout the Connexion, over thirty thousand probationers had been added to the Church. Many of us feared that at the decease of Bishop Asbury dissensions and divisions would arise and injure our beloved Zion; but we had no question that gave us much trouble at that time. It is true, slavery was a troublesome matter to legislate on; but the one-eyed creature called Rabid Abolitionism had, at that time, been just born, and had but just cut its teeth, and could not bite hard; and it is a notorious fact, that all the preachers from the slaveholding states denounced slavery as a moral evil; but asked of the General Conference mercy and forbearance on account of the civil disabilities they laboured under, so that we got along tolerably smooth. I do not recollect a single Methodist preacher, at that day, that justified slavery. But O, how have times changed!

Methodist preachers in those days made it a matter of conscience not to hold their fellow-creatures in bondage, if it was practicable to emancipate them, conformably to the laws of the state in which they lived. Methodism increased and spread; and many Methodist preachers, taken from comparative poverty, not able to own a Negro, and who preached loudly against it, improved, and became popular among slaveholders; and many of them married into those slavehold-ing families, and became personally interested in slave property, (as it is called.) Then they began to apologize for the evil; then to justify it on legal principles; then on Bible principles; till, lo and behold! it is not an evil, but a good! it is not a curse, but a blessing! till really you would think, to hear them tell the story, if you had the means and did not buy a good lot of them, you would go to the devil for not enjoying the labour, toil, and sweat of this degraded race, and all this without rendering them any equivalent whatever!

I will here repeat what I have elsewhere stated in this narrative: that I verily believe, if the Methodist preachers had gone on as in olden times, bearing a testimony against the moral evil of slavery, and kept clear of it themselves, and never meddled with it politically, and formed no free-soil or abolition societies, and given all their money and the productions of their pens in favour of the colonization organ-izations, that long before this time many of the slave States would have been free states; and, in my opinion, this is the only effectual way to get clear of slavery. If agitation must succeed agitation, strife succeed strife, compromise succeed compromise, it will end in a dissolution of this blessed Union, civil war will follow, and rivers of human blood stain the soil of our happy country.

At this General Conference I heard, for the first time in my life, whisperings and innuendoes against the government of the Church. I suppose radicalism had just pipped. Many of our preachers that had travelled, had, as I said before, married into slaveholding and other-wise wealthy families. Some of the first order of talent, that had located, began to say that local preachers ought to have a voice in the lawmaking department of the Church; and in order to make friends, they said the laity ought to have a voice in all the Conferences; but there was no special outbreak at this General Conference. But the unhallowed leaven of disaffection spread; the friends of reform (so

called) established a press, and formed what they called Union
Societies; so that by public lectures, the Union Societies, and the
press, by 1820, when the General Conference met again in Baltimore,
it was astounding to see what evil disaffections had taken place.

They then came out boldly. They wanted to revolutionize the
whole government of the Methodist Episcopal Church. Many of our
old and talented preachers were loud and bitter in complaints against
our Church government; and I was greatly alarmed to see so many
strong, talented men carried away. Some of the hardest and bitterest
things ever written or spoken against the power of the bishops, or the
despotism of the itinerant preachers' administration, were spoken and
written by men who were afterward made bishops of the Methodist
Episcopal Church and the Southern Church. Motion after motion
was made, resolution after resolution was introduced, debate followed
debate, for days, not to say weeks. The radicals wanted to take away
the power of the bishops to appoint preachers to their fields of labour;
especially to deprive them of the power to appoint presiding elders,
and make them elective by the Annual Conferences; to have a lay
delegation, and many other things.

Finally, they concentrated all their arguments to make presiding
elders elective; but on counting noses, they found we had a majority,
though small; and, rather than be defeated, they moved for a committee of compromise. Strong men from each side were chosen; they
patched up a sham compromise, as almost all compromises are, in
Church or State. The committee reported in favour, whenever a presiding elder was needed for any District, the bishop should have the
right to nominate three persons, and the Conferences should have the
right to elect one of the three. This report passed by a vote of about
sixty; there were twenty-three, if my recollection is correct, in the
minority against it.

This report having passed, the radicals had a real jubilee. It was
the entering wedge to many other revolutionary projects; and they
began to pour them in at a mighty rate I had, in my speech in
debate on the subject, predicted that this would be the case. Our
friends began to see their error, but it was well-nigh too late.

In the meantime Bishop Soule, now of the Church South, had been
elected to the office of a bishop, and he informed the General Conference that he could not be ordained, because he could not conscientiously administer the government according to this inglorious compromise. Perhaps this was the best act that Bishop Soule ever
performed.

In the meantime I visited the room of Bishop M'Kendree, who was
too feeble to preside in the Conference. He wept, and said this compromise would ruin the Church for ever, if not changed, and advised

that we make a united effort to suspend these rules or regulations for·
four years; and we counted votes, and found we could do it, and introduced a resolution to that effect.   And now the war commenced
afresh; and after debating the resolution for several days, the radicals
found that if the vote was put we would carry it, and they determined
to break the quorum of the house, and for two or three times they
succeeded.   Bishop Roberts at length rebuked them sharply, and said,·
" If you cannot defeat the measure honourably, you ought not to do it
at all   Now," said he, "keep your seats, and vote like men."   This
awed several of them, and they kept their seats; the vote was put and
carried, and these obnoxious rules were suspended for four years.

But peace and harmony were very far from being restored to the
Church.   A strong and violent effort was made for the next four years
by the revolutionists to carry their radical measures, and thousands of
our members became disaffected, and by their constant agitations disturbed the peace, and endangered the harmony, of the Church, until it
really became imperatively necessary to arrest these lawless disturbers
of the peace of the Church.   They were arrested, brought to trial,
and expelled for rebellion against the constituted authorities of the
Church.

These wholesome and salutary measures were, by these self-styled
reformers, denounced as tyranny and despotism.   At our next General
Conference, in Baltimore, in 1824, the radical war against the Church
still raged with unabated fury, but we still had a majority in favour
of our old and well-tried government, and we succeeded, after long
and tedious debate, in suspending those heretical rules for four years
more.   This was the death-warrant to the revolutionists.   From this
time, many of the preachers and members began calmly to review their
ground of reform, and became well satisfied that it was all wrong;
and they retraced their steps, and became able and efficient expositors
of the polity of the Methodist Episcopal Church.

The reaction threw death and destruction into the radical ranks, and
created, as they thought, the necessity of a separate organization.
Accordingly, they set to work, and formed what they were pleased to
call the Protestant Methodist Church, in which they incorporated all
those radical measures for which they so strenuously contended before
their amputation or secession   They carried off thousands of our members, and many of our very talented preachers, and now they thought
that they would sweep the world; and truly they have swept it, for
they formed a complete trash-trap, and a great many of our unfaithful
members and preachers, that walked disorderly, and would not be reproved or cured, have gone into it, and upon the whole they have
saved the Methodist Episcopal Church a great deal of trouble in trying
and expelling disorderly preachers and members; for whenever they

were expelled or arraigned for misconduct, they fled to these seceders. They took them in, regardless of the crimes laid to their charge, and by 1828, when our General Conference sat in Pittsburgh, this little radical brat gave its last squeak among us, and we repealed those obnoxious rules and regulations. The Church was restored to peace and harmonious action, and we have done infinitely better without them than we did with them.

That this professed reform has proved, beyond any reasonable doubt, an entire failure, I think cannot be questioned by any impartial and unprejudiced mind. Over thirty years have rolled by since they organized. They boasted that they commenced with over twenty thousand members, headed by a strong corps of talented preachers: and after gathering up thousands of the expelled and disaffected members of the Methodist as well as other Churches, their numerical strength at this day is not, perhaps, over seventy thousand. They have tried to their hearts' content their Presbyterian form of government and their lay delegation. Their operations remind one of an old horse-mill with about one third of the cogs out of the main wheel. There is a mighty jarring and jolting, and often a mighty strife about who shall be the big man. Woe to them that kick against the pricks!

And now I say, and I speak with a respectful deference, Was there ever a heresy in doctrine or Church government that was not started by preachers? Look at the ten thousand and one erroneous doctrines, schisms, and divisions, that have sprung up almost in every country and clime, and in almost every age, and then ask, Was there not a preacher or preachers at the head of it? And here I may speak with confidence, and say, so far as the Methodist Church is concerned, from the days of John Wesley down to the present, there never has been a schism or a division in our Church but it was headed by a preacher or preachers, that have become wise above what is written. Witness the seven divisions among the Wesleyan Methodists in England; then view the secessions in these United States, in the Methodist Episcopal Church. Look at Hammet in the South, at Stillwell in New York; see James O'Kelly in Virginia; then behold the radical secession from 1820 to 1828 throughout the length and breadth of the land; then come to the great secession of the South in 1844.

If these secessions had been left to the voice of our members, would they ever have taken place? "No, verily, no," will be the answer of every intelligent man, woman, and child. But these preachers took an ungodly advantage of the members who stood firmly and strongly opposed to a division of the Methodist Episcopal Church; and now, to keep up appearances, these very preachers, with their bribed judges, sneeringly call the Methodist Episcopal Church *the Methodist Church, North,* and say we are all rabid abolitionists, when they do verily

know it is all false. At their late General Conference they have fully
disclosed the cloven foot of the slavery-loving preachers ; for they have
stricken out of their Discipline every rule on the subject of slavery,
and had well nigh stricken out that part of the General Rules that interdicts the slave trade, (according to their interpretation.) I should
not be greatly surprised if, in a few years, this rule goes by the board,
and some of these slavery-loving preachers are engaged in importing
them by the thousands into this land of the free, and home of the brave.
O, kind Heaven, prevent it, and reclaim these wretched wanderers ! *

And now, though we have spoken freely of preachers and their
faults, their errors ought not to be concealed. But this fact is not, as
we conceive, any triumph to infidelity, nor should it discourage the
Church. Among the first twelve that Christ called to the blessed work
of the ministry there were two that fatally erred : Judas betrayed and
Peter denied Him ; the love of money and the fear of man were too
strong for their religious attachment to Christ, and only proves the
necessity of sacrificing everything for the immortal honours of the
cross ; and although our sins are as near and dear to us as a right eye,
hand, or foot, they must be plucked out, or cut off, and cast from us,
knowing it is better, infinitely better, to make these sacrifices than re-
tain them all, and be cast into hell. What a sad account will many
preachers have to give in the day of judgment, who have preached a
free salvation to listening thousands, while their poor degraded slaves
are deprived of many of the blessings of life, and privileges of civil
and religious liberty ! These preachers must and do know that slavery
is at war with the attributes and perfections of God, who will never
punish the innocent or let the guilty go free.

Who ever before knew of a professed slavery Church ? that is, one
which justified slavery by the word of God ? Well may some of them
be ashamed of their assumed name, *Methodist Episcopal Church, South,*
and wish to change it ; for it is evident that they can never preach the
Gospel successfully in any country that opposes slavery ; for they could

* The author's fears have unhappily been realized. At the General Conference
of the Methodist Episcopal Church, South, in 1858, it was resolved that " *the rule
forbidding the buying and selling of men, women, and children, with an intention
to enslave them, be expunged from the General Rules of the Methodist Episcopal
Church, South,*" and further, "that in adopting the foregoing resolution, this
Conference *expresses no opinion in regard to the African slave trade,* to which the
rule in question has been understood to refer." To the eternal disgrace of this body,
be it known that only eight out of nearly 150 ministers of God's word could be
found to protest against such a violation of every feeling of humanity. One hundred
and forty ministers *express no opinion of the African slave trade,*—a traffic which
has been nurtured by human blood, and supported by the perpetration of every
crime that can stain humanity. If God's ministers are silent on a subject so
revolting as this, what claim can they urge to condemn lesser crimes ?

not, by possibility, have any confidence in such preachers; and the poor slaves, in proportion to their capabilities of reasoning on the subject, just in that ratio must they lack confidence in such preachers. Nay, they must lack confidence in that God and religion that these preachers recommend to them, and I am solemnly afraid that thousands of these poor slaves will be lost under the influence of these slaveholding preachers; but I predict the downfall of such a Church, and hope by other men and means God will yet save the thousands of the South, and preserve our happy *Union* until it shall give liberty, civil and religious, to unnumbered millions of the human family.

CHAPTER XIV.

FORMATION OF EARLY CIRCUITS IN THE WEST.

Our Annual Conference this year was held at Franklin, Tennessee, October 20th, 1816. Our increase this year in the West, including the Ohio and Tennessee Conferences, was 1,203. Our increase of travelling preachers in these two Conferences was but two, owing to many locating for want of the means of support. My four years on the Wabash and Green River District having expired, Bishop M'Kendree told me he desired me to go to the Holston District, but it was a long journey to move, and I had a young and increasing family, and I was poor. I asked him to be excused, but if he thought it best I would go, but he appointed me to the Christian Circuit, in the Green River District, James Axley presiding elder. this was the year 1816-17.

It must be borne in mind that in the West we always received our appointments for the year in the fall of the previous year. The General Conference of 1816 formed the Missouri Conference, which covered that State, and Arkansas, Illinois, and Indiana States. It was composed of Illinois and Missouri Districts, covering the principal settlements in four large States, though only two Districts. The same General Conference formed the Mississippi Conference. The Ohio Conference was composed of Ohio, Muskingum, Scioto, Miami, and Kentucky Districts, five in number.

It is probable that the first introduction of Methodism in the State of Indiana was in 1802 or 1803. In the fall of 1804 Illinois Grant, which was opposite and north of Louisville, was then included in the Salt River and Shelbyville Circuits, and Brother Benjamin Lakin and myself crossed the Ohio River, and preached at Brother Robertson's and Prather's. In this grant we had two classes, and splendid revivals of religion; and, if my recollection serves me correctly, this Illinois

Grant was formed into a Circuit in 1807–8, and Moses Ashworth was appointed to travel it; it was called Silver Creek Circuit. This was the first regular Circuit ever formed in the State of Indiana, and composed of 188 members. The next Circuit formed in the State of Indiana was called Vincennes Circuit, which I formed in 1808, at the time I fought the memorable battle with the Shakers, in the Busroe Settlement, elsewhere named in this narrative. This Circuit was temporarily supplied probably till 1811; it then had 125 members, and Thomas Stillwell was its first regular preacher; it belonged to the Green River District. The first introduction of Methodism in the State of Illinois is hard to determine.

The real pioneer and leader of Episcopal Methodism in the State of Illinois was Captain Joseph Ogle, who came to Illinois in 1785, and was converted under the preaching of James Smith, (Baptist,) of Kentucky, who visited and preached in Illinois in 1787. The first Methodist preacher was Joseph Lillard, who visited this State in 1793, and formed a class in St. Clair County, and appointed Captain Ogle leader. The next Methodist preacher was John Clarke, who was originally a Circuit rider in South Carolina, from 1791 to 1796, when he withdrew on account of slavery. He was the first man that preached the Gospel west of the Mississippi, in 1798. The Rev. Hosea Riggs was the first Methodist preacher that settled in Illinois, and he revived and reorganized the class at Captain Ogle's, formed by Lillard, which had dropped its regular meetings.

From 1798 there seems to have been no regular preacher in Illinois till 1804; then Benjamin Young was sent as a missionary. In the fall of 1805 he returned sixty-seven members, and Joseph Oglesby was appointed to succeed Brother Young on the Illinois Circuit. This Circuit was in the Cumberland District, Western Conference, and Lewis Garrett presiding elder, though I think he never visited Illinois. In 1806 Charles Methany was appointed to the Illinois Circuit. In 1807 Jesse Walker was appointed to this Circuit, and in 1808 John Clingan. All these early pioneer preachers have long since passed away and gone to their reward. "Blessed are the dead that die in the Lord; they rest from their labours, and their works do follow them."

The Tennessee Conference was composed of Salt River, Nashville, Cumberland, Green River, Holston, and French Broad Districts. The Mississippi Conference was composed of Mississippi and Louisiana Districts. Our old Western Conference had now, in four years from its first division, increased to four Annual Conferences, and they started in this form with the following ministers and members. According to the Minutes of 1817, Ohio had 22,171 members, and 62 preachers; Missouri had 3.173 members, and 23 travelling preachers; Tennessee had 19,401 members, and 53 travelling preachers; Mississippi Conference had 1,941 members, and 11 travelling preachers. Our four Conferences now covered the following States : Ohio, Indiana, Illinois, Missouri, Arkansas, Louisiana, Mississippi, Alabama, Tennessee, Kentucky, and Western Virginia, and some appointments in North Carolina. In the fall of 1813 I had left the Christian Circuit for the District, with 743 members, and I now found 546 ; but parts of the Circuit and membership had been merged into other Circuits. I was without any helper, and it was a full four weeks' Circuit.

This year we had some glorious revivals. There was a small society of good members some five miles north of Hopkinsville ; one of our quarterly meetings was holden here, and a blessed work broke out ; some seventy were converted and joined the Church. Several of these young converts made useful ministers in the Methodist Episcopal Church.

Down near the Tennessee State line, there moved and settled two wealthy Methodist families ; but they were surrounded by a strong settlement who were very rigid Calvinists, raised to hate the Methodists. I took them in the Circuit, but, it being a week-day appointment, and strong prejudices against us, our congregations were small These two families had over one hundred and twenty slaves, and the slaves were dreadfully wicked ; they were a drunken, Sabbath breaking, and thievish set of slaves. The masters were very humane and indulgent. There were but two, I believe, among them that were professors at all ; two old grey-headed men. One of them was a Methodist, the other was a Baptist ; both were exhorters among the people of colour. The brother at whose house I preached was a plain, old-fashioned Methodist in almost everything save slavery I was opposed to slavery, though I did not meddle with it politically ; yet I felt it my duty to bear my testimony against the moral wrong of slavery. The old brother took some exceptions to my testimony against it. I saw very plainly that in all probability these slaves must be lost. On week-days they were under an overseer, and not permitted to hear preaching. Sundays they were out drinking and trading, selling brooms, baskets, and the little articles they manufactured. I felt distressed at the thought that they would be lost. At length I asked the old brother to give me the privilege to go to their cabins and preach to them ; he thought this too great a degradation for a preacher. I told him, if something was not done for them, they would all be lost, and that God held him in a strong sense accountable, and that something must be done. He said he was willing I should preach to them, if I would preach to them in his house. I told him I had this objection to that : "You white people will be present, and your very presence will embarrass them and me both. I want to talk to them as ignorant Negroes, and tell them of all their drunkenness, stealing, acts of adultery, and Sabbath breaking; and I cannot do it if the white people are present." He then proposed to give the Negroes the large room and entry, and that he and his brother-in-law's family would retire to another room   I said, " If you will let me lock you up, I will agree to it." He assented.

The appointment was made, and all the slaves of the two families directed to attend   I told John and Harry, the two black men that were exhorters, that if any impression was made on any of them, they must set out a mourners' bench, and assist me in talking to and praying with them.

The day rolled on; I attended. The room was full, and entry too. I locked up the white people in another room, and went in and took my stand. There was belonging to the old brother a large, likely mulatto man, the carriage-driver; he dressed much finer than his master; he came and took his stand in the door, his bosom full of ruffles. He looked scornfully on me, as good as to say, " Yes, you think you are going to do great things in preaching to us coloured people." I sung and prayed; took my text; explained the plan of salvation through Jesus Christ; then told them of all their dirty deeds in as plain language as I could command; and then, in as warm an exhortation as I could give, I warned them to flee from the wrath to come: and, just as I closed, the large ruffle-shirted carriage-driver fell full length on the floor, and made the house jar and tremble. In a few minutes they fell right and left, till the place was strewed with them in every direction. John and Harry, my two armour-bearers, set out a bench, and gathered them to it, till they could get no more, for the crowd; and the first thing I knew, here were the old brother and his wife, his brother-in-law and wife, talking to and praying with the Negroes, and several of their children down with the Negroes praying for mercy at a mighty rate. Our meeting lasted all the afternoon and night, and there were forty conversions; several of the white children among the rest. From this a blessed revival spread among the slaves, and many of them, I believe, were soundly converted. I took some seventy into the Church, baptized them and their children. Several of these coloured men made respectable local preachers to preach to the slaves around the country.

These two old Methodist men said I had in a temporal sense bettered or enhanced the value of their servants more than a thousand dollars; they ceased getting drunk, stealing, and breaking the Sabbath. This revival among the slaves, with many others that I have been engaged in, fully satisfies me that the Gospel ought to be carried to slaves and owners of slaves; for if the religion of Jesus Christ will not finally bring about emancipation of the slaves, nothing else will. I am greatly astonished at many good Methodist preachers that say,

"Don't carry the Gospel into slave States, but deliver over to the uncovenanted mercies of God slaves and their masters ; " for they say virtually, none of them can be saved. But I know better; and unless freedom for the slaves is accomplished under the redeeming influence of religion, this happy Union will be split from centre to circumference, and then there will be an end to our happy and glorious Republic. And if we do not carry the Gospel to these slaves and their masters, who will ? Surely not the ministers who justify slavery by perverting the word of God; and still more surely not abolition preachers, who by political agitation have cut themselves off from any access to slave-holders or slaves

I wish we had a trained band of the Methodist Episcopal Church who are willing to let our Discipline be as it is, to send into every slave State in the Union. Surely here is missionary ground that ought to be occupied with great care, for the salvation of the perishing thousands of the South, and for the final overthrow of slavery, under the benign influences of the Christian religion.

There was another incident occurred this year, that I will mention in this place. Many of the early Methodists somehow imbibed the notion that a quarter of a dollar meant what we call quarterage ; and although many of them were wealthy, it was hard to convince them that twenty-five cents were not quarterage, and that every member should pay according to his ability. This was one cause why so many of our preachers were starved into a location, and of necessity had to retire from the itinerant field

There were two wealthy families moved into my Circuit from one of the old States, and settled in a very wicked neighbourhood. They came to me, and insisted that I should take them into the Circuit, and preach to them. I did so ; and formed a class of five white members, and one old black man. The round on the Circuit before the next quarterly meeting I told them, as none of them would go to the quarterly meeting, that if they had anything to send up as their quarterage to support the Gospel, if they would hand it to me, I would credit it to their names on the class-paper.

The old Negro man stepped forward and laid down his quarter of a dollar. Next came his mistress ; she handed me two dollars ; then came her husband and the master of the old black man, and threw down twenty-five cents.

Said I, "Colonel, what is this twenty-five cents for ? "

Said he, "It is my quarterage "

"Surely, colonel," said I, "you are going to give more than that."

"No, sir," said he ; "I will have you to know beggars are not to be choosers."

"Well, sir," said I, "I will have you to know I am no beggar. I have a just claim on you, and you owe it to me; and if you will not give me more than that, I will not have it."

"Very well," said he.

So I left the money on the table. "And now, sir," said I, "if you will not support the Gospel, I shall not leave any other appointment here, but will go and preach to those who are willing to support the Gospel."

The old brother was considerably riled. His good lady expostulated with him; but he was inexorable. The sister told me afterward that the colonel spent a sleepless night; he kept twisting and turning from side to side, and groaning all night. She spoke to him several times, and told him if he would resolve to be more liberal, his bad feelings would go off, and he would sleep better. The old brother got up the next morning, and after family worship he said to me :—

"Brother, what ought I to give as quarterage?"

"O," said I, "brother, I can't answer that question, that is a matter between God and your conscience. But," said I, "brother, solve the following question, and you will know what you ought to give: If your old Negro man, not worth ten dollars, gave twenty-five cents a quarter, what ought Colonel T., who has seventy slaves, two thousand acres of good land, several thousand dollars out at interest, and worth, at least, fifty thousand dollars, to give?"

The solving of this question stumped him, and his quarterage ever afterward, as long as I knew him, came by dollars, and not cents. And when last I saw him, as I moved to Illinois, he stopped me in the road, and said,—

"Brother, I owe you a thousand dollars, and here's part of it," handing me a fifty-dollar bill.

His excellent wife, leaning on his arm, said to me, " I owe you as much as my husband, take a part," and handed me a twenty-dollar bill. Thus I cured a quarter-of-a-dollar-quarterage member, and, my dear reader, if you are one of these old dispensationists, look out for a perfect cure, or come and be healed of this parsimonious leprosy.

In travelling the Christian Circuit, which crossed the Tennessee State line, and lay partly in Tennessee, and partly in Kentucky, in one of my exploring routes, hunting up new ground and new appointments to preach at, late one evening, in or near the Cumberland River Bottom, I called at a gentleman's gate, and asked the privilege of staying all night. The gentleman very readily granted my request. He was a wealthy farmer, the owner of several slaves. I found a mild, good, easy, fashionable family. After supper, several neighbours came in to spend an evening in social chat. Being a stranger among them,

I turned the conversation on religious subjects, inquired if they had any preaching. I soon found they had very little preaching of any kind. I told the gentleman my business was to preach anywhere I could get peaceable and orderly hearers, and asked him if I might not leave an appointment to preach at his house. He pleasantly said, if he had heard me preach and liked my preaching, he could better determine whether to grant me the privilege to leave an appointment or not. I told him, as he had a large family, black and white, and as there were some five or six visitors present, if he had no objections, and would call them together, I would preach to them, and he could the better judge how he liked my preaching, and determine whether I should leave a future appointment. He agreed to the proposition, and called all in. I sung and prayed, took my text, and preached to them about an hour as best I could. The coloured people wept; the white people wept; the man of the house wept; and when I closed, he said, " Do leave another appointment, and come and preach to us; for we are sinners, and greatly need preaching." I left an appointment; but before I came round, the devil stirred up opposition. One man told the gentleman at whose house I preached, that if he let the Methodist preachers preach at his house, it would not be long before they would eat him out of house and home. He said his father had taken in Methodist preachers, and in a few years they ate him out, and brought him to poverty; and, besides, these Methodist preachers were a very bad set of men. Mr. B. told this man that he thought he could stand it a while, and if he found there was any danger of being eaten out, he would send us adrift.

When I came to my appointment, there was a large congregation; the house and porch were literally crowded. I preached to them with great freedom, and almost the whole congregation were melted into tears. I sung, prayed, and went through the congregation, and shook hands with a great many of them. When I came to the man of the house, he wept, and fell on his knees, and begged me to pray for him. Soon his wife and children, and several others, knelt by his side, and cried aloud for mercy It was late at night before our meeting closed, and not until the swelling shouts of five or six went to heaven, that the dead were alive and the lost were found. I opened the doors of the Church for the reception of members, and some ten persons joined,— the man of the house, his wife, two children, and two servants. This was the first-fruits of a gracious revival and a large society in this neighbourhood; and while I lived in that country, we held a sacramental meeting at this place every year. After the first sacrament we held there, Brother B. rose and addressed the large assembly. He said, " Some of you kindly warned me not to take in these Methodist preachers. You said they would eat me out and bring me to poverty; but, neighbours, I have raised more corn, more wheat, more hemp, more tobacco, and never lived as well and plentifully in all my life. I could feed a regiment of Methodist preachers all the time, and then get rich; for God blesses me in my basket and in my store."

During this year, while on this Circuit, something like the following occurred: An Englishman, a Wesleyan Methodist, moved into a very wicked and high-strung Predestinarian settlement. He came several miles, and made himself known. He invited me to preach at his house. I told him the people were so prejudiced against the Methodists, that we could not get them out to hear on a week-day; but he insisted, and I gave him an appointment. When I came, there were only five besides the family. I preached: two of the little company wept. I left another appointment. For several times that I preached to them, my congregation increased, and were orderly and somewhat affected. At length the Englishman, being wealthy, told me he was going to build a church. I tried to dissuade him from it. I told him he could get no help to build; that there was no Society, and not much probability that there would ever be a Methodist Society there; but, he said, he thought a man lived to very little purpose in this world, if he did not live so as to leave his mark, that would tell when he was dead and gone. "Now," said he, "if you will promise me that you will hold a protracted meeting, and give us a sacrament, and get some help, and come and dedicate the church, it shall be up and finished in eight or ten weeks." I told him I would do so, if spared: in the meantime, while the church was in process of building, we had two or three conversions at our little meetings. The church being finished, I got the help needed, appointed a protracted sacramental meeting to dedicate the church, and invited people far and near to attend; and, it being a new thing in the settlement, when the day came there was a very large concourse of people. The first sermon on Saturday was attended with great power; that night there were several mourners and two sound conversions. On Sunday, under the sermon of dedication, the word was attended with great power; many fell under the mighty power of God. Our meeting lasted all that day and night, with very little intermission, and about twenty were converted.

Our meeting continued several days and nights; many were the happy conversions to God, and forty joined the Church. My Englishman was so happy, he hardly knew whether he was in the body or out of it. Methodism was firmly planted here. Long since my English brother died in great peace, and rests in heaven from his labours, and his works do follow him: but surely he made his "mark," and it will be owned in heaven.

From the earliest of my recollection up to this time, 1816, there were scarcely any books of any kind in this now mighty West; but especially was there a great scarpity of Bibles and Testaments. We were young and poor as a nation; had but a few years gained our liberty; had hardly begun to live as a Republic after a bloody and devastating war for our independence; and although Congress, the very first year after the declaration of our independence, had wisely taken steps for furnishing the struggling infant for independence with the word of God, and did order that precious book, yet there was a great lack of the Bible, especially in the wilderness of the West; but this year the Lord put it into the hearts of some of His people to organize a Bible Society, which was done on the 11th of May, 1816; and although at first it was a feeble concern, yet God has prospered it, and millions upon millions of this precious book have been printed and circulated, and it is pouring streams of light, life, and knowledge upon almost every nation of this sin-stricken world. The man of sin has quailed before it; the false religion of the God-dishonouring prophet is tottering before its mighty truths; the dying idolatrous pagan millions are receiving its soul-converting truths, and we hope for its universal spread till every crowned head shall be brought down to the dust, every oppressive yoke broken, universal civil and religious liberty enjoyed by our fallen race, and the benefits of the redeeming stream be enjoyed by all mankind.

Nothing but the principles of the Bible can save our happy nation or the world, and every friend of religion ought to spread the Bible to the utmost of his power and means. Then let us look for the happy end of the universal spread of truth, when all flesh shall see the salvation of God.

CHAPTER XV.

EARTHQUAKE IN THE SOUTH.

THE Conference was held in Franklin, Tennessee, October 30th, 1817. I was appointed to travel on the Christian Circuit, Green River District, James Axley, presiding elder. Our increase this year was 5,163 members, and seven preachers, in the four Conferences. In the winter of 1812 we had a very severe earthquake, it seemed to stop the current of the Mississippi, broke flat-boats loose from their moorings, and opened large cracks or fissures in the earth. This earthquake struck terror to thousands of people, and under the mighty panic hundreds and thousands crowded to and joined the different

Churches. There were many very interesting incidents connected with the shaking of the earth at this time . two I will name. I had preached in Nashville the night before the second dreadful shock came, to a large congregation. Early the next morning I arose and walked out on the hill near the house where I had preached, when I saw a Negro woman coming down the hill to the spring, with an empty pail on her head. (It is very common for Negroes to carry water this way without touching the pail with either hand.) When she got within a few rods of where I stood, the earth began to tremble and jar; chimneys were thrown down, scaffolding around many new buildings fell with a loud crash, hundreds of the citizens suddenly awoke, and sprang into the streets; loud screaming followed, for many thought the day of judgment was come. The young mistresses of the above-named Negro woman came running after her, and begging her to pray for them. She raised the shout, and said to them, "My Jesus is coming in the clouds of heaven, and I can't wait to pray for you now; I must go and meet Him. I told you so, that He would come, and you would not believe me. Farewell. Hallelujah! Jesus is coming, and I am ready. Hallelujah! Amen." And on she went, shouting and clapping her hands, with the empty pail on her head.

Near Russellville, Logan County, Kentucky, lived old Brother Valentine Cook, of very precious memory, with his wife Tabitha. Brother Cook was a graduate at Cokesbury College at an early day in the history of Methodism in these United States. He was a very pious, successful pioneer preacher; but for the want of a sufficient support for a rising and rapidly-increasing family, he had located, and was teaching school at the time of the above-named earthquake. He and wife were in bed when the earth began to shake and tremble. He sprang out of bed, threw open the door, and began to shout, and started with nothing on but his night-clothes He steered his course east, shouting every step, saying, "My Jesus is coming." His wife took after him, and at the top of her voice cried out, "O Mr. Cook, don't leave me."

"O Tabby," said he, "my Jesus is coming, and I cannot wait for you;" and on he went, shouting every jump, "My Jesus is coming; I can't wait for you, Tabby."

The years of the excitement by these earthquakes hundreds joined the Methodist Episcopal Church; and though many were sincere, and stood firm, yet there were hundreds that no doubt had joined from mere fright. My predecessors had for several years held the reins of discipline with a very loose hand; and when Bishop M'Kendree told me privately he wished me to go to the Red River Circuit at the Conference of 1817, my heart was troubled within me, for I knew the state of the Circuit. There were many wealthy, fashionable families in the Church; slavery abounded in it, and the members had been allowed to buy and sell without being dealt with; moreover, these were the days of common, fashionable dram-drinking, before the great temperance reformation was started; and extravagant dressing was the unrestrained order of the day; and there were about twenty talented local preachers in the Circuit, many of them participators in these evils, and I dreaded the war that must follow. Under this conviction I begged Bishop M'Kendree not to send me there. He very gravely replied, "There are many members in that Circuit that may be saved by a firm, judicious exercise of discipline, that otherwise will be lost, and I wish you to go and do for them the best you can."

"Enough said," replied I; "I'll go."

At the upper end of the Circuit, not more than eight or nine miles from Nashville, there was a large society and a meeting-house. My predecessor had left a conditional appointment for his successor. I was a total stranger in this region. The day of my conditional appointment was a dark day, misting with rain, but I got there in due time. After waiting till half-past twelve o'clock, one man came, who had had the misfortune to lose one of his eyes. We sat a little while, and I asked him if there was not an appointment for preaching that day.

"Yes," said he; "but there will be no preacher or people, I suppose." I saw from his answer he did not suspect me for the preacher.

He further said, "As it is late, and no preacher nor people, we had as well go Come, go home with me, and get some dinner."

"No," said I, "we must have meeting, and if you will preach, I will conclude after you."

"No, no," said he; "if you will preach, I will conclude after you."

"Agreed," said I, and up I rose in the stand, sung and prayed, took my text, and preached as best I could for forty-five minutes, and then called on him, and he rose, sung and prayed, and prayed well.

I went home with my one man, my entire congregation, and found him to be a pious, religious elder in the Presbyterian Church. From the novelty of the effort of the day, my friend professed to think it was one of the greatest sermons he had ever heard in all his life.

I left another appointment, and went on my way round the Circuit. For weeks my one-man congregation proclaimed and circulated my next appointment, telling the people what a great preacher had come to the Circuit; and when I came to my next appointment, the whole hill-side was covered with horses and carriages, and the church crowded to overflowing. My heart almost fainted within me for fear

I should not meet the expectations of the people; but the Lord helped me, and we had a mighty shaking among the dry bones, and a blessed revival broke out. Our meeting lasted several days and nights, and many souls were happily converted to God and joined the Church on my first round on this Circuit.

When I got to the lower end of the Circuit I found a large society, a fine class-leader, and a very pious, old, superannuated travelling preacher.   He told me the society was in a most wretched condition; that there was a very popular local preacher in the society, who married a great many people, and was in the habit of drinking too much at almost every wedding he attended; and that he had a large connexion, all in the Church, and that for years the preachers were afraid to do anything with him.

The next day, which was Sabbath, we had a large congregation, and after preaching, as my uniform custom was, I met the class.   My popular local preacher was present.   In examining the leader of the class I, among many other questions, asked him if he drank drams. He promptly answered me, No, he did not.

"Brother," said I, "why do you not?"   He hesitated; but I insisted that he should tell the reason why he did not.

"Well, brother," said he, "if I must tell the reason why I do not drink drams, it is because I think it is wrong to do so."

"That's right, brother," said I; "speak it out; for it is altogether wrong for a Christian, and a class-leader should set a better example to the class he leads, and to all others."

When I came to the local preacher, I said, "Brother W., do you drink drams?"

"Yes," said he.

"What is your particular reason for drinking drams?" I asked him.

"Because it makes me feel well," he answered.

"You drink till you feel it, do you?" said I.

"Certainly," said he.

"Well, how much do you drink at a time?"

He replied, gruffly, that he never measured it.

"Brother, how often do you drink in a day?"

"Just when I feel like it, if I can get it."

"Well, brother, there are complaints that you drink too often and too much; and the Saturday before my next appointment here you must meet a committee of local preachers at ten o'clock, to investigate this matter, therefore prepare yourself for trial."

"O!" said he, "if you are for that sort of play, come on; I'll be ready for you."

I had hard work to get a committee that were not dram-drinkers themselves. The trial came on; the class-leader brought evidence that the local preacher had been intoxicated often, and really drunk several times. The committee found him guilty of immoral conduct, and suspended him till the next quarterly meeting; and then the quarterly meeting, after hard debate, expelled him. The whole society nearly were present.

After his expulsion, and I had read him out, his wife and children, and connexions, and one or two friends, to the number of thirteen, rose up, and withdrew from the society. I told the society, if there was anything against their moral character, they could not withdraw without an investigation; but if there was nothing against their moral character, they could withdraw. The leader said there was nothing immoral against them, so I laid down the gap and let them out of the Church. They then demanded a letter. I told them there was no rule by which they had a right to a letter, unless they were going to move and join some other society of the Methodist Episcopal Church. They said they never intended to join the Methodist Episcopal Church again. I then told them that they came to us without a letter, and must go without a letter. I then read the Rules; exhorted the leader to be punctual, faithful, and pious; the members I urged to attend all the public and private means of grace, especially class-meetings, love-feasts, and the sacraments, and to bring and dedicate their children to God by having them baptized.

From this very day the work of religion broke out in the society and settlement, and before the year closed I took back the thirteen that withdrew, and about forty more joined the Church, and not a dram-drinker in the whole society; but the poor local preacher who had been expelled, I fear, lived and died a drunkard.

This was a four weeks' Circuit, and I had no helpers; and on examination of the class papers I found over one hundred and fifty delinquent members; some, yea, many of them, had not been in a class-meeting for one, two, and three years. I determined, with a mild and firm hand, to pull the reins of our discipline, and by the aid of the leaders, and by my personally visiting the delinquents, we managed to see every one of them, and talk to them.

Through the blessing of God upon our labours, we saved to the Church about sixty of them, the others we dropped, laid aside, or expelled. This was awful work, to turn out or drop ninety persons in about nine months; it bowed me down in spirit greatly; it looked like as if a tornado had fearfully swept over the Church; but there was a stop put to trading in slaves, and the dram-drinkers became very few, and many threw off their jewellery and superfluous dressing; prayer-meetings sprung up, class-meetings were generally attended, our congregations increased, our fasts were kept. Toward the last quarter of the year I beat up for a general camp-meeting, and there was a general rally. We had a large camp-ground, seats for thousands prepared, a large shed built over the altar and pulpit that would shelter more than a thousand people. The square of our camp-ground was well filled. The camp-meeting lasted eight days and nights; the preachers preached, the power of God attended, sinners by the score fell; the altar, though very large, was filled to overflowing; and while many managed and laboured in the altar with mourners, we erected another stand at the opposite end of the encampment, and there the faithful minister proclaimed the word of life. The power of God came there as the sound of a mighty rushing wind; and such was the effect, that crowds of mourners came forward and kneeled at the benches prepared, and, indeed, the work spread all over the encampment and almost in every tent. There were two hundred and fifty who professed religion, and one hundred and seventy joined the Church, besides about forty coloured people. Glory to God! Zion travailed, and brought forth many sons and daughters to God.

Many of these converts and accessions to the Church were from different and distant Circuits around; for people in those days thought no hardship of going many miles to a camp-meeting. I was continued two years on this Circuit: the first year J. Axley, presiding elder; the second year M. Lindsey was my presiding elder. There were many interesting incidents that occurred during my stay on this Circuit. A few I will name.

At Mount Zion meeting-house there was a good class of poor, simple-hearted Methodists that desired to hold class-meetings according to rule with closed doors, admitting persons not members of the Church only two or three times, unless they intended to join. There was an old lady in the settlement, a New Light by profession, who hated the Methodists and despised class-meetings with closed doors, but would stay in in spite of the leader. She would take her seat near the door, and open it while the leader was speaking to the class. They had tried to stop her many ways, but did not succeed. When I came round, the leader complained to me, alleging that they were greatly annoyed by her disorderly conduct I preached, then read the Rules, then requested all to retire but the class, or such as desired to join the Church, and then closed the door, and proceeded to examine the class. I knew this lady was in, and sat near the door as usual. I asked the leader if there were any in but members. He answered, "Yes, there are three that are not members." I told him to take me to them first. He did so. The first was a man. I asked him his intention in staying in class-meeting. He told me he wanted to serve

God, and join the Church. "Very well," said I. The next was a woman, whom I questioned, and who answered in the same way. While I was talking to her, my New Light got up and opened the door, and took her seat close by it. I approached her, and asked her what was her motive for staying in class-meeting.

She said she wanted to be with the people of God.

"Do you wish to join our Church?"

"No, I don't like the Methodists."

"Madam, you ought not to violate our Rules."

"Indeed, I do not care a fig for your Rules; I have stayed in class-meetings many times, and will stay in when I please."

"You must go out."

"I will not, sir."

"Then I will put you out."

"You can't do it," she replied; and sprung to her feet, and began to shout and clap her hands; and as she faced to the door, I took hold of her arms behind her shoulders, and moved her toward the door. She threw up her hands against the cheek of the door, and prevented me from putting her out. I saw a scuffle was to take place, and stooped down and gathered her in my right arm, and with my left hand jerked her hand from the cheek of the door, and lifted her up, and stepped out and set her on her feet. The moment I set her down she began to jump and shout, saying, "You can't shut me out of heaven." I sternly ordered her to quit shouting; for, said I, "you are not happy at all, you only shout because you are mad and the devil is in you." When she quit shouting, I said, "I knew you were not happy; for if God had made you happy, I could not have stopped it; but as it was the devil in you, I have soon stopped your shouting." I then stepped back and shut the door, and met my class standing against it; and we had a very good time, and effectually foiled our old New Light tormentor, and she never troubled me any more during my two years on this Circuit.

· The Tennessee Conference sat in Nashville, October 1st, 1818, when I was re-appointed to Red River. Our increase this year, in the four Western Conferences, was 5,164. Our increase of travelling preachers was only nine.

At the Nashville Conference an incident occurred, substantially, as well as my memory serves me, as follows : The preacher in charge had risen from very humble beginnings, but was now a popular, fashionable preacher. We talk about "Young America" these times; but Young America was as distinctly to be seen in those days among our young, flippant, *popularity*-seeking preachers, as now.

Brother Axley and myself, though not very old, were called old-fashioned *fellows;* and this popular young aspirant was afraid to appoint Brother Axley or myself to preach at any popular hour, for fear we would break on slavery, dress, or dram-drinking. But at length the old staid members and the young preachers began to complain that Axley and Cartwright were slighted, and an under-current of murmuring became pretty general. The city preacher had been selected to appoint the time and place where we were to preach. Brother Axley and myself had our own amusement. At length, on Saturday of the Conference, this preacher announced that Brother Axley would preach in the Methodist Church on Sunday morning at sunrise, thinking there would be but few out, and that he could do but little harm at that early hour.

When we adjourned on Saturday afternoon, I rallied the boys to spread the appointment; to rise early and get all out they could. The appointment circulated like wildfire, and sure enough at sunrise the church was well filled. Brother Axley rose, sung, prayed, took his text: "Be not conformed to this world, but be ye transformed by the renewing of your minds;" and if the Lord ever helped mortal man to preach, He surely helped Brother Axley. First he poured the thunders of Sinai against the Egyptians, or slave-oppressors; next he showed that no moderate dram-drinker could enter heaven; and then the grape-shot of truth rolled from his mouth against *rings*, ruffles, and all kind of ornamental dress. Dr. Bascom was sitting right before him. He had a gold watch-chain and key, and two very large gold seals. He was so excited, that unconsciously he took up one of the seals, and began to play with the other seal with his right hand. Axley saw it, stopped suddenly, and very sternly said to him, "Put up that chain, and quit playing with those seals, and hear the word of the Lord." The claret rushed to the surface of his profile.

The sermon went off admirably, and really it seemed as though a tornado had swept the ruffles and veils; and the old members of the Church shouted for joy. Having achieved another signal victory over error and pride, the ministers and ruling elders of other sister Churches had opened their pulpits, and invited us to preach to their people during Conference Among the rest, Dr. Blackbourn had opened his church. Dr. Blackbourn was a strong, popular Presbyterian minister.

In the course of the Sabbath, the city preacher informed me that I was to preach on Monday evening in Dr. Blackbourn's church, and charged me to be sure and behave myself. I made him my best bow, and thanked him that he had given me any appointment at all; and I assured him I would certainly behave myself the best I could "And now," said I, "Brother Mac, it really seems providential that you have appointed me to preach in the doctor's church; for I expect they never heard Methodist doctrine fairly stated and the dogmas of Calvinism exposed, and now, sir, they shall hear the truth for once." Said the preacher, "You must not preach controversy." I replied, "If I live to preach there at all, I'll give Calvinism one riddling." "Well," said the preacher, "I recall the appointment, and will send another preacher there, and you must preach in the Methodist church Monday evening, and do try and behave yourself." "Very well," said I; "I'll do my best."

The preacher's conduct toward me was spread abroad, and excited considerable curiosity. Monday evening came; the church was filled to overflowing; every seat was crowded, and many had to stand. After singing and prayer, Brother Mac took his seat in the pulpit. I then read my text: "What shall it profit a man if he gain the whole world and lose his own soul?" After reading my text I paused. At that moment I saw General Jackson walking up the aisle; he came to the middle post, and very gracefully leaned against it, and stood, as there were no vacant seats. Just then I felt some one pull my coat in the stand, and turning my head, my fastidious preacher, whispering a little loud, said, "General Jackson has come in; General Jackson has come in." I felt a flash of indignation run all over me like an electric shock, and facing about to my congregation, and purposely speaking out audibly, I said, "Who is General Jackson? If he don't get his soul converted, God will damn him as quick as he would a Guinea Negro!"

The preacher tucked his head down, and squatted low, and would, no doubt, have been thankful for leave of absence. The congregation, General Jackson and all, smiled, or laughed right out, all at the preacher's expense. When the congregation was dismissed, my city-stationed preacher stepped up to me, and very sternly said to me, "You are the strangest man I ever saw, and General Jackson will chastise you for your insolence before you leave the city." "Very clear of it," said I, "for General Jackson, I have no doubt, will applaud my course; and if he should undertake to chastise me, as Paddy said, 'There is two as can play at that game.'"

General Jackson was staying at one of the Nashville hotels. Next morning, very early, my city preacher went down to the hotel to make an apology to General Jackson for my conduct in the pulpit the night before. Shortly after he had left, I passed by the hotel, and I met the general on the pavement; and before I approached him by several steps, he smiled, and reached out his hand and said,—

"Mr. Cartwright, you are a man after my own heart. I am very much surprised at Mr. Mac, to think he would suppose that I would be offended at you. No, sir ; I told him that I highly approved of your independence ; that a minister of Jesus Christ ought to love every-body and fear no mortal man. I told Mr. Mac that if I had a few thousand such independent, fearless officers as you were, and a well-drilled army, I could take old England."

General Jackson was certainly a very extraordinary man. He was, no doubt, in his prime of life, a very wicked man, but he always showed a great respect for the Christian religion, and the feelings of religious people, especially ministers of the Gospel. I will here relate a little incident that shows his respect for religion.

I had preached one Sabbath near the Hermitage, and, in company with several gentlemen and ladies, went, by special invitation, to dine with the general. Among this company there was a young sprig of a lawyer from Nashville, of very ordinary intellect, and he was trying hard to make an infidel of himself. As I was the only preacher pre-sent, this young lawyer kept pushing his conversation on me, in order to get into an argument. I tried to evade an argument,—in the first place, considering it a breach of good manners to interrupt the social conversation of the company. In the second place, I plainly saw that his head was much softer than his heart, and that there were no laurels to be won by vanquishing or demolishing such a combatant ; and I persisted in evading an argument. This seemed to inspire the young man with more confidence in himself; for my evasiveness he construed into fear. I saw General Jackson's eye strike fire, as he sat by and heard the thrusts he made at the Christian religion. At length the young lawyer asked me this question.—

"Mr. Cartwright, do you really believe there is any such place as hell, as a place of torment ? "

I answered promptly, " Yes, I do."

To which he responded, " Well, I thank God I have too much good sense to believe any such thing."

I was pondering in my own mind whether I would answer him or not, when General Jackson for the first time broke into the conversa-tion, and, directing his words to the young man, said, with great earnestness,—

" Well, sir, I thank God that there is such a place of torment as hell."

This sudden answer, made with great earnestness, seemed to astonish the youngster, and he exclaimed,—

" Why, General Jackson, what do you want with such a place of torment as hell ? "

To which the general replied, as quick as lightning.—

"To put such d——d rascals as you are in, that oppose and vilify the Christian religion."

I tell you this was a poser. The young lawyer was struck dumb, and presently was found missing

In the fall of 1819, our Tennessee Conference sat again in Nashville. This year the Minutes show an increase of members in the four Western Conferences of 5,085 ; of travelling preachers, 38 : our whole membership in the West, 56,945 ; our travelling preachers, 194. Our Tennessee Conference lay partly in Tennessee and partly in Kentucky. In Kentucky our rules of discipline on slavery were pretty generally enforced, and especially on our preachers, travelling and local. Whenever a travelling preacher became the owner of a slave or slaves, he was required to record a bill of emancipation, or pledge himself to do so; otherwise he would forfeit his ministerial office. And under no circumstances could a local preacher be ordained a deacon or an elder, if he was a slaveholder, unless he gave the Church satisfactory assurances that he would emancipate at a proper time. In Tennessee some of our prominent preachers fell heir to slaves They were unwilling to emancipate them, and they sought refuge in the plea of their disabilities, according to the laws of the State

At this Conference I complained of 'some of our strong preachers living in constant violation of the discipline of the Church They tried to make out a fair excuse, and to show that it was impracticable, according to the laws of the State; and I, in order to sustain my charges of violating the discipline of the Church, had to show that they could at any time emancipate their slaves by becoming surety that their Negroes, when emancipated, did not become a county charge. They employed a distinguished lawyer, F. Grundy, and I went to General Jackson for counsel. The case was fairly stated and explained in open Conference, and these preachers were required to go to court and record a bill of emancipation.

When the great Southern secession took place in 1844–45, Dr. Bascom wrote a pamphlet, and there represents the circumstance above alluded to as a great abolition move. Now there is nothing more foreign from the truth. Ultra abolition was not then known among us in the West; and if it was, we never meddled politically with slavery, but simply required our preachers and members to emancipate their slaves whenever it was practicable, according to the laws of the State in which they lived, and which permitted the liberated slave to enjoy freedom.

The discussion on the subject of slavery waked up some bad feeling, and as we had at this Conference to elect our delegates to the General Conference, which was to hold its session in Baltimore, in May, 1820, these slaveholding preachers determined to form a ticket, and exclude every one of us who were for the Methodist Discipline as it was, and is to this day. As soon as ever we found out their plan, we formed an opposite ticket, excluding all advocates of slavery, and, on the first ballot, we elected every man on our own ticket save one, and he was a young preacher who had only travelled six years. He and their strongest man tied in the vote. Of course, we had to ballot again, but on the second ballot we elected our man by a large majority. This triumph made the slavery party feel very sore. They then went to work and wrote a very slanderous pamphlet, in which they misrepresented us, and sent a copy of it to each member of the General Conference. But they missed their mark; for instead of lowering us in the estimation of the members of the General Conference, that body approved our course fully.

It was at this General Conference of 1820, in Baltimore, that radicalism threatened to shake the foundations of the Church; but as I have freely spoken of these trying scenes to the Church elsewhere in this sketch, I forbear making any further remarks. At this General Conference, the Kentucky Conference was organized, which made five annual Conferences out of the old *Western* Conference, namely,—

1. Ohio Conference, composed of the following presiding-elder Districts:—Ohio, Muskingum, Lancaster, Scioto, Lebanon, and Miami; with a membership of 34,178, and 87 travelling preachers.

2. Missouri Conference, with the following Districts:—Indiana, Illinois, Cape Girardeau, and Arkansas; with a membership of 7,458, and 39 travelling preachers.

3. Kentucky Conference, with five Districts:—Kenhawha, Kentucky, Salt River, Green River, and Cumberland; with a membership of 23,723, and 84 travelling preachers.

4. Tennessee, composed of Nashville, Tennessee, French Road, Holston, and Duck River Districts; 17,633 members, and 51 travelling preachers.

5. Mississippi, with Louisiana, Mississippi, and Alabama Districts; 4,147 members, and 19 travelling preachers.

Making in 1820–21 our membership 87,139, and our travelling preachers 280. See what God has done for our "*far West.*" From the time I had joined the travelling ranks in 1804 to 1820–21, a period of sixteen years, from 32 travelling preachers, we had increased to 280; and from 11,877 members, we had now over 87,000; and there was not a single literary man among those travelling preachers.

In the fall of 1820, our Conference sat in Hopkinsville, Kentucky. I was re-appointed to the Christian Circuit, M. Lindsey, presiding elder. About this time, owing to my having reprinted and circulated two small pamphlets, one called, "The Dagon of Calvinism," and the other, "A useful Discovery," both of them satires on Calvinism, some Presbyterian clergymen, judging me to be the author of these pamphlets, and not being willing publicly to debate the points at issue between us, concluded to take satisfaction of me by writing me a letter in the name of the devil, complimenting me for promoting the interests of his Satanic majesty's kingdom by spreading the Arminian doctrine. Whereupon I wrote a rejoinder, and both these letters, the one to me and my answer, were published in pamphlet form, and created a considerable buzz for a while. Those clergymen called a council in order to answer me, but considering prudence the better part of valour, realizing that—

> "He that lived to run away,
> Might live to fight another day;"

so they abandoned the project of answering me altogether. This was regretted by many of my friends, who wanted them to speak out in their own proper names, and not skulk behind the name of the devil to hide their errors or malice. And perhaps it was best that they did not answer back again.

CHAPTER XVI.

THE MOUNTAIN PREACHER.

I WILL now relate an incident or two that occurred in 1820-24.

Old Father Walker, of excellent memory, and myself, set out in the month of April, 1820, to the General Conference, in Baltimore, on horseback. We travelled hard all the week. Late on Saturday afternoon we came to the spurs of the Alleghany Mountains, and were within a few miles of the toll-gate, when a gentleman overtook us. We inquired of him if he knew of any quiet tavern on the road near by, where two weary travellers could rest over Sabbath, as we did not intend travelling on that day. He said there was no such house on the road for many miles; but if we would turn off the road a mile or such a matter, he could take us to a good, quiet, religious family, where we could rest till Monday very comfortably; for he, being a local preacher, had an appointment next day. We thankfully consented to go with this local brother, and, following him, we soon came to a poor but decent house and family, and were made very welcome. The brother, on learning that we were preachers, insisted that we should preach for the people in the morning and evening, to which we consented.

At eleven o'clock, Brother Walker held forth. The people were all attention, but there was no excitement. At night I tried to preach, and although I had profound attention from a cabinful of these mountaineers, yet the preaching did not seem to have any effect whatever. When I closed, I called on our kind local preacher to conclude. He rose and began to sing a mountain song, and pat his foot, and clap his hands, and ever and anon would shout at the top of his speech, "Pray, brethren." In a few minutes the whole house was in an uproarious shout. When Brother Walker and I got a chance to talk, I said, " Well, sir, I tell you this local preacher can do more in singing, clapping, and stamping, than all our preaching put together."

" Verily," said Walker, " he must be a great man, and these are a great people living here in these poor dreary mountains."

In passing on our journey going down the mountains, on Monday, we met several waggons and carriages moving west. Shortly after we had passed them, I saw lying in the road a very neat pocket-pistol. I picked it up, and found it heavily loaded and freshly primed. Supposing it to have been dropped by some of these movers, I said to Brother Walker, " This looks providential; " for the road across these mountains was, at this time, infested by many robbers, and several daring murders and robberies had lately been committed. Brother Walker's horse was a tolerably good one, but my horse was a stout, fleet, superior animal. As we approached the foot of the mountains, and were about two miles from the public-house where we intended to lodge that night, the sun just declining behind the western mountains, we overtook a man walking with a large stick as a walking cane, and he appeared to be very lame, and was limping along at a very slow rate. He spoke to us, and said he was travelling, and a poor cripple, and begged us to let him ride a little way, as he was nearly given out, and was fearful he could not reach the tavern that night.

Brother Walker said, " O yes," and was in the attitude of dismounting and letting him ride his horse. Just then a thought struck me, that this fellow's lameness was feigned, and that it was not safe to trust him. I said to Walker, " Keep your horse; we are a long way from home, have a long journey before us; under such circumstances trust no man ; " and we trotted on down the hill, and thought we had left our lame man more than a hundred yards behind. Walker was rather ahead of me. All at once my horse made a spring forward; I turned to see what was the matter; and, lo! and behold, here was my lame man, within a few steps of me, coming as fleet as a deer. I grasped my pistol, which was in my over-coat pocket, cocked it, wheeled about, and rushed toward him; he faced about, and in a few jumps more I should have been on him, but he plunged into the thick brush, and I could not follow him. When we got to the tavern, the landlord said we had made a very fortunate escape; for these robbers in this way had decoyed and robbed several travellers lately.

Brother Walker being the oldest man and rather infirm, we had agreed that he should conduct all religious ceremonies, and that I should call for lodging, attend to horses, pay off bills, &c. When we had gotten down into Virginia some distance, we called one evening at a Mr. Baly's, who kept a tavern on the road: his wife and daughters were very kind and clever, but the man of the house was a drunken Universalist. He was not sober when we called, but granted us the liberty to stay all night. While I was out seeing to the horses, Brother Walker and the landlord got into a strong debate on the universal restoration plan. Brother Walker was very mild and easy in debate; the landlord was abrupt and insulting, as well as very profane. I stood it a good while, but at length I got tired of it, and said to Brother Walker that the way he debated was of no use; that it was casting pearls before swine. The old landlord at this let loose a volley of curses on me. I did not attempt any debate, but shook my brimstone wallet over him till he was sick and tired of it. The old lady and daughters were very much mortified at their husband and father. By this time it became proper that we should retire to bed. Brother Walker told the landlord that we were preachers, and asked leave to pray in the family before we went to bed. The landlord flatly denied us that privilege, and swore he would have none of our praying about him, saying he knew we only wanted to pray off our bill. Brother Walker mildly expostulated with him, and insisted on having the privilege to pray; but all in vain. He said he would have no praying about his house. I then asked him if he did not keep a house of public entertainment.

He replied, "Yes."

"Then," said I, "do you not allow men to curse and swear, and get drunk in your house, if they pay for it?"

He said, "Yes."

"Well, then, we have as good a right to pray and serve God in your house, if we pay for it, as they have to serve the devil and pay for it; and I insist that we have our rights. We have plenty of money, and don't wish to pray off our bill." So said I to Brother Walker, "Go to prayer; and if he cuts up any capers, I'll down him, and hold him still till you are done praying; for," said I, "' the kingdom of heaven suffereth violence, and the violent take it by force.'" So Brother Walker prayed, and I watched the old landlord, who sat very quiet, and looked sullen. After this we retired to bed, and his wife and daughter made many apologies for him, and hoped

I

we would not be offended. I told them, No, not at all; that he was heartily welcome to all he had made of us. They laughed, and said they had never seen him so completely used up before.

In the morning we rose early; our horses were fed, and breakfast on the table. We prayed and took our meal, the old man still in bed. I then asked the landlady for our bill. She frankly said she would not have anything; that we were welcome to all we had from them, and invited us to call and stay with them as we returned. I insisted that she should receive pay, "for you know," said I, "the old gentleman said we wanted to pray off our bill," but she utterly refused. So we bade farewell, and went on our way rejoicing; for we had said our prayers and prayed off our bill in the bargain.

On our return from the General Conference in Baltimore, in 1820, in the month of June, which was very warm, and we having to travel on horseback, it may be supposed that our journey in this way for a thousand miles was very fatiguing. When we got to Knoxville, East Tennessee, the following incident in substance occurred:—

Brother Walker and myself had started early in the morning, had travelled about twenty-five miles, and reached Knoxville at noon. We rode up to a tavern with a view of dining, but, finding a great crowd of noisy, drinking, and drunken persons there, I said to Brother Walker, "This is a poor place for *weary travellers*, and we will not stop here." We then rode to another tavern, but it was worse than the first, for here they were in a real bully fight. I then proposed to Brother Walker that we should go on, and said we would soon find a house of private entertainment, where we could be quiet; so on we went. Presently we came to a house with a sign over the door of "*Private Entertainment, and New Cider.*" Said I, "Here's the place; and if we can get some good light bread and new cider, that's dinner enough for me."

Brother Walker said, "That is *exactly what I want.*"

We accordingly hailed. The old gentleman came out. I inquired if we could get our horses fed, and some light bread and new cider for dinner.

"O yes," said the landlord; "alight, for I suspect you are two Methodist preachers, that have been to Baltimore, to the General Conference."

We replied, we were. Our horses were quickly taken, and well fed. A large loaf of good light bread and a pitcher of new cider were quickly set before us. This gentleman was an *Otterbein Methodist.* His wife was very sick, and sent from the other room for us to pray for her. We did so, and then returned to take our bread and cider dinner. The weather was warm, and we were very thirsty, and began to lay in the bread and cider at a pretty liberal rate. It, however, seemed to me that our cider was not only new cider, but something more, and I began to rein up my appetite. Brother Walker laid on liberally, and at length I said to him, " You had better stop, brother ; for there is surely something more than *cider here*."

" I reckon not," said he.

But as I was not in the habit of using spirits at all, I knew that a very little would keel me up, so I forbore ; but with all my forbearance presently I began to feel light-headed. I instantly ordered our horses, fearing we were snapped for once.

I called for our bill; the old brother would have nothing. We mounted, and started on our journey. When we had rode about a mile, being in the rear, I saw Brother Walker was nodding at a mighty rate. After riding on some distance in this way, I suddenly rode up to Brother Walker, and cried out, "Wake up! wake up!" He roused up, his eyes watering freely. "I believe," said I, "we are both drunk. Let us turn out of the road, and lie down and take a nap till we get sober." But we rode on without stopping. We were not drunk, but we both evidently felt it flying into our heads; and I have thought proper, in all candour, to name it, with a view to put others on their guard.

We journeyed on till we came to the Crab Orchard, where was kept a toll-gate This gate was kept at this time by two very mean men; they also kept a house of entertainment, and, it being late, we concluded to tarry all night. The fare was very indifferent. We asked the privilege to pray with them. It was granted, and we prayed with them night and morning; took breakfast, and then asked our bill. The landlord told us, and I drew out my pocket-book, in which I had several hundred dollars in good current bank bills. He told me he would not take any of them; he must have *silver*. I told him I had no silver, and no coin but a few cents. He very abruptly swore he knew better; he knew I had the silver. I assured him again that I had no silver, but he persisted in swearing he knew I had, and that we could not leave or pass the toll-gate till we paid our bill of fare. Our horses were all ready to mount, and I had fresh loaded my pistol over night, for I did not like the signs about the house, and as I had a good deal of money in bills about me, I had determined I would not be robbed without leaving my mark. Brother Walker tried to reason the case with him, but to no purpose. I then threw down the amount of his charge, and told him he had to take that or nothing, and mounted my horse and started. He ordered one of his servants to shut and lock the toll-gate, and not let me through. I spurred my horse, and was at the gate nearly as quick as his servant, and drew my horsewhip, and told the Negro, if he attempted to close the gate, I would down him. The Negro took fright, and let go the gate, and took to his heels for safety. The moment I passed through the gate I wheeled my horse, and called for Brother Walker to come on; I would bear him harmless. The landlord called for his pistols, swearing he would follow me. I told him to come on, and wheeled my horse, and started on my way independently. But he took the "second, sober thought," and declined pursuing me. This was to me a pretty trying and tempting circumstance, but I survived it.

Shortly after this Brother Walker left me to visit some of his old friends and relatives in West Tennessee, and I journeyed on toward my home in Christian County, Kentucky. Saturday night came on, and found me in a strange region of country, and in the hills, knobs, and spurs of the Cumberland Mountains. I greatly desired to stop on the approaching Sabbath, and spend it with a Christian people; but I was now in a region of country where there was no Gospel minister for many miles around, and where, as I learned, many of the scattered population had never heard a Gospel sermon in all their lives, and where the inhabitants knew no Sabbath only to hunt and visit, drink and dance. Thus lonesome and pensive, late in the evening, I hailed at a tolerably decent house, and the landlord kept entertainment. I rode up and asked for quarters. The gentleman said I could stay, but he was afraid I would not enjoy myself very much as a traveller, inasmuch as they had a party meeting there that night to have a little dance. I inquired how far it was to a decent house of entertainment on the road; he said seven miles. I told him if he would treat me civilly and feed my horse well, by his leave I would stay. He assured me I should be treated civilly. I dismounted and went in. The people collected, a large company. I saw there was not much drinking going on

I quietly took my seat in one corner of the house, and the dance commenced. I sat quietly musing, a total stranger, and greatly desired to preach to this people. Finally, I concluded to spend the next day (Sabbath) there, and ask the privilege to preach to them. I had hardly settled this point in my mind, when a beautiful, ruddy young lady walked very gracefully up to me, dropped a handsome courtesy, and pleasantly, with winning smiles, invited me out to take a dance with her. I can hardly describe my thoughts or feelings on that occasion. However, in a moment I resolved on a desperate experiment. I rose as gracefully as I could; I will not say with some emotion, but with many emotions. The young lady moved to my right side; I grasped her right hand with my right hand, while she leaned her left arm on mine. In this position we walked on the floor.

The whole company seemed pleased at this act of politeness in the young lady, shown to a stranger. The coloured man, who was the fiddler, began to put his fiddle in the best order.   I then spoke to the fiddler to hold a moment, and added that for several years I had not undertaken any matter of importance without first asking the blessing of God upon it, and I desired now to ask the blessing of God upon this beautiful young lady and the whole company, that had shown such an act of politeness to a total stranger.

Here I grasped the young lady's hand tightly, and said, "Let us all kneel down and pray," and then instantly dropped on my knees, and commenced praying with all the power of soul and body that I could command. The young lady tried to get loose from me, but I held her tight. Presently she fell on her knees. Some of the company kneeled, some stood, some fled, some sat still, all looked curious. The fiddler ran off into the kitchen, saying, "Lord a marcy, what de matter? what is dat mean?"

While I prayed, some wept, and wept out aloud, and some cried for mercy. I rose from my knees and commenced an exhortation, after which I sang a hymn. The young lady who invited me on the floor lay prostrate, crying earnestly for mercy. I exhorted again, I sang and prayed nearly all night. About fifteen of that company professed religion, and our meeting lasted next day and next night, and as many more were powerfully converted. I organized a Society, took thirty-two into the Church, and sent them a preacher   My landlord was appointed leader, which post he held for many years. This was the commencement of a great and glorious revival of religion in that region of country, and several of the young men converted at this Methodist preacher dance became useful ministers of Jesus Christ.

I recall this strange scene of my life with astonishment to this day, and do not permit myself to reason on it much. In some conditions of society I should have failed; in others I should have been mobbed; in others I should have been considered a lunatic. So far as I did permit myself to reason on it at the time, my conclusions were something like these : These are a people not Gospel taught or hardened. They at this early hour have not drunk to intoxication, and they will at least be as much alarmed at me and my operations, as I possibly can be at theirs. If I fail, it is no disgrace; if 1 succeed, it will be a fulfilment of a duty commanded, to be "instant in season and out of season." Surely, in all human wisdom, it was out of season, but I had, from some cause or other, a strong impression on my mind, from the beginning to the end of this affair, (if it is ended,) that I should succeed by taking the devil at surprise, as he had often served me, and thereby be avenged of him for giving me so much trouble on my way to General Conference and back thus far.

The actions prompted by those sudden impressions to perform religious duty, often succeed beyond all human calculation, and thereby inspire a confident belief in an immediate superintending agency of the Divine Spirit of God. In this agency of the Holy Spirit of God I have been a firm believer for more than fifty-four years, and I do firmly believe that if the ministers of the present day had more of the unction or baptismal fire of the Holy Ghost prompting their ministerial efforts, we should succeed much better than we do, and be more successful in winning souls to Christ than we are. If those ministers, or young men that think they are called of God to minister in the word and doctrine of Jesus Christ, were to cultivate, by a holy life, a better knowledge of this supreme agency of the Divine Spirit, and depend less on the learned theological knowledge of Biblical Institutes, it is my opinion they would do vastly more good than they are likely to do; and I would humbly ask, Is not this the grand secret of the success of all early pioneer preachers, from John Wesley down to the present day?

Now I say for one, who has been trying to preach in the wilderness for more than fifty years, that I take no flattering unction to my soul from those who pretend to speak in such lofty terms of the old and early pioneers of Methodism; for in the very next breath they tell us that such preachers and preaching will not do now, and at one fell swoop sweep us, as with the besom of destruction, from the face of the earth.

I am often reminded by the advocates of learned and theologically trained preachers of a circumstance that occurred years gone by in Kentucky, after the wilderness state of the country had passed away, and the people had grown up into improved life, and many of them had become wealthy.

In the region alluded to there was a large and wealthy Presbyterian congregation that, by growing tired of their old and early preacher, had become vacant. They sought a popular successor, one that was up with the improved and advanced state of the times. They finally, by the offer of a large call, or salary, succeeded in engaging a very pious young minister as their pastor. At his first appointment, he took for his text, "Repent ye, therefore, and be converted, that your sins may be blotted out, when the times of refreshing shall come from the presence of the Lord." (Acts iii. 19.) He preached an excellent sermon from this passage, in the judgment of the congregation, and they were very much delighted. The next Sabbath rolled on. Their new pastor rose in the pulpit and took the same text, and delivered substantially the same sermon. This produced a little whispering among their wise and knowing elders; but they attributed it all to absence of thought. The third Sunday rolled on, and up rose the preacher, reading off the same text, and preaching the same sermon. Well, the elders concluded that this was outrageous and insufferable, and that they must really talk to him, and put a stop to this way of preaching. So they called on their young pastor, and tabled their complaints very feelingly before him, asking him if he really had but the one sermon. If so, they must call the congregation together and dismiss him. To all of which the pastor responded, the Bible was full of as good texts as the one he had preached from, and he had an abundance of good sermons ready; but he thought that as the signs of this improved age and state of society required an improved and advanced ministry, so did the advanced age require that the congregation should fully keep up with an improved ministry; "and," said the minister, "do you really think the congregation has complied with the requirements of my sermon? If you think they have,—and you shall be the judges,—I am ready at all times to take another text and preach a new sermon."

The elders at that moment were possessed of a dumb devil, and they never afterward called their minister to chide with him. As the old truths of the Gospel were behind the times, the Lord did signally own and bless the labours of this young minister, and made him a savour of life unto life to many of his hearers, giving ample evidence that He will own and bless His word.

A few more incidents will close this chapter. ʳIt is very astonishing how easily and generally mankind fall into idle and sinful habits. I have often been astonished at the far-seeing wisdom of John Wesley. In the General Rules of his United Societies he interdicts dram-drinking; and while the whole religious world, priests, preachers, and members, rushed into this demoralizing practice, Mr. Wesley made desisting from dram-drinking a condition of membership in the Methodist Societies; and although the Methodist Episcopal Church, in her organization, as a wise provision in her General Rules, forbids dram-drinking, yet how often and how long did it remain a dead letter! From my earliest recollection drinking drams, in family and social circles, was considered harmless and allowable sociality. It was almost universally the custom for preachers, in common with all others, to take drams; and if a man would not have it in his family, his harvest, his house-raisings, log-rollings, weddings, and so on, he was considered parsimonious and unsociable; and many, even professors of Christianity, would not help a man if he did not have spirits and treat the company. I recollect, at an early day, at a court time in

Springfield, Tennessee, to have seen and heard a very popular Baptist preacher, who was evidently intoxicated, drinking the health of the company in what he called the health the devil drank to a dead hog—Boo! I have often seen it carried and used freely at large baptizings, where the ordinance was administered by immersion.

In 1821, the last year I travelled the Christian Circuit, I took in a preaching-place in a densely populated settlement that was long destitute of the Gospel, and had many notorious drunkards in it. Here the Lord owned and blessed my labours; religion spread through the settlement. Among the rest there was one interesting family; the man was a drunkard; the family became deeply interested about religion and joined the Church, and were remarkably friendly to me; the old man was also very friendly. On a certain occasion I met him in a store in Hopkinsville, and—although I was never intoxicated but once in my life, yet I had wholly abandoned the social glass; for, according to my best conviction, it was a bad and dangerous habit, and that the rules of the Methodist Church required it—this drinking gentleman called for some cherry-bounce, and sweetened it for me expressly, out of pure love to me, as he said, and then invited me to drink with him. I declined. He urged me. I refused. I told him I had wholly given up the practice. Nothing would satisfy him; he said, if I did not drink with him, I was no friend of his, or his family, and he would never hear me preach again. I told him that it was all in vain to urge me; my principles were fixed, and that I would not violate my principles for the friendship of any man or mortal. He flew into a violent rage, and cursed and abused me. I walked off and left him in his glory. He never forgave me, I suppose, and made his family leave the Church, and would not let them come to hear me preach, and he lived and died a drunkard.

In 1824, Jesse Walker, Samuel H. Thompson, F S., and myself, were elected delegates to the General Conference in Baltimore. the first three from Missouri, myself from Kentucky. We started on horseback, and travelled together. Two of the company would call for spirits when we stayed at public-houses. Brother Thompson and myself would not drink spirits at all. We made it a rule to pray in families wherever we stayed, if it was agreeable. I felt hurt that two Methodist preachers, delegates to the General Conference, and our travelling companions, would call for and drink spirits in those public-houses. Thompson and myself remonstrated with them. They defended the practice. I told them at length that if they did not quit the practice, I would not travel with them, and in this Thompson joined me. Brother Walker was a good man, and for our sakes he agreed to and did quit it altogether, and we got along much better.

In the fall of 1821 our Conference was held in Lexington, Kentucky, and I was appointed by Bishop M'Kendree to Cumberland District, containing the following appointments, namely, Green River, Somerset, Wayne, Roaring River, Goose Creek, Fountain Head, Barren, and Bowling Green Circuits; it lay partly in Kentucky and partly in Tennessee, and was a large and populous District, containing between five and six thousand members, many of whom had grown wealthy; there was also a great number of talented local preachers.

On my first round of Quarterly Meetings—I was on my way to Somerset Circuit, had rode on Friday about fifty miles, and my horse and myself were both very much tired—I called at several houses on the public highway, and asked to stay all night, but was denied. About dusk I hailed another house, and asked leave to stay. The man said I could not stay. I inquired how far to the next house where he thought they would take me in. He said, "Seven miles." Said I, "My dear sir, I have rode to-day fifty miles, and I cannot go seven more. If you will give me a faggot of fire, I will camp out rather than go any further."

He stepped into a little kitchen hard by for the fire, and I heard his old lady say to her husband, "You had better let that man stay. If he gets the fire, he will burn up the barn because you turned him off." And as she spoke out loud, I replied, equally as loud, "Yes, you had better let me stay, if you don't, some mischief will befall you before morning."

He threw down his chunk of fire, and said, "Well, I suppose you must stay."

Down I got, stepped to the kitchen door, and said, "Good lady, will you give me supper quick? for I could get no dinner on the road to-day."

"O yes," said the old lady.

My horse put up, my supper eaten, I felt much better. Presently I began to inquire about religion and religious denominations. I soon found out that the old gentleman and old lady were real high-toned Predestinarian Baptists. The old gentleman informed me that, a few miles off, most all the people were Methodists, and that he was really afraid they would take the country, and that they had a quarterly meeting the next day, (Saturday,) a few miles from there.

Said I, "A quarterly meeting; what sort of a meeting is that?" He did not know, he replied.

Said I, "What did you call the name of this religious sect?"

Said he, "Methodist."

"Methodist," said I; "what's that? What sort of people are they?"

"Ah," said he, "they are the strangest people you ever saw; they shout and halloo so loud you may hear them for miles; they hold that all will be saved, and a man can live without sin in this life, and yet that a Christian can fall from grace; and all this," said he, "is not half; they are the worst people you ever saw. They had a camp-meeting just over here last year, and they had a tent they called the preachers' tent, and there, by night and day, the preachers carried on all sorts of wickedness; and," said he, "they are begging and taking all the money out of the country."

"Mercy defend us!" I exclaimed; "why don't you raise a company and drive them out of the country?"

"O!" said he, "they are too strong for us; if we were able to drive them they should soon go, you may depend."

Said I, "What a wretched set they must be! But it may be they are misrepresented, and are not as bad as you say."

"No, sir," said he; "I was there at the camp-meeting, and their bad conduct I saw with my own eyes."

"Well," said I, "if these things be so, it is too bad for a civilized country." By this time they thought that it was near bedtime, and he said, "If you wish to lie down, there is a bed."

"But," said I, "my friend, I learn you are a professor of religion, and religious people ought always to pray with their families. I am a friend to religion, and hope you will pray with us before we go to bed."

"Ah!" said he, "I am a poor weak creature, and can't pray in my family."

"O!" said I, "you must certainly pray for us; you ought to pray for the benefit of these interesting children of yours."

"No," said he; "I can't do it."

"Well, sir," said I, "we must have prayers before we lie down, and I am a weak creature, too; but if you will not pray, may I?"

"Do as you please," said he.

So I read a chapter, rose, gave out a hymn, and commenced singing. There were two young ladies present, one a daughter, the other a niece, of the old man; they both rose and sung with me. Finally, I knelt down, and so did the girls; I prayed, but the old man and old lady kept their seats all the time. In prayer I told the Lord what a poor weak old man lived there, and asked the Lord to give him strength and grace to set a better example before his family. I also prayed the Lord to have mercy on those deluded Methodists, if they were half as bad as my old friend had represented them; but if he had misrepresented them, to forgive him, and prosper them. As soon as prayer was over, the old gentleman and lady went into the kitchen, and the niece said to me, "You need not believe a word uncle has said about the Methodists, and the doings at their camp-meeting; for I was there, and they are a good people, and my uncle is prejudiced." His daughter said the same. Presently I stepped out at the door, and I heard the old lady say to her husband, "He is a Methodist preacher."

The old man said, "No, he is not."

"Well," said she, "he is, and you have done it now."

The old man said, "I don't care if he is; it 's good enough for him."

Shortly after this I retired to bed, and the two young ladies began to sing some of the Methodist camp-meeting songs, and really they sang delightfully. I rose early next morning, and went on to my quarterly meeting, and we had a real good one.

I will just say here, in this connexion, the next summer I held a large and splendid camp-meeting on the ground where this old gentleman had told me there was such bad conduct, and he and his family were out; and right in their presence I told the congregation what this man had said about them to me. The old man could not face it, and slunk off and went home. His daughter and niece both were powerfully converted, and joined the Methodist Church.

When I got over on the southern part of my District, the summer following, to a camp-meeting in the Roaring River Circuit, having been detained a little by affliction in my family, and not being able to reach my camp-meeting till Sunday, Brother Simon Carlisle was in the stand preaching. He was a real Boanerges, an able and successful New Testament preacher. The congregation was large and very disorderly. Brother Carlisle reproved them sharply, but they behaved very rudely. When he closed, I rose to preach, but the congregation was so disorderly that I found it would be very difficult for me to proceed; so at length I told the vast crowd if they would give me their attention a few moments, I would relate an incident or two worthy of their attention. I commenced by relating several short anecdotes. They began to draw up nearer, and nearer still, the anecdotes were well calculated to excite their risibilities. Right before me sat an old, grey-headed man, with straight-breasted coat; he did not like the laughter that my anecdotes produced, and he spoke out loudly to me and said, "Make us cry, make us cry; don't make us laugh."

As quick as thought I replied to him thus.—

"I don't hold the puckering strings of your mouths, and I want you to take the Negro's eleventh commandment; that is, Every man mind his own business."

"Yes, sir, yes, sir," said the old man, and sank down perfectly still.

This produced considerable mirth in the congregation, but by this time the vast crowd had gathered up as close as they well could, and were all eyes and ears. I then announced my text: "To the unknown God. Whom ye ignorantly worship, Him declare I unto you." And for two hours I held listening thousands spell-bound, while, to the very best of my abilities, I defended the supreme Divinity of Jesus Christ, and riddled Arianism as best I could. Arianism was rife through all that country, although they called themselves "Christians," and were called by the world New Lights, Marshallites, or Stoneites.* The two Baptist preachers that would not receive me into the Baptist Church without re-baptizing, in Stogden's Valley, at an early day, elsewhere stated in this narrative, were present on this occasion. The circumstance of that encounter was one of the incidents that I had just related to gain audience with the people, and the old man with straight coat that bade me make them *cry* and not *laugh*, whom I had taken to be a Methodist from his straight coat, proved to be an old Baptist man that had long been in the habit of speaking out to the preachers in time of preaching; but, alas for these Baptist preachers! they, with many more of their co-labouring ministerial brethren, had been carried off into the whirlpool of Arianism. While I was preaching, I not only gained audience, but there was a solemn silence and profound attention; for, by the blessing of God, I succeeded in interesting the whole congregation in the sublime subject under discussion. And when I came to show that if Jesus Christ was not the supreme God, all heaven and earth was filled with idolatrous devotions, and angels and men, and redeemed spirits had been, were now, and eternally would be, nothing more or less than gross idolaters . "Now," said I, "if there is a single man, minister, woman, or child, in this assembly, that will dare to ascribe Divine honours to Jesus Christ and not believe in His supreme Divinity, let them show it by raising their hand."

I then paused, but not one hand went up. It was an awful solemn time; every soul seemed to feel that the supreme Divinity brooded over the assembly. I then said, I wanted one more triumphant testimony of our holy religion, that should overwhelm all the legions of devils that rose from the stagnant pools of Arianism, Unitarianism, and Socinianism. I then desired every one in that vast crowd that believed that Jesus Christ was justly entitled to supreme honour and glory, and expected to get to heaven through His merits alone, to

* Marshall and Stone were two leading Presbyterian ministers, that, in the time of a great revival in Kentucky, were disowned by the Synod of Kentucky. They headed the New Light party, and gratuitously assumed the name of "Christian," yet they evidently imbibed the Arian sentiment, and spread their errors, and did great mischief in corrupting the scriptural doctrine of the true Divinity of Jesus Christ.

give me the sign by raising their right hand : the hands went up by the thousand, and with hands triumphant shouts of glory ascended by hundreds, and many sinners were seen with streaming eyes, and even exulting shouts, giving glory to Jesus Christ. The vast multitude fell almost in every direction, and I sat down under a deep sense that God was there. Mourners were found all through the crowd, to be numbered by the hundred. Many of the Arians recanted ; and, after the legions that had distracted them for years were cast out, came to their right minds, were clothed, and once more esteemed it their highest honour to sit at the feet of Jesus Christ. There was no more preaching for that day and the next. The cries of the penitents, and shouts of the young converts and the old professors, went up without intermission, day and night. Two hundred professed religion, and one hundred and seventy joined the Methodist Episcopal Church before the close of the camp-meeting, and it was remarked by many, that it seemed the easiest thing for sinners to get religion here of any place or time they ever saw, and they could not account for it ; but I told them that it was plain to me the Lord had given marching orders to the legions of little Arian devils to the lake, as He had done to the swine in the days of old, and, when these were cast out, it was quite easy to come to their right minds. Perhaps there never was a more manifest display of God's saving mercy on a small scale than on the present occasion, since the confounding of tongues at the building of the tower of Babel. Many Arians returned to their old folds, perfectly tired of their wanderings ; and having cast anchor once more in a safe harbour, they gave their wanderings o'er. Those that remained among the New Lights, so called, split into many factions, and fought each other till they ate each other up all to the tail, and that was immersion. This remains, and perhaps will, until the millennial glory shall inundate the whole world. A remarkable incident occurred on this occasion which I must not omit relating.

There was a very confirmed Arian lady in the congregation who denied the supreme Divinity of Jesus Christ. Late on Monday, she professed to get very happy, and shouted out aloud ; but said, while shouting, among other things, she knew I was wrong in my views of Jesus Christ, but she desired some one to go and bring me to her, for she wanted to show me, that though I was in error, she could love her enemies and do good for evil At first I refused to go ; but she sent again. I then thought of the unjust judge, and, lest by her continual coming she might weary me, I went

She told me she knew I was wrong, and that she was right, and that God had blessed her and made her happy.

Said I, " Sister, while I was preaching, did you not get mad ? "

She answered, " Yes, very mad; I could have cut your throat.
But I am not mad now, and love you, and God has blessed me."

Said I, " I fear you are not happy; you have only got in a little
better humour, and think this is happiness. But we will test this
matter. Let us kneel down here, and pray to God to make it manifest
who is wrong."

" But," said she, " I don't want to pray; I want to talk."

" Well," said I, " I have no desire to talk; I always go to God in
prayer; and I now believe God, in answer to prayer, will recover you
out of the snare of the devil, for you certainly are not happy at all."

So I called upon all around (and they were many) to kneel down
and help me to pray God to dislodge the lingering Arian devil that
still claimed a residence in this woman's heart. We knelt, and by the
score united in wrestling, mighty prayer; and while we prayed, it
seemed that the bending heavens came near; and if the power of God
was ever felt among mortals, it was felt then and there. The woman
lost her assumed good feelings, and sunk down into sullen, dumb
silence, and so she remained during the meeting; and for weeks afterward many of her friends feared she would totally lose her balance of
mind. She became incapable of her business, till one night she had a
dream or vision, in which she afterward declared she saw her Saviour
apparently in all His supreme glory, and He told her she was wrong,
but He frankly forgave her; and when she came to herself, or awoke,
she was unspeakably happy, and never afterward, for one moment,
doubted the supreme Divinity of Jesus Christ. She joined the
Methodists, and lived and died a shining and shouting Christian.

There is another circumstance I wish to state before I close this
chapter.

The brother, Simon Carlisle, before mentioned, had been a regular
Circuit preacher somewhere down South, and there was a wealthy
family at or near one of his appointments. The old gentleman and
lady were members of the Church; but they had a very profligate son,
who behaved disorderly at one of Carlisle's appointments, and Carlisle
sharply reproved him for his disorderly conduct, at which the young
man took great umbrage, and swore he would have satisfaction out of
Carlisle. The house of the father of this young man was the preacher's
home. When Carlisle came round next time, he was, as usual, invited
by this old brother home with him. Brother Carlisle said, as he had
offended his son, perhaps he had better not go; but the old brother
and sister insisted he should go; for they knew their son was to blame
altogether, and that Carlisle had done nothing but his duty in reproving
him; so he went. This young man was at home, but slunk about,
and would not be social with Carlisle; and next morning, while Car-

lisle was fixing his horse to ride on to his next appointment, he took a brace of pistols, and slipped into the room where Carlisle's saddle-bags were lying, and put those pistols in the bottom of his saddle-bags, unperceived and unsuspected by Carlisle, or anybody else. Shortly after Carlisle started, the young man pretended to miss the pistols, and declared he knew that Carlisle had stolen them. The old people remonstrated against any such imputation, but he persisted in affirming he knew that the preacher had stolen his pistols, and off he started, got a writ and an officer, and pursued Carlisle, and before he reached his next appointment they overtook him. The officer informed him of the allegation, and that he had a writ for him, and that he was his prisoner. Carlisle, conscious of his innocence, told the officer that he was welcome to search him, and handed over his saddle-bags, when, lo and behold, there were the pistols at the bottom of them. What could he say? He protested his innocence, but submitted to the law, was found guilty, and only escaped being incarcerated in prison by the father of this mean young man going his bail till further trial.

We will not narrate the trouble and cost Carlisle was put to before he got clear of this malicious prosecution. Suffice it to say, during the pendency of this prosecution, the Annual Conference came on, and Carlisle had to answer to this criminal charge; but what could he say? He had no evidence of his innocence, and by possibility could have none. The Conference did not believe him guilty, but his guilt was sworn to by this young man. In this dilemma, into which the Conference was thrown, Carlisle rose and requested the Conference, for the honour of the cause of God, that they would expel him until God should, in some way, vindicate his innocence. He affirmed he was innocent, and that he believed God would shortly make his innocence manifest to all.

The Conference very reluctantly, and by a bare majority, expelled him. Able counsel, believing in his innocence, volunteered in his defence. He was cleared. Believing it to be his duty and privilege, he married, and when I saw him he had an interesting rising family. The Church restored him to his former standing, offered him a Circuit, but for the present he declined travelling, and went to work to support his family, and did it with credit to himself and them.

But the circumstance that triumphantly vindicated his innocence remains yet to be told. The young man who pursued him so maliciously, in about nine months after Carlisle was arrested, was taken down with a fever common to that region of country. The best medical aid was called in, he was faithfully attended and administered unto. His parents were much alarmed for his safety and his salvation.

He was talked to and prayed with, but to no purpose. His physicians told him he must die. He then said he could not die until he disclosed one important matter. His parents were called in, and he frankly told them and others that he put his pistols in Carlisle's saddle-bags himself; and shortly after the disclosure he expired, without hope of mercy.

CHAPTER XVII.

SERMON ON BAPTISM AT CAMP-MEETING.

THERE was, in the bounds of the Goose Creek Circuit, a Baptist minister, who was a tolerably smart man, and a great proselytizer from other Churches, and who almost always was harping on immersion as the only mode of Christian baptism, and ridiculing what he called "baby-sprinkling." We had an appointment for a camp-meeting in this Circuit, in what was called Poplar Grove. There was a fine little widow woman, a member of the Methodist Episcopal Church, lived here; and this Baptist preacher tried his best to proselyte her, and make a Baptist of her. She at length got tired of his water talk, and told him if he would come to the camp-meeting, and patiently hear the presiding elder, Peter Cartwright, preach one sermon on baptism, on Sunday, she would give him a new suit of clothes, out and out. He agreed to it; but he was to sit patiently, and hear the sermon through; if he did not, then he was not to have the suit of clothes.

When I got to the camp-ground, my little spunky Methodist widow was tented on the ground. She came and invited me to her tent, and then told me the proposition she had made to Mr. W., the Baptist preacher. "And now," said she, "do your best. if he runs, the suit of clothes is yours; and if he stands his ground, and you do your very best, you shall have as good a suit, any how."

This was a very large encampment, well arranged; and there were about twenty strong, talented Methodist preachers, from the travelling and local ranks, present. The meeting commenced and progressed with great interest, and there were many melting Gospel sermons preached. Many sinners were awakened and converted, both among the whites and coloured people. Sunday morning came, and my Baptist preacher arrived; and we were soon made acquainted. He proposed that he, if he felt like it, should have the privilege of replying to me. "Certainly," said I, "with all my heart."

Eleven o'clock arrived, the hour appointed me to commence my sermon on baptism. It was supposed that there were ten thousand people on the ground. My heart rather quailed within me; but I prayed for light, a ready mind, and success. I took no text in particular, but submitted the four following propositions for discussion :—

First. The design and intent of water baptism.

Second. Who were the divinely-appointed administrators of water baptism ?

Third. The proper mode of water baptism.

Fourth. Who were the qualified subjects of baptism ?

My Baptist minister took his seat in the altar, in front of me. He listened with tolerable attention while I was on the first and second propositions. As I approached the third point, the galled jade winced a little; but when I came to the fourth point, and took my position that all infants had the first and only indisputable title to baptism, and that all adults must become converted, and be like little children, before they could claim any valid title to water baptism, my preacher became very restive. Finally, I propounded this question : " Is not that Church which has no children in it more like hell than heaven ?" I then added, " If all hell was searched, there would not be a single child found in it; but all children are in heaven; therefore, there being no children in the Baptist Church, it was more like hell than heaven "

The Baptist preacher here rose to his feet, and started I called out to him to stop and hear me out; but he replied he could not stand it, and kept on, and cleared the ground ; so he lost his suit of clothes, and I gained one. But what was much better than all this, I was listened to for three hours ; and the attention of the multitude seemed not to falter, but they heard with profound interest, and it was the opinion of hundreds that this discussion did a vast amount of good.

Our camp-meeting progressed with increasing interest , many were awakened, and about forty were converted and added to the Church.

In the course of the summer of 1822, we held a camp-meeting in Logan County, Kentucky, the county in which I was chiefly raised. At this meeting there came a strange kind of preacher among us, who held that a Christian could live so holy in this life, that he would never die, but become all immortal, soul, body, and all He seemed like a good, innocent, ignorant kind of creature. He asked of me the liberty to preach ; but I told him that was altogether out of the question; that as the manager of the meeting, I felt myself accountable to the people, as well as to the Lord, for the doctrines advanced from the stand.

K

One night, while I was outside of the encampment settling some rowdies, he thought, I suppose, he would flatter my vanity a little; and, stepping up to me, he told me he had a heavenly message for me.

"Well," said I, "what is it?"

He said it had just been revealed to him that I was never to die, but to live for ever.

"Well," said I, "who revealed that to you?"

He said, "An angel."

"Did you see him?" I asked.

"O yes," was the reply; "he was a white, beautiful, shining being."

"Well," said I, "did you smell him?"

This stumped him, and he said he did not understand me.

"Well," said I, "did the angel you saw smell of brimstone?" He paused, and I added, "He must have smelled of brimstone; for he was from a region that burns with fire and brimstone, and consequently from hell; for he revealed a great lie to you, if he told you I was to live for ever!"

At this he slipped off, and never gave me any more trouble during the meeting.

There were a great many people in attendance at this meeting, and among the rest some youngsters who called themselves gentlemen, some from the country, and some from Russellville. These fellows would occupy the seats we had prepared for the ladies. I announced from the stand that the gentlemen and ladies were to sit apart, and requested every gentleman to remove to the seats on the left prepared for them.

There were some twenty who did not move. I said, "We request every gentleman to retire from the ladies' seats, that I may see how many country clowns and town fops there are; for these will not move!" All then left but five, and I began to count them; they then left in a hurry, but were very angry.

Among them was a young sprig of the bar, the son of a Major L. He was in a mighty pet, and told his father, who happened not to be present. His father and I dined together that day at a friend's house. He brought up the subject, and said I was wrong, that many young men did not know any better, and that he thought hard of me for exposing his son.

Said I, "Major, do you not believe if a company of Shawnee Indians were to come into one of our religious assemblies, and see all the women seated on one side and most of the men on the other side, that they would have sense and manners enough to take their seats on the men's side?"

He answered me abruptly, "No ; I don't believe they would."

" Well," said I, " it is my opinion they would, and that they have more manners than many of the pretended young gentlemen of the day."

He flew into a violent passion, and said, if we were not in the presence of ladies, he would abuse me. I told him if he thought to abuse and frighten me from doing my duty in keeping order in the congregation, he was very much mistaken, and I would thank him to mind his own business, and I would most assuredly attend to mine. Here the subject dropped for the present. I returned to the camp-ground. Presently he sent for me to talk the matter over. I told the messenger, Brother Cash, a local preacher, that I should not go ; for the major was very irritable, and only wanted to insult and abuse me, and that I was not of a mind to take abuse. I did not go. Presently Brother Cash returned, and said that the major pledged his word and honour that he would not insult me, but that he wanted to talk the matter over in a friendly way.

I then consented, and went to him with Brother Cash, and we had passed but a few words when he commenced a tirade of abuse. Brother Cash tried to check him, but he would not be stopped. I then told him that he had forfeited his word and honour, and therefore was beneath my notice, and turned off. He flew into a desperate rage, and said, if he, thought I would fight him a duel, he would challenge me.

" Major," said I, very calmly, " if you challenge me, I will accept it."

" Well, sir," said he, " I do dare you to mortal combat."

" Very well, 1 'll fight you ; and, sir," said I, " according to the laws of honour, I suppose it is my right to choose the weapons with which we are to fight ? "

" Certainly," said he.

" Well," said I, " then we will step over here into this lot, and get a couple of corn stalks ; I think I can finish you with one."

But, O ! what a rage he got into ! He clinched his fists and looked vengeance Said he, " If I thought I could whip you, I would smite you in a moment."

" Yes, yes, Major L.," said I, " but, thank God, you can't whip me ; but don't you attempt to strike me ; for if you do, and the devil gets out of you into me, I shall give you the worst whipping you ever got in all your life," and then walked off and left him.

His wife was a good, Christian woman, and the family was tented on the ground. At night, after meeting was closed, I retired to bed ; and about midnight there came a messenger for me to go to Major

K 2

L.'s tent and pray for him, for he was dying. Said I, "What is the matter with him?"

."O, he says he has insulted you, one of God's ministers; and if you don't come and pray for him, he will die, and go to hell."

"Well," said I, "if that's all, the Lord increase his pains! I shall not go; let him take a grand sweat; it will do him good; for he has legions of evil spirits in him, and it will be a long time before they are all cast out."

I did not go nigh him at that time. After an hour or two he sent for me again. I still refused to go. By this time he got into a perfect agony; he roared and prayed till he could be heard all over the camp-ground. Presently his wife came and entreated me, for her sake, to go and pray for, and talk to, the major. So I concluded to go; and when I got into the tent, there he was lying at full length in the straw, and praying at a mighty rate. I went to him and said,—

"Major, what is the matter?"

"O!" said he, "matter enough; I have added to my ten thousand sins another heinous one of insulting and abusing you, a minister of Jesus Christ, for labouring to keep order and do good. O will you, can you, forgive me?"

"Yes, major, I can and do forgive you; but remember, you must have forgiveness from God, or you are lost and ruined for ever."

"Can you possibly forgive me," said he, "so far as to pray for me? If you can, do pray for me, before I am swallowed up in hell for ever."

I prayed for him, and called on several others to pray for him. He continued in great distress all the next day, and some time the following night it pleased God to give him relief, and he professed comfort in believing.

This case plainly shows how the devil often overshoots his mark; but, perhaps, it more clearly shows how God, in His infinite goodness and mercy, makes the wrath of man to praise Him. It seems to me that at least a legion of very dirty little devils were cast out of this Major L.

We had a very interesting quarterly meeting the past spring in Russellville, and a considerable number in the higher and wealthier walks of life, especially among the ladies, gave signs of repentance, and a disposition to devote themselves to a religious life. I had given them a special and pressing invitation to attend our camp-meeting, and accordingly they came, and there was a glorious work going on in the congregation from time to time. Many came to the altar as penitents, and sought and found mercy of the Lord. And although these wealthy ladies would weep under the word, yet we could not get them to the altar, and I was afraid it was pride that kept them back, and frankly told them so, assuring them, if this was the case, they need not expect to obtain religion.

They told me that it was not pride that kept them away, but that the altar was so crowded, not only with mourners, but idle professors and idle spectators, and that in many instances the mourners were unceremoniously trodden on and abused, and the weather being very warm, the mourners in the altar must be nearly suffocated These were the reasons why they did not come into the altar as seekers, and not pride; and I assure the reader I profited very much by these reasons given by those ladies; for I knew all this and much more might, with great propriety, be said about our altar operations. So I determined, at all hazards, to regulate, renovate, and cleanse the altar of God, and turn out, and keep out, all idle, strolling, gaping lookers-on; and when the evening sermon closed, I rose in the stand, and I told them all these objections of the ladies, and I deliberately endorsed them as valid objections to our altar exercises, and told them I was going to invite every seeker of religion to come into the altar, and assured them they should be protected from these abuses; and, in order to a fair start, I invited all to rise up and retire out of the altar except seekers, and directed that the avenues leading to the altar be kept clear at all times; that there was to be no standing on the seats, and no standing up around the pales of the altar; that no person whatever should come into the altar unless invited, and that no person was to talk to, or pray with, the mourners uninvited, unless they got very happy. I appointed and named out my men to keep order. Thus arranged, and our large altar being cleared, and the aisles kept open, I invited the mourners to come as humble penitents, and kneel in the altar, and pray for mercy; and we all were astonished at the number that distinguished themselves as seekers. I suppose there were not less than one hundred, and almost all of them professed comfort that night, and, among the rest, many of those fine, wealthy ladies from town. It was supposed that this was one among the best camp-meetings ever held in Logan County, where there had been many, very many, glorious camp-meetings; where camp-meetings started in modern times; and they had been in progress for twenty-two years, every year more or less. The fruits of this camp-meeting I hope to see with pleasure in vast eternity.

The Methodist Church received an impetus and strength at this meeting, that vastly increased her usefulness, her members, and religious respectability. I sincerely hope it is going on and increasing to this day. And here permit me to remark, from many years' experience, that *sanctified* wealth will always prove a blessing to the Church of God; but unsanctified wealth, though poured into the Church by the million, never fails to corrupt and curse the Church. If our wealthy people will come themselves and bring their wealth, and consecrate the whole without any reserve to God, it is almost incalculable to tell the instrumental good that can and will result to the cause of religion; but, on the other hand, if religion must be defeated, the obligations of the Gospel loosened, the rules of the Church not exacted, a time-serving ministry employed and supported, this is, and has been, the death-knell to all Churches, so far as inward piety is concerned. Look at the needless, not to say sinful, expenditures in our older cities and districts of country; the unnecessary thousands expended, not in building needful and decent churches,—for this is right,—but ornamental churches, to make a vain show and gratify pampered pride. Look at the ornamented pulpits, pewed and cushioned seats, organs, and almost all kinds of instruments, with salaried choirs, and as proud and graceless as a fallen ghost, while millions upon millions of our fallen race are dying daily, and peopling the regions of eternal woe for the want of the Gospel of Jesus Christ; and as scarce as ministers are in some places in our own happy country, yet there are thousands that are ready and willing to go to the utmost verge of this green earth, and carry the glad tidings of mercy to those dying millions, if they had the means of support. Would it not the better comport with the obligations of our holy Christianity to refrain from those superfluous expenditures, and with a liberal hand and devoted heart apply, or furnish the means to carry the glad tidings of salvation to those that sit in the region and shadow of moral death, than to apply them as is done in many directions in this Christian land? Say, ye professed lovers of Jesus Christ, are not your responsibilities tremendously fearful? There is wealth enough in the Churches, and among the friends of the different Christian denominations in this happy republic, if rightly husbanded and liberally bestowed, to carry the Bible and a living ministry to every nation on the face of the whole earth. And may we be permitted to hail with Christian rapture the rising glory of this liberal spirit, when we shall see it as the apocalyptic angel flying in the midst of heaven, having the everlasting Gospel to preach to every nation, kindred, and tongue! Say, O say! when shall we see this happy day? May the Lord hasten it in His time, and we be co-workers together with Him! Will the Christian world say, "Amen?"

During my presidency on this District up to the fall of 1824, there was a blessed revival in many parts of the District, and many joined the Methodist Episcopal Church. There are several interesting incidents, no doubt, that have clean escaped my recollection; but there are some I remember, and I will embody them here as well as I can.

At a camp-meeting held in the edge of Tennessee, a considerable revival took place, and some tall sons and daughters of Belial were brought down to cry for mercy. Religion made its mark in several wealthy families. Persecution was pretty fierce; the rowdies sent off and got whiskey, drank freely, and disturbed us considerably. We arrested some of them, and they were fined. Finally, they collected their forces in the woods, a short distance from the camp-ground, and resolved to break up our camp-meeting; they then elected their captain and all other subordinate officers. Their plan was to arm themselves with clubs, to mount their horses, and ride bravely through the camp-ground, and break down officers, preachers, and anybody else that would oppose them.

Saturday afternoon was the time appointed for them to drive us from the ground, but in the meantime we found out their plans, and many of their names. Their captain called his name Cartwright; all their officers assumed the name of some preacher. We made our preparations accordingly, and were perfectly ready for them. They drank their whiskey, mounted their horses, armed with sticks and clubs, and then came, almost full speed, into our camp. As I was captain of the interior, I met the captain of the Philistines, and planted myself near the opening between the two tents, where they were to enter the enclosure. As the mounted captain drew near the entering place, I sprang into the breach; he raised his club, bidding me to stand by, or he would knock me down.

I cried, "Crack away."

He spurred his horse and made a pass at me, sure enough; but, fortunately, I dodged his stroke. The next lick was mine, and I gave it to him, and laid him flat on his back, his foot being in the stirrup. His horse got my next stroke, which wheeled him "*right about;*" he dragged his rider a few steps and dropped him, and then gave this redoubtable captain leg-bail at a mighty rate. The balance of the mounted rowdies, seeing their leader down and kicking, wheeled and ingloriously fled. We took care of the captain, of course, and fined him fifty dollars This gave us entire control of the encampment, and peace in all our borders during our meeting.

Connected with this meeting was another incident of thrilling interest, something like the following There were two young men in this settlement, of wealthy and respectable parentage, who were distantly related. They both were paying attention to a very wealthy young lady. Some jealousy about rivalship sprung up between them; they were mutually jealous of each other, and it spread like an eating cancer. They quarrelled, and finally fought; both armed themselves, and each bound himself in a solemn oath to kill the other. Thus

sworn, and armed with pistols and dirks, they attended camp-meeting.
I was acquainted with them, and apprised of the circumstances of this
disagreeable affair. On Sunday, when I was addressing a large congregation, and was trying to enforce the terrors of the violated law of
God, there was a visible power more than human rested on the congregation. Many fell under the preaching of the word. In closing
my discourse I called for mourners to come into the altar. Both these
young men were in the congregation, and the Holy Spirit had convicted
each of them; their murderous hearts quailed under the mighty power
of God, and with dreadful feelings they made for the altar. One
entered on the right, the other on the left. Each was perfectly ignorant
of the other being there. I went deliberately to each of them, and
took their deadly weapons from their bosoms, and carried them into
the preachers' tent, and then returned and laboured faithfully with
them and others (for the altar was full) nearly all the afternoon and
night. These young men had a sore struggle; but the great deep of
their hearts was broken up, and they cried hard for mercy; and while I
was kneeling by the side of one of them, just before the break of day,
the Lord spoke peace to his wounded soul. He rose in triumph, and
gave some thrilling shouts. I hastened to the other young man, at
the other side of the altar; and in less than fifteen minutes God
powerfully blessed his soul, and he rose and shouted, "Victory!" and
as these young men *faced* about, they saw each other, and, starting
simultaneously, met about midway of the altar, and instantly clasped
each other in their arms. What a shout went up to heaven from these
young men, and almost the whole assembly that were present! There
were a great many more who were converted that night, and, indeed,
it was a night long to be remembered for the clear conversion of
souls. One of these young men made an able itinerant preacher. He
travelled a few years, had a brilliant career, and spread the holy fire
wherever he went. He then fell sick, lingered a little while, and died
triumphantly. There was a remarkable instance of the power of
religion manifested in the change of these two young men. A few
hours before they were sworn enemies, thirsting for each other's blood;
but now all those murderous feelings were removed from them, and,
behold! their hearts were filled with love. "Old things were done
away, and all things became new."

I will relate another circumstance, though a little out of the order of
time, which will serve to show the malignity of an unrenewed human
heart. In a little town in Breckenridge County, Kentucky, called
Hardinsburgh, there lived a notorious infidel, who delighted, on almost
all occasions, to treat the Christian religion with scorn and contempt.
It was his special pride to mortify the feelings of professors of religion

and ministers of the Gospel. In the course of my travelling excursions it fell to my lot, almost a total stranger in the place, to be detained here several days and nights. The citizens, having little or no preaching in the place, invited me to preach to them of evenings. I consented to do so, and there were very good congregations and some very good signs of a revival of religion. The people were very friendly to me, and several respectable citizens gave me an invitation to dine with them, and I did so. This infidel had attended my preaching in common with the rest, and in common with the rest of the citizens he gave me a very friendly invitation to dine with him. Having learned his infidel character, the first time I declined. Several respectable citizens urged me to accept his invitation, saying, surely something strange had come over Mr. A., for he was never known to invite a preacher to his house before in all his life, and they urged me to go. Accordingly, the next day he invited me home with him to dinner. I went, and when we came to the table, instead of requesting me to ask a blessing, he said, as we drew up to the table, "Mr. Cartwright, I never permit any man to ask a blessing at my table, nor do I do it myself; for it is all hypocrisy"

I had not seated myself. Said I, "Mr. A., did you not invite me, as a preacher, to dine with you?"

"Yes, sir"

"Do you not know that preachers are in the habit of asking a blessing at table, sir?"

"Yes, sir," said he; "but I will have none of it at my table"

"Very well, sir," said I, "if I am denied the privilege of asking a blessing at your table, I assure you I will not eat with you," wheeled off, took up my hat, and started, bidding him good bye.

"O, Mr. Cartwright," said he, "you must not leave without eating with me."

"I tell you, sir," was my reply, "I will not," and went out. His manner of treating me soon flew all over the village, and the wickedest people in it cried out shame, shame, on Mr. A., and greatly applauded me for not eating with him. He rendered himself very unpopular by this mean act, and I shrewdly suspect he never treated another preacher as he had treated me. "Lord, what is man that Thou art mindful of him, or the son of man that Thou visitest him?"

The Kentucky Conference sat in Lexington again this fall, September, 25th, 1822; in Maysville, September 24th, 1823 Here we elected our delegates to the fourth delegated General Conference, which sat in Baltimore, May 1st, 1824. This was the third General Conference to which I was elected. Our Kentucky Conference was held in Shelbyville, September 23rd, 1824, and up to this time we had approximated to the following number of travelling preachers and members :—

	Members.	Travelling Preachers.
Ohio Conference	36,541	122
Kentucky Conference	24,683	92
Tennessee Conference	25,509	87
Mississippi Conference	9,009	46
Missouri Conference	11,773	55
	107,515	402

This year closed my twentieth year of regular travelling, from the time I was admitted on trial in the old Western Conference in 1804. Then we had one Conference, now we had eight, for the General Conference had formed three more in the West, namely, Holston, Illinois, and Pittsburgh; then we had two bishops, now we had five; then we had four presiding-elder Districts, now we had thirty; then we had 32 travelling preachers, now we had over 400, then in all the western world we had 11,877 members, now we had over 120,000, including the membership of the Pittsburgh Conference, which properly belonged to the West; then we had in all these United States and the Canadas seven annual Conferences, now we had fifteen; then we had, in the entire Methodist Episcopal Church in these United States and the Canadas altogether, of members, 113,134, of travelling preachers, 400, now we had of members, 328,523, travelling preachers, 1,272.

Thus you have a very small view of the progress and prosperity of the Methodist Episcopal Church in twenty years of her history. In these estimates we make no account of the thousands that were awakened and converted by her instrumentalities, and had joined other branches of the Church of Christ, nor of the thousands that had died in the triumphs of faith, and gone home to heaven.

When we consider that these United States had just emerged from colonial dependence, and had passed a bloody revolution of seven years' continuance, and were yet surrounded by hundreds of thousands of bloody savages, hostile to the last degree, and that we were without credit abroad and without means or money at home, we may well join with the venerable founder of Methodism, Mr. John Wesley, and say, that " God had strangely set us free as a nation " And, on the other hand, in reference to the Methodist Episcopal Church, when we consider that her ministers were illiterate, and not only opposed and denounced by the Catholics, but by all Protestant Churches; that we were everywhere spoken against, caricatured, and misrepresented; without colleges and seminaries, without religious books or periodicals, without missionary funds, and almost all other religious means; and our ministers did not for many years, on an average, receive over fifty dollars for a support annually, and a Methodist preacher's library almost entirely consisted of a Bible, Hymn Book, and a Discipline, may we not, without boasting, say with one of old, "What hath God wrought?"

A Methodist preacher in those days, when he felt that God had called him to preach, instead of hunting up a college or biblical institute, hunted up a hardy pony of a horse, and some travelling apparatus, and with his library always at hand, namely, Bible, Hymn Book, and Discipline, he started, and, with a text that never wore out nor grew stale, he cried, "Behold the Lamb of God, that taketh away the sin of the world!" In this way he went through storms of wind, hail, snow, and rain; climbed hills and mountains, traversed valleys, plunged through swamps, swam swollen streams, lay out all night, wet, weary, and hungry, held his horse by the bridle all night, or tied him to a limb, slept with his saddle-blanket for a bed, his saddle or saddle-bags for his pillow, and his old big coat or blanket, if he had any, for a covering. Often he slept in dirty cabins, on earthen floors, before the fire; ate roasting ears for bread, drank butter-milk for coffee, or sage tea for imperial; took, with a hearty zest, deer or bear meat, or wild turkey, for breakfast, dinner, and supper, if he could get it. His text was always ready, "Behold the Lamb of God," &c. This was old-fashioned Methodist preacher fare and fortune. Under such circumstances, who among us would now say?—"Here am I, Lord; send me!"

CHAPTER XVIII.
REMOVAL TO ILLINOIS.

My three years on the Cumberland District were years of immense labour and toil, and of great peace and prosperity to the Church. I had seen with painful emotions the increase of a disposition to justify slavery; and our preachers, by marriage and other ways, became more and more entangled with this dark question, and were more and more disposed to palliate and justify the traffic and ownership of human beings, and the legislatures in the slave States made the laws more and more stringent, with a design to prevent emancipation. Moreover, rabid abolitionism spread, and dreadfully excited the South. I had a young and growing family of children, two sons and four daughters; was poor; owned a little farm of about one hundred and fifty acres; lands around me were high, and rising in value. My daughters would soon be grown up. I did not see any probable means by which I could settle them around or near us. Moreover, I had no right to expect our children to marry into wealthy families, and I did not desire it, if it could be so ; and by chance they might marry into slave families. This I did not desire. Besides, I saw there was a marked distinction made among the people generally, between young people raised without work and those that had to work for their living ; and though I had breasted the storms and suffered the hardships incident to an itinerant life for more than twenty years, chiefly spent in Southern Kentucky and Western Tennessee, and though I had just as many friends as any man ought to have, and hundreds that claimed me as the humble and unworthy instrument of their salvation, and felt not the least fear that I should not be well supported during life as a Methodist preacher, the whole country having grown up into improved and comfortable living ; and although many, very many of my friends in the Church and out of the Church remonstrated against the idea of my moving to a new country, yet, after much prayer and anxious thought, I very clearly came to the conclusion that it was my duty to move ; and although the thought of leaving thousands of my best friends was severely painful to me, and sometimes almost overwhelmed me, and shook my determination, yet I saw, or thought I saw, clear indications of Providence that I should leave my comfortable little home, and move to a free State or Territory, for the following reasons : First, I would get entirely clear of the evil of slavery.   Second, I could raise my children to work where work was not thought a degradation.   Third, I believed I could better my temporal circumstances, and procure lands for my children as they grew up.   And, Fourth, I could carry the Gospel to destitute souls that had, by their removal into some new country, been deprived of the means of grace.   With these convictions, I consulted my wife, and found her of the same mind ; and in the spring of 1823, with my brother-in-law, R. Gaines, a local preacher, and old Father Charles Holliday, set out to explore Illinois in quest of a future home.

We made the journey on horseback ; packed horse feed, and, in part, our own provisions, as best we could, and camped out several times.   We knew the country was thinly settled, especially the north-eastern, north, and north-western parts of the State ; and our inclination led us in these directions.   We took our course, without roads, up the big Wabash valley, till we struck the Illinois River above Fort Clark (now Peoria City) ; thence wound our way north of said river, through a part of what was then called the Military Tract ; recrossed the river at what is now called Beardstown, (then there was only one solitary family and a small cabin,) and made our way up the Sangamon

River to a small settlement on Richland Creek, in Sangamon County, the then extreme northern county in the State, to the place on which I now live, and where I have lived ever since I moved to the State, and at which I expect my friends will deposit my mortal remains in our family cemetery. Here I found a very decent family, with a small improvement, having a double cabin, about the best the country afforded. They were settled on Congress land; and, indeed, though the land had been surveyed by government, it had not been brought into market. I gave him two hundred dollars for his improvement and his claim; bought some stock, and rented out the improvement, with a view to have something to live on in the fall of 1824, when I expected to move to it.

We then retraced our steps homeward through Springfield. There were in this place, now the seat of government, a few smoky, hastily-built cabins, and one or two very little shanties, called " stores;" and, with the exception of a few articles of heavy ware, I could have carried at a few loads all they had for sale on my back. When we returned home, I made sale of my little property, all with a special view to our removal in 1824; and at the Conference, which sat in Shelbyville, Kentucky, I asked and obtained a transfer to the Illinois Conference from Bishop Roberts, and was appointed to travel the Sangamon Circuit.

When the Conference adjourned, and I was about to leave the body of preachers of the Kentucky Conference, many of whom I had laboured with for ten, fifteen, or twenty years, it seemed to me that I never felt such a rush of feeling before. As we took the parting hand, our eyes mutually filled with tears. Few of us ever expected to meet again till we met at the judgment-seat. I shook their hands, made my best bow to the brethren of the Kentucky Conference, asked an interest in their prayers, and hastened away home; and in a few days all my little plunder was packed up and my family mounted, and we started for Illinois.

Although the Illinois Conference, at the General Conference, had been stricken off from Missouri Conference, yet the Annual Meeting this fall of both these Conferences was to be held at Padfield's, Looking-glass Prairie, October 23rd, 1824. It was my intention to meet this Conference on my way to Sangamon County; but I was prevented by the following fatal accident on our way. Just before we struck the prairies, the man that drove my team contrived to turn over the waggon, and was very near killing my oldest daughter. The sun was just going down; and by the time we righted up the waggon and reloaded, it was getting dark, and we had a difficult hill to descend; so we concluded to camp there for the night, almost in sight of two cabins containing families. I was almost exhausted reloading my waggon; the evening was warm, and my wife persuaded me not to stretch our tent that night; so I struck fire, and kindled it at the root of a small, and, as I thought, sound, tree. We laid down and slept soundly.

Just as day was appearing in the east, the tree at the root of which we had kindled a small fire fell, and it fell on our third daughter, as direct on her, from her feet to her head, as it could fall; and I suppose she never breathed after. I heard the tree crack when it started to fall, and sprang, alarmed very much, and seized it before it struck the child; but it availed nothing. Although this was an awful calamity, yet God was kind to us; for if we had stretched our tent that night, we should have been obliged to lie down in another position, and in that event the tree would have fallen directly upon us, and we should all have been killed instead of one The tree was sound outside to the thickness of the back of a carving knife, and then all the inside had a dry rot; but this we did not suspect. I sent my teamster to those families near at hand for aid; but not a soul would come nigh. Here we were in great distress, and no one to even pity our condition. My teamster and myself fell to cutting the tree off the child, when I discovered that the tree had sprung up, and did not press the child; and we drew her out from under it, and carefully laid her in our feed trough, and moved on about twenty miles to an acquaintance's in Hamilton County, Illinois, where we buried her.

Here I will state a fact worthy of record. There was in the settlement a very wicked family, total strangers to me and mine. The old gentleman and two sons heard of our affliction, and they hastened to our relief, and every act of kindness that they possibly could do us was rendered with undisguised and undissembled friendship; and they would on no account have any compensation. This was true friendship, and it endeared them to me in a most affectionate manner. I met and conversed with them years afterward, and although they are now dead and gone to the spirit-land, I hope they will be in heaven rewarded for their kindness to us in our deep and heart-rending affliction; for surely this was giving more than "a cup of cold water to a disciple." By the blessing of Providence, we prosecuted our journey; and on the 15th of November, 1824, we arrived where we now live.

Sangamon County was not only a newly-settled country, but embraced a large region. It was the most northern and the only northern county organized in the State. It had been settled by a few hardy and enterprising pioneers but a few years before. Just north of us was an unbroken Indian country, and the Indians would come in by scores and camp on the Sangamon River bottom, and hunt and live there through the winter. Their frequent visits to our cabins created sometimes great alarm among the women and children. They were a very degraded and demoralized people, and the white people were very much to blame in dealing out the fire-water so freely among them. But the whites kept advancing further and further into their country, and the Indians kept constantly receding and melting away before their rapid march, until they are now mostly removed west of the Mississippi, the great Father of Waters.

The Sangamon Circuit had been formed about three years when I came to it. Brother J. Sims, I think, formed the Circuit Brother Rice followed, and J. Miller, of one of the Indiana Conferences, travelled it in 1823–4. The Circuit was in what is called the Illinois District, Samuel H. Thompson presiding elder. I found about two hundred and sixty members in Society. The Circuit embraced all the scattered settlements in the above-named county, together with parts of Morgan and M'Lean Counties. We were almost entirely without ferries, bridges, or roads. My mode of travelling, with a few exceptions, was to go from point to point of timber, through the high grass of the prairie. My Circuit extended to Blooming Grove in M'Lean County, near where the city of Bloomington now stands. A few fine Methodist families had settled in this grove; some local preachers from Sangamon Circuit first visited them; then Jesse Walker, who was appointed missionary to the Indians in and about Fort Clark and up the Illinois River toward Lake Michigan I took it into the Sangamon Circuit, and, in conjunction with Brother Walker, appointed a sacramental meeting at the house of Brother Hendricks, he and his wife being excellent members of the Church, and he was appointed classleader. Brother Hendricks has long since gone to his reward, while Sister Hendricks still lingers among us, a shining example of Christian piety.

An incident occurred at this sacramental meeting worthy of note. The ordinance of baptism was desired by some, and some parents wanted their children baptized, and the brethren desired me to preach on or explain the nature and design of Christian baptism I did so on the Sabbath. There was present a New Light preacher, who had settled in the grove, and was a very great stickler for immersion, as the only proper mode. That afternoon there arose a dark cloud, and presently the rain fell in torrents, and continued almost all night; nearly the whole face of the earth was covered with water; the streams rose suddenly and overflowed their banks. A little brook near the house rose so rapidly that it swept away the spring house and some of the fences. Next morning I was riding up the grove to see an old acquaintance. I met Mr. Roads, my New Light preacher, and said, " Good morning, sir."

" Good morning," he replied.

Said I, " We have had a tremendous rain."

" Yes, sir," said he; " the Lord sent that rain to convince you of your error."

" Ah!" said I, " what error?"

" Why, about baptism. The Lord sent this flood to convince you that much water was necessary."

" Very good, sir," said I; " and He in like manner sent this flood to convince you of your error."

" What error?" said he.

" Why," said I, " to show you that water comes by pouring and not by immersion."

The preacher got into this mad fit because I had satisfied one of his daughters that immersion was not the proper mode of baptism, and she had joined the Methodists; and I am told that this flood to this day is called " Cartwright's Flood," by way of eminence; and though it rained hard, and my New Light preacher preached hard against us, yet he made little or no impression, but finally evaporated and left for parts unknown. His New Light went out because there was " no oil in the vessel."

I had an appointment in a settlement in a certain brother's cabin. He had a first-rate wife and several interesting daughters; and I will not forget to say, had some three hundred dollars hoarded up to enter land. For the thin settlement we had a good congregation. The meeting closed, and there was but one chair in the house, and that was called " the preacher's chair." The bottom was weak and worn out, and one of the upright back pieces was broken off. We had a hewed puncheon for a table, with four holes in it, and four straight sticks put in for legs The hearth was made of earth, and in the centre of it was a deep hole, worn by sweeping. Around this hole the women had to cook, which was exceedingly inconvenient, for they had no kitchen. When we came to the table, there were wooden trenchers for plates, sharp-pointed pieces of cane for forks, and tin cups for cups and saucers There was but one knife besides a butcher's knife, and that had the handle off. Four forks were driven down between the puncheons into the ground; for bedsteads, cross poles or side poles put in those forks, and clapboards laid crosswise for cords. The old sister kept up a constant apology, and made many excuses. Now, if the brother had been really poor, I could have excused everything; but, knowing he had money hoarded up, I thought it my duty to speak to him on the subject. I was at first a little careful; so I commenced by praising his good-looking daughters, and noticed what a good cook his wife was, if she had any chance. " Now, brother," said I, " do fill up this hole in the hearth, and go to town and get you a set of chairs, knives and forks, cups and saucers, and get you a couple of plain bedsteads and bed-cords. Give your wife and daughters a chance. These girls, sir, are smart enough to marry well, if you will fix them up a little." I saw in a moment the women were on my side, and I felt safe. The old brother said he had seen proud preachers before, and that he knew I was proud the moment he saw me with my broadcloth coat on, and he did not thank me for meddling with his affairs.

" Brother," said I, " you have been a member of the Church a long time, and you ought to know that the Discipline of our Church makes it the duty of a Circuit preacher to recommend cleanliness and decency everywhere; and, moreover, if there was nothing of this kind in the Discipline at all, my good feelings toward you and your family prompt me to urge these things on you; and you ought to attend to them for your own comfort, and the great comfort of your family."

The old sister and daughters joined with me in all I said.

" Brother," said I, " you have two fine boys here, and they will help you to do up things in a little better style; and I tell you, if you don't do it by the time I come round in four weeks, I shall move preaching from your cabin somewhere else."

The old brother told me I could move preaching; for if I was too proud to put up with his fare, he did not want me about him. I went on, but left another appointment; and, when I came on to it, I tell you things were done up about right. The females had taken my lecture to the old brother for a text, and they had preached success-fully to him, for the hole in the hearth was filled up, two new bed-steads were on hand, six new split-bottomed chairs were procured, a new set of knives and forks, cups and saucers, and plates, were all on hand. The women met me very pleasantly, and the old brother him-self looked better than usual; and, besides all this, the women all had new calico dresses, and looked very neat. We had a good congrega-tion, a good meeting, and things went on very pleasantly with me and the whole family during the two years that I rode the Circuit. And, better than all this, nearly all the children obtained religion and joined the Church, and those of them who still live I number among my fast friends.

On Horse Creek we had an appointment, and a good society; old Brother Joseph Dixon was class-leader and steward. I think he was one of the best stewards I ever saw. The country was new; our little market was at St. Louis, distant one hundred miles or more; and

some of the people had to go sixty miles for their grinding and bread-
stuff ; and this country was generally settled with poor, but very kind,
people ; money was very scarce, and what little there was, was generally kept close to enter lands when our Congress should order sales ;
almost universally we were settled on Congress or government lands.
In this condition of affairs, the support of a travelling preacher was
exceedingly small.   The first year I travelled the Sangamon Circuit,
with a wife and six children, I received forty dollars all told ; the
second year I received sixty.   This was considered a great improvement in our financial affairs.   I state these things that the reader
may see the extreme difficulties our early preachers had to contend
with.   The round before each quarterly meeting, Brother Dixon, the
steward, would take his horse and accompany the preacher, and after
preaching, and the class had met, he would rise and call on the Church
for their aid in supporting the Gospel. . He invariably made it a rule
to see that every member of his own class paid something every
quarter to support the Gospel ; and if there were any too poor to pay,
he would pay for them.

Brother Dixon had been a real backwoodsman, a frontier settler, a
great hunter and trapper to take furs.   Among other early and enterprising trappers, he prepared himself for a hunting and trapping
expedition up the Missouri River and its tributaries, which at that
early day was an unbroken Indian country, and many of them hostile
to the whites.   He made himself a canoe or dug-out, to ascend the
rivers, laid in his traps, ammunition, and all the necessary fixtures for
such a trip, and he and two other partners slowly ascended the Missouri.   After ascending this stream for hundreds of miles, and escaping
many dangerous ambuscades of the Indians, winter came on with
great severity.   They dug in the ground and buried their furs and
skins at different points, to keep them from being stolen by the
Indians.   They then dug a deep hole on the sunny side of a hill,
gathered their winter meat and fuel, their leaves and grass, and carried
them into the hole, and took up their winter quarters.   The snows
were very deep, the weather intensely cold ; but they wintered in
comparative safety till returning spring, which they hailed with trans-
ports of joy.   They were robbed several times by the Indians, had
several battles with them, and killed two or three of them.   The next
fall his partners fell out with him, bought a canoe of the Indians, left
him alone, descended the river, dug up their furs, and returned home.
Dixon fortunately secured most of the ammunition they had on hand.
He again found a dreaded winter approaching.   He resorted to the
former winter's experiment, and dug his cave in the side of a steep
hill, laid up his winter provisions, and took up his winter quarters all

alone. In this perilous condition, his eyes became inflamed, and were very much affected from constant gazing on the almost perpetual snows around him, until, such was their diseased state, he could not see anything. Here he was, utterly helpless and hopeless. He began to reflect on his dreadful condition, while he felt nothing but certain death, and realized himself to be a great sinner and unprepared to die. For the first time in his life, almost, he kneeled down and asked God for mercy and deliverance from this awful condition. Then and there he promised God, if He would spare and deliver him, he would from that solemn moment serve Him faithfully the rest of his life. This promise, he told me, he had faithfully kept, and there is not in my mind a single doubt but he kept his covenant till he was safely housed in heaven.

When he made this covenant with God in his desperate condition, all of a sudden there was a strong impression made on his mind, that if he would take the inside bark of a certain tree that stood a few steps from the mouth of his earthy habitation, and beat it up, soft and fine, soak it in water, and wash his eyes with it, he would soon recover his sight. He groped his way to the tree, got the bark, prepared it as impressed, bathed his eyes, bound some of this bark to them, and lay down and slept, not knowing whether it was day or night. When he awoke, his eyes felt easy; the inflammation was evidently subsiding, and in a short time his sight began to return, and soon was entirely restored. When he gained confidence in his restoration to sight, he fell on his knees to return thanks to God; a sweet and heavenly peace ran all through his soul, and he then and there, all alone, shouted aloud the high praises of God. He then felt that God had forgiven his sins, blessed his soul, restored his sight, and that he ought to praise and give glory to His holy name.

When the weather opened for trapping, he said, he had astonishing good luck; took a great amount of the very best furs, and, collecting them, began to descend the river. He had an Indian village to pass on the bank of the river, and, as they were a deceitful, sly, bad tribe of Indians, he determined to keep his canoe as far from their shore as possible. They made many friendly signs for him to stop; so he concluded to land and trade a little with them. He had his rifle well loaded, and was a very strong man. When his canoe struck the bank, a large, stout Indian jumped into it, and others were following. He, accordingly, shoved off, when one on the bank raised his rifle and aimed to shoot him. As quick as thought, Dixon jerked the Indian that was in the canoe between him and the other that raised his rifle; the gun fired, and lodged its contents in the heart of the large Indian in the canoe, who fell overboard dead. Dixon paddled with all speed down the river, and escaped being robbed or killed. When he returned to St. Louis, he sold his furs for several thousand dollars, and returned to his family, after having been absent nearly three years. He then packed up, moved to Horse Creek, in Sangamon County, took preaching into his cabin, joined the Methodist Episcopal Church, and continued to be a faithful member, leader, and steward for many years. His children mostly grew up, married, and left him; his most excellent wife at length died, witnessing a good confession; his youngest son he named Missouri, in memory of his conversion on the trapping expedition up that turbid stream, and also to keep fresh in his recollection the solemn vow he had made in his perilous condition. After the death of his wife he lingered a few years, and then died in peace, at his daughter's, in Morgan County.

It may be gratifying to some to see what has grown out of what was within the bounds of the old Sangamon Circuit in 1824–5. There is Beardstown Station, Virginia Circuit, Havana Circuit, Delavan Mission, East and West Charges in Bloomington, Randolph's Grove Circuit, Waynesville Circuit, Mount Pleasant Circuit, Clinton, Honey Creek, Mount Pulaski, Decatur Station and Circuit, Taylorsville, Sulphur Spring, Virden Island Grove, and Springfield Station. Thus the old hive has sent forth twenty swarms, and still retains its old name, *Sangamon*. Perhaps this Circuit has retained its first name longer than any Circuit in the State or Conference. At the close of my second year I returned 400 members, being an increase, in two years, of 160. At our Conference in Charlestown, Indiana, August 25th, 1825, Bishop M'Kendree attended and presided; and I was reappointed to Sangamon Circuit. At the time of this Conference I was taken down with a violent attack of bilious fever. Three friendly doctors attended me. They succeeded in stopping the fever. My doctor advised me to travel homeward slowly, and only a few miles a day, till I gained strength, and to take good care of myself. Some of the preachers secured a preacher acquainted with the country through which I had to pass, to go with and take care of me; for I was very feeble. This preacher was under marriage contract, and the day set for the ceremony, but I knew it not. The first day we rode twenty-eight miles. I urged him to stop long before we did. But no; he knew of a Judge Somebody, a fine Methodist, and a good place, &c.; he lived in the west end of a little town. As we passed the tavern, I urged the preacher again to stop; but no, he rode up to the judge's, told my name and condition, but he would not take us in. There was present a kind-hearted man, who, on learning my condition, took me home with him and treated me well. Next morning we started on, and when we got into another little town, having rode that day twenty miles, I begged my preacher to let me stop. "O no, no," said he; "there is a fine place three miles down here; we must get there." At that moment I saw a doctor who had been a travelling preacher in Kentucky, and I knew him and called to him, and begged him to take me somewhere that I could rest. I then told my preacher guide to move on and move off, for certainly I would not travel with him a step further. So he left, and the doctor took me home with him, and treated me kindly. On Sunday morning he took me a few miles up the country, on Honey Creek, to a camp-meeting that was in progress. Here I tarried and rested a while. I was aiming to cross the Wabash, and get to J. W. M'Reynold's, near Paris.

The day I left the camp-meeting my fever returned, just while I was crossing Honey Creek Prairie. It seemed to me I should die for want of water, there being no house on the road. I was immensely sick, and the day was intensely warm. At length I found a little green bush that afforded a small shade. Here I lay down to die. I saw a house a little way off, over a field, but was unable to get to it. In a few minutes a lady rode up to me, and although I had not seen her for twenty years, I instantly knew her, and she recognised me, and after a few minutes she rode off briskly after help.

In a little time there came a man and buggy, and a small boy. The boy mounted my horse. The man helped me into the buggy, and drove up to his house, and took me in, and placed me on a bed between two doors, where I had a free circulation of air. This was the house where the lady lived. The man was her husband. They took all possible care of me till I got a little better, then I started, and got safe to Brother M'Reynold's. And now I had the Grand Prairie to cross, ninety miles through. To go alone seemed out of the question, and Brother Mac's family was not in a situation for him safely to leave, and carry me in a carriage through; but he said he would go, as I must not go alone.

We arranged to start next morning early; and just as we were about leaving, I saw a carriage with a span of horses drive up to the steps with three persons, and who should they be but Brother and Sister Springer, my neighbours, and my wife, who had heard of my sickness, and had come to convey me home.

A bed was placed in the carriage, and we started. There was but one house for eighty miles across this Grand Prairie, and no water but a few ponds. I thought that these two days that we were crossing, I should surely die for the want of good water. I drank freely of these ponds, and it made me very sick every time; and I threw off great quantities of bile, and this, perhaps, saved my life. After all my fever abated, I gradually grew better, and finally recovered my wonted health.

We had a glorious camp-meeting this year on what was called Waters' Camp Ground, on Spring Creek, six miles west of Springfield. It lasted five days and nights. Over forty professed religion, and joined the Church; and the Circuit generally was in a healthy condition.

The country this year settled up very rapidly, and improvements went up equally as rapid in almost every direction.

CHAPTER XIX.

POLITICAL LIFE.

OUR Conference met in Bloomington, Indiana, September 28th, 1826. Bishop Soule and Bishop Roberts attended and presided. S. H. Thompson's time on the Illinois District having expired, he was appointed to the Illinois Circuit, and I was appointed to succeed him in the District, which was composed of the following Circuits or appointments: Illinois, Kaskaskia, Shoal Creek, Sangamon, Peoria, Mississippi, Atlas, and the Pottawattomie Mission. This District thus extended from Kaskaskia River to the extreme northern settlements, and even to the Pottawattomie nation of Indians, on Fox River; up that river into the heart of the nation. And there were only about three thousand members of the Church in it, and only half of another presiding-elder District in the State. The Wabash District, Charles Holliday presiding elder, lay on the west side of the Wabash River, in Illinois, and on the east side of that river, in Indiana.

The following appointments were in Illinois: Mount Carmel, Wabash, Carmi, Mount Vernon, and Cash River, with a membership of about thirteen hundred and fifty; a little over four thousand in the entire State. My District was four hundred miles long, and covered all the west side of the Grand Prairie, fully two thirds of the geographical boundaries of the State. The year before I moved to the State, there had been a strong move, by a corrupt and demoralized legislature, to call a convention with a view to alter the constitution, so as to admit slavery into the State. I had left Kentucky on account of slavery, and, as I hoped, had bid a final farewell to all slave institutions; but the subject was well rife through the country; for, although the friends of human liberty had sustained themselves, and carried the election by more than one thousand votes, yet it was feared that the advocates of slavery would renew the effort, and yet cause this "abomination of desolation to stand where it ought not." I very freely entered the lists to oppose slavery in this way, and, without any forethought of mind, went into the agitated waters of political strife. I was strongly solicited to become a candidate for a seat in the legislature of our State. I consented, and was twice elected as representative from Sangamon County.

But I say, without any desire to speak evil of the rulers of the people, I found a great deal of corruption in our legislature; and I found that almost every measure had to be carried by a corrupt bargain and sale; which should cause every honest man to blush for his country.

The great national parties were now organized, and, as my honest sentiments placed me in the minority in my county, of course I retired from politics. But I say now, if the people would not be led by party considerations, but would select honest and capable men, I cannot see the impropriety of canvassing for office on Christian principles.

· There is an incident or two connected with my little political experience that I will give.

The first time I ran for office in Sangamon County, I was on the north side of the Sangamon River, as we say in the East, electioneering, or rather trying to get acquainted with the people; for I was at that early day a great stranger to many of them. Passing through a brushy point of undergrowth, near a ferry where I intended to cross the river, I heard just before me some one talking very loud. I reined my horse to listen. I heard some one say that Peter Cartwright was a d—d rascal; and so were all Methodist preachers; they would all steal horses; and that it was a scandal to the country that such a man as Cartwright should offer for a representative of the county; and that the first time he saw him, he intended to whip him for his impudence. This surprised me a little, and I looked round for some way to pass without coming in contact with this company; but there was no path that I could see, and the brush was so thick I could not get through. So I summoned all my courage, and rode boldly up, and spoke to the man. There were six of them; and, as I learned, but one of them had ever seen me. So I said, "Gentlemen, who is it among you that is going to whip Cartwright the first time you see him?" The man who had threatened spoke out and said, "I am the lark that's going to thrash him well." Said I, "Cartwright is known to be much of a man, and it will take a man to whip him, mind you." "O no," said he; "I can whip any Methodist preacher the Lord ever made." "Well, Sir," said I, "you cannot do it; and now I tell you my name is Cartwright, and I never like to live in dread; if you really intend to whip me, come and do it now."

He looked a little confused, and said, "O, you can't fool me that way; you are not Cartwright."

"Well," said I, "that is my name, and I am a candidate for the legislature, and now is your time; if you must whip me, do it now."

He said, "No, no, you are not Cartwright at all; you only want to fool me."

By this time we had moved slowly to the boat, and when we got on it, he broke out in a fresh volley of curses on Cartwright. I said to a gentleman on the boat, "Here, hold my horse;" and stepping up to this cursing disciple, I said sternly to him, "Now, sir, you have to whip me as you threatened, or quit cursing me, or I will put you in the river, and baptize you in the name of the devil; for surely you belong to him." This settled him; and strange to say, when the election came off, he went to the polls and voted for me, and ever afterward was my warm and constant friend.

Take another instance of what an honest man has to bear, if he mixes in the muddy waters of political strife; and what powerful temptations it throws in his way to do wrong, and thereby wound his tender conscience, if he has any. There was a man, whom I never knowingly saw, and he did not know me by sight, as I clearly proved. At a large gathering in Springfield, he stated that he had lived my neighbour in Kentucky, and that he saw and heard me offer to swear off a plain note of my indebtedness; and this statement was gaining and spreading like wildfire. Those opposed to my election were chuckling over it at a mighty rate; some of my friends came to me and told me of it, and said, I must meet it and stop it, or it would defeat my election. Said I,—

"Gentlemen, if you will take me to, and show me, this man, I will give you clear demonstration that his statements are false."

So a crowd gathered around me, and I walked up to the public square where this man was defaming me. I said to the company, "Take me right up to the man, and I will show you that he never saw me, and never knew me." They did so; and when we came to him, one said to me, "This is Mr. G."

Looking him in the eye, said I, "Well, sir, I want to know something about this lying report you have been circulating about me." There was a large crowd gathered around.

"Who are you, sir?" said he. "I don't know you."

"Did you ever see me before?"

"No, sir, not that I know of."

"Well, sir, my name is Peter Cartwright, about whom you have circulated the lying statement, that I, in your presence, in Kentucky, offered to swear off a plain note of my indebtedness; and I have proved to this large and respectable company that you are a lying, dirty scoundrel; and now,.if you do not here acknowledge yourself a liar and a dirty fellow, I will sweep the streets with you to your heart's content; and do it instantly, or I will give you a chastisement that you will remember to your latest day."

The crowd shouted, "Down him, down him, Cartwright; he ought to catch it."

After the crowd was a little stilled, my accuser said, "Well, gentlemen, I acknowledge that I have done Mr. Cartwright great injustice, and have, without any just cause, lied on him." At this, the crowd gave three cheers for Cartwright.

Now, you see, gentle reader, the muddy waters that a candidate for office in our free country has to wade through; and well may we pray, "Lead us not into temptation, but deliver us from evil."

I will relate an incident that occurred in the legislature. After we were sworn in as members of that body, there was a flippant, loquacious lawyer elected from Union County. He was a pretty speaker, but not very profound, and had a very high opinion of his own tact and talent. He was also a great aspirant, and had a thirst for popularity; and there were several congregations of Dunkers, or Seventh-day Baptists, in the district. This lawyer represented that they kept Saturday for the Christian Sabbath, and thought, or professed to think, it was altogether wrong that they should pay taxes, work on roads, perform military duty, or serve on juries, &c.

He wanted to have a law passed, favouring them in all these particulars, and thus exclusively legislating for their particular benefit, thereby making a religious test, and making a sectarian distinction, and legislating for their pretended scruples of conscience. He accordingly introduced a Bill for their special benefit. I opposed the passage of the Bill, and briefly remarked, that, as a nation, we all acknowledged Sunday as the Christian Sabbath, and that there ought to be no distinctions in Churches, or among the people; and as to bearing arms, that the people who were unwilling to take up arms in the defence of their country, were unworthy of the protection of the government; and as for not working on roads, if there were any unwilling to work on roads, they should not be allowed the privilege of travelling them; as to serving on juries, if anybody was unwilling to serve on them, he ought to be deprived of the privilege of having the right of trial by jury; and if there were any unwilling to pay taxes to support government, they should be declared outlaws, and denied the protection of government. The representative from Union, at this, flew into a mighty rage, and, instead of arguing the case, began to eulogize the Dunkers, and drew a contrast between them and the Methodists. He said the Dunkers were an honest, industrious, hard-working people; their preachers worked for their own support; there was no hypocritical begging among them; no carrying the hat round in the congregation for public collections, and hypocritical whining among them for support, as was always to be seen among Methodist preachers. Thus he laid on thick and fast. It was my good fortune to know, that a few years before, this same lawyer was a candidate for Congress, and the lamented S. H. Thompson was the presiding elder, and his District covered the congressional district this lawyer desired to represent; and as Brother Thompson was very popular among the people, and had a number of camp and quarterly meetings in the bounds of this congressional district, this said lawyer had pretended to be serious on the subject of religion; and here he followed Brother Thompson from appointment to appointment, appearing to be very much concerned about religion, threw in liberally at every public collection, offering to carry the hat round himself when collections were taken.

When he closed his tirade of abuse, I rose and said, "Mr. Speaker, I award to the gentleman from Union the honour of being one of the best judges of hypocrisy in all the land;" and then narrated the above facts. He rose and called me to order; but the Speaker said I was in order, and directed him to sit down. Presently, he rose again, and said if I was not called to order, he would knock me down at the bar. The Speaker again pronounced me in order, and bade me proceed. I finished my speech, and left my mark on this belligerent son of the law.

When we adjourned, our clerk told me to be on my guard; that he heard this lawyer say, the moment I stepped out of the state house door he intended to whip me. I walked out and stepped up to him, and asked, "Are you for peace or war?"

"O," said he, "for peace; come, go home with me and take tea."

We locked arms, and I went. When we got there, we found the governor and his lady, and a number of genteel people. We sat down to tea, and I found they were going to eat with graceless indifference. Said I, "Governor, ask a blessing." He blushed, apologized, and begged me to do it. I did so; and then remarked that I had called on his excellency by way of reproof, for I thought the governor ought to be a good man and set a better example. He readily admitted all I said to be true; and this was the last time during the session that I ate at any of their houses without being requested to ask a blessing.

At a quarterly meeting I held in Kaskaskia in 1827, an incident occurred which I will relate. S. L. Robinson and A. E. Phelps were the Circuit preachers, both of whom have passed away, witnessing a good confession. E. Roberts and Colonel Mather lived in Kaskaskia at this time; and although neither of them was a professor of religion, yet they were both friendly to religion, and treated Methodist preachers with great kindness. We stayed with them during the quarterly meeting; and although neither of them was a drinking man, yet they sometimes took a little rum; so also did Methodist and other preachers. These two men, in all kindness, poured out some wine, as they supposed, into glasses, and sent it round in a waiter to us preachers, but, through mistake, it happened to be brandy. The most of the preachers turned off their wine as was supposed, and they did it so suddenly and unsuspiciously, the mistake was not detected till it was drunk. Fortunately for me, I got the smell of the brandy, and held back from drinking at all.

Said I, " Gentlemen, this is brandy as sure as you live."

Mr. Roberts and Mr. Mather were greatly surprised at their mistake, and were mortified. The preachers who had drunk their brandy through mistake were alarmed, fearing they would be intoxicated, being so little in the habit of using ardent spirits. No serious intoxication was the result of this mistake; but how much better it would have been wholly to abstain from all, and then these accidents would never happen! Suppose any, or all of us, through this mistake, had become intoxicated, what a dreadful reproach we would have caused to religion, and the worthy name of Christ would have been blasphemed through an idle, not to say sinful, habit!

The last year Brother Thompson was on this District, it being very large, he requested me to attend some of his quarterly meetings; and, among others, I attended one in Green County, near what is now called Whitehall. John Kirkpatrick, a local preacher from 'the Sangamon Circuit, went down and arrived there a little before me. When I came, he approached me and said,—

" Brother, I sincerely pity you from my very heart."

" Why, what 's the matter ? "

" The people have heard that you are one of the greatest preachers in the West, and their expectations are on tiptoe, and no bishop could satisfy them; but do your best."

These statements somewhat disconcerted me, though I never was very anxious to gratify idle curiosity: I knew my help must come from God, and unless the Lord helped me, every effort would be vain; but if God would help me, I asked no other aid. At length the hour arrived, and I rose in the stand, and tried to preach the best I knew how. The people gave me their kind attention, but I saw in their

countenances they were disappointed.   During the intermission,
Brother Kirkpatrick came to me and said,

"I told you so; you have fallen several degrees under the people's
expectations.   You must try again."

Accordingly, on Sunday I took the stand, and tried to look wise,
and I not only tried to look so, but I tried to preach so, and in all
good conscience I went at the top of my speed, and did my very best;
but it was a failure.   Brother Kirkpatrick came to me again, and
deeply sympathized with me.

Said I, "Brother, I know what is the matter; I'll come it the next
time."

So on Sunday night I mounted the stand, took my text, and, though
I had loaded in a hurry, drew the bow at a venture, and let fly arrows
in almost all directions : some laughed ; some cried ; some became
angry; some ran; some cursed me right out; some shouted; some
fell to the earth; and there was a general uproar throughout the whole
encampment.   Our meeting lasted all night, and the slain of the Lord
were many; and although this discourse was ·delivered without connexion, system, or anything else but exhortation, I redeemed myself,
and now it was admitted that I was a great preacher.

I attended several camp-meetings in this neighbourhood during my
continuance on the District, and we always had good times; there was,
however, considerable opposition and persecution.   At one of these
camp-meetings, the wicked young men, who were chiefly children of
religious people, or professors in other Churches, brought their whiskey
and hid it in the woods, where they would collect together and drink,
and then come and disturb the worshipping congregation.   I closely
watched them, and after they had gone out to their whiskey and drunk
freely, and returned to interrupt us, I captured their keg of whiskey,
and brought it in and placed it under guard.   After a while they
missed it, and there was great confusion amongst them.   They finally
suspected me, and sent me word, if I would give up their whiskey, they
would behave themselves, or go away.   I sent them word, that I never
hired people to behave; and if they did not behave, I would make them.
They then sent me word, if I did not give up their whiskey, they
would stone the preachers' tent that night, and one of them had the
impudence to tell me so.   I utterly refused to give up the whiskey,
and told him to stone away, that I would be ready for them.

There was, close by the camp-ground, a beautiful running stream,
with a gravelly bottom, and many little rocks or pebbles   After dark
a while, the camp-ground was brilliantly lighted up; I went and borrowed some old clothes, and dressed myself in disguise, and obtained
an old straw hat.   Thus attired, I sallied out, and presently, unper-

ceived, I mixed among these rowdies, and soon got all their plans : they were to wait till the congregation was dismissed, the lights put out, and the people retired to rest; and then they were to march up and stone the preachers' tent; and if I made my appearance to annoy them in any way, they were to give me a shower of stones. I mixed freely among them, and do not suppose any one even suspected me at all. Meeting closed, the lights were blown out, and the people mostly retired to rest; in the meantime I had slipped down to the brook, and filled the pockets of the old overcoat that I had borrowed with little stones; and as I came up to them, they were just ready to commence operations on the preachers' tent; but before they had thrown a single stone, I gathered from my pockets my hands full of stones, and flung them thick and fast right in among them, crying out, at the top of my voice, "Here they are! here they are! Take them! take them!" They broke at full speed, and such a running I hardly ever witnessed. I took after them, hallooing, every jump, "Take them! take them!" Thus ended the farce. We had no more interruption, and our camp-meeting went on gloriously, and we had many conversions clear and powerful.

There lived in this settlement a very pious sister, who was much afflicted; she was poor, and money was scarce, and hard to get; but this sister believed it to be her duty, and the duty of every member of the Church, to aid in the support of the Gospel. She was very liberal, and very punctual in paying her quarterage; but circumstances entirely beyond her control prevented her from getting the money to pay her quarterage. The above-named camp-meeting was the last quarterly meeting before Conference, and the thought that her preachers were to go away without their pay greatly afflicted her, she talked to me about it, and felt greatly distressed, and even wept over it. On Monday morning she went home, living but a short distance from the camp-ground, to get a fresh supply of provisions, and, as she returned to the camp-ground, she found, lying in the road, a silver dollar; she picked it up, and came to the camp-ground greatly rejoicing, and said, the Lord had given her that dollar to pay her preachers, and she gave it to the support of the Gospel with great cheerfulness. Now, if all our Church members would act as conscientiously as this beloved sister, our preachers would never go without their pay. This sister lived and died a noble pattern of piety; her end was peace, and well might she say, on her dying couch, to her surrounding friends, who wept by her bedside, "Follow me, as I have followed the Lord Jesus Christ."

Before I take leave of this camp-meeting, I will relate an incident, to show what lengths people can go in wild and unjustifiable fanaticism. There came a man to this meeting from one of the Carolinas, who had professed religion in some of the revivals in that country. He was a man of good education, and wealthy, of polite manners, of chaste and pleasant conversation; he had joined no Church, had no licence to preach from any accredited branch of the Christian Church, had no testimonials of his good character, or of being in fellowship with any Christian body whatever; and yet he professed to be called of God to the ministry of the word, and that God had appointed him to travel all over the world, and to travel on foot too.

First, he was to bring about a universal peace among all nations; secondly, he was to unite all the branches of the Christian Church, and make them one. Until then he was forbidden to ride, or go in any other way than on foot; and when he had accomplished the object of his mission, the closing of which was to be attended by the bringing in of the Jews, and their return to Palestine, and the rebuilding of Jerusalem, and the rearing up of the Temple; then Christ was to descend bodily as He ascended, and reign a thousand years on earth in the midst of His saints; and then, and not till then, he, the preacher, was to ride, and ride in triumph into the new Jerusalem, and this was to be the commencement of the millennium. This man would talk on the subject until his feelings would be wrought up to an ecstatic rapture; and he would shout in apparent triumph, as if he had performed the greatest work ever accomplished on earth, saving the redemption of the world. Although his whole conversation on the subject was replete with supreme absurdities, yet it was astonishing to see with what earnest attention the people heard him in his private conversations. I say private, because I would not let him occupy the pulpit, and deliver his discourses from the stand, although he, and others, importuned me to let him do so; but I told them, No, I could not, in view of my responsibility to God and man, permit any such religious foolishness to disturb and divert the minds of the people from the sober truths of the Gospel; and gave, as my decided opinion, that God would not swerve one hair's breadth from the system of truth recorded in the Gospel, to save or to damn the world. This gave him great offence, and shortly he left us; and I was exceedingly glad when he took his departure. During the time he stayed among us I tried to reason him out of his absurd notions, to show the great folly and inconsistency of his views, but all in vain; he construed it into persecution, and a disposition to fight against God. I have lived to see many of these insane enthusiasts on the subject of religion, and I have never seen any good resulting from giving them any countenance at all; but, in several instances, great harm was done by showing them countenance. They can manufacture more fanatics, and in a shorter time, than twenty good, sound Gospel ministers can turn five sinners from the error of their ways to the service of the living and true God. Perhaps it may not be considered out of place to indulge here in a few remarks on the subject of this wild, frenzied fanaticism.

There are several classes of these fanatics, according to the best observations that I have been able to make, and I have had many opportunities in the course of my fifty years' ministry. First. There are many that are truly awakened and soundly converted to God, and are pious; but instead of taking the word of God for their only infallible guide, and trying the spirits, and their impressions, or feelings, by that as a standard, they take all their impressions and sudden impulses of mind as inspirations from God, and act accordingly. If you oppose them, they say and believe you are fighting against God. If you try to reason them out of their visionary flights, and settle them down on the sure foundation, the word of God, they construe it all into the want of religion, and cry out, "Persecution!"

Secondly There is another class of enthusiastic persons, that not only seem, but actually are, so supremely wrapped up in self, that all they do, or say, or perform, is to be seen of men; and if they can only get the ignorant multitude to run after them, and cry, "Hosannah! blessed is he that cometh in the name of the Lord," they wrap themselves in their mantle of supreme self-complacence. They surely have not the fear of God before their eyes, and their fearful responsibilities seem not to enter into their calculations from first to last. Woe unto them! If they want to go to hell, they had better take the most obscure route to that dismal region, and go single-handed and alone, than to draw the ignorant and gaping crowds, the riff-raff of all God's creation, after them; but all rebels against the government of God love company. The devil himself is a fearful witness of this fact, when, under his mutinous and revolting conspiracy against the eternal Majesty of Heaven, he drew the third part of the stars of heaven after him in his rebellion against God. It is impossible to calculate the mischief done by this class of fanatics, and the many souls they have ruined for ever.

Thirdly. There is a dark, motley crowd of wizards, witches, and spiritual rappers, so called, that have, sooner or later, infested all lands, and are the common property of the devil. They must have a fee for divining and soothsaying, and make a gain of their pretended art; and some of them pretend to be ministers of Christ and followers of the Lamb. By the indulgence of my readers I will give a very brief and, of course, imperfect statement of a case that will set this matter in a true light.

There was, in one of our Eastern Conferences, a very talented, shrewd travelling preacher, whose piety was of a doubtful complexion.

If his piety had been equal to his talents as a pulpit orator, he certainly could have done a great deal of good; but being weighed in the balances of the public mind, and, in point of piety, found wanting, he thought he must rise somehow; so he fell in with those locusts of Egypt, the spiritual rappers, took a few lessons, and then commenced operations, and really astonished the ignorant multitudes, himself with the rest. He pretended to call up the dead from every country and clime; he summoned them from heaven, earth, and hell; he not only could tell who was happy in heaven, as he said, but who were miserable in hell; he could hold communion with God, with angels, spirits, and the devil also. The last part I am not disposed to doubt. Indeed, I have very little doubt that he was in constant communion with the devil.

The Church was grieved with this state of things, and the ministers thought it their duty to arrest him, not only for these presumptuous pretensions, but for sundry other moral delinquencies. They tried him, and expelled him from the Church. He appealed to the General Conference that sat in Pittsburgh in 1848. On examination the General Conference thought that there was some informality in his trial in the annual Conference to which he belonged, and they remanded it back to his Conference for a new trial. The Conference took up the case again, found him guilty of several immoralities, and expelled him again. From this act of expulsion he appealed to the General Conference that sat in Boston in 1852. In his defence before that body, he openly avowed that he could tell what was going on in heaven, earth, and hell; that he had foretold the results of many of the important battles in Mexico, under Generals Taylor and Scott, before the battles were fought; and that he knew how the decision of that General Conference would go, before the trial ended. When the special pleadings in his case were over, and he was requested to retire, in order that the Conference should make up their verdict, I slipped out at the door after him, and said to him, "Now, Brother S., can you tell how this Conference will decide in your case beforehand?"

"Yes, I can," said he.

"Well," said I, "if you will tell me now, and they should decide as you say, you can very easily make a convert of me. Do tell me here privately; I will say nothing about it till the verdict is rendered."

"Get away," said he; "I will not do it."

"No," said I, "because you cannot." The General Conference, with great unanimity, affirmed the decision of the court below, and he was expelled.

While I was on my way to the quarterly meeting in Mississippi Circuit, at Brother J. Pickett's, in what was then Madison County, south of the Macoupin Creek, there had fallen a tremendous rain, and the creek was out of its banks. There was a little, old, crazy horse-boat; and although within a few miles of the place where the quarterly meeting was to be held, there was no chance of getting there without risking life in this old, crazy boat across this rapid stream. When I rode up to the creek, there sat a good old local preacher on the bank, holding his horse by the bridle. After the usual salutations, he said,—

"Brother, I started to go to the quarterly meeting; but I have no money, and the ferryman will not set me over, even on trust."

"How much does he charge?" said I.

He replied, "Twelve and a half cents."

"Very well, brother," said I; "go with me, and I will pay the ferriage."

So we crossed and got out safely. That night this old brother preached, and the power of the Lord was present to kill and make alive. Three souls were converted and six joined the Church, and we had an excellent meeting. I state this little circumstance to show the great good that can be done with a small sum of money. I do not think that I ever laid out twelve and a half cents to better advantage in all my little pilgrimage on earth.

From this quarterly meeting I crossed the Illinois river on to the military tract, aiming for the Atlas Circuit quarterly meeting. Late in the evening I rode up to a temporary building, a total stranger, and asked for quarters for the night, which was readily granted. I found that my landlord's family had moved from some of the New England States, and were a well-informed and clever family. The gentleman's name was Colonel Ross. Several families had moved out here, and had been living here three or four years, and, perhaps, had never heard a sermon since they had settled in this new country. I was invited to pray in the family night and morning. Our conversation chiefly turned on religious subjects. When I started on next morning, they would receive no compensation from me; and as they were kind, and would have nothing for my night's lodging, having in my saddle-bags a few religious books, I drew out "The Letters and Poems of Caroline Matilda Thayer," and made a present of this little book to my landlady, and went on my way.

I was happy afterwards to learn from this landlady's own mouth that God made this little book the means of her sound conversion. She led a happy Christian life, and died a peaceful, triumphant death. I name this little circumstance to show, in a small way, what good can be done by the distribution of religious books among the people. It has often been a question that I shall never be able to answer on earth, whether I have done the most good by preaching or distributing religious books. If we as a Church had been blessed with a flourishing Book Concern such as we now have, and our preachers had scattered books broad-cast over these western wilds, or any other wilds, it would be impossible to tell the vast amount of good that would have been done. And, indeed, this is one of the grand secrets of the success of our early Methodist preachers.

Well do I remember reading in early life Russell's Seven Sermons, Nelson's Journals, and such books as those, which would make me weep, and pray too. For more than fifty years I have firmly believed that it was a part and parcel of a Methodist preacher's most sacred duty to circulate good books wherever they go among the people. And I claim to have come as nigh my duty in this as any other, and perhaps more so. I have spread thousands of dollars' worth among the people; sometimes a thousand dollars' worth a year. But I fear a change for the worse has come over our Methodist preachers on this subject : many of them, since the country has grown up into improved life, and wealth abounds, feel themselves degraded in peddling books, as they call it, and want to roll this whole duty on to the *colporteurs*. But I believe, with our most excellent Discipline, that we should "be ashamed of nothing but sin." The religious press is destined, in the order of Providence, to give moral freedom to the perishing millions of earth. "My people," saith the Lord, "perish for lack of knowledge." Think of this, ye ministers of Jesus Christ; lay aside your pride, and call to your aid, in disseminating religious knowledge from the pulpit, religious books, and God will own the effort, and prosper the work of your hands everywhere.

I suppose I was the first preacher who ever held a camp-meeting in the military tract, in what is now called Pike, Adams, Schuyler, and Hancock Counties. We had a camp-meeting in Pike County in 1827. We had but one tent on the ground, and that was called the "Preachers' Tent." The people rolled on to the ground in their waggons; brought their victuals, and ate at the waggons. We held this meeting several days and nights in this way, and we had a prosperous meeting. We held one in Schuyler County the same season, and many souls were blessed.

Our Pottawattomie Mission was located on Fox River. Jesse Walker was missionary, and I was appointed superintendent; and it belonged to the Illinois District. During the two years that I superintended this mission I received not one cent from the missionary funds. We had near one hundred miles of unbroken wilderness country to pass through to get to this mission. I had to pack provisions for myself and horse to and from the mission. There being no roads, I had to hire my pilot, and camp out

Having made preparations for the journey, and an appointment to meet the chiefs of the nation at the mission, I started from the Peoria quarterly meeting with my pilot and several volunteers for the mission. We shaped our course from point to point of timber. Late in the evening we struck the timber of the Illinois Vermilion, and, finding plenty of water, we camped, struck fire, cooked, and took supper and dinner all under one. We had prayer, fixed our blankets and overcoats, and laid us down, and slept soundly and sweetly till next morning. We rose early, took breakfast, fed our horses, and started on our way across the Illinois River, swimming our horses beside a canoe, and just at night reached the mission. We called the mission family together and preached to them. The next day the chiefs appeared; we smoked the pipe of friendship with them, and, through an interpreter, I made a speech to them, explaining our object in establishing a mission among them All the chiefs now shook hands with us, as their custom is, and gave us a very sociable talk, and all bid us a cordial welcome save one, who was strongly opposed to our coming among them. He did not wish to change their religion and their customs, nor to educate their children. I replied to him, and met all his objections. I tried to show them the benefits of civilization and the Christian religion. There was present a Chippewa chief, with his two daughters, at the mission. This chief made a flaming speech in favour of the mission, and in favour of our " Great Father," the President, and the American people He had fought under the American colours in the last war with England, and had his diploma from the President as a brave captain, and showed it with great exultation. His two daughters were dressed like the whites, and could read pretty well. When our " great talk " was over, I asked them the liberty to preach to them, which was granted I tried to explain to them the original state of man, the fall of man, and the redemption through Christ; the condition of salvation, namely, faith in Christ, and obedience to all the precepts of the Gospel, as revealed in the Holy Scriptures; and urged them to repent, and forsake all their sins, and come to Christ.

It was an awkward and slow way to preach, through an interpreter; but I succeeded much better than I anticipated. One Indian woman, who had obtained religion, as we believed, desired baptism, and the ordinance was administered to her. Several couples, from the scattering white people that hung around the mission, applied to be married.

After directing matters, according to my instructions as superintendent, we started for home After travelling near fifty miles, night came on at a point of timber called Crow Point, and there we camped. A dreadful storm of wind arose, which blew a severe gale; but Providence favoured us in withholding the rain, and we considered this a great blessing. The next day we reached the settlement, in health and safety.

We expended several thousand dollars of missionary money in improving these mission premises, and succeeded in civilizing and Christianizing a few of these Indians; but the whites kept constantly encroaching on them till they became restless, and, finally, the government bought them out. The mission premises, with a section of land, were reserved for one of the half breed, so that the Missionary Society lost all that they had expended. It is true, the chiefs of the nation gave Brother Walker a thousand dollars of their annuities, as a compensation for the improvements he had made with the missionary money; and this money properly belonged to the Missionary Society, but they never realized it; and the Indians moved, finally, west of the Mississippi. There is still a lingering, wasting remnant of that nation; they have a missionary among them, and a good many of them are pious Christians.

Before this mission was broken up, there appeared another of those wandering stars, or visionary preachers, by the name of Paine. He visited a camp-meeting held near Springfield. He had no proper credentials to preach, and yet he professed to be commissioned from heaven to convert the world, whites, Indians, and all. He wanted to preach at my camp-meeting, but I would not permit him to occupy the stand. He called off the loose crowd some distance into the woods, and gave us a terrible tongue-lashing, and then departed north to preach to the Indians. In the meantime the Black Hawk Indian war had broken out, and they were killing our people on the outskirts of the settlements fearfully. This Paine had gotten up somewhere this side of Chicago, and wanted to come down the country toward the old mission. He was admonished not to venture, and was assured the Indians would kill him; but he was so visionary that he said he was not afraid to go alone, right in among them; for the Lord would protect him, and the Indians would not hurt a hair of his head. He, in despite of every warning, started alone, through a long prairie. The Indians were waylaying the trail, and, as he drew near a point of timber, they shot and killed him, and then cut off his head; after scalping it, they placed it on a pole, and stuck the pole erect in the ground. They then took his horse and riding apparatus, clothes, &c. The next day, as a company of men passed, they saw Paine's head sticking on a pole, and his body greatly mangled by the wolves; and this was an end of his commission to convert the world, Indians and all. "As the fool dieth, so died he."

In the fall of 1827, September 20th, our Conference was holden in

Mount Carmel, and I was continued on the Illinois District, and the name of Mississippi Circuit changed to Apple Creek Circuit. At the Mount Carmel Conference we elected our delegates that sat in Pittsburgh, May 1st, 1828. This was our fifth delegated General Conference, and the first we ever had in the West, this side of the mountains.

In the month of April Brother Dew, Brother Thompson, and myself, met at St. Louis, to take passage on board a steamboat to the General Conference in Pittsburgh. We had never been on board a steamboat before, at least I never had. They were then a new thing among us. So we took passage on board the "Velocepede," Mr. Ray captain. Before we went aboard, Brothers Dew and Thompson, with the kindest feelings imaginable, thought it their duty to caution me to be very quiet; for these steamboat fellows, passengers and all, were desperadoes. They knew I was outspoken, loved everybody and feared nobody. They were afraid I would get into some difficulty with somebody. I thanked them very kindly for their special care over me. "But," said I, "brethren, take care of yourselves, I think I know how to behave myself, and make others behave themselves, if need be"

When we got aboard, we had a crowded cabin, a mixed multitude, some Deists, some Atheists, some Universalists; a great many profane swearers, drunkards, gamblers, fiddlers, and dancers. We dropped down to the barrack, below St. Louis, and there came aboard eight or ten United States officers, and we had a jolly set, I assure you. They drank, fiddled, danced, swore, played cards, men and women too. I walked about, said nothing, but plainly saw we were in a bad snap, but there was no way to help ourselves. Brother Thompson came to me and said, "Lord have mercy on me! what shall we do?"

"Go to your berth," said I, "and stay there quietly."

"No," said he; "I'll reprove them."

"Now, brother," said I, "do not cast your pearls before swine."

"Well," said he, "I won't stay in the cabin; I'll go on deck."

Up he started, and when he got there, behold, they were playing cards from one end of the deck to the other. Back he came and said, "What shall I do? I cannot stand it."

"Well," said I, "Brother Thompson, be quiet and behave yourself; you have no way to remedy your condition, unless you jump overboard and swim to shore."

So things went on several days and nights. At the mouth of the Ohio there came aboard a Captain Waters. He had a new fiddle and a pack of cards. He was a professed infidel. Card-playing was renewed all over the cabin. The captain of the boat was as fond of drinking and card-playing as any of them. There was a lieutenant of

the regular army on board, and although he was very wicked, yet he had been raised by religious parents. His wife, as he told me, was a good Christian. In walking the guard this lieutenant, whose name was Barker, and myself fell into conversation, and, being by ourselves, I took occasion to remonstrate with him on the subject of his profanity. He readily admitted it was wrong, and said, "I have been better taught. But O," said he, "the demoralizing life of a soldier!"

There was also a Major Biddle on board, a professed infidel, but gentlemanly in his manners; he afterward fell in a duel, in or near St. Louis. I got a chance to talk to him in private, and alone; I remonstrated against his profanity; he agreed with me in all I said. In this way, I got to talk to many of them, and they mostly ceased to swear profanely in my presence. Presently, they gathered around the table, and commenced playing cards. I walked carelessly up, and looked on. Lieutenant Barker and Captain Waters looked up at me; I knew they felt reproved. Said one of them to me, "We are not blacklegs; we are not playing for money, but just to kill time." I affected to be profoundly ignorant of what they were doing, and asked them what those little spotted things were. Mr. Barker said,—

"Sit down here, and I will show you what we are doing, and how we do it."

"No, no," said I, "my friends; I am afraid it is all wrong."

They insisted there was no harm in it at all.

"Well," said I, "gentlemen, if you are just playing for fun, or to kill time, would it not be much better to drop all such foolishness, and let us talk on some topic to inform each other? Then we could all be edified. As it is, a few of you enjoy all the pleasure, if, indeed, there is any in it; while the rest of us, who have no taste for such amusements, are not at all benefitted Come, lay aside those little spotted papers, that are only calculated to please children of a larger size, and let us talk on History, Philosophy, or Astronomy; then we can all enjoy it, and be greatly benefitted."

Captain Waters said, "Sir, if you will debate with me on the Christian religion, we will quit all our cards, fiddles, and dances."

"I will do it with pleasure, captain," said I. "I have only one objection to debate with you. You are in the habit, I see, of swearing profanely, and using oaths, and I can't swear back at you; and I fear, a debate, mixed up with profane oaths, would be unprofitable."

"Well, sir," said he, "if you will debate with me on that subject, I will pledge you my word and honour that I will not swear a single oath."

"Very well, sir," said I; "on that condition, I will debate with you." By this time there were gathered around us a large crowd.

"Well," said Lieutenant Barker, "take notice of the terms on which this debate is to be conducted." Said he, "Now, gentlemen, draw near, and take your seats, and listen to the arguments; and by the consent of the two belligerent gentlemen, I will keep order."

We both agreed to his proposition. The captain opened the discussion by a great flourish of trumpets, expressing his great happiness at having one more opportunity of vindicating the religion of reason and nature, in opposition to the religion of a bastard. To all of these flourishes, I simply replied, that the Christian religion was of age, and could speak for itself; and that I felt proud of an opportunity to show that infidelity was born out of holy wedlock; and, therefore, in the strictest sense, was a bastard; and that I thought it ill became the advocate of a notorious illegitimate to heap any reproaches on Christ. These exordiums had one good effect; they fixed and riveted the attention of almost all the passengers, the captain of the boat, ladies and all. My opponent then proceeded to lay down his premises, and draw his conclusions. When his twenty minutes expired, I replied, and in my reply quoted a passage of Scripture.

"Hold, sir," said my opponent, "I don't allow a book of fables and lies to be brought in; nothing shall be admitted here but honourable testimony."

"Very well, sir," said I; "the Bible shall be dispensed with altogether as evidence; and then I feel confident I can overturn your system on testimony drawn from the book of nature;" and proceeded in the argument.

In his second replication he quoted Tom Paine as evidence.

"Hold, sir," said I; "such a degraded witness as Tom Paine can't be admitted as testimony in this debate."

My opponent flew into a violent passion, and swore profanely, that God Almighty never made a purer and more honourable man than Tom Paine. As he belched forth these horrid oaths, I took him by the chin with my hand, and moved his jaws together, and made his teeth rattle together at a mighty rate. He rose to his feet, so did I. He drew his fist, and swore he would smite me to the floor. Lieutenant Barker sprang in between us, saying,—

"Cartwright, stand back; you can beat him in argument, and I can whip him; and, if there is any fighting to be done, I am his man, from the point of a needle to the mouth of a cannon, for he is no gentleman, as he pledged his word and honour that he would not swear; and he has broken his word, and forfeited his honour."

Well, I had then to fly in between them, to prevent a bloody fight; for they both drew deadly weapons. Finally, this ended the argument. My valorous captain made concessions, and all became pacified. From this out, Barker was my fast friend, and would have fought for me at any time; and my infidel, Captain Waters, became very friendly to me; and when we landed in the night at Louisville, he insisted that I should go home with him and partake of his very best hospitalities.

But, to return a little to my narrative, the whole company that witnessed the encounter with my infidel captain were interested in my favour. Our boat was old and crazy, and we made but little speed; consequently, we were detained on the river over Sunday. Early on Sabbath morning, the passengers formed themselves into a kind of committee of the whole, and appointed a special committee to wait on me, and invite me to preach to them that day on the boat. Lieutenant Barker was the committee. He came to me, and presented the request. I said,—

"Lieutenant, I never travelled on a steamboat before, and it will be a very awkward affair for me to preach on the boat; and, besides, I don't know that the captain would like such an arrangement: and the passengers will drink, and perhaps gamble, and be disorderly; and every man on a steamboat is a free man, and will do pretty much as he pleases, and will not be reproved."

Said the lieutenant, "I have consulted the captain of the boat, and he is willing, and pledges himself to keep good order. And now, sir," said he, "we have annoyed you and your fellow-clergymen all the week, and I pledge you my word, all shall be orderly, and you shall enjoy your religious privileges on Sunday undisturbed, and you must preach to us. We need it, and the company will not be satisfied if you don't comply."

I gave my consent, and we fixed on the following times for three sermons,—one immediately after the table was cleared off after breakfast, one after dinner, and one after supper. I led the way, taking the morning hour. The cabin was seated in good order, the deck passengers were invited down. We had a very orderly, well-behaved congregation. Brother Dew preached in the afternoon, and Brother Thompson at night, and I rarely ever spent a more orderly Sabbath anywhere within the walls of a church. From this out we had no more drunkenness, profane swearing, or card-playing. What good was done, if any, the judgment-day will alone declare. I cannot close this sketch and do justice to my feelings without saying a few things more.

After the adjournment of the General Conference, on our return trip home, the river had fallen very much. We could not pass over the falls, and the canal was not finished around them. Of course we had to land and reship at the foot of the falls. The "Maryland," a good steamboat, lay here waiting for passengers. When I entered this boat, almost the first man I met was Lieutenant Barker, who, when he recognised me, sprang forward and seized me by the hand, and said, " O, is this Mr Cartwright ? " and really seemed as glad to see me as if I had been his own brother. He had been East, and was returning with his wife to some of the Western military posts.

" Now, sir," said he, " I told you I had a good little Christian woman for my wife. She is in the ladies' cabin. I have talked to her of you a thousand times. Come, you must go right in with me, and I will introduce her to you. I know she will be glad to see and form an acquaintance with you."

I went, and was introduced to this, as I believe, Christian lady. We had a number of preachers on board, returning delegates from the General Conference, and we had preaching almost every day and night from that to St. Louis ; for we had almost entire command of the boat.

CHAPTER XX.

GENERAL CONFERENCE OF 1828.

In the fall of 1828 our Conference sat in Madison, Indiana, October 9th. This was the only Annual Conference that I ever missed attending in fifty years. My wife was sorely afflicted, and was supposed to be at the gates of death, so that I did not think it my duty to leave her ; though a kind Providence spared her to me a little longer, and she still lives. I was re-appointed to the Illinois District. The Oneida Annual Conference was formed at the General Conference in May, 1828. This made nine Annual Conferences east, and eight west of the mountains. They had a membership in the nine Eastern Conferences of 270,210. In the East there were of travelling preachers 984. We had in the West, of travelling preachers, 519. Of members the West had 150,894. Total number of members, 421,104 ; of travelling preachers, 1,503.

The New Hampshire and Vermont Conference was formed in the interim, or between the General Conferences of 1828 and 1832. It will also be remembered that Canada had existed as a separate Annual Conference, and was in union, as a Conference, with the Methodist Episcopal Church in these United States, and was regularly supplied with American preachers, and superintended by our American bishops. Being under the British laws, that established the Catholic Church in Lower Canada, and the Church of England in Upper Canada, our people, members and preachers, laboured under many civil disabilities. They thought, under all the circumstances, that it would be better to be separated from the Methodist Episcopal Church in these United States, and organized into a distinct Methodist Episcopal Church in Canada, elect from among themselves a bishop, that should be resident among them; and thereby avoid many of those disabilities that had fallen so heavily upon them, in consequence of being under the jurisdiction of American bishops. Accordingly, they petitioned the General Conference of 1828, at Pittsburgh, to set them off as a separate and distinct Church; but, after careful consideration and investigation, the General Conference, with great unanimity, resolved, that they were not vested with any constitutional power to divide the Methodist Episcopal Church; and, therefore, declined granting them their request; but said, if they really thought their civil disabilities were a burden too grievous to be borne, they would throw no difficulties in their way, but leave them to make their own choice, whether they would remain as an integral part of the Methodist Episcopal Church in the United States, or organize themselves into a separate Church. They chose the latter first, and then merged themselves into the great Wesleyan Connexion of England.

There is one circumstance that befell me at the General Conference at Pittsburgh in 1828, that I wish briefly to state; but, for the sake of honourable feelings, I must be sparing of names. Brother Waterman, who was considerably radicalized, had the duty assigned him of billeting out the preachers among the families that had agreed to take care of them during the General Conference. When I arrived in Pittsburgh I went to know where I was to stay, and he gave me a ticket to a gentleman's house in Alleghany Town. He was nominally a ruffle-shirted Methodist; he was rich, and abounded in almost all the good things of this world. His lady was a very genteel, fine, fashionable woman, but a stiff-starched Presbyterian; so I was told. One of the bishops was stationed here, and two D.D.'s, both preachers. I, of course, very confidently made my way to this gentleman's house. As I approached the dwelling, I cast my eye upward, and through a window I saw the bishop and another preacher sitting in an upper room. When I reached the portico, the gentleman met me at the entrance. Addressing him, I said,—

" Does Colonel —— live here ? "

" Yes, sir."

" Brother Waterman informed me, as one of the delegates to the General Conference, that I was to board with you during the Conference· my name is Peter Cartwright; I hail from Illinois "

" Yes, sir," said he, seriously; " we had intended to take four of the preachers, but my wife thinks she can't take but two ; and Bishop —— and Dr. —— are here already, and we can't accommodate you."

I felt a little curious; but so foolish was I, that I hastily concluded that the thing was a trick, played off to plague me. He never invited me in.

". Well, said I, " I must see the bishop anyhow, and I reckon you'll let me stay;" so in I went. After entering,—

"Please, sir," said I, "direct me to the bishop's room." He did so, and up I went, and ushered myself into his magisterial presence. After the accustomed salutations, which I thought came from the bishop with unusual coolness, I said to him,—

"And is it so that I am not to stay here, after Brother Waterman has sent me?"

"Too true, too true," said he; "the lady of the house is not a Methodist, and says she is not willing to take but two."

The reader may be sure I began to feel bad at a mighty rate, the bishop seated himself, and began to write, looking dry, sour, and cool, but paid no further attention to me. I took my hat, and started down stairs in a mighty hurry, gathered my saddle-bags, and started off. Just as I mounted the steps leaving his ornamented lot, the landlord hailed me, and requested me to stop. He came near, and in a cold, stiff manner informed me that his wife had concluded that I might stay, and invited me to return.

"No, sir," said I, "it is too late; I can't, under the circumstances, return; I have money enough to pay my way; and I had rather pay my way than to be treated as I have been."

"But," said the gentleman, "you must not leave my house in this way; it will be a great reproach to me and my family."

"Yes, sir," said I, "you ought to have thought of that sooner."

"Well," he asked, "where are you going?"

"To a tavern," said I, "if I can find an orderly one."

So on I went. After proceeding some distance I saw a tavern sign; and after looking around a little, I said to the tavern-keeper,—

"Can I board with you for a month, and be accommodated with a private room?"

He said I could.

"Do you keep an orderly house, or shall I be annoyed by drunkards and gamblers?"

"My house, sir," said he, "is kept orderly; you shall not be annoyed by any rude company whatever. Be seated, sir," said he; "you shall have a room fitted up directly. I judge," said he, "you are one of the delegates to the General Conference."

"Yes, sir, I am," was my reply.

Said he, "Mr. Waterman was to have sent me two preachers, but none have come, unless you are one assigned me."

"No, sir, I am not sent; I come on my own responsibility."

Said he, "I am a member of no Church, but my wife is a Methodist, and she will be glad for you to stay with us."

I soon began to feel that I had got into another atmosphere. I fared well, was treated kindly, and had nothing to pay.

Shortly after I had settled down, the landlord of my first place sought me out, and entreated me to return to his house. He said his wife had fitted up a comfortable room, and desired me to return.

"No, sir," said I, "I shall not do it; I am not dependent on you or yours at all, and I am well provided for here, and I mean to stay."

He went home, and sent —————— to invite me back again. The messenger said I ought to return; that the family were very much mortified at the circumstance that had taken place. I told him that I felt under no obligations to him or them; that they had treated me very cavalierly, and I should abide my determination not to return; but by invitation I visited them, and stayed with them some; but I think I effectually humbled their pride for once.

I was at this first place several evenings; but everything seemed to come wrong. The bishop seemed as cold as an icicle, and as stiff in his manners as if he had been the autocrat of all the Russias. I felt that there was not the least congeniality in them, and that I was alone in such company. The time of evening devotions came on. The master of ceremonies asked me to lead the devotions; but the moment I was requested to do so, it appeared to me that thick darkness fell on me; and if ever I felt the power of the devil physically and mentally, it was just then. I turned almost blind, literally blind, and the great drops of sweat rolled off my face. I was so blind I feared I could not see to read a chapter; hence I turned to the first Psalm, which I could and had repeated often by memory; but I found my memory as defective as my sight, and surely, memory, sight, and all gone, I made a very stammering out at repeating the first Psalm; but I stammered over it in some sort. My voice was usually clear in those days, and I could sing tolerably well. I rose and commenced singing a verse of one of our familiar hymns, but not a soul in the crowd, by name or nature, would sing with me. I stopped short, and kneeled down to pray, but in all my life I was never in a worse plight to pray but once, and that was the first time my leader called on me to pray in public after I had professed religion. I then thought my head was as large as a house, and I now thought I had no head at all. It seemed to me that the devil was veritably present, and all around, and in everybody and everything. I stammered over a few incoherent sentences, and closed by saying, "Amen." And you may rely on it, while in this wretched state of feeling, and before I was delivered from the hour and power of temptation, I felt as though the devil reigned triumphant, and had a bill of sale of us all. The next day, when the General Conference adjourned, at noon, the presiding bishop called on me to close by prayer. O, how awful I felt! I fell on my knees, and uttered only a few words, and said, "Amen," before one half of the preachers had fairly got on their knees. They looked round and scuffled up, and looked queer; and I assure you I have no language at my command by which I could describe my feelings, for I felt "unutterable woe." This state of bad feelings lasted during a whole week.

One night I heard of a prayer-meeting near by where I lodged. I determined to go; and it pleased God that night to roll back the clouds that had covered me in such thick darkness. I was very happy, and the next evening hastened to the house where I had made such a dreadful out in reading, singing, and praying. It so happened that when the family got ready for prayer, and sent up for the preachers to come down, they were all very much engaged in finishing an interesting report. The bishop said he could not go, and that he wished some one would go and hold prayer with the family, and let the rest stay. I spoke up and said, "Let me go; for I feel so much better than I did when I tried to pray with them before, I want to go and try again." He bade me go. I went, took the book, read a chapter readily, sung a hymn clearly, knelt and prayed with more than my accustomed liberty, and got happy. The family wept. We talked, wept, and sung together, and I felt as independent of the devil and a stiff bishop as if there were no such beings in the world.

When the General Conference adjourned, and I had started for the steamboat, the landlady that I thought was so stiff, formal, and proud, followed me to the boat, and sent by me a present of a silk dress to my wife. Why this dispensation of darkness should be permitted to fall upon me I cannot tell, but there is no doubt on my mind there was a special providence in it, if I only understood the matter; but I leave all to the revelations of the great day of judgment. "The Lord reigneth."

At our Conference, in the fall of 1828, Galena Charge was added to the Illinois District; so that my District reached nearly from the mouth of the Ohio River to Galena, the extreme northwest corner of the State, altogether six hundred miles long. This was a tremendous field of travel and labour. Around this District I had to travel four times in the year, and I had many rapid streams to cross, mostly without bridges or ferry-boats. Many of these streams, when they were swollen, and I had to cross them to get to my quarterly meetings, I would strike for some point of timber, and traverse up and down the stream until I could find a drift or a tree fallen across. I would then dismount, strip myself and horse, carry my clothes and riding apparatus across on the fallen tree or drift, and then return and mount my horse, plunge in and swim over, dress, saddle my horse, and go on my way, from point to point of timber, without roads. Often night would overtake me in some lonesome, solitary grove. I would hunt out some suitable place, strike fire,—for I always went prepared with flint, steel, and spunk,—make as good a fire as circumstances called for, tie up or hopple out my horse, and there spend the night. Sometimes, in travelling from point to point of timber, darkness would come upon me before I could reach, by miles, the woods; and it being so dark that I could not see the trees I was aiming for, I would dismount and hold my horse by the bridle till returning light, then mount my horse, and pursue my journey.

The northern part of my District was newly settled; and where it was settled at all, a few scattered cabins, with families in them, were all that could be looked for or expected in a vast region of the north end of my District; and I assure my readers that when I came upon one of these tenanted cabins, in those long and lonesome trips, it was a great treat, and I have felt as truly thankful to God to take shelter in one of those little shanties and get the privilege of a night's lodging, as I have, under other circumstances, been when I have lodged in a fine house, with all the comforts of life around me. I recollect, in one of my northern trips, I had a very large and uninhabited prairie to cross; about midway across the prairie, twenty miles from any house, I came to a deep and turbid stream; twenty miles beyond was the point I was aiming for that day. The stream looked ugly and forbidding. I was mounted on a fine large horse, and I knew him to be an excellent swimmer I hesitated for a moment. To retrace my steps I could not consent; and if I advanced, a swim, on my horse, was to be performed, no timber being in sight. I got down, readjusted my saddle, girded it tolerably tight, tied my overcoat on behind, put my watch and pocket papers in my saddle-bags, and then tied them around my neck, letting the ends rest on my shoulders, and said, " Now, Buck," (that was the name of my horse,) " carry me safe to the other bank." In we went; he swam over easily, and rose on the opposite bank safely. I readjusted my affairs, and went on my way rejoicing, and was not wet but a trifle. Three times this day I swam my horse across swollen streams, and made the cabin I was aiming for. Here lived a kind Methodist family, who gave me a hearty welcome; gave me good meat and bread, and a strong cup of coffee; and I was much happier than many of the kings of the earth. I arrived safe at my quarterly meeting. All the surrounding citizens had turned out, twenty-seven in number.

We had five conversions; seven joined the Church; and we were nearly all happy together.

In one of these northern trips I was earnestly solicited to cross the Mississippi and preach to the few new settlers near what is now called Burlington City, on the west of the Father of Waters. My son-in-law, William D R Trotter, perhaps was the first travelling preacher who broke ground in the Iowa State, and I followed a short time afterward. I had sent them an appointment to hold a two days' meeting, just back of where Burlington City stands. Then there were only a few cabins in the place; now it is a growing city, containing, perhaps, ten thousand souls.

When I went to my appointment, although there was but a scattered population, yet when they came out to meeting, the cabins were so small that there was not one in the whole settlement which would hold the people. We repaired to the grove, and hastily prepared seats. Years before this time an old tree had fallen down across a small sapling and bent it near the earth. The sapling was not killed, and the top of it shot up straight beside the tree that fallen on it, and it had grown for years in this condition. The old tree had been cut off, and they scalped the bark off of that part of the sapling that lay parallel with the ground. They drove a stake down, and nailed a board to it and the top of the sapling that grew erect, and this was my band-board, and I stood on that part of the sapling that lay near and level with the ground. This was my pulpit, from which I declared the unsearchable riches of the Gospel of Jesus Christ; and we had a good meeting.

On the 23d of August, 1828, one of our beloved bishops, Enoch George, fell a victim to death. He had been an itinerant preacher thirty-eight years, and had honourably discharged the duties of a bishop in the Methodist Episcopal Church for twelve years. One has said of him, "Bishop George was a man of deep piety, of great simplicity of manners, a very pathetic, powerful, and successful preacher; greatly beloved in life, and very extensively lamented in death."

The Illinois Conference met this fall (September 18th, 1829) at Edwardsville. Our country was rapidly filling up, our work constantly enlarging, and Bishop Roberts, at Conference in Vincennes, September 30th, 1830, found it necessary to divide the Circuits, and multiply the presiding-elder Districts. The following new Districts were formed in the bounds of the Illinois Conference, namely: the Illinois District was divided into two: the Kaskaskia and Sangamon Districts. The Kaskaskia District embraced the following appointments: Kaskaskia, Brownsville, Jonesborough, Golconda, Mount Vernon, Shoal Creek, and Shelbyville,—in all seven. The Sangamon

District embraced the following appointments : Lebanon, Apple Creek, Atlas, Spoon River, Sangamon, Salt Creek, Peoria, Fox River Mission, and Galena Mission,—nine.　Samuel H. Thompson was appointed to the Kaskaskia District, and I was appointed to the Sangamon District. This District still covered a large field of labour, embracing from opposite St. Louis to the northern limits of the State.

Within the bounds of this District there lived a local preacher, who was a small, very easy, good-natured, pleasant man ; he was believed to be also a very pious man, and a good and useful preacher.　His wife was directly the reverse of almost everything that was good, saving it was believed she was virtuous.　She was high-tempered, overbearing, quarrelsome, and a violent opposer of religion.　She would not fix her husband's clothes to go out to preach, and was un-willing he should ask a blessing at the table, or pray in the family. And when he would attempt to pray, she would not conform, but tear around and make all the noise and disturbance in her power.　She would turn the chairs over while he was reading, singing, or praying ; and if she could not stop him any other way, she would catch a cat and throw it in his face while he was kneeling and trying to pray. Poor little man ! surely he was tormented almost to desperation.　He had invited several preachers home with him to talk to her, and see if they could not moderate her ; but all to no purpose ; she would curse them to their face, and rage like a demon.　He had insisted on my going home with him several times, but I frankly confess I was afraid to trust myself.　I pitied him from my very heart, and so did every-body else that was acquainted with his situation.　But at length I yielded to his importunities, and went home with him one evening, intending to stay all night.　After we arrived, I saw in a minute that she was mad, and the devil was in her as large as an alligator ; and I fixed my purpose, and determined on my course.　After supper he said to her very kindly, " Come, wife, stop your little affairs, and let us have prayer."　That moment she boiled over, and said, " I will have none of your praying about me."　I spoke to her mildly, and expostulated with her, and tried to reason ; but no, the further I went, the more wrathful she became, and she cursed me most bitterly.　I then put on a stern countenance, and said to her, " Madam, if you were a wife of mine, I would break you of your bad ways, or I would break your neck."

"The devil you would ! " said she.　" Yes, you are a pretty Christian, ain't you ? "　And then such a volley of curses as she poured on me, was almost beyond human endurance.

"Be still," said I ; " we must and will have prayer."　But she declared we should not.

"Now," said I to her, "if you do not be still, and behave yourself, I'll put you out of doors." At this she clinched her fist, and swore she was one half alligator, and the other half snapping-turtle, and that it would take a better man than I was to put her out. It was a small cabin we were in, and we were not far from the door, which was then standing open. I caught her by the arm, and, swinging her round in a circle, brought her right up to the door, and shoved her out. She jumped up, tore her hair, foamed; and such swearing as she uttered was seldom equalled, and never surpassed. The door, or shutter of 'the door, was very strongly made, to keep out hostile Indians. I shut it tight, barred it, and went to prayer, and I prayed as best I could, but I have no language at my command to describe my feelings; at the same time, I was determined to conquer, or die in the attempt. While she was raging and foaming in the yard and around the cabin, I started a spiritual song, and sung loud, to drown her voice as much as possible. The five or six little children ran and squatted about and crawled under the beds. Poor things! they were scared almost to death.

I sang on, and she roared and thundered on outside, till she became perfectly exhausted, and panted for breath. At length, when she had spent her force, she became calm and still, and then knocked at the door, saying, "Mr Cartwright, please let me in."

"Will you behave yourself, if I let you in?" said I.

"O yes," said she, "I will;" and throwing myself on my guard, and perfectly self-possessed, I opened the door, took her by the hand, led her in, and seated her near the fireplace. She had roared and foamed till she was in a high perspiration, and looked pale as death After she took her seat, "O," said she, "what a fool I am!"

"Yes," said I, "about one of the biggest fools I ever saw in all my life. And now," said I, "you have to repent for all this, or you must go to the devil at last." She was silent. Said I, "Children, come out here; your mother won't hurt you now," and, turning to her husband, said, "Brother C., let us pray again." We kneeled down, and both prayed. She was as quiet as a lamb.

And now, gentle reader, although this was one of the hardest cases I ever saw on this earth, I must record it to the glory of Divine grace, I lived to see, in less than six months after this frolic with the devil, this woman soundly converted to God; and if there was ever a changed mortal for the better, it was this said woman. Her children, as they grew up, all, I believe, obtained religion, and the family became a religious, happy family, and she was as bold in the cause of God as she had been in the cause of the wicked one.

When I came to the County of Sangamon in 1824, and rode the

Sangamon Circuit in 1825–26, Springfield, our present seat of government for the State, was a very small village.   Even the county seat
was not located at it, and for several years there was no regular
society of any denomination organized there, save the Methodist. We
had a respectable society in point of numbers and religious moral
character, but they were generally very poor.   There was no meeting-
house or church in the place.   We preached in private houses almost
altogether for several years.   The first Presbyterian minister who
came to the town, that I have any recollection of, was by the name of
———.   He was a very well educated man, and had regularly studied
theology in some of the Eastern States, where they manufacture young
preachers like they do lettuce in hot-houses. He brought with him a
number of old manuscript sermons, and read them to the people; but
as to common sense, he had very little, and he was almost totally
ignorant of the manners and usages of the world, especially this new
Western world; yet he came here to evangelize and Christianize us
poor heathen.   He did not meet with much encouragement; but he
certainly was a pious, good man, much devoted to prayer.   He came
to my appointments, and we became acquainted.   He, in part,
travelled with me round my Circuit, anxious to get acquainted with
the people, and preach to them.   He soon saw and felt that he had
no adaptation to the country or people.   I told him he must quit
reading his old manuscript sermons, and learn to speak extempora-
neously; that the Western people were born and reared in hard times,
and were an out-spoken and off-hand people; that if he did not
adopt this manner of preaching, the Methodists would set the whole
Western world on fire before he would light his match. He tried it a
while, but became discouraged, and left for parts unknown.

Shortly after this others came in, but still there was no church in
the town of Springfield to worship in for any denomination.   The
Methodists were poor, the Presbyterians few, and not very wealthy.
At length the citizens put up a small school-house, which was appropriated to religious purposes on the Sabbath; but it was often attended
with difficulty, as different ministers of different denominations would
make their appointments in this little school-house, and their appointments would often come together and clash.   This was attended with
no good results, and at length a proposition was made for the Methodists and Presbyterians to unite and build a church between them,
and define each denomination's time of occupancy and legal rights in
the church, till such time as one or the other could be able to build
separately, and then sell out to the other denomination.   A subscription was set on foot, and five or six hundred dollars subscribed.

Thinking all was right, I left to fill my appointments; but when the deed to this property was to be made, it was settled on Presbyterian trustees, and the Methodists only occupied it by grace. There was a very honest old gentleman, who was an intelligent lawyer, that had not subscribed anything, but intended to; but he wanted equal rights and privileges secured to the Methodists, though he himself was a Universalist. He saw how things were driving, and sent for me. I went, and, on examination, found that the agreement between the two denominations was violated in the deed. I expostulated with them, but all in vain; they persisted. I then went, and immediately drew up a subscription to build a Methodist church, and subscribed seventy-five dollars. My old honest lawyer told me he would either give two lots in the new town, above where the most of the town then was, or he would give fifty dollars. I took the two lots, on which the Methodist church now stands.

The Presbyterians went on and built the little brick shanty that stands near where the first Presbyterian church now stands; and in one day I obtained about six hundred dollars, and the Methodists built their old frame meeting-house that stood as a monument of their covetousness for many years, and, indeed, till lately, when they saw their folly, and now have a fine church. But still they ought to have at least two more good churches in a city containing ten thousand souls, and constantly increasing in population, and which, undoubtedly, is destined to become a large inland city, and, from its central position and railroad facilities, will, in a very few years, contain fifty thousand inhabitants.

The securing those two lots at an early day in Springfield clearly shows the sound policy of taking early measures in every new country, city, town, village, and prospectively strong settlement, to secure lots for churches and parsonages when they can be obtained at a nominal price, and often as a donation. Our people and preachers are often too negligent in this very thing. They wait till lots rise in value, and sometimes have to give for a suitable one, on which to build a church or parsonage, as much as would erect a decent house in which to worship God. The two lots above named were, by their owner, valued at fifty dollars. They would now sell, I suppose, for seven or eight thousand dollars. They will soon be in the heart of the city, and are as beautiful lots, for church purposes, as are to be found in the city.

A few years ago our beloved Bishop Janes, in a visit to Springfield, saw clearly its rapid growth, and the slowness of the members of the Church in that place in regard to church extensions, and he advised, and organized, through the Mission Committee, the establishment of a mission in Springfield. But such was the short-sighted policy of many of the members of the Church belonging to the old charge, that they directly and indirectly opposed the establishment of this mission.

But, through the strong and persevering efforts of the missionaries and the superintendent of the mission, we succeeded in procuring a lot, and erecting a neat little mission church, at a cost of something like twenty-seven hundred dollars.

When the church was finished, it was in debt some four hundred dollars, and instead of the members of the old charge, and the mission charge, making an effort to pay this indebtedness, they suffered the church to be sold for less than three hundred dollars; and even the members of the old charge devised a plan to buy it in, and diverted it from its original purpose of a church, to an academy, for the benefit of the old charge; and, consequently, our mission was blown out, our labour, for from two to four years, lost, and, in open violation of the provisions of the Discipline of the Church, the mission property was converted from church to academical purposes; and a house and lot, that had cost near three thousand dollars, was thus sacrificed for a debt of less than three hundred dollars. This very transaction will stand out to future generations as evidence of the folly and stupidity of the members of the Methodist Church in Springfield, and will bar our approach to the citizens for years to come, when we desire to solicit aid to erect houses of worship in our metropolis.

Somewhere about this time, in 1829–30, the celebrated camp-meeting took place in Sangamon County and Circuit; and, as I suppose, out of incidents that then occurred was concocted that wonderful story about my fight with Mike Fink, which has no foundation in fact. We had this year two fine camp-meetings on the same ground, a few weeks apart · at the first, it was thought, over one hundred professed religion, and most of them joined the Methodist Church. At the second camp-meeting, over seventy joined the Church. Our encampment was large, and well seated, and we erected a large shed, that would, it was supposed, shelter a thousand people.

. While I was on the Sangamon District, I rode one day into Springfield, on some little business. My horse had been an excellent racking pony, but now had the stiff complaint. I called a few minutes in a store, to get some little articles; I saw in the store two young men and a young lady; they were strangers, and we had no introduction whatever; they passed out, and off. After I had transacted my little business in the store, I mounted my stiff pony, and started for home. After riding nearly two miles, I discovered ahead of me a light, two-horse waggon, with a good span of horses hitched to the waggon; and although it was covered, yet the cover was rolled up. It was warm weather, and I saw in the waggon those two young men and the young lady that I had seen in the store. As I drew near them, they began to sing one of our camp-meeting songs, and they appeared to sing with great animation. Presently the young lady began to shout, and said, "Glory to God! Glory to God!" The driver cried out, "Amen! Glory to God!"

My first impressions were, that they had been across the Sangamon River to a camp-meeting that I knew was in progress there, and had obtained religion, and were happy. As I drew a little nearer, the young lady began to sing and shout again. The young man who was not driving fell down, and cried aloud for mercy; the other two, shouting at the top of their voices, cried out, "Glory to God! another sinner's down." Then they fell to exhorting the young man that was down, saying, "Pray on, brother; pray on, brother; you will soon get religion." Presently up jumped the young man that was down, and shouted aloud, saying, "God has blessed my soul. Hallelujah! hallelujah! Glory to God!"

Thinking all was right, I felt like riding up, and joining in the songs of triumph and shouts of joy that rose from these three happy persons; but as I neared the waggon, I saw some glances of their eyes at each other, and at me, that created a suspicion in my mind that all was not right; and the thought occurred to me that they suspected or knew me to be a preacher, and that they were carrying on in this way to make a mock of sacred things, and to fool me I checked my horse, and fell back, and rode slowly, hoping they would pass on, and that I should not be annoyed by them any more; but when I checked my horse and went slow, they checked up and went slow too, and the driver changed with the other young man; then they began again to sing and shout at a mighty rate, and down fell the first driver, and up went a new shout of "Glory to God! another sinner's down. Pray on, brother; pray on, brother; the Lord will bless you." Presently up sprang the driver, saying, "Glory to God! He has blessed me." And both the others shouted, and said, "Another sinner's converted, another sinner's converted. Hallelujah! Glory to God!" A rush of indignant feeling came all over me, and I thought I would ride up and horsewhip both of these young men, and if the woman had not been in company, I think I should have done so; but I forbore. It was a vexatious encounter: if my horse had been fleet, as in former days, I could have rode right off, and left them in their glory; but he was stiff, and when I would fall back and go slow, they would check up; and when I would spur my stiff pony, and try to get ahead of them, they would crack the whip and keep ahead of me; and thus they tormented me before, as I thought, my time, and kept up a continual roar of "Another sinner's down! Another soul's converted! Glory to God! Pray on, brother! Hallelujah! hallelujah! Glory to God!" till I thought it was more than any good preacher ought to bear.

It would be hard for me to describe my feelings just about this time. It seemed to me that I was delivered over to be tormented by the devil and his imps. Just at this moment I thought of a desperate mudhole about a quarter of a mile ahead; it was a long one, and dreadful deep mud, and many waggons had stuck in it, and had to be prised out. Near the centre of this mudhole there was a place of mud deeper than anywhere else. On the right side stood a stump about two feet high; all the teams had to be driven as close to this stump as possible to avoid a deep rut on the left, where many waggons had stuck; I knew there was a small bridle way that wound round through the brush to avoid the mud; and it occurred to me that when we came near this muddy place, I would take the bridle way, and put my horse at the top of his speed, and by this means get away from these wretched tormentors, as I knew they could not go fast through this long reach of mud. When we came to the commencement of the mud, I took the bridle path, and put spurs and whip to my horse. Seeing I was rapidly leaving them in the rear, the driver cracked his whip, and put his horses at almost full speed; and such was their anxiety to keep up with me, to carry out their sport, that when they came to this bad place, they never saw the stump on the right. The fore wheel of the waggon struck centrally on the stump, and as the wheel mounted the stump, over went the waggon. Fearing it would turn entirely over and catch them under, the two young men took a leap into the mud, and when they lighted they sunk up to the middle. The young lady was dressed in white, and as the waggon went over, she sprang as far as she could, and lighted on all fours; her hands sunk into the mud up to her armpits, her mouth and the whole of her face immersed in the muddy water, and she certainly would have strangled if the young men had not relieved her. As they helped her up and out, I had wheeled my horse to see the fun. I rode up to the edge of the mud, stopped my horse, reared in my stirrups, and shouted at the top of my voice,—

"Glory to God! Glory to God! Hallelujah! another sinner's down! Glory to God! Hallelujah! Glory! Hallelujah!"

If ever mortals felt mean, these youngsters did; and well they might; for they had carried on all this sport to make light of religion, and to insult a minister, a total stranger to them. But they contemned religion, and hated the Methodists, especially Methodist preachers.

When I became tired of shouting over them, I said to them,—

" Now, you poor, dirty, mean sinners, take this as a just judgment of God upon you for your meanness, and repent of your dreadful wickedness; and let this be the last time that you attempt to insult a preacher; for if you repeat your abominable sport and persecutions, the next time God will serve you worse, and the devil will get you."

They felt so badly that they never uttered one word of reply. Now I was very glad that I did not horsewhip them, as I felt like doing; but that God had avenged His own cause, and defended His own honour, without my doing it with carnal weapons; and I may here be permitted to say, at one of those prosperous camp-meetings named in this chapter, I had the great pleasure to see all three of these young people converted to God. I took them into the Methodist Church, and they went back to Ohio happy in God. They were here on a visit among their relations from that State, and went home with feelings very different from those they possessed when they left.

There is another small incident connected with these two prosperous camp-meetings before named. There was a great and good work going on in our congregation from time to time; and on Sunday there were a great many from Springfield, and all the surrounding country. A great many professors of religion in other Churches professed to wish their children converted, but still they could not trust them at a Methodist meeting, especially a camp-meeting. A great many of these young people attended the camp-meetings, and on Sunday the awful displays of Divine power were felt to the utmost verge of the congregation. When I closed my sermon, I invited mourners to the altar, and there was a mighty shaking among the dry bones; many came forward, and among the rest there were many young ladies whose parents were members of a sister Church; two in particular of these young ladies came into the altar. Their mother was present; and when she heard her daughters were kneeling at the altar of God, praying for mercy, she sent an elder of her Church to bring them out. When he came to tell them their mother had sent for them, they refused to go. He then took hold of them, and said they must go. I then took hold of him, and told him they should not go, and that if that was his business, I wanted him to leave the altar instantly. He left, and reported to their mother; and while we were kneeling all round the altar, and praying for the mourners, the mother in a great rage rushed in. When she came, all were kneeling around, and there was no place for her to get in to her daughters. As I knelt and was stooping down, talking, and encouraging the mourners, this lady stepped on my shoulders, and rushed right over my head. As, in a fearful rage, she took hold of her daughters to take them out by force, I took hold of her arm, and tried to reason with her; but I might as well have reasoned with a whirlwind. She said she would have them out at the risk of her life.

"They are my daughters," said she, " and they shall come out."

Said I to her,—"This is my altar, and my meeting ; and I say, these girls shall not be taken out."

She seized hold of them again. I took hold of her, and put her out of the altar, and kept her out. Both of these young ladies professed religion, but they were prevented by their mother from joining the Methodists. She compelled them to join her Church, sorely against their will. They married in their mother's Church, but I fear they were hindered for life, if not finally lost.

I have often thought of the thousands who have been awakened and converted under Methodist preaching, but, from the prejudice of their husbands, wives, parents, or children, and friends, have been influenced to join another branch of the Church. What a fearful account will many have to give who, through prejudice or bigotry, have opposed their relatives or friends in joining the Church of their choice ! If these souls are lost, who will have to answer for it at the bar of God ? "Lord, we saw some casting out devils in Thy name, and we forbade them, because they followed not us." "Forbid them not," was the reply of our Saviour ; "for there is no man can do a miracle in My name, and speak lightly of Me." Let us be careful on this subject; for the loss of a soul is a fearful consideration to all.

We had a camp-meeting in Morgan County, Sangamon District. While I was on this District, the following remarkable providence occurred: there were large congregations from time to time, many awakened and converted to God, fifty joined the Church. G. W. Teas, now a travelling preacher in the Iowa Conference, made the fiftieth person that joined the Church. We had worship for several days and nights. On Monday, just after we had dismissed for dinner, there was a very large limb of a tree that stood on the side of the ground allotted for the ladies, which, without wind or any other visible cause, broke loose and fell, with a mighty crash, right in among the ladies' seats ; but as the Lord would direct it, there was not a woman or child there, when the limb fell. If it had fallen at any time while the congregation was collected, it must have killed more than a dozen persons. Just in the south of Morgan, near Lynnville, we had another camp-meeting, perhaps the same summer. In the afternoon, at three o'clock, I put up a very good local preacher to preach. He was not as interesting as some, and the congregation became restless, especially the rowdies. I went out among them, and told them they ought to hear the preacher.

"O," said they, "if it was you, we would gladly hear you."

"Boys," said I, "do you really want to hear me ? "

"Yes, we do," said they.

"Well," said I, "if you do, go and gather all those inattentive groups, and come down in the grove, two hundred yards south, and I will preach to you."

They collected two or three hundred. I mounted an old log; they all seated themselves in a shade. I preached to them about an hour, and not a soul moved or misbehaved. In this way I matched the rowdies for once.

CHAPTER XXI.

CAMP ROWDIES.

IN the fall of 1831, our Conference was holden in Indianapolis, Indiana, October 4th; Bishop Roberts presided. At this Conference, we elected our delegates to the General Conference, which was to sit in Philadelphia, May 1st. This was the fifth delegated General Conference to which I was elected, and, perhaps, it is the proper place to say, this was the only General Conference that I ever missed attending, from 1816 to this date. My family were in great affliction, which prevented my attendance. Brothers Andrew and Emory were elected, and ordained bishops in the Methodist Episcopal Church; and the Indiana Conference was formed; so that there were now twelve annual Conferences East and South, and ten West and South, all the latter formed out of the old Western Conference. Our numbers in the West had risen to 217,659. Our travelling preachers numbered 765. The others, Eastern and Southern, had, in members, 382,060, travelling preachers, 1,454. Total, in round numbers, 600,000. Of travelling preachers, 2,219.

The reader will see our increase in the old Conferences in members, in four years, was 111,850; and in the West was 66,775; total, 177,625. We had increased in travelling preachers, in the same length of time, 716: this was a greater increase than all the branches of the Protestant Christian Churches in the Union could number, and surely all the factories in the Union that make preachers, did not, in the same length of time, graduate as many preachers; and, in point of learning and real ability, our increase of preachers will compare favourably with any of them.

As 1832 closed my three years on the Sangamon District, I will relate an incident or two which occurred in Fulton County. We held a camp-meeting, at which good preparations were made; many attended, and our prospects for an interesting meeting were fair, and there was an increasing interest. But some low and unprincipled fellows, in the adjoining village of Canton, fitted out a man, who was perfectly bankrupt, and sent him down to set up a huckster's shop, with tobacco, segars, cakes, candies, pies, and almost all kinds of ardent spirits. I went to him, and told him he should not disturb us in vending those articles, and that he must desist; he swore he would not, and hurled defiance at me; I got a writ and an officer, and took him; he employed a young lawyer to defend him; I prosecuted the suit, and the jury fined him ten dollars and costs. On saying that he had nothing, and was not worth a cent in the world, the court told him, he had to pay his fine or go to jail; he said he must go to jail then, for he could not pay the fine. There was a black-legged gang, that were his chief customers, who swore, if we attempted to put him in jail, which was about ten miles off, that they would rescue him, and give those who attempted to convey him there a sound drubbing. The officer was scared, and hesitated; in the meantime, I ordered out an execution, and levied on his whole grocery. He declared that these articles were not his, but belonged to other men. I said, I did not care a fig who they belonged to, and ordered the officer to levy on them, and I would indemnify him. When we had secured the grocery, and put it under guard, our officer still hesitated to take the criminal to jail. I told him to summon me, and four other stout men that I named, and I would insure the criminal a safe lodgment in jail, or risk the consequences. This was done, and we hoisted our prisoner on a horse, mounted our own horses, well armed with bludgeons, and started on a merry jog. When we got about half way, I told the prisoner that he had better pay his fine, and not disgrace himself by lying in jail. No, he swore he would not; so on we went. The rowdies that were to waylay us and release the prisoner, never appeared. When we got in sight of the town, in which the jail was, the prisoner asked me very seriously, if we really intended to put him in jail. I told him, yes, certainly we did. "Well," said he, "I can't go into jail;" and then pulled out the money and paid his fine and costs.

We returned to the encampment, and the rowdies were in a mighty rage because they could get no drink; for we had the groggery under guard. They swore if we did not release it, they would break up the camp-meeting. I told them to ride on, that we would not release the grocery, and we could whip the whole regiment. At candle-lighting we had preaching; they were still and quiet till most of the tent-holders had gone to bed. They then began their dirty deeds. I had ordered out a strong watch, and directed the lights to be kept burning all night. They began at a distance to bark like dogs, to howl like wolves, to hoot like owls; they drew near and crowed like chickens; they tried to put out our lights, and threw chunks at the tent; but the guard beat them back, and kept them off nearly all night. Toward day they drew nearer and nearer still, and would slap their hands, and crow like chickens. One ringleader among them came right before the preachers' tent, slapped his hands, and crowed and passed on. I stepped to a fire close by, and gathered a chunk of fire, and threw it, striking him right between the shoulders, and the fire flew all over him. He sprung and bounded like a buck. I cried out, "Take him; take him;" but I assure you it would have taken a very fleet man to have taken him, for he ran as though the very devil was in him and after him. When I returned to the tent, one of the guard came and told me that they were taking wheels off the waggons and carriages; and looking through an opening in the tent, I saw one of them busy in loosening my carriage behind the tent, where I had tied it to a sapling for fear they would run it off. I slipped round, gathered a stick in my way, and came up close behind him, and struck at him, not with much intent to hurt, but to scare him. However, the stroke set his hat on one side of his head; he dashed off in a mighty fright, and his hat not being adjusted right, it blinded him, and, fleeing with all speed, he struck his head against a tree, knocked himself down, bruised his face very much, and lay senseless for several minutes; but when he came to himself, he was as tame as a lamb, and his dispensation of mischief was over. This put an end to the trouble of the rowdies, and afterward all was peace and quiet.

We had a very singular and remarkable man among us, a travelling preacher in the Illinois Conference; his name was Wilson Pitner. He was at this camp-meeting. He was uneducated, and it seemed impossible for him to learn; but, notwithstanding his want of learning, and in common he was an ordinary preacher, yet at times, as we say in the backwoods, when he swung clear, there were very few that could excel him in the pulpit; and perhaps he was one of the most eloquent and powerful exhorters that was in the land.

On Monday he came to me, and desired me to let him preach at eleven o'clock, saying,—

"I have faith to believe that God will this day convert many of these rowdies and persecutors."

I consented; and he preached with great liberty and power. Nearly the whole congregation were powerfully moved, as he closed by calling for every rowdy and persecutor to meet him in the altar; for, said he,—

"I have faith to believe that God will convert every one of you that will come and kneel at the place of prayer."

There was a general rush for the altar, and many of our persecutors, and those who had interrupted and disturbed us in the forepart of the meeting, came and fell on their knees, and cried aloud for mercy; and it is certainly beyond my power to describe the scene; but more than fifty souls were converted to God that day and night. Our meeting

doubt it was swimming for twenty yards. There were no bridges, no canoe, and I could not find any fallen tree that could possibly reach across, so that I would have to swim, and all alone. If any accident should happen to me, I would certainly be drowned.

The prospect looked gloomy, and I felt some misgivings come over me; and the reasons and arguments of my friend were not without considerable effect on my mind. I paused for a few moments, reasoning on the subject. Just then my old Methodist preacher motto occurred to my mind, that is, "Never retreat till you certainly know you can advance no further." And as my motto occurred to my mind, my purpose was unalterably fixed to go ahead.

"Brother," said I, "as there is no road, get on your horse and ride a little distance with me, till I can clearly see the point of timber that is to guide me."

He readily consented, and did so. We rode two miles, and the point of timber was plain in view. As he turned back, he said, "I should not be surprised if I never saw you again."

"Well," said I, "if I fall, and you never see me again, tell my friends that I fell at my post, trying to do my duty. Farewell."

I had a fine, large, faithful horse under me, and a Divine Providence above me, and, in a few minutes after my friend and myself separated, I felt that I had nothing to fear. On I moved, sometimes in and sometimes out of sight of my landmark; sometimes nearly swimming in the little branches, but every step I left the prairie in the distance, and neared my point of timber. There was so much water, and the ground was so soft, I could make but slow progress; but every time I rose on the high ground, from the low valleys in the prairie, my point of timber seemed nearer and nearer still. At length, about three o'clock, I reached the timber in safety, rode up and hailed the cabin, but there was no person at home. I saw in the distance, about fourteen miles off, my next point of timber, and contiguous to the place of holding my quarterly meeting. I concluded to make a hard push and go through that afternoon; but here was the large creek to cross, only two hundred yards ahead of me. I concluded to go above the timber and cross it; but when I came to it, I found it had swollen and spread out at least two hundred yards on the level ground. I could not tell how far I would have to swim on my horse. I rode in about one third the apparent distance across. My horse was nearly swimming. I concluded it would be too far for me to risk a swim on horseback. It occurred to me that "prudence was the better part of valour," so I retreated. I then pursued the creek down the timber, in search of a drift or tree across the stream, where I could carry my things over, and then return and swim my horse, without wetting all my travelling apparatus. At length I found a tree that had been felled across a narrow part of the creek, that I thought answered my purpose admirably; but by this time it was nearly night, and if I got safe over the creek, I could not make the distance to the next point of timber, and should have to lie out without food for myself or my horse. I came to a halt, and, thinking that the occupants of the cabin I had just passed would be in at night, I concluded to retrace my steps and get quarters for the night. So back I came to the cabin, but still there was no one at home. I concluded, at home or not at home, I should lodge there that night. So down I got, opened the door of the cabin, and ushered myself in I found they had covered up some fire in the ashes, to keep in their absence, which made me still hope they would come home some time that night. I went out and stripped my horse, and put him up and fed him, and then my next care was for something to eat myself. By this time I had a good appetite. I went and made up a little fire, and in a small corner cupboard, made of clapboards, backwoods fashion, to my great joy I found a pan of corn bread, nicely baked, and, though cold, it relished well. In one corner of the wooden chimney there hung some excellent dried venison. I pulled out some coals and broiled my venison, and had a hearty meal of it. And now, thought I, if I only had a good cup of coffee, I should have the crowning point gained of a good and pleasant meal. In looking about in the cupboard I found a tin bucket full of excellent honey, in the comb. I took it out, got some water in a tin cup that was on the shelf, sweetened the water with the honey, and found in it an excellent substitute for coffee. There was a nice clean bed, in which I slept unusually sound. Next morning I rose early, fed my horse, prepared my breakfast, much after the fashion of my supper, saddled my horse, and started on my journey.

When I came to the creek, it had fallen considerably, but was still swimming. I carried all my travelling fixtures over perfectly dry; stripped myself, went back, mounted my horse, went over safe, dressed myself, knelt down and offered up my sincere thanks to God for His providential care over me, and the mercy He had showed me, and went on my way shouting and happy.

I arrived at the place of the quarterly meeting, and found the few scattered members, six in all, and about eight who were not members; and these comprised the whole settlement, save one family who lived close by, the head of which was a great persecutor of the Methodists. He said he had moved there, in that new and out-of-the-way place, especially to get rid of those wretched people called Methodists; but he had scarcely got into his rude cabin before here was the Methodist preacher, preaching hell-fire and damnation, as they always did.

On Monday morning I went over to see him. He was a high-strung predestinarian in his views; believed, or professed to believe, that God had decreed everything that comes to pass. After introducing myself to him, he presently bristled up for an argument. . I told him I had not come to debate, but to invite him to the Saviour. He said he could not receive anything from me, for he cordially despised the Methodists. I told him, if God had decreed all things, he had decreed that there should be Methodists, and that they should believe precisely as they did, and that they were raised up by the decree of God to torment him before his time, and that he must be a great simpleton to suppose that the Methodists could do or believe anything but what they did; "and now, my dear sir, you must be a vile wretch to want to break the decrees of God, and wish to exterminate the Methodists;" that if his doctrine was true, the Methodists were as certainly fulfilling the glorious decrees of God, which were founded in truth and righteousness, as the angels around the burning throne; and several admonitions I gave him, and, by the bye, he had some feeling on the subject. I talked kindly and prayed with him, and left.

After I left, he began to think on the topics of conversation, and the more he thought the more his mind became perplexed about these eternal decrees. When he would sit down to eat, or ride, or walk the road, he would soliloquize on the subject. After cutting off a piece of meat and holding it on his fork, ready to receive it into his mouth, he would say, "God decreed from all eternity that I should eat this meat, but I will break that decree," and down he would dash it to the dogs. As he walked the paths in the settlement and came to a fork, he would say, "God from all eternity decreed that I should take the right-hand path, but I 'll break that decree," and he would rush to the left. As he rode through the settlement, in coming to a stump or tree, he would rein up his horse and say, "God has from all eternity decreed that I should go to the right of that stump or tree, but I will break that decree," and would turn his horse to the left.

·· Thus he went on until his family became alarmed, thinking he was deranged. The little settlement, also, was fearful that he had lost his balance of mind. At length, deep conviction took hold of him; he saw that he was a lost and ruined sinner, without an interest in Jesus Christ. He called the neighbours to come and pray for him, and, after a long and sore conflict with the devil and his decrees, it pleased God to give him religion, and almost all his family were converted and joined the Methodist Church, and walked worthy of their high and holy calling.

At another quarterly meeting in this mission on Sunday, we had twenty-seven for our congregation; and yet the scattered population were all, or nearly all, there, for many miles around; and when we administered the sacrament on Sabbath, we had just seven communicants, preachers and all. Brother Barton Randle, now a superannuated member of the Illinois Annual Conference, was the missionary. Though a man of feeble health and strength, yet he was faithful in hunting up the lost sheep in this new and laborious field of labour. He suffered many privations and hardships, but he endured all as seeing Him who is invisible, and I have thought that he was one among the very best missionaries I was ever acquainted with. He did great good in this new and rising country, and laid firmly the foundation of future good, which the increasing and now densely populated country has realized. Long since this mission has formed many large Circuits and self-supporting stations, and no doubt many, in the great day of retribution, will rise up and call Brother Randle blessed, and he will hail many of his spiritual children in heaven from this field of labour. Brother Randle was the first missionary that was sent to and formed this mission, and, at the close of his year, he returned seventy-five members.

The Rock Island mission was formed in 1832, and Philip T. Cordier was appointed missionary. He was a man of feeble talents, unstable, and did but little good. He was finally expelled. I do not know what has become of him. On my first visit to Rock Island Mission, which was chiefly located in what was then called Wells's Settlement, a few miles above the mouth of Rock River, the river had been very high, but was fallen considerably. There was an old ferry-boat at the lower ford. The ferryman was a very mean man, charged high, and imposed very much on travellers. Some thought the river might be forded, others thought that it would swim. I was a total stranger, and although I had no money to pay my ferriage, yet I did not wish to swim, if I could well avoid it, so I rode up and hailed the ferryman. I asked him if the river was fordable.

"No," said he, "it is swimming from bank to bank nearly, and it is a very dangerous ford in the bargain."

"Well," said I, "what do you do with strangers who have no money? I am out, but shall return this way on Monday. If you will ferry me over, you shall then be sure of your pay."

"I won't do it," said he. "You must leave something in pawn till you return, or I will not set you over."

"What shall I leave?"

"Your overcoat," said he.

"No, sir, perhaps I shall need it before that time; and if you will not trust me, I am afraid to trust you."

"Well," said he, "you can't get over. I won't trust you."

o

I felt a little indignant, and turned off, saying, "My horse is a much better ferry-boat than your own, and he'll trust me." So I determined to take a swim. Just as I turned off from the ferryman, I saw a man on horseback ride down to the river's edge on the other side. He waded his horse in, and came over without swimming at all. This stranger told me there was no better ford on any river in the world, and that there was not the least danger on earth. I told him what the ferryman said.

"Ah," said he, "you have made a blessed escape; for if you had left your overcoat, you never would have got it again. He is a great rascal, and makes his living by foul means."

So I passed over in safety, and had the pleasure of keeping my overcoat. When I got to Brother Wells's, I found a good little society, all in peace, and we had a very pleasant little quarterly meeting.

Here, on the north side of Rock River, on the rising ground from the Mississippi bottom, stands the site of one of the oldest Indian towns in the North or North-west. It is a beautiful site for a city. There were to be seen lying, bleached and bleaching, the bones of unnumbered thousands of these poor, wild, and roaming races of beings. It was the centre of the vast, and powerful, unbroken, war-like tribes of the North-west. This particular spot was claimed by the notorious Black Hawk and his tribe. If they had been a civilized people, and had known the real arts of war, it would have been utterly impossible for the Americans to have vanquished and subdued them as they have done. When I looked over the fields in cultivation by the whites, where the ground had, for ages, been the country of thousands of Indians, a spirit of sorrow came over me. Had they been an educated and civilized people, there no doubt would now be standing on this pre-eminent site as splendid a city as New York. But they are wasted away and gone to their long home. I saw a scattered few that were crowded back by the unconquerable march of the white man.

On another visit to a quarterly meeting on the Rock Island Mission, Brother H. Summers, a travelling presiding elder in the Rock River Conference, accompanied me. We had a pleasant meeting, and it was believed that good was done. I had taken and distributed a good many religious books in the mission, which were eagerly sought for by the community. Brother Summers and myself concluded to cross at the upper ford on Rock River. About midway in the river was a very slippery rock, which could be avoided by keeping up stream considerably; but somehow I missed the safe track, and my horse got on this slippery rock, and all of a sudden he slipped and fell. My saddle turned; off I went, and the first thing I knew I saw my saddle-bags floating down with great rapidity, for the water ran very swift. I left my horse to get up as best he could, and took after my saddle-bags. I had a tight race, but overtook them before they sunk so as to disappear. They were pretty well filled with water. My books and clothes had all turned Campbellites, for there was much water; and I escaped, not by the skin of my teeth, but by the activity of my heels. My horse rose, and, with all the calmness of old Diogenes, waded out, and left me to do the same. Brother Summers could not maintain his usual gravity, but I assure you all his fun was at my expense. I had scarcely a dry thread about me; but on we went, and reached Pope River settlement that night.

The Galena Mission, I think, was formed in 1827. It was a singular providence, somehow, that, notwithstanding Galena was in my District for several years, yet, by high waters, sickness of my horses, myself, and family, I was never able to reach a single appointment in Galena, and to this day I have never seen her hills, walked her streets, or explored her rich mineral stores or mines; and although I have always borne the name of a punctual attendant on my appointments, it seems strange to me that I never reached that interesting point.

In the fall of 1834 and 1835, William D. R. Trotter rode and preached on the Henderson River Mission; he was my son-in-law. On one occasion when I attended one of his quarterly meetings, there was no parsonage, and but few families comfortably situated to board with. During the meeting it rained almost constantly, and then turned cold, and there fell a considerable quantity of snow. I was in my gig or one-horse sulky. As I was to return home from this quarterly meeting, my daughter concluded that she would go with me, and spend a few weeks with her mother. I told her I knew the streams were very high, and it was doubtful whether we could get along. She said she thought if I could get along, she could. So we started in my two-wheeled vehicle. In a few miles we reached Spoon River. At a little village called Ellisville, the river was very full, and rapidly rising; no ferry-boat, no comfortable house to stay at. One of the citizens of the village had a canoe; but how was I to take my carriage over a rapid stream on a canoe? The man said he could do it; and, rather than stay for any length of time among a drunken, swearing, rowdy crowd, I concluded to try it. Down we went; I took out my horse, took off the harness, and took the harness and all the travelling appendages into the canoe; took in my daughter; took my harness, bridle, and led my horse in, and swam him over, by the side of the canoe. I landed all safe, and then returned with the manager of the canoe for my carriage; we rolled it into the water, centred it as well as we

o 2

could; balanced it, and I held on to it while he paddled and managed the canoe; and over we went safe and sound; geared up, hitched to, and started on through the mud for Lewistown, and got there safe. We put up with Judge Phelps, a fine man, and his wife an excellent woman, and very friendly family; and we were not only made welcome, but comfortable. That night it snowed, and covered the ground several inches. Next morning we started early, and crossed the Illinois River just above the mouth of Spoon River, which we had crossed the day before. We met some travellers in the afternoon, who told us that the waters of the Sangamon River were out for five miles, and that we could not reach the ferry-boat without swimming. We then turned our course up Salt Creek, which emptied into the Sangamon River above where we had intended to cross it. Just before sundown we reached Salt Creek, where was a miserable old rotten ferry-boat, and Salt Creek out of its banks a mile. The ferry-man told us he could ferry us over the main channel of the stream, and he had no doubt we could wade out without swimming, if we could find the way. It was at least a mile to the bluff, he said, if we kept the road, we would swim. We could only tell where the road was by a little space along, clear of weeds and grass. He said if we kept on ground where we could see the tops of the weeds and grass, there was no danger , but if we could not see these, not to venture; for there were many ponds clear of weeds and grass as well as the road. This seemed to me to be a very dangerous undertaking. But my daughter urged me on. I had great confidence in my horse; he was large and strong, and an excellent swimmer, so over we went. There were a few rods of earth uncovered with water; and then we took water for the bluffs. We could see very distinctly the windings of the road by the little space that was clear of weeds and grass; but presently we would come to a large space clear of weeds and grass , these we took to be ponds, and would wind round them and come back to our watery road. In this tedious way we got along slowly, though making all the speed we could without injuring my horse. As we neared the bluffs, darkness was closing in on us very fast; at length we got within about three rods of the bluffs, and we could not see the tops of weeds and grass, neither to the right, nor left, nor in front; I turned up stream, and then down stream, but all my pilots had disappeared. I was brought to a stand. Said I to my daughter,—

"Let's swim it; Gray will ferry us over safe."

"Agreed," said she.

Said I, "Take a firm hold of the gig, and, sink or swim, never let go, and Gray will make land."

So in I drove, when, behold! it was not swimming, and my horse waded out safe. We then had four miles to go, without road or pilot, and very dark. I took my course by the evening star, and soon arrived at a friend's house; was kindly received and comfortably entertained by my old brother, Dr. Ballard, in New-Market, then Sangamon County. He has long since fallen asleep, left earth for heaven, and is reaping his reward among the blessed.

I have thus given a small sketch of some of the perilous scenes through which early Methodist preachers had to pass, to show the Methodist preachers of the present day the difference between walking on Turkey carpets and eating yellow-legged chickens, and walking on mud and water and eating nothing for days at a time.

The Fort Edwards Mission was formed, I believe, in 1832–33. D. B. Carter was the first missionary appointed to this mission; he returned at the next Conference fifty-three members. Brother Carter was a man of small literary acquirements. When he professed religion, he could not read a hymn intelligibly; but believing God had called him to preach the Gospel, he industriously applied himself to books, and soon learned to read very well. He was not a brilliant or profound theologian; but he was a pious, zealous, useful minister of Jesus Christ; and during his short ministerial career, many were the seals of his ministry. He was much beloved in life, and greatly lamented in death. After a few years of zealous, useful labours, the fell disease, consumption, seized on him; he lingered in a superannuated relation a year or two, and then died a peaceful and happy death. Many in the great day of judgment will rise up and call him blessed.

The Fort Edwards Mission lay up and down the east bank of the Mississippi, from Quincy City to Fort Edwards, which stood where the City of Warsaw now stands; thence up the Mississippi to the celebrated foot of what is called the Lower Rapids, where, in after times, was erected the idolatrous city of Nauvoo, under the supervision of the grand impostor Joseph Smith, who was and is claimed as the Mormon Prophet.

CHAPTER XXII.

MORMONISM.

PERMIT me to make a few remarks about the blasphemous organization called the Mormons, or Latter-Day Saints. The original absurdity and trifling character of Joe Smith and his coadjutors is a matter of history, known and understood of all the intelligent reading community that have sought information on the subject, and therefore need not be stated here by me. But there are a few facts I will state that have come under my own personal knowledge; for it has fallen to my lot to be appointed to travel in the region of country in Illinois most infested with this imposture.

After the Mormons were driven from Missouri for their infamous and unlawful deeds, they fled to Illinois, Joe Smith and all, and established themselves at Nauvoo, or the foot of the Lower Rapids, on the east side of the Mississippi. At an early day after they were driven from Missouri and took up their residence in Illinois, it fell to my lot to become acquainted with Joe Smith personally, and with many of their leading men and professed followers. On a certain occasion I fell in with Joe Smith, and was formally and officially introduced to him in Springfield, then our county town. We soon fell into a free conversation on the subject of religion, and Mormonism in particular. I found him to be a very illiterate and impudent desperado in morals, but, at the same time, he had a vast fund of low cunning.

In the first place, he made his onset on me by flattery, and he laid on the soft sodder thick and fast. He expressed great and almost unbounded pleasure in the high privilege of becoming acquainted with me, one of whom he had heard so many great and good things, and he had no doubt I was one among God's noblest creatures, an honest man. He believed that among all the Churches in the world the Methodist was the nearest right, and that, as far as they went, they were right; but they had stopped short by not claiming the gift of tongues, of prophecy, and of miracles; and then quoted a batch of Scripture to prove his positions correct. Upon the whole, he did pretty well for clumsy Joe. I gave him rope, as the sailors say, and, indeed, I seemed to lay this flattering unction pleasurably to my soul.

"Indeed," said Joe, "if the Methodists would only advance a step or two further, they would take the world. We Latter-Day Saints are Methodists, as far as they have gone, only we have advanced further; and if you would come in and go with us, we could sweep not only the Methodist Church, but all others, and you would be looked up to as one of the Lord's greatest prophets. You would be honoured by countless thousands, and have of the good things of this world all that heart could wish."

I then began to inquire into some of the tenets of the Latter-Day Saints. He explained. I criticized his explanations till, unfortunately, we got into high debate, and he cunningly concluded that his first bait would not take, for he plainly saw I was not to be flattered out of common sense and honesty. The next pass he made at me was to move upon my fears. He said that in all ages of the world the good and right way was evil spoken of, and that it was an awful thing to fight against God.

"Now," said he, "if you will go with me to Nauvoo, I will show you many living witnesses that will testify that they were, by the saints, cured of blindness, lameness, deafness, dumbness, and all the diseases that human flesh is heir to; and I will show you," said he, "that we have the gift of tongues, and can speak in unknown languages, and that the saints can drink any deadly poison, and it will not hurt them;" and closed by saying, "The idle stories you hear about us are nothing but sheer persecution."

I then gave him the following history of an encounter I had at a camp-meeting in Morgan County, some time before, with some of his Mormons, and assured him I could prove all I said by thousands that were present.

The camp-meeting was numerously attended, and we had a good and gracious work of religion going on among the people. On Saturday there came some twenty or thirty Mormons to the meeting. During the intermission after the eleven o'clock sermon they collected in one corner of the encampment, and began to sing, and they sang well. As fast as the people rose from their dinners, they drew up to hear the singing, and the scattering crowd drew up until a large company surrounded them. I was busy regulating matters connected with the meeting. At length, according, I have no doubt, to a preconcerted plan, an old lady Mormon began to shout, and after shouting a while she swooned away and fell into the arms of her husband. The old man proclaimed that his wife had gone into a trance, and that when she came to she would speak in an unknown tongue, and that he would interpret. This proclamation produced considerable excitement, and the multitude crowded thick around. Presently the old lady arose and began to speak in an unknown tongue, sure enough.

Just then my attention was called to the matter. I saw in one moment that the whole manœuvre was intended to bring the Mormons into notice, and break up the good of our meeting. I advanced instantly toward the crowd, and asked the people to give way and let me in to this old lady, who was then being held in the arms of her husband. I came right up to them, and took hold of her arm, and ordered her peremptorily to hush that gibberish; that I would have no more of it; that it was presumptuous, and blasphemous nonsense. I stopped very suddenly her unknown tongue. She opened her eyes, took me by the hand, and said,—

"My dear friend, I have a message directly from God to you."

I stopped her short, and said, "I will have none of your messages. If God can speak through no better medium than an old, hypocritical, lying woman, I will hear nothing of it." Her husband, who was to be the interpreter of her message, flew into a mighty rage, and said,—

"Sir, this is my wife, and I will defend her at the risk of my life."

I replied, "Sir, this is my camp-meeting, and I will maintain the good order of it at the risk of my life. If this is your wife, take her off from here, and clear yourselves in five minutes, or I will have you under guard."

The old lady slipped out and was off quickly. The old man stayed a little, and began to pour a tirade of abuse on me. I stopped him short, and said, "Not another word of abuse from you, sir. I have no doubt you are an old thief; and if your back was examined, no doubt you carry the marks of the cowhide for your villany." And sure enough, as if I had spoken by inspiration, he, in some of the old States, had been lashed to the whipping-post for stealing; and I tell you the old man began to think other persons had visions besides his wife, but he was very clear from wishing to interpret my unknown tongue. To cap the climax, a young gentleman stepped up and said he had no doubt all I said of this old man was true, and much more; for he had caught him stealing corn out of his father's crib. By this time, such was the old man's excitement that the great drops of sweat ran down his face, and he called out,—

"Don't crowd me, gentlemen; it is mighty warm."

Said I, "Open the way, gentlemen, and let him out." When the way was opened, I cried, "Now start, and don't show your face here again, nor one of the Mormons. If you do, you will get Lynch's law."

They all disappeared, and our meeting went on prosperously; a great many were converted to God, and the Church was much revived and built up in her holy faith.

My friend, Joe Smith, became very restive before I got through with my narrative; and when I closed, his wrath boiled over, and he cursed me in the name of his God, and said, "I will show you, sir, that I will raise up a government in these United States which will overturn the present government, and I will raise up a new religion that will overturn every other form of religion in this country!"

"Yes," said I, "Uncle Joe; but my Bible tells me, 'The bloody and deceitful man shall not live out half his days;' and I expect the Lord will send the devil after you some of these days, and take you out of the way."

"No, sir," said he; "I shall live and prosper, while you will die in your sins."

"Well, sir," said I, "if you live and prosper, you must quit your stealing and abominable whoredoms!"

,Thus we parted, to meet no more on earth ; for in a few years after this, an outraged and deeply-injured people took the law into their own hands, and killed him, and drove the Mormons from the State. They should be considered and treated as outlaws in every country and clime.   The two great political parties in the State were nearly equal, and these wretched Mormons, for several years, held the balance of power, and they were always in market to the highest bidder ; and I have often been put to the blush to see our demagogues and stump orators, from both political parties, courting favours from the Mormons, to gain a triumph in an election.   Any man or set of men that would be mean enough to stoop so low as to connive at the abominations of these reckless Mormons, surely ought to be considered unworthy of public office, honour, or confidence.   But this is the way with all demagogues ; and if our happy and glorious Union is destroyed, it will be done by these office-seekers, who go for their own little insignificant selves, while the true love of country is an eternal stranger in their traitorous hearts

One fact I wish here to mention, that ought to be made public. When Joe Smith was announced a candidate for President of these United States, almost every infidel association in the Union declared in his favour.   I travelled extensively through the Eastern States and cities, as well as in the West, that year ; and I must say this was literally true, as far as I conversed with, or obtained reliable information of, those infidel associations or individuals.   Does not this speak volumes ? and ought it not to teach the friends of religion an impressive lesson ?

Great blame has been attached to the State, the citizens of Hancock County, in which Nauvoo is situated, as well as other adjoining counties, for the part they acted in driving the Mormons from among them.   But it should be remembered they had no redress at law ; for it is beyond all doubt that the Mormons would swear anything, true or false.   They stole the stock, plundered and burned the houses and barns of the citizens, and there is no doubt they privately murdered some of the best people in the county ; and owing to the perjured evidence always at their command, it was impossible to have any legal redress.   If it had not been for this state of things, Joe Smith would not have been killed, and they would not have been driven with violence from the State.   Repeated efforts were made to get redress for these wrongs and outrages, but all to no purpose ; and the wonder is, how the people bore so long as they did with the outrageous villanies practised on them, without a resort to violent measures.   I claim to know all about the dreadful conduct of the Mormons, and could state in detail .the facts in these cases, but think it unnecessary.   This much I think it my duty to state, at least to palliate the seeming high-handed measures of our wronged and oppressed citizens.

In the fall of 1833, our Illinois Conference was held in Union Grove, Padfield's, St. Clair County, September 25th. It fell to the lot of Bishop Soule to take this Western tour, in the summer previous to our Conference. He came to my house on his Western round of Conferences. He travelled in a two-horse carriage, with an excellent span of horses; and he needed such; for the Missouri Conference sat in Arkansas Territory, at Salem, Washington County, a long way in the interior, and west of the Mississippi. He had mountains to climb and large rivers to cross, through a sparsely-populated country. My son-in-law, William D. R. Trotter, rode the Blue River Mission, which was in Pike and Calhoun Counties, and lay directly in the bishop's route. My quarterly meeting was in this mission. Trotter, the missionary, was at my house; so we started in company with the bishop. After we crossed the Illinois River, we had a hilly country to pass through to get to the quarterly meeting, almost without roads. So steep were some of the hills, and so deep the hollows and ravines, that we had to loose the horses from the bishop's carriage and let it down by hand; then hitch on and drive up the hills. It seemed to me that if these were episcopal honours, I would beg to be excused from wearing them; and really it appeared to me that it was enough to discourage a bishop himself. But those who know Bishop Soule, know him to be a man of indomitable courage.

After much labour to man and beast, we got safe to the quarterly meeting. The bishop stayed with us over Sabbath, and preached two excellent sermons, which had a good effect on the congregations; and the curiosity of many was gratified; for if circumstances had not transpired to bring him to our camp quarterly meeting, they would have lived and died without ever seeing a Methodist bishop.

Our Western country, in certain locations, was, in 1832 and 1833, fearfully visited with that dreadful scourge, the cholera. On Monday of our camp-meeting, a very severe case of cholera took place with a hearty young man, that terminated fatally in eight or ten hours. The people generally believed it to be contagious; hence we deemed it most prudent to close the meeting, though our prospects for a good meeting were very encouraging. Bishop Soule, with great labour and fatigue, prosecuted his journey, and reached the Missouri Conference, but was taken sick with a violent attack of fever, so that he did not reach our Conference till the last hour of its session. The Conference had elected me as their president. We had done all our business, and the council had made out all the appointments, and we were just about adjourning, when the bishop arrived. I sent a messenger to him, and inquired of him if he wished to say anything to the Conference; but he declined coming into the room, and requested all those who had been elected to office to wait until he had rested a little, being much fatigued, and he would ordain them. They did so, and were ordained accordingly.

At this Conference, in the fall of 1833, the brethren in Jacksonville, though few in number and comparatively poor, petitioned for a stationed preacher. Their request was granted, and Thomas J. Starr was appointed their preacher. Few and poor, however, as the brethren in Jacksonville were, there was a great improvement, in point of numbers and wealth, from the time of their first organization as a class till now. I am sorry that it is out of my power to give the date of the organization of the first class in Jacksonville, but I think it was in 1827, when it was embraced in what was then called the Mississippi Circuit, and Thomas Randle and Isaac House were the Circuit preachers. In the course of this year, the first quarterly meeting ever held in Jacksonville was held in a log-house, owned by old Father Jordan. It was held up-stairs, and I well remember it was an interesting quarterly meeting. In 1831 the Jacksonville Circuit was formed from part of the old Mississippi Circuit, and John Sinclair, now of the Rock River Conference, was the Circuit preacher; but from the rapid growth of the town, and increase of population, the Methodists have two large churches and pastoral charges, and there are many more churches in the city, belonging to other denominations. The Presbyterians have a flourishing college located here, and the Methodists have a female college, numerously attended. There is also another flourishing female college in Jacksonville, but to what denomination it belongs, or whether to any particular one, I am not prepared to say. The Illinois State Hospital for the Insane, the Deaf and Dumb Asylum, the Institute to Educate the Blind, all under the fostering care of the State, are located in Jacksonville. Indeed, it is the Athens of Illinois, and speaks loudly in favour of the State, and of the citizens of Jacksonville and surrounding country in particular. These institutions have high claims on all benevolent sympathizers in human woe, and all the real friends of a sanctified literature that will issue streams of light and life, to bless unnumbered thousands of our fallen race.

Our Illinois Conference, for 1834, was holden at Mount Carmel, October 1st. This year the brethren in the town of Rushville desired to be organized into a station, and pledged themselves for the support of a preacher. I consented, and appointed T. N. Ralston, and it has remained a station ever since.

At one of our early camp-meetings in Schuyler County, Rushville Circuit, there was a general religious excitement. Many professed religion and joined the Church. Among the rest was a very intelligent and interesting young lady, a Roman Catholic She was deeply convicted, and knelt at the altar and prayed fervently for mercy, and, after a sore conflict, she found peace in believing in the Lord Jesus Christ. Her conversion was a very clear one. She joined the Methodist Church, and desired me to baptize her. I inquired of her whether she had not been baptized. She told me she had been baptized by the Roman priest, but she was aware of her own knowledge that the priest was a very wicked man, and that she did not believe he had any right to administer the ordinances of the Church on account of his wickedness, and, therefore, she was dissatisfied with her baptism. After mature reflection on the subject I baptized her, and she proved to be a worthy member of the Church.

CHAPTER XXIII.

CONVERSION OF A FAMILY.

In the course of this year, 1834, we had a camp-meeting in Knox County, Henderson River Mission. There was a goodly number tented, and a fine turn-out of people, for the number of settlers in this new and rising country. Our encampment was pitched in a beautiful little grove, on an eminence, surrounded by prairie on every hand.

There was in this settlement an interesting and intelligent family from one of the Eastern States. The younger members of the family consisted of several young men and young ladies. The young people liked the Methodists, and were deeply convicted; the old people, particularly the old lady, were very much opposed to them. Living, as they did, close by the camp-ground, they put their Yankee ingenuity to work to keep their children away from the meeting; but finding they could not accomplish it, they at once determined to pitch their tent on the camp-ground, and then they thought they would have a better opportunity to watch the children, and counteract any influence we might exert upon them. They pretended to be very friendly, to save appearances. The old lady, for the purpose of disarming me, treated me very kindly, and invited me to eat with them, which I did. In the meantime one of the daughters, who was deeply convicted, told me all about her mother's opposition to the Methodists, and her schemes to prevent her children from being influenced to become religious.

One Saturday evening I invited the seekers of religion to come forward to the altar for the prayers of the Church. Two of her daughters came forward and knelt in prayer. A younger sister, almost as much opposed to the Methodists as her mother, went into the altar with a vial of hartshorn, and, while her two sisters were trying to pray, she slipped the hartshorn to their nose, in order to drive them up, and prevent their seeking religion. I very soon detected her in her operations, and took hold of her hand, wrenched the vial from her, led her out of the altar, and told her, if I caught her in there any more on such business, I would pitch her out and publicly expose her.

While I was talking to and praying with these two young ladies and others, I saw the old lady, their mother, come and take her seat outside of the altar, immediately opposite her daughters; and if at any time she thought I was not watching her, she would kick them in their sides to drive them up. I watched her very closely, and when in the act of kicking them, I took hold of her foot and gave her a strong push backward, and over she tumbled among the benches. Being a large, corpulent woman, she had some considerable tussle to right herself again. So in this way I defeated the scheme of the devil once more. The girls became very much engaged, but while there were many still pressing to the altar, and my attention for a moment was called off, the old lady contrived to get them out of the altar into the tent. As soon as I discovered what was done, I gathered two or three good singers and praying persons, and followed them into the tent, and commenced singing; I then gave them an exhortation; then said, "Let us pray," and called on the father of the girls to pray for his children, but he refused; I then called on their mother to kneel down and pray for her children, and she refused. In the meantime two of the boys, as well as the two girls, became very much affected, and cried for mercy; and presently the third daughter, that had used the hartshorn in the altar, got awfully convicted, and begged all present to pray for her, as she would be lost and damned for ever. This was too much for the old people; they became awfully alarmed, and wept bitterly; and you may be sure the whole tent was in a mighty uproar. The singing, praying, and exhortations were kept up nearly all night. Four of the family were powerfully converted, and the sectarian devil in the old father and mother was effectually disarmed, and from that blessed night they became a religious family; all joined the Methodist Church, and, as far as I know, walked worthy of their high vocation May they all prove faithful till death, and then receive a crown o' life!

While on the Quincy District,—the town of Quincy was a very

small and sickly place,—I remember spending near two weeks in it when, if my recollection serves me, there was but one family where there was no affliction. In some families there were one, two, or three confined to their beds with fever, and sometimes the whole family were sick together, and not one able to help another. I went from house to house, not only to minister to their temporal wants, but to pray with them, and point the sick and dying to Christ. Many died, and it was with great difficulty that we could muster enough persons able to bury the dead.

There was one case which, in a very special manner, affected my mind. Under the hill, close by the brink of the river, there was what was called a "tavern." It was a poor, filthy place at best; the general resort of boatmen; and, in a word, all kinds of bad company resorted to this house. A young man, from some of the Eastern States, had come out to explore the West, and was taken sick on the boat, on the river, and was left at this miserable house. He was a professed Christian, and a member of the Methodist Church. No medical aid could be obtained, no nurse, and, in a word, no care was taken of him. In this deplorable condition, he heard that there was a Methodist preacher in town, visiting the sick. He sent for me, and I went to see him. He told me who he was, where his parents lived, and that he had a considerable sum of money with him, and he wanted me to take charge of it; for he was sure, if it was known he had money, he should be robbed of it. I took charge of his money, told the landlord to give him all the attention he could, and I would see him paid. The sick man said he was sensible he must die, but that he was not willing to die at that house, and begged me to have him removed, if possible. I knew of a very comfortable place, a few miles in the country, and caused his removal there. Here he lingered for a while, and then died. He had requested me, in case of his decease, to have him decently buried, pay out of his money his tavern bill, his funeral expenses, and write to his parents, that they might come to get his clothes and money. I did as requested. His younger brother came, got his money and clothes; and although it was a mournful dispensation to his relatives, yet it afforded them great comfort to know that he died among friends, though strangers.

This is one among many cases of the kind that from an early day came under my notice, in which enterprising men have come to the far West, have been taken sick, and died among strangers, uncared for.

We had a camp-meeting in Adams County, Quincy Circuit, and it was numerously attended. There was a gracious work of religion going on among the people, and there was a pretty clever, intelligent old gentleman, who had moved into the settlement from Kentucky, who, in that State, had been a Baptist preacher, but had got his mind confused with Alexander Campbell's dogmas about experimental religion. He had a fine family, and some of them knew what real religion was. He and family attended our camp-meeting. He was very fond of argument on almost all theological subjects He tried to get me into debate during the meeting, but I told him I was there for other and better business. He denied the operations of the Spirit, its testimony, bearing witness with our spirits that we are the children of God; and [asserted] that all those happy feelings professed by Christians were nothing but excitement; that there was no religion in it.

On Sunday night a most tremendous power fell on the assembly, and a general shout went up to heaven from hundreds of Christians. Among the crowd of happy and shouting Christians this gentleman's wife and daughter were exceedingly happy, and shouted aloud. The old gentleman could not stand it; he fled behind the tent, lighted his pipe, and tried to smoke away his bad feelings. After labouring in the altar a long time, I stepped back to get a drink of water, and there sat this old Campbellite preacher, and the cloud of smoke from his pipe was fearful; he seemed to be insensible of what he was about, and the pipe and tobacco were paying tribute to his reveries at a mighty rate. I stepped up to him and tapped him on the shoulder, and said, "Come, Mr. ——, go with me, and I will show you more happy Christians than you ever saw among the Campbellites in all your life."

"Sir," said he, "it is all delusion; they are not happy."

"But," said I, "your wife and daughter are among the foremost shouters in the crowd. Come," said I, "you must come with me to the altar; I want to pray for you there, that you may get religion, and be happy too. Come, sir, I want to see you converted, and shouting-happy." I took him by the arm, to lead him to the altar, but he drew back. I gathered him again, and pulled him along; but the moment he saw his wife and daughter shouting, and making toward him, he tore loose from my grasp, and actually ran. Poor man, he was so confused by fishing in the muddy waters of Campbellism, that he lost his mental balance. He would not yield to the Spirit of God, and submit to be an humble, shouting, happy Christian. Sometimes he would talk rational; sometimes quote and apply the Scriptures right; then, again, he became sceptical. But the great difficulty was, the pride of his professed ministerial standing would not let him yield, and renounce his errors. Thus he worried on for a considerable time, and was carried into the whirlpool of doubt and unbelief. His friends talked to him, but talked in vain. He became more and more flighty in his mind, till at length, in a paroxysm of insanity, he shot himself. This event fell like a thunderbolt on his family and the surrounding community, and proves that it is a hard thing to fight against God.

CHAPTER XXIV.

MISSIONARIES FROM THE EAST.

ABOUT this time there were a great many young missionaries sent out to this country to civilize and Christianize the poor heathen of the West. They would come with a tolerable education, and a smattering knowledge of the old Calvinistic system of theology. They were generally tolerably well furnished with old manuscript sermons, that had been preached, or written, perhaps a hundred years before. Some of these sermons they had memorized, but in general they read them to the people. This way of reading sermons was out of fashion altogether in this Western world, and of course they produced no good effect among the people. The great mass of our Western people wanted a preacher that could mount a stump, a block, or old log, or stand in the bed of a waggon, and, without note or manuscript, quote, expound, and apply the word of God to the hearts and consciences of the people. The result of the efforts of these Eastern missionaries was not very flattering; and although the Methodist preachers were in reality the pioneer heralds of the cross throughout the entire West, and although they had raised up numerous societies and churches every five miles, and notwithstanding we had hundreds of travelling and local preachers, accredited and useful ministers of the Lord Jesus Christ; yet these newly-fledged missionaries would write back to the old States hardly anything else but wailings and lamentations over the moral wastes and destitute condition of the West.

These letters would be read in their large congregations, stating that they had travelled hundreds of miles, and found no evangelical minister, and the poor perishing people were in a fair way to be lost for the want of the bread of life; and the ignorant or uninformed thousands that heard these letters read would melt into tears, and their sympathies would be greatly moved, when they considered our lost and heathenish state, and would liberally contribute their money to send us more missionaries, or to support those that were already here. Thus some of these missionaries, after occupying our pulpits, and preaching in large and respectable Methodist congregations, would write back and give those doleful tidings. Presently their letters would be printed, and come back among us as published facts in some of their periodicals.

Now, what confidence could the people have in such missionaries, who would state things as facts that had not even the semblance of truth in them? Thus I have known many of them destroy their own usefulness, and cut off all access to the people; and, indeed, they have destroyed all confidence in them as ministers of truth and righteousness, and caused the way of truth to be evil spoken of. On a certain occasion, when these reports came back known to contain false statements, the citizens of Quincy called a meeting, mostly out of the Church, and, after discussing the subject, pledged themselves to give me a thousand dollars *per annum*, and bear all my travelling expenses, if I would go as a missionary to the New England States, and enlighten them on this and other subjects, of which they considered them profoundly ignorant. But, owing to circumstances beyond my control, I was obliged to decline the acceptance of their generous offer.

If it had been consistently in my power, how gladly and willingly would I have undertaken this labour of love, and gloried in enlightening them down East, that they might keep their home-manufactured clergy at home, or give them some honourable employ better suited to their genius, than that of reading old musty and worm-eaten sermons! If this matter is rightly looked into, it will astonish every well-informed man to see the self-importance and self-complacence of these little home-manufactured fellows. If they would tarry at Jericho till their beards were grown out, it would certainly be more creditable to themselves, and to all others concerned, and especially to the cause of God.

It will be perceived that in the fall of 1834 the Galena and Chicago Districts were formed, which gave us six presiding-elder Districts in our Conference. Our Conference met in Springfield, October 1st, 1835. At this Conference I was returned to the Quincy District, which now consisted of the following appointments, namely, Pittsfield, Quincy Circuit, Quincy Mission, Rushville Station, Rushville Circuit, Canton, Fort Edwards Mission, Henderson River Mission, and Knoxville Mission; eight. At this Conference in Springfield, we again elected our delegates to the General Conference, which was holden in Cincinnati, May 1st, 1836. To this General Conference I was elected; and it was the fifth General Conference in which I was entitled to a seat by the suffrages of my brethren in the ministry.

At the General Conference of 1832, that body had granted the privilege to the West to publish a religious paper at Cincinnati, on the hard condition that we obtained five thousand subscribers. However, by strong effort we obtained that number, and Thomas A. Morris

P

was its first editor. At the General Conference of 1836, he, as well as Brother Beverly Waugh, and Dr. Fisk, were elected bishops of the Methodist Episcopal Church, and Doctor C. Elliott, the present incumbent, was elected editor of the "Western Christian Advocate," John F. Wright our Western book agent, and Leroy Swormstedt assistant book agent.

It was at this General Conference of 1836, that the ground was taken by a majority of the delegates from the slaveholding States, that slavery was right, and a blessing, instead of a curse, to the slaves themselves. We had from the North O. Scott and his coadjutors, who were ultra abolitionists; and we had some warm debates on the subject. The Southern delegates met in private caucus to devise a plan of separation from the Methodist Episcopal Church, unless we would so modify the Discipline as to tolerate slavery, or make it no bar to membership or office in the Church. This movement was headed by the Rev. William A. Smith, of Virginia, and others of the same cloth and kidney. I was invited by John Early, of Virginia, now bishop of the Southern Church, to attend one of these caucuses. I went. Some of them took strong ground, and urged a division, or a separation from the Methodist Episcopal Church. Others of them said they would never consent to a division; that they would rather suffer martyrdom than to divide the Church. Finally, I think they did not harmonize on any plan of division at that time; but William A. Smith said to me, he never would be satisfied unless we would agree to expunge everything from the Discipline of the Methodist Church on the subject of slavery; and, true to the dark principles of his creed, he never rested until he divided the Methodist Church; and at the late General Conference of the Church, South, they swept, as with the besom of destruction, every rule from their Discipline on the subject of slavery, and only lacked a few votes of erasing from the General Rules that part which forbids "the buying and selling of men, women, or children, with an intention to enslave them " *

This rule the advocates of slavery at the South have always interpreted to apply to the slave-trade, and that trade alone   Taking them to be sincere in this interpretation of this General Rule, what is the conclusion that we must draw from their late move in their General Conference? It is, plainly, that they wish every disciplinary barrier moved out of the way, and the slave-trade, with all its damning, murdering influences, revived again, notwithstanding it is denounced by all Christian philanthropists, and made piracy by the laws of our happy country; notwithstanding all their pretensions to patriotism, their love of country, and all their law-loving and law-abiding pro-

See note, ante, p. 90.

fessions, as being " obedient to the powers that be," they would open the way to revive this abominable traffic in human souls and bodies; and while this slave-trade stands reprobated by every Christian nation that deserves the name, and has the broad seal of reprobation set on it by God Himself, they wish to see its dark wheels set in motion again, without let or hindrance.

And why should they not desire this, if they are sincere in their expressed opinions ?   They tell us that slavery " is a political, domestic, and religious blessing;" if so, why not enter into the slave-trade, wholesale and retail? go with armed ships, kidnap human beings by the thousand, bring them to America, sell them into perpetual bondage ? Never mind the parting of husband and wife, parents and children; the encouraging the savage ferocity of these poor degraded heathen.   Tell them the Christian religion sanctions their bloody wars among themselves ; and that it is to make Christians of them that you buy and transport them to " the land of the free and the home of the brave."   Have no scruples of conscience about the thousands that are murdered in these wars, instigated by Christians, or that die on their passage from the land of barbarism to this Christian land of universal freedom; " the great end will sanctify the means."   Crowd the slave-ships or " floating hells;" all, all is to better their condition.   It is a god-like deed of mercy, and why should not Methodist preachers, bishops and all, have a large share in this benevolent and Christian affair ?   Who can forbid ?   And let the officers of these slave vessels never forget to tell these savage tribes that there is at least one very popular Church in America that sanctions all these operations, and will justify them ; namely, the Methodist Episcopal Church,-South.

Prior to the General Conference of 1836, the run-mad spirit of rabid abolitionism had broken out in some of the Eastern and Northern Conferences ; and Methodist preachers were found by the dozen to quit their appropriate fields of labour, and their holy calling of saving souls, and turn out and become hired lecturers against slavery. So zealous were they, that they forgot their pastoral duties ; and they went so far as violently to oppose colonization as a slaveholding trick. Dr. Fisk was a good man and true, and was as much opposed to slavery as any of them ; yet he was for occupying real Methodist preacher ground, and bearing his plain, honest testimony against the moral evil of slavery, and not meddling with it politically, only in a constitutional way.   He, seeing that this rabid abolitionism would rivet the chains of slavery the tighter, rouse the jealousies of the slave-holders, and disrupt the Methodist Church, flung himself into the breach, and met those lecturers in open combat; vanquished them in argument, and compelled them to retreat, or bolt, and set up for themselves. O. Scott and his coadjutors formed themselves into a separate party organization, calling themselves the "True Wesleyans;" but long since they have found, to their sorrow, that they misnamed the brat; for the secession that they produced was a very feeble, little, illegitimate child. But they nursed it till it took the rickets; and the last I heard of it, it was fast wasting away, and "the last state of it is worse than the first."

. Under these circumstances, Dr. Fisk stood in the general confidence of the Methodist Episcopal Church, North and South, East and West; and although he was not present at the General Conference at Cincinnati, yet when we were about to elect three new bishops, Dr. Winans, of Mississippi, a thorough Southern man, and a great defender of slavery, rose, and in open Conference nominated Dr. Fisk for episcopal honours; and if I am not greatly mistaken, nearly the entire Southern delegation voted for him, and he was elected by a great majority of the members of the General Conference. But Dr. Fisk, thinking that the episcopate was strong enough without him, declined being ordained, and lived and died without episcopal consecration. It is a pity that more Methodist preachers do not follow the illustrious course pursued by Dr. Fisk. Then we should benefit the slaves more than we do.

At the General Conference of 1836, there were six new Conferences formed; two in the West, namely, Arkansas and Michigan, and four in the East, namely, Erie, North Carolina, Oneida, and New Jersey. The number of members in the West was about 262,690; our travelling preachers in the West had increased to 1,069. The number of members in the Eastern Conferences was about 396,000; their travelling preachers numbered about 3,560. Total membership, 658,690; total travelling preachers, 4,629. Our increase in the West, in four years, was something like 45,000; in travelling preachers we had increased about 300. The increase in the Eastern Conferences, according to the Minutes, was 14,000; their increase in travelling preachers was something like 200. Total increase through the Connexion, in four years, 59,000.

Thus, I think, without any disposition to boast in the least degree, I may say, in the fear of God, that, under the Divine guidance of the Great Redeemer, the Methodist Episcopal Church, in point of prosperity and increase of number in her ministry and membership, stands without an equal in the Protestant world since the days of the apostles. O that she may keep humble, and never move her old land-marks!

Our venerable Bishop M'Kendree, of whom I have spoken freely in another part of this narrative, who laboured long and suffered much as a travelling preacher, had closed his mortal probation on March the 5th, 1835. At the General Conference at Cincinnati, in May, 1836, Bishop Soule preached the funeral sermon of this eminent minister and unrivalled bishop of the Methodist Episcopal Church. That sermon has been published and thrown broadcast over the world, and I therefore have no need to say anything in relation to its merits. But I wish to say a few brief things of Bishop M'Kendree himself.

If my information be correct, he was born in King William County, Virginia, 6th of July, 1757. In an extensive and glorious revival of religion, under the ministerial labours of John Easter, a real son of thunder and of consolation too, M'Kendree embraced religion and joined the Methodist Episcopal Church. In a few months he was licensed to preach, and was appointed to a Circuit. He was very diffident and distrustful of his own abilities as a preacher. The members of the Church did not receive him kindly. This he told me himself; and under the discouragement he met with from his brethren, he left his Circuit, conceiving that he was mistaken about his call to the ministry, but he fell into good hands among the preachers, and they advised, cheered, and comforted him, and soon he entered the work again.

These were the times of the schism created in the Church by James O'Kelly, who had a great influence over M'Kendree, and for a little while he inclined to leave the Methodist Episcopal Church and go with this popular schismatic. But he was not hasty, and narrowly watched the spirit and course of O'Kelly, until he became thoroughly satisfied that O'Kelly was of a wrong and wicked spirit, and that the great moving cause of O'Kelly's disaffection was disappointed ambition. He then gave up O'Kelly, fully satisfied that Bishop Asbury and his preachers were right, and from this to the day of his death he never wavered or doubted on the grand land-marks of Episcopal Methodism.

Bishop M'Kendree was the gentleman as well as Christian minister. He was a profound theologian, and understood thoroughly the organic laws of ecclesiastic government; he was a dignified, shrewd parliamentary presiding officer, a profound judge of human nature, and one of the strongest debaters and logical reasoners that ever graced an American pulpit. At an early period of his ministry he was transferred to the Western Conference, and, considering the hardships, privations, and sufferings of frontier life, and the delicacy of his constitution, he bore it all with great cheerfulness and resignation, and truly he was, in his feelings and habits, a Western man and a Western bishop. When his end drew near, death found him duly prepared for his change, and on his dying pillow and amid surrounding friends he was enabled to proclaim, " All is well." He died in Sumner County,

Tennessee State, at his brother's, Dr. M'Kendree, and was buried in his brother's family burying ground, where all that is mortal of Bishop M'Kendree will repose till the general resurrection.

Dr. Jennings, of Baltimore, was employed to write his life for publication, and, after making some progress in the work, declined its prosecution any further. Then the General Conference of the Methodist Episcopal Church, in 1840, requested Bishop Soule to prepare a history of his life and labours for publication; but, by some strange neglect, Bishop Soule delayed doing so till the unhappy division of the Church, and then Bishop Soule seceded from the Methodist Episcopal Church, and joined the Church, South; and I suppose if ever the life of Bishop M'Kendree is published at all, the Methodist Episcopal Church will be deprived of the benefit of it. It is to be regretted that this work has been so long delayed, and we think unnecessarily so.

CHAPTER XXV.

THE NEW-SCHOOL PREACHER.

In the fall of 1836, our Conference was holden in Rushville, Illinois State. Bishop R. R. Roberts attended and presided. My field of labour had for four years been the Quincy District. My constitutional time was out, and I was again appointed to the Sangamon District, which was composed of the following appointments: Jacksonville Station, Jacksonville Circuit, Winchester, Springfield Station, Sangamon, Flat Branch, Athens, Pecan Mission, Beardstown Mission; nine in all. It will be perceived that Beardstown was this year first formed into a distinct station, and Dr. P. Akers appointed missionary. It will also be noticed that the Illinois Conference, at this date, not only reached to the northern limits of the State, but had spread with the constantly increasing population into Wisconsin and Iowa Territories, and covered, in its missionary stations, almost the entire unbroken Indian country, now called the Minnesota Territory; and we had thirteen presiding-elder Districts, and at our annual Conference, held in Jacksonville, Morgan County, September 27th, 1837, we had over 130 travelling preachers, and over 21,000 members. Any one of our travelling preachers was liable to be sent from the mouth of the Ohio and Wabash Rivers nearly to the head waters of the Mississippi, a thousand or twelve hundred miles, and all the northern part of our Conference was frontier work or Indian wilds. Hard were our labours, but glorious was our success.

This year, 1837, J. T. Mitchell was appointed to the Jacksonville Station, and we had a blessed revival of religion in the station, and a number were added to the Church. At one of our quarterly meetings there was a minister who was what was called a New-School minister, and he was willing to work anywhere. When the mourners presented themselves at the altar of prayer, he would talk to them, and exhort them to "change their purpose," and assured them that all who changed their purpose were undoubted Christians. I plainly saw he was doing mischief, and I went immediately after him, and told them not to depend on a change of purpose in order to become a Christian, but to believe in the Lord Jesus Christ with a heart unto righteousness, and they should be saved. Thus I had to counteract the false sentiments inculcated by this New-School minister. It is very strange to me to think these educated and home-manufactured preachers do not understand the plain, Bible doctrine of the new birth better. They say man is a free agent in so far as to change his purpose, and in changing his purpose he is constituted a new creature. Thus he makes himself a Christian by his own act without the Spirit of God.

This year we had a gracious work of religion in the town of Winchester, in the Winchester Circuit. We had no meeting-house or church built there at this time to worship in; and when our quarterly meeting came on, the friends had procured an unfinished frame building, large and roomy, to hold the quarterly meeting in. There was a very large concourse of people in attendance. The house was crowded to overflowing; our seats were temporary; no altar, no pulpit: but our meeting progressed with great interest. The members of the Church were greatly revived, many backsliders were reclaimed, and scores of weeping and praying sinners crowded our temporary altar that we had erected.

There happened to be at our quarterly meeting a fresh, green, live Yankee from down East. He had regularly graduated, and had his diploma, and was regularly called, by the Home Missionary Society, to visit the far-off West,—a perfect moral waste, in his view of the subject; and having been taught to believe that we were almost cannibals, and that Methodist preachers were nothing but a poor, illiterate set of ignoramuses, he longed for an opportunity to display his superior tact and talent, and throw us poor upstarts of preachers in the West, especially Methodist preachers, into the shades of everlasting darkness. He, of course, was very forward and officious. He would, if I had permitted it, have taken the lead of our meeting. At length I thought I would give him a chance to ease himself of his mighty burden; so I put him up one night to read his sermon. The frame building we were worshipping in was not plastered, and the wind blew hard; our candles flared and gave a bad light, and our ministerial hero made a very awkward out in reading his sermon. The congregation paid a heavy penance and became restive; he balked, and hemmed, and coughed at a disgusting rate. At the end of about thirty minutes the great blessing came : he closed, to the great satisfaction of all the congregation.

I rose and gave an exhortation, and had a bench prepared, to which I invited the mourners. They came in crowds; and there was a solemn power rested on the congregation. My little hot-house reader seemed to recover from his paroxysm of a total failure, as though he had done all right, and, uninvited, he turned in to talk to the mourners. He would ask them if they did not love Christ; then he would try to show them that Christ was lovely; then he would tell them it was a very easy thing to become a Christian; that they had only to resolve to be a Christian, and instantly he or she was a Christian. I listened a moment, and saw this heterodoxy would not do; that it produced jargon and confusion. I stepped up to him, and said,—

. "Brother, you don't know how to talk to mourners. I want you to go out into the congregation, and exhort sinners."

He did not appear the least disconcerted, but at my bidding he left the altar, and out he went into the crowd, and turned in to talking to sinners. There was a very large man, who stood a few steps from the mourners, who weighed about 230 pounds; he had been a professor, but was backslidden. The power of God arrested him, and he cried out aloud for mercy, standing on his feet. My little preacher turned round, and pressed back through the crowd; and, coming up to this large man, reached up, and tapped him on the shoulder, saying,—

"Be composed; be composed."

. Seeing and indistinctly hearing this, I made my way to him, and cried out at the top of my voice,—

"Pray on, brother; pray on, brother; there's no composure in hell or damnation."

And just as I crowded my way to this convicted man, who was still crying aloud for mercy, the little preacher tapped him again on the shoulder, saying,—

"Be composed; be composed, brother."

I again responded,—

"Pray on, brother; pray on, brother; there is no composure in hell."

I said to the throng that crowded the aisle that led to the altar,—

"Do, friends, stand back, till I get this man to the mourners' bench."

But they were so completely jammed together that it seemed almost impossible for me to get through with my mourner. I let go his arm, and stepped forward to open the way to the altar, and just as I had opened the aisle, and turned to go back, and lead him to the mourners' bench, the Lord spoke peace to his soul, standing on his feet; and he cried, " Glory to God!" and, in the ecstasy of his joy, he reached forward to take me in his arms; but, fortunately for me, two men were crowded into the aisle between him and myself, and he could not reach me. Missing his aim in catching me, he wheeled round and caught my little preacher in his arms, and lifted him up from the floor , and being a large, strong man, having great physical power, he jumped from bench to bench, knocking the people against one another on the right and left, front and rear, holding up in his arms the little preacher. The little fellow stretched out both arms and both feet, expecting every moment to be his last, when he would have his neck broken. O ! how I desired to be near this preacher at that moment, and tap him on the shoulder, and say, " Be composed; be composed, brother ! " But as solemn as the times were, I, with many others, could not command my risibilities, and for the moment it had like to have checked the rapid flow of good feeling with those that beheld the scene; but you may depend on it, as soon as the little hot-bed parson could make his escape, he was missing

Our annual Conference was held in Alton this fall, September 12th, 1838. Owing to the low stage of water in the Ohio River, Bishop Soule was detained on the way, and did not reach Alton till the fourth day of the Conference. He not being present when we organized, I was elected president of the Conference till the bishop arrived.

In the fall of 1839, onr Illinois Conference was held in Springfield, Sangamon County ; here we elected our delegates to the eighth delegated General Conference of the Methodist Episcopal Church. I was one of the delegates, and this was the seventh General Conference to which I was elected. Our General Conference sat in Baltimore, May 1st, 1840. At this Conference, the unhappy agitation of slavery was revived. The two ultra parties had their representatives there. The slavery party from the South contended that slavery was no disqualification for the episcopal office. The abolitionists from the North contended that slavery was a sin under all circumstances. This party was led on by O. Scott ; and they urged that it should not only be a test of office, but of membership, in the Methodist Episcopal Church, in the slaveholding States as well as the free States. Our Committee on Episcopacy had recommended the election of two more bishops : believing that if we went into an election of these officers of the Church, a conflict on the subject would soon ensue, and believing that the then present incumbents of that office could discharge all the labours necessary for the healthy action of the Church, I flung myself against the election of any more bishops at that Conference.   In this, nearly all the conservative members of the General Conference joined me, and thereby defeated the designs of both the ultra parties, and every aspiring expectant for that office, for the time being, and, in all probability, a rupture in the Church.   At this General Conference, the following additional annual Conferences were formed : Rock River, North Ohio, Memphis, and Texas, all in the West and South-west. Rock River Conference was stricken off from the Illinois Conference, and consisted of the following presiding-elder Districts : Chicago, Ottawa, Mount Morris, Burlington, Iowa, Indian Mission, Plattville, and Milwaukie; eight in number.

The Illinois Conference consisted of the following presiding-elder Districts, namely, Danville, Mount Vernon, Vandalia, Lebanon, Jacksonville, Springfield, Quincy, Knoxville, and Bloomington; nine in number.   We had in Rock River Conference 6,585 members, and 75 travelling preachers; in Illinois Conference we had 24,687 members, and 103 travelling preachers.   North ·Ohio Conference was stricken off from Ohio Conference; the Memphis Conference was stricken off from the Tennessee Conference; the Texas Conference was taken from the Mississippi Conference, and had three presiding-elder Districts, namely, San Augustine, Galveston, Rutersville; having 18 travelling preachers, and 1,853 members.   Thus you see in the two original divisions of the work, namely, East and West, the East had 16 annual Conferences ; and the West, with her enlargements, had 16 annual Conferences; making, in all, 32, besides the Liberia Mission Conference and the Canadas, which were under foreign governments.

The Eastern division of the work had, in members, 466,561 ; in travelling preachers, 3,125 ; the membership in the West was, 375,433 ; travelling preachers we had, 1,447.   Total in members, 841,994 ; in travelling preachers, 4,572.   Increase in four years in the East was, in members, 60,500 ; in the Western division was over 11,200.

Here I wish to remark that the abolition party up to this time had universally, as far as I knew, opposed most strenuously the Colonization Society; and it really appeared to me that if they could not effect an immediate emancipation, and a restoration of the people of colour to equal rights and privileges with the whites, they did not care what became of them. · I will state a case.   In Natchez, Mississippi, the Methodist Episcopal Church had erected a good, substantial church at a considerable cost. The galleries of the church were appropriated for the use and benefit of the coloured people. Some time in 1839 or 1840, a fearful tornado had swept over the town of Natchez, and done a great deal of damage; and among the rest, it had well-nigh overturned the Methodist church, so that it was not safe to worship in it. The society was weak, and comparatively poor. In this situation they were deprived of any suitable place to worship in, either the whites or blacks.

The delegates from the Mississippi Conference came on to the General Conference, and asked aid of their Eastern brethren, and of the members of the General Conference, to rebuild or refit their church; and a collection was taken up in the Conference for this purpose; and if my memory serves me, the members of the General Conference gave them over one thousand dollars; but our abolition brethren would not give anything, alleging that the church or the Gospel could do no good to either the slaves or slaveholders, so long as slavery existed among them. I went to those members of the General Conference who refused, and tried to reason the case with them; but all in vain. I urged that these poor slaves could not help themselves; they were in bondage, not of choice, but from circumstances beyond their control; and we ought not to withhold the Gospel from them; for it was all the comfort these poor slaves could have in this life, or to fit them for happiness in the life to come. But no; it was upholding and countenancing slavery, and, therefore, their consciences would not let them contribute anything. Now look at it; who does not see that there was a wrong and fanatical spirit which actuated them, and that their consciences, for solidity and rotundity, very much resembled a ram's horn? But this false view has prevented many, very many, from doing their duty by these poor children of Ham.

In the fall of 1840–41, I was appointed to Jacksonville District; and on September 15th, 1841, our annual Conference was holden in Jacksonville. Bishop Morris presided. The Jacksonville District embraced the following appointments, namely, Carrollton Station, Carrollton Circuit, Grafton, Whitehall, Winchester, Jacksonville Station, Jacksonville Circuit, and Manchester; eight appointments. In the course of this year, we had a camp quarterly meeting, for the Winchester Circuit, in what was called Egypt. We had a beautiful camp-ground, a few miles from Winchester. There was a general turn-out among the members, who tented on the ground. William D. R. Trotter was the Circuit preacher.

We had been threatened by many of the baser sort, that they would break up our camp-meeting; and there was a general rally from the floating population of the river, and the loose-footed, doggery-haunting, dissipated renegades of the towns and villages all round. They came and pitched their tents a few hundred yards from the camp-ground. Many also came in waggons and carriages, bringing whiskey and spirits of different kinds, pies, cigars, tobacco, &c. We had many respectable tent-holders and proper officers on the ground, but I plainly saw that we were to have' trouble; so I summoned the tent-holders and friends of good order together, and we adopted rules to govern the meeting, and then urged them, one and all, to aid me in executing those rules for the maintenance of good order. But I thought there was a disposition in some of the friends to shrink from responsibility, and that they must be roused to action.

When we were called to the stand by the sound of the trumpet, I called the attention of the congregation to the absolute necessity of keeping good order. I stated that my father was a revolutionary soldier, and fought for the liberties we enjoyed, and all the boon he had left me was liberty; and that, as the responsible officer of the camp-meeting, if the friends of order and the sworn officers of the law would give me backing, I would maintain order at the risk of my life. My lecture roused the friends of order, and they gave me their countenance and aid; but the whiskey-sellers and whiskey-drinkers, nothing daunted, commenced their deeds of darkness. Some were soon drunk, and interrupted our devotions very much. I then ordered several writs, and took into custody several of those whiskey-vendors and drunken rowdies; but these rowdies rose in mob force, and rescued the whiskey-seller and his waggon and team from the officer of the law. The officer came running to me, and informed me of the rising of the mob, and that the whiskey man was given up, and was making his escape, and it appeared to me he was very much scared. I told him to summon me and five other men that I named, and I would insure the retaking of the transgressor, in spite of any mob. He did so. We rushed upon them and stopped the team. The man that had transgressed drew a weapon, and ordered us to stand off; that he would kill the first man that touched him: and as one of the men and myself that were summoned to take him rushed on him, he made a stroke at my companion with his weapon, but missed him. I then sprang upon him, and caught him by the collar, and jerked him over the waggon bed, in which he was standing, among his barrels. He fell on all-fours. I jumped on him, and told him he was my prisoner, and that if he did not surrender I should hurt him. The deputy she-riff. of the county, who was with the mob, and a combatant at that, ran up to me, and ordered me to let the prisoner go. I told him I

should not. He said, if I did not, he would knock me over. I told
him, if he struck, to make a sure lick; foi the next was mine. Our
officer then commanded me to take the deputy sheriff, and I did so.
He scuffled a little; but finding himself in iather close quaiters, he
surrendered.

We then took thirteen of the mob, the whiskey-seller, and the sheriff, and marched them off to the magistrate, to the tune of good
order. They were fined by the justice of the peace; some paid their
fine, some appealed to court. This appealing we liked well, because
they then had to give security, and this secured the fine and costs,
which some of them were not able to pay.

This somewhat checked them for a while, but they rallied again,
and gave us trouble. There was one man, a turbulent fellow, who
sold whiskey about a quarter of a mile off. He had often interrupted
us by selling whiskey at our camp-meetings. He generally went
armed with deadly weapons, to keep off officers. I sent the constable
after him; but he had a musket, well loaded, and would not be taken.
He kept a drinking party round him nearly all night however, toward morning they left him, and went off to sleep as best they could;
and he lay down in his waggon, and went to sleep, with his loaded
musket by his side.

Just as day dawned, I slipped over the creek, and came up to his
waggon. He was fast asleep. I reached over the waggon bed and
gathered his gun and ammunition; then struck the waggon bed with
the muzzle of the musket, and cried out, "Wake up! wake up!" He
sprang to his feet, and felt for his gun. I said, "You are my prisoner; and if you resist, you are a dead man!" He begged me not
to shoot, and said that he would surrender. I told him to get out of
the waggon, and march before me to the camp-ground; that I was
going to have him tried for violating good order and the laws of his
country. He began to beg most piteously, and said if I would only
let him escape that time, he would gear up and go right away, and
never do the like again. I told him to harness his team, and start.
He did so. When he got ready to go, I poured out his powder, and
fired off his musket, and gave it to him; and he left us, and troubled
us no more.

On Sunday night, the rowdies all collected at the Mormon camp.
It was so called, because some Mormons had come and pitched a tent
a quarter of a mile from our encampment, with whiskey and many other
things to sell. They ate and drank; and by way of mockery, and in
contempt of religion, they held a camp-meeting; they preached,
prayed, called for mourners, shouted, and kept up a continual annoy-
ance. They sent me word they would give me ten dollars if I would

bring an officer and a company to take them; that they could whip our whole encampment. They fixed out their watchers.

I bore it, and waited till late in the night; and when most of our tent-holders were retired to rest, I rose from my bed, dressed myself in some old shabby clothing that I had provided for the purpose, and sallied forth. It was a beautiful moonlight night. Singly and alone I went up to the Mormon camp. When I got within a few rods of their encampment, I stopped, and stood in the shadow of a beautiful sugar-tree. Their motley crowd were carrying on at a mighty rate. One young man sprang upon a barrel, and called them to order, saying he was going to preach to them, and must and would have order, at the risk of his life. Said he, "My name is Peter Cartwright; my father fought through the old war with England, and helped to gain our independence, and all the legacy he left me was liberty. Come to order, and take your seats, and hear me!"

They obeyed him, and took their seats. He then sung and prayed, rose up, took his text, and harangued them about half an hour. He then told them he was going to call for mourners, and ordered a bench to be set out; and it was done. He then invited mourners to come forward and kneel down to be prayed for. A vast number of the crowd came and kneeled, more than his bench could accommodate. This self-styled preacher, or orator of the night, then called lustily for another bench; and still they crowded to it. A thought struck me that I would go and kneel with them, as this would give me a fine chance to let loose on them at a proper time; but as I had determined to rout the whole company, and take their camp single-handed and alone, I declined kneeling with the mourners. So this young champion of the devil called on several to pray for these mourners; he exhorted them almost like a real preacher. Several pretended to get religion, and jumped and shouted at a fearful rate. The preacher by this time was pretty much exhausted, and became thirsty. He ordered a pause in their exercises, and called for something to drink; he ordered the tent-holder to bring the best he had.

Just at this moment I fetched two or three loud whoops, and said, "Here! here! here, officers and men, take them! take them! every one of them, tent-holders and all!" and I rushed on them. They broke, and ran pell-mell. Fortunately, five or six little lads were close by, from our encampment, who had been watching me raise the shout, and rushed with me into their camp; but all the motley crowd fled, tent-holders and all, and the lads and myself had not only peaceable but entire possession of all their whiskey, goods, chattels, and some arms, and not a soul to dispute our right of possession. Thus you see a literal fulfilment of Scripture. "The wicked fleeth when no man pursueth;" or, "One shall chase a thousand, and two put ten thousand to flight."

There are but very few hardened wretches who disturb religious worship but what at heart are base cowards: this I have proved to my entire satisfaction throughout my ministerial life, for more than fifty years. I will here say, on Monday, the day after the rout of the Mormon camp, the power of God fell on our congregation, and the whole encampment was lighted with the glory of God. The Church, or members of the Church, were greatly blessed, and felt fully compensated for all the toil and trouble that they had been at in pitching their tents in the grove, and waiting upon the Lord a few days and nights. Hardened sinners were brought to bow before the Lord, and some of them were soundly converted. And I will record it to the glory of the stupendous grace of God, that the young man who had been the ringleader in the ranks of these disturbers of God's people, and the mock preacher in the Mormon camp the night before, was overtaken by the mighty power of God, and awfully shaken as it were over hell. He fell prostrate before God and all the people he had so much disturbed and persecuted, and cried for mercy as from the verge of damnation, and never rested till God reclaimed him; for he was a wretched backslider. I had known him in Tennessee, and had often preached in his father's house

Of the disorderly fellows who had been arrested and *fined*, and had appealed to the court, hardly one of them came to a good end, or died a natural death, some ran away to Texas, some were stabbed in affrays of different kinds · it seemed as if God had put a mark on them, and His fearful judgments followed them even into strange and distant lands. When their appeals came on for trial in court, there were two distinguished lawyers who volunteered to conduct the prosecution against them; one of them was the lamented General Hardin, of Morgan County, who afterward fell in Mexico in General Taylor's army, at the memorable battle of Buena Vista, while fighting, or contending with Santa Anna's unprincipled minions; but he died like a brave soldier and subordinate officer. Peace to his memory! He was considered a worthy member of the Presbyterian Church, and a staunch friend to good order.

The other lawyer, Mr. Sanbourn, though somewhat dissipated at times, was a talented gentleman of the bar, and a friend to religious order. These gentlemen, without fee or reward, volunteered their services to prosecute these wretched disturbers of the worship of God, and by their eloquent appeals to the jurors made these transgressors quail before the public bar of their country; and these suits, first and last, cost those offenders against the morals of their country over three hundred dollars, showing them clearly that the way of the transgressor is hard. I must remark here that I was much pleased with the decision of Judge Lockwood, who presided at the trial; his decision was substantially this, that no matter what the articles were that were sold at a place of worship, if it disturbed the peace and quiet of the worshippers, it was punishable by the statute that was enacted for the protection of worshipping assemblies; that as a free people, where there was no religious test, we had a right to assemble and establish our own forms, or rules of order; and that anything which infracted those rules of order made to govern a worshipping congregation, the law made a high misdemeanour, and therefore those who transgressed those rules were punishable by the law. Our present law to protect worshipping congregations is too loose and obscure. In the hands of good officers of the law, the present statute will protect people in the sacred right to worship God; but in the hands of corrupt officers it is often construed to screen offenders, and thereby give encouragement to disorderly persons to trample with impunity on the rights of religious people. I have often wondered why legislative bodies of men should be so reluctant to pass a stringent law on this subject. If people don't like the forms of worship of any religious denomination, let them stay away; but if they will attend their religious assemblies, they ought to behave themselves; and if they will not behave and conform, they ought by law to be compelled to do it, or punished severely for trampling under foot the rights of a free people assembled for the express purpose of peaceably worshipping God. The good Book is right when it declares, "When the wicked bear rule, the land mourneth," and that "righteousness exalteth a nation, but sin is a reproach to any people:" but we still hope to see better days, better laws, and better administrators of law. The Lord hasten it in His time!

CHAPTER XXVI.

CHURCH IN A CABIN.

In the fall of 1842 'our Illinois Conference was holden in Winchester, Scott County, September 14th; Bishop Roberts presided, and I was continued on the Jacksonville District. The reader will indulge me in saying a few things about my own immediate neighbourhood. When I settled here in 1824, there was no society nearer than five miles on Rock Creek, to which place my family had to go for Circuit preaching and class-meeting every Sunday, if they attended anywhere. There was in my immediate settlement but one single member of the Methodist Church, besides my own family. This member was a widow lady, a very fine woman, and I think a consistent Christian.

The country was entirely new, and almost in a state of nature : we had no churches to worship in; nearly all the citizens lived in newly built cabins. We thought we would open our cabin for preaching, and did so, and invited the neighbours to come and hear the word of God, and worship with us. I formed a small class of about twelve, including three of my own family ; and we kept Circuit preaching in our humble dwelling for fourteen years, during which time our little class continued with various successes and depressions from year to year. Sometimes by emigration we increased considerably, and then, when these new emigrants would select homes for themselves, and move off, we would be reduced almost to the number with which we started.

About this time my wife's health was very poor, so that entertaining preaching every two weeks, and class-meeting every Sunday, became a little too much for her strength. I determined to build a church ; but how was it to be done ? The society was small and poor; the citizens outside of the society were comparatively poor, and not friendly to the Methodists, but I determined to build a house to worship God in, and accordingly I opened a subscription, had trustees appointed, gave a lot of ground to build the church on, and subscribed one hundred dollars toward its erection. But when I presented my subscription paper to neighbours round, there were many objections and excuses ; some wanted it for school purposes as well as a church ; some said, if I would make it a Union Church for all denominations, they would then help, but they would not give anything if it was to be deeded to the Methodist Episcopal Church. To these objections I answered, "No, friends ; a church shall never be a school-house ; and as for a Union Church, I never knew one built on this principle but what became a bone of contention, and created strife, and ended in confusion ; " that a church should always belong to some religious denomination that would take care of it, and I was going to build a church for the Methodists ; if they would help me, I would thank them; and if they did not see proper to do so, I would try without their help as best I could. Our help amounted to but little, but we commenced, and finally succeeded in building a neat little church, twenty-four by thirty feet, which cost us about six hundred dollars, of which I had to pay about three hundred. I struggled hard, and sometimes thought my load was too heavy to get along with ; but my creed was never to back out, unless I found myself wrong.

Shortly after we finished the house, Brother Heath, now of California, and Brother H. Wallace, of the Griggsville District, Illinois

Q

Conference, were our Circuit preachers; and it pleased the Lord to pour out His Holy Spirit upon our congregation and settlement generally, and we had a glorious revival, resulting in about forty conversions and accessions to the Church. I then thought that the use I had made of the 300 dollars in building the church was the best investment I had ever made in all my life. We called the house " Pleasant Plains church."

Long since our little church became too small, and we have enlarged it so that it is now thirty feet by fifty. Our society increased so that a division has taken place, and another very respectable church has been built a few miles off, and the two societies number near one hundred and eighty members, and the time is not distant when another church must be erected a few miles south of the old stand. See what the Lord has done for us, under all the forbidding circumstances that attended our little history in the last thirty years. Praise the Lord !

I beg leave here to say that the first church, as far as I know, ever built in Sangamon County and Sangamon Circuit, was on Spring Creek, six miles west of Springfield. It was really a log cabin, about eighteen feet by twenty, with a log partition cutting off a small part of it for a class-room. Here was one of the oldest classes ever formed in Sangamon Circuit. In this little house the society met and worshipped for many years; and, on the lot donated for the church and burying-ground, the Circuit erected a large and comfortable camp-ground, and many, very many, glorious camp-meetings were held here ; and I may safely say that hundreds of souls were born into the kingdom of God on this consecrated ground ; and many of those who sung and shouted the high praises of God on this ground have long since fallen victims to death, and are now employed in singing praises to God and the Lamb, around the throne in heaven.

This camp-ground was called " Watters's Camp-Ground." He lived near it, but years gone by he left the Church militant for the Church triumphant above. This spot is sacred to me, as several of my children were converted on it, and many of my best friends in heaven, as well as on earth, were converted here ; and we have sung, and prayed, and shouted together ; and I have a strong hope that we shall shortly sing together in heaven, and this singing and shouting will last for ever. Amen.

In 1840–41, Alton Station, that had been attached to the Lebanon District, Charles Holliday presiding elder, was attached to the Jacksonville District, N. Hobart in charge. In the fall of 1842–43, N. S. Bastion and C. J Houts were appointed to Alton. Our quarterly meeting came off in the dead of this winter; and although it was

bitter cold weather, we had a good congregation, and Divine power
was present to heal. Many were converted and deeply penitent, and
we found it necessary to protract the meeting. Mourners, in crowds,
came to the altar for the prayers of the Church. Right in the midst
of our revival, the keeper of the Eagle Tavern took it into his heart
(not head, for that was nearly brainless) that he would stop our
revivals; so he proclaimed that he was going to have a splendid free
ball the next evening at the Eagle Tavern, and dispatched his runners,
and ticketed nearly the whole city. Among the rest he sent me a
ticket to the church, where we were having a very good meeting. Just
before the congregation was dismissed, I rose in the pulpit, and read
my ticket to the ball, and then announced that I could not attend the
Eagle Tavern ball, for the reason that I was going to have a Methodist ball in the church the same evening, and requested the whole
congregation to attend the Methodist ball, and get as many more to
come with them as they could; that my invitation they might consider
as a free ticket; that I was sure we would have a better fiddler than they
possibly could scare up at the Eagle Tavern. The thing took like
wildfire. The wickedest persons in the congregation electioneered
for the Methodist ball, and cried out shame on the tavern-keeper.
When the evening came, after all the drilling and drumming of the
tavern-keeper, he could not get ladies enough to dance a four-handed
reel. He succeeded in getting two little girls and some men, and
these mean fellows had well-nigh danced the children to death. Our
church was crowded to overflowing. That night the arm of the Lord
was made bare, and the mighty power of God was felt through the
numerous crowd. Many came to the altar as weeping penitents, but
rose therefrom with triumphant shouts of "Glory to God in the
highest, peace on earth, good-will toward men."

I now beg leave to relate an incident which occurred at this
meeting; I will do it as delicately as I well can. Among the crowd
that came to the altar there were many women, and among them
two good-looking, well-dressed young ladies, who were deeply
affected; it seemed as if the great deep of their hearts was broken up.
I was informed that they were under ill-fame, and an old sister in the
Church was so disturbed about them that she wanted me to drive them
from the altar, for fear we should be reproached, and bring down persecution on the Church. I told her to be quiet, and let them alone;
"for," said I, "they must have religion, or be lost for ever."
But the old sister would not rest; she ran to Brother Bastion and told
him. He was a very sensitive man. He came to me and whispered,
telling me they must be ordered away directly; it would ruin our
meeting and stop the work. I begged him to let them alone.

"Now," said I, "brother, on the other side of the altar there are a dozen men that, in all probability, are guilty of as base conduct as these young women; why don't you go and drive them from the altar? Do let them alone. Do you go and talk to the men, and I will attend to these females; they must not be driven from the altar of prayer." But two of our old, squeamish sisters, when I turned away from Brother Bastion, renewed their importunities with Bastion, and, while my attention was called to regulate the congregation, Bastion went and ordered these two women from the altar. They retired away back to a vacant seat and sat down, and wept bitterly. As soon as I discovered what was done, I followed those women to their seats, and talked with them and encouraged them, saying, "Although you may be rejected by mortals, God will not reject or spurn you from His presence. Mary Magdalene had seven devils, yet Christ cast them all out; the man in the tombs had a legion of devils in him, but Christ dispossessed them all." They asked me to pray for them. "Yes," said I, "with all my heart," and we knelt down and prayed. It seemed as if their hearts would break with the sorrow and anguish they felt; and then to punish those sensitive old sisters, I went and made them come and pray for them; and before we closed our meeting, one of them professed to be converted, and I have no reason to doubt it. The other left the house weeping. She never returned to our meeting. Perhaps she was for ever lost on account of this uncalled-for rebuke.

The next time we opened the doors of the Church, to take in members, a number came and joined. This young woman, who had experienced religion, advanced to the foot of the altar, but would not come and give me her hand. I saw she wanted to join, but was afraid, not having confidence to do so; and she said, afterwards, she thought the Church would not receive her. I went to her, took her by the hand, and asked her if she did not desire to join the Church. She said, with streaming eyes, "Yes, if the Church can possibly receive me, and grant me the lowest seat among God's people."

I lived to see this woman in other and after years, and with firm and unfaltering steps she lived up to her profession, and thoroughly redeemed herself from degradation, in the estimation of all who knew her. Now, dear reader, think of it. Did Christ reject the woman taken in adultery, or the woman of Samaria at the well, or any other poor wretched sinner, male or female, that ever came to Him with a broken and contrite heart? Think of the significant words of the poet,—

> "None are too vile, who will repent.
> Out of one sinner legions went;
> The Lord did him relieve," &c.

It is a little singular why men, and women too, should feel such sensitiveness concerning females of ill-fame more than they do in relation to men; especially when they make efforts to reform their lives and live religious; but it is so, though I cannot see any just reason for it.

This Conference year, 1842–43, was a memorable one in many parts of our beloved Zion. Jacksonville District shared largely in revival influences. Several hundreds were soundly converted, and over five hundred joined the Methodist Episcopal Church in the bounds of the District. We not only had the above-named revival in Alton, but Brother Bird had a prosperous year on the Carrollton Circuit; Brother J. B. Houts considerable prosperity on the Whitehall Circuit; Brother Grubbs had a fine revival in the Jacksonville Station; but perhaps it was a jubilee to the Winchester Circuit, under the labours of Brother Norman Allen, and those that worked side by side with him pretty near the whole year.

Naples, a beautiful little town on the east bank of the Illinois River, was one of the appointments in the Winchester Circuit. The citizens were kind and friendly; but, with a few exceptions, they were very wicked, and had long resisted and rejected the offers of mercy; but at a protracted meeting gotten up and superintended by Brother Allen, this wicked little town was awfully shaken by the power of God; many tall sons and daughters of dissipation were made to quail under the power of God. From day to day, from evening to evening, they crowded the place of worship, and, with unmistakable signs of penitence, prostrated themselves at the mourners' bench. The cries of the penitent and the shouts of the converted were heard with awe and wonder by the wicked multitude that stood around. Deism gave way, Universalism caved in, scepticism, with its coat of many colours, stood aghast, hell trembled, devils fled, drunkards awoke to soberness, and, I may safely say, all ranks and grades of sinners were made to cry out, "Men and brethren, what shall we do to be saved?" The cries of penitents were not only heard in the church, but in the streets, in almost all the houses, by day and by night. Many were the thrilling incidents that attended this revival in Naples. More than one hundred were converted, and joined the Church, and the whole face of the town was changed; and although some of them fell back into their old habits of vice, yet many of them stood firm as pillars in the house of God. The subjects of this revival were from the child of ten or twelve years to the hoary-headed sinner that stood trembling on the verge of the grave.

Before this meeting closed in Naples, which was crowned with such signal success, our quarterly meeting commenced in a little town in the same Circuit, called Exeter. There Satan had long reigned without a rival, wickedness of all kinds abounded; and what made it the more deplorable, the wickedness of the people was sanctified by a Universalist priest or preacher, who assured them all of eternal salvation in heaven, irrespective of their moral conduct here on earth. I have thought, and do still think, if I were to set out to form a plan to contravene the laws of God, to encourage wickedness of all kinds, to corrupt the morals and encourage vice, and crowd hell with the lost and the wailings of the damned, the Univeisalist plan should be the plan, the very plan, that I would adopt. What has a Universalist, who really and sincerely believes that doctrine, to fear? Just nothing at all; for this flesh-pleasing, conscience-soothing doctrine will not only justify him in his neglect of duty to God and man, but gives fallen nature an unlimited licence to serve the devil with greediness, in any and every possible way that his degenerate, fallen soul requires or desires.

A few years ago I had a neighbour who professed to be a confirmed Universalist. He contended with me that there was no devil but the evil disposition in man, and that there was no hell but the bad feelings that men had when they did wrong; that this was all the punishment anybody would suffer. When this neighbour's father lay on his dying bed, (a confirmed Universalist, professedly,) there was a faithful minister of Christ believed it his duty to visit this old Universalist, and warn him of his danger, and try to awaken his conscience, if not seared, to a just view of his real situation. The minister, however, failed in his faithful attempt and well-meant endeavours; for the old man, then on his dying pillow, was greatly offended at the preacher, and told him he did not thank him for trying to shake his faith in his dying moments. This neighbour of mine, and son of this old, hardened sinner, was greatly enraged at the preacher, and cursed and abused him in a violent manner. A few days after the demise of the old man, he, in a furious rage, began to abuse and cuise the preacher in my presence, and said,—

"D—n him, I wish he was in hell, and the devil had him."

I stopped him short by saying, "Pooh, pooh, man, what are you talking about? There is no hell but the bad feelings that a man has when he does wrong, and no devil but the evil disposition that is in man;"—thus answering a fool according to his folly.

"Well," said he, "if there is no hell, there ought to be, to put such preachers in."

"Now, sir," said I, "you see the utter untenableness of your creed; for a man, even in trying to do good honestly, draws down

your wrath, and, in a moment, you want a hell to put him into, and a
devil to torment him, for giving you an offence, and for doing what
no good man ought to be offended about. But God must be insulted,
His name blasphemed, His laws trampled under foot; yet He must
have no hell to put such wretches in, no devil to torment them. Now,
I would be ashamed of myself if I were in your place, and let the seal
of truth close my lips for ever hereafter."

Although he was confounded, he still clave to his God-dishonouring
doctrine, waxing worse and worse, till it was generally believed he
was guilty of a most heinous crime.

But to return to the narrative. From the first sermon in Exeter,
at the quarterly meeting, there were visible signs of good; and
although the weather was intensely cold, yet our church was crowded
beyond its utmost capacity. The power of God arrested many careless sinners, and waked up many old formal professors of religion.
There was a large company of young unfledged Universalists who came
to look on and mock, and so ignorant were they, that they did not
imagine they would run into any possible danger of taking these
"Methodist fits," as they called the exercises that were going on.
There were two sisters, young ladies, carried off with the soul-
destroying doctrines of the Universalists, in attendance. In pressing
through the crowd, I saw one of them was deeply affected, and weeping. I went and talked with her. She saw her wretched condition.
I invited her to go to the altar with the mourners; she consented,
and I led her there. I talked and prayed with her; she was deeply
engaged. Her sister did not know for some time that she was at the
mourners' bench, but presently some one told her. At this she flew
into a violent rage, and said, at the risk of her life, she would have
her out of that disgraceful place. I happened to turn my face toward
the door, and saw her coming, the house was very much crowded;
some tried to stop her, but she rushed on. I rose and met her in the
crowded aisle, and told her to be calm, and desist. She made neither
better nor worse of it than to draw back her arm and give me a severe
slap in the face with her open hand. I confess this rather took me by
surprise, and, as the common saying is, she made the fire fly out of
my eyes in tremendous sparkling brilliancy; but, collecting my best
judgment, I caught her by the arms near her shoulders, and wheeled
her to the right-about, and moved her forward to the door, and said,
"Gentlemen, please open the door; the devil in this Universalist lady
has got fighting hot, and I want to set her outside to cool" The
door was opened, and I handed her out with this assurance, that when
she got into a good humour, and could behave herself like a decent lady
ought to do, then, and not till then, she might come in again   I

then closed the door, and set a watch to keep it, to avoid further disturbance.

I had hardly returned to the altar when the young lady I had led there rose and gave us a heavenly shout, and then another, and another, till five in rapid succession raised the shout. It ran like electricity through the congregation; sinners wept, quaked, and trembled, and saints shouted aloud for joy. Thus our meeting continued 'for a number of nights and days, and many souls were born into the kingdom of God. The whole country around for miles came to our meetings, were convicted and converted, and great was the joy of the people of God. Over one hundred professed religion, and nearly that number joined the Methodist Episcopal Church.

There was a gentleman in this place who had been very wicked, a noted gambler, by the name of W——t; he was an esquire. He had got under serious concern for his salvation, and sent for me; I went and prayed with him. After talking with him a little, he got up deliberately, went to his desk, took out his cards, stepped to the fire, and pitched them in, making a whole burnt-offering of them. Shortly after this he found peace, and was, as I believe, soundly converted to God. He seemed to have the innocence and simplicity of a child. He was very zealous for God, and gave great promise of doing good. He had a brother-in-law and sister in Nauvoo, among the self-deluded Mormons. His sister professed to have the gift of tongues, and his brother-in-law the gift of healing all manner of diseases, and the interpretation of tongues

This brother, in his zeal for God, was impressed that he must go to Nauvoo to convince his brother-in-law and sister, and all the rest of the Mormons, that they were wrong. I tried to dissuade him, knowing they were artful and cunning, and adepts in practising frauds and religious jugglery, and that he was just in a state of mind to be deceived, without any experience of the devices of the devil, especially of his power to transform himself into an angel of light; but, despite all my remonstrances, go he must, and go he did; and, as I predicted, they were ready for him. They told him that he was just right as far as he had gone; that the Methodists were right as far as they had gone, and next to the Latter Day Saints, *alias* Mormons, were the best people in all the land, but they had stopped short of their grand and glorious mission; that they were afraid of persecution, and had shrunk from their duty; that if they had followed the light, they would have taken the world; and that the best and holiest men and women among the Mormons had been members of the Methodist Church. They told him, if he would join the Mormons and live faithful, that in a very little time he would have the gift of tongues, and the gift of healing, so that by faith he would raise the dead as did the first Christians. The fatal bait was gulped down; they took him to the river and ducked him; and when I last saw him, he was in daily expectation of these great gifts. I told him he would never receive them; and he promised me, if he did not, he would leave them. What has become of him I know not, but it is probable he is at Utah, and has fifteen or twenty wives.

I will name another incident connected with this revival. There was an interesting young man, well educated, and gentlemanly in all his conduct, from some of the Eastern States. He boarded at a house I frequently visited. He was serious; I talked to him, and he frankly admitted the real necessity of religion, and said, for his right hand he would not lay a straw in the way of any person to prevent him from getting religion; but he said he was not ready to start in this glorious cause, but that he fully intended at some future time to seek religion. I urged him to submit now; that in all probability he never would live to see so good a time to get religion as the present. He admitted all I said, and wept like a child; but I could not prevail on him to start now in this heavenly race.

As our meeting was drawing to a close, I was uncommonly anxious to see this young man converted, but I was not permitted to see it. Some little time before we closed the meeting, a messenger arrived for me to go to another town where the work of religion had broken out, and they greatly needed ministerial aid. The day after I left this young man he was taken violently ill. His disease was rapid, all medical aid failed, and he was shortly given over by his physicians to die. He sent post-haste for me to come to him. I hastened to him, but never to the last moment of my recollection shall I ever forget the bitter lamentations of this young man. "O!" said he, "if I had taken your advice a few days ago, which you gave me in tears, and which, in spite of all my resistance, drew tears from my eyes, I should have now been ready to die. God's Spirit strove with me powerfully, but I was stubborn, and resisted it. If I had yielded then, I believe God would have saved me from my sins; but now, racked with pain almost insupportable, and scorched with burning fevers, and on the very verge of an eternal world, I have no hope in the future; all is dark, dark, and gloomy. Through light and mercy I have evaded and resisted God, His Spirit, and His ministers; and now I must make my bed in hell, and bid an eternal farewell to all the means of grace, and all hope of heaven; lost! lost! for ever lost!"

In this condition he breathed his last. It was a solemn and awful scene; mournfully I turned away and wept bitterly. I never think of this scene but with mournful feelings. God forbid that I should die the death of such a one! But how many are there that have lived and died like this pleasant young man; approve the right, but choose the wrong; put off the day of their return to God; wade through tears and prayers of ministers and pious friends; till they make the dreadful plunge, and have to say, "Lost! lost! lost! for ever lost!" O, sinner, stop and think before you further go! Turn, and turn now.

I hastened to Winchester, where the brethren had rallied, and were engaged in a glorious revival of religion. They had sent off for Brother Akers, who had been with them several days, battling successfully for the cause of true religion, and was made the honoured instrument of much good to many souls. I met Brother Akers between Jacksonville and Winchester; he was compelled to leave for his regular field of labour. When I met him, he exclaimed, "One woe is past, and, behold, another cometh!" The Campbellite preachers, and many of their members, had rushed into our meeting, and tried to hinder or stop the blessed work by drawing our people into foolish controversy. Brother Akers had used the artillery of truth very successfully against this false form of religion. To this he referred when I met him, as he was leaving, and I was hastening to, the field of battle.

When I got to the meeting, I found a blessed work in prosperous progress. It really seemed to me that the Campbellites, and especially their preacher, were as restless as fallen demons. They tried to draw off our labouring members into vain and hurtful debates; and instead of encouraging mourners to seek on, they tried to confuse their minds, and throw doubts and difficulties in their way; and all round, and in the congregation, they were busy in this way, to confuse the minds of the people, and draw them off from seeking God. At once I saw through their plan,·and the bad effects of such a course, if permitted to be carried on. When, at our first coming together after my arrival, I forbade all controversy of this kind, and told our brethren they must not indulge in it any more, and said to all that were opposed to the glorious work in progress, if they did not like it they must and should desist from entering into debates about it in the congregation, the most of the Campbellites desisted, or slily opposed; but their preacher continued boldly to provoke debate. He rudely attacked, in the time of our altar exercises, one of our local preachers.

When I was informed of it, I went straight to him, and told him he must not do so. He said he was a free man, and would do as he pleased. "Now," said I, "Mr. S., if you do not desist, and behave yourself like a decent man ought to do, I will have you arrested as a disturber of our religious order."

He said that all this work was wrong; that it was undue excitement, and it was his duty to oppose it; and he would like to attack it at head-quarters, and just then and there to debate the question with me.

"Now, sir," said I, "if you think to provoke me to condescend to turn aside from carrying on this glorious work to debate with you, the evil spirit that prompts you does but deceive you; for it seems to me it would be like loading a fifty-six to kill a fly; and if you don't like the work and our meetings, go away and stay away; your room will be better than your company."

I nonplussed him considerably, and measurably silenced his batteries, but he was very restive. At length the power of God arrested some of the members of his Church. A very fine and meek woman in their Church, who had been baptized for the remission of sins, but never felt any evidence of her acceptance with God, and was not satisfied with her condition, became very much affected, and wept bitterly on account of her unconverted state. I went to her, at the request of her husband, who, though not at that time a professor of religion, had been raised by Methodist parents, and was friendly. I asked her if she was happy.

She said, "No, far from it."

I asked her if she was willing to go and kneel at the altar, ask God to bless her, and give her a sensible evidence of the pardon of her sins.

She said, "Yes."

I started to lead her to the altar, when one of her Campbellite sisters took hold of her, and said, "What are you going to do?"

She said, "I am going to the altar, to pray for religion."

"O," said the other, "you have religion. You were baptized, and in that act of obedience your sins were all washed away; and you ought to be satisfied with your religion, and not disgrace your Church by going to a mourners' bench, among the deluded Methodists."

She replied, "I know I was baptized for the remission of sins, and you all told me that in this act of obedience to Christ I should be forgiven, and be made happy; but I know it is all a deception, and false; for I know I have no religion; and I am determined to seek it with these Methodists; for, if I die as I am, I must be lost for ever."

"O," said the Campbellite lady, "you must not go."

I then interposed, and said to the lady, "Let her go. She shall go to the altar if she wants to;" and I accordingly led her there. She dropped on her knees, and shortly afterward her husband kneeled at the same altar, with the great deep of his heart broken up; and they never rested till they were both soundly converted to God, and were enabled to sing,

"How happy are they, who their Saviour obey!"

with a zest which they never had felt or enjoyed before.

The work of God went on with great power, and the slain of the Lord were many. Presently, in going through the congregation to hunt up the wounded sinners and lead them to the altar, to my great astonishment and surprise I found my Campbellite lady, who tried to prevent the one I had led to the altar first, sitting down with her face in her hands, and her eyes suffused in tears. She was much agitated. I laid my hand on her shoulder, and said to her, " Sister, what is the matter? Have these deluded Methodists got hold of you? or have you got a Methodist spasm?"

She screamed right out, and said, " God be merciful to me, a poor, deluded, Campbellite sinner!"

" O," said I, " will not water save you?"

" O, no, no," she responded; "I am a poor, deluded sinner, and have no religion, and, if I die as I am, must be lost, and lost for ever. Will you pray for me?"

" Yes," said I; " but now you must go to the Methodists' despised mourners' bench."

" With all my heart," said she; and I partly led and partly carried her there, and if I ever heard a poor sinner plead with God for mercy, she was one.

When it was known that Mrs. ——, a Campbellite, was at the mourners' bench, it awfully shocked some of her fellow-members in that watery regiment. She was in such an agony and such good earnest, I almost knew it would not be long till she found the blessing; and while I was leading some other convicted persons to the altar, the Lord powerfully converted this Campbellite heroine. She sprang to her feet, and shouted over the house like a top, and she fell directly to pulling and hauling her Campbellite friends to the Methodist altar, exhorting them to come and get religion, and not for a moment longer to depend on water for salvation, but come and try the Methodist fire, or the fire of the Holy Ghost; and the way she piled up the Campbellite friends at the altar was sublimely awful. After she had got a great number there, she took after her preacher, and exhorted him to come and get religion; " For," said she, "I know you have none;" but he resisted and fled. Several of his members' children had obtained religion, and several more were seeking it. He then started a meeting in his own church to draw off his members and others from the Methodist meeting; and if ever you saw a water divinity grow sick and pale, it was just about this time. Things were so cold at his church that the little effort soon failed. There were over 120 professed religion and joined the Methodist Church during this meeting, and, according to my best recollection, thirteen of them were Campbellites.

And now let me say, my little experience and observation for many years goes to establish the following fact · Whenever and wherever the ministry and membership of the Church live faithful, and keep alive to God, and enjoy the life and power of religion, they can bid an eternal defiance to all opposition, schism, divisions, ceremonial diversities, and all the false prophets that may arise can never stop, to any great extent, the heavenly march and triumphs of true religion; but when we have a formal, negligent ministry, that wish to substitute education for the power of faith, and our members begin to ape the world, or even other proud and fashionable Churches, you may depend upon it that, like Samson with his eyes put out, we shall make sport for the Philistines. For, however education may be desirable, and however much the progress of this age may demand an improved ministry, especially an improved pulpit eloquence, I would rather have the gift of a devil-dislodging power than all the college lore or Biblical Institute knowledge that can be obtained from mortal man. When God wants great and learned men in the ministry, how easy it is for Him to overtake a learned sinner, and, as Saul of Tarsus, shake him a while over hell, then knock the scales from his eyes, and, without any previous theological training, send him out straightway to preach Jesus and the resurrection! When God calls any man to preach His Gospel, if he will not reason with flesh and blood, but do his duty and live faithful, my experience for it, God will qualify him for the work if he never saw a college.

Perhaps I may say a few things right here that may be of some little benefit to my brethren in the ministry. You know these are the days of sore throats and bronchial affections among preachers Some have laid the predisposing causes to coffee, and some to tobacco; some to one thing, and some to another. Now, without professing to have studied physiology, or to be skilled in the science of medicine, I beg leave, with very humble pretensions, to give it as my opinion that most cases of these diseases are brought on by carelessness and inattention of public speakers themselves. I had, for several years previous to this great revival of which we have been speaking, been greatly afflicted with the bronchial affection; so much so that I really thought the days of my public ministry were well-nigh over. This revival lasted near five months, through a hard and cold winter. I preached, exhorted, sung, prayed, and laboured at the altar, I need not say several times a day or night, but almost day and night for months together. With many fears I entered on this work, but from the beginning I threw myself under restraint, took time to respire freely between sentences, commanded the modulation and cadence of my voice, avoided singing to fatigue, avoided sudden transitions from heat to cold, and, when I left the atmosphere of the church, heated by the stoves and breath of the crowd, guarded my breast and throat, and even mouth, from a sudden and direct contact with the chilling air, or air of any kind, got to my room as quick as possible, slept in no cold rooms if I could help it, bathed my throat and breast every morning with fresh, cold water from the well or spring, wore no tight stocks or cravats, breathed freely, and, strange to tell, I came out of the five months' campaign of a revival much sounder than when I entered it. The only medicine I used at all was a little cayenne pepper and table salt dissolved in cold vinegar, and this just as I was leaving a warm atmosphere to go into the cold air or wind; and although several years have passed since, I have been very little troubled with that disease, and can preach as long and as loud as is necessary for any minister to be useful. Keep your feet warm, your head cool, and your bowels well regulated, rise early, go to bed regularly, eat temperately, avoiding high-seasoned victuals, pickles and preserves, drink no spirits of any kind, and there will be no need of your ever breaking down till the wheels of life stop, and life itself sweetly ebbs away.

Our Conference this year, 1843, was held in Quincy, Adams County, Illinois, September 13th. Bishop Andrew presided. This was the only annual Conference that Bishop Andrew ever presided in with us. The Illinois Conference was now large, and there were some men of fine talents among us. Bishop Andrew presided with great acceptability, and had, among our preachers, many fast friends. At this Conference we elected our delegates to the ninth delegated General Conference, that was to sit in New York, May 1st, 1844. P. Akers, J. Vancleve, J. Stamper, N. G. Berryman, and myself were elected, which made the eighth General Conference that the brethren saw proper to send me to, to represent their interests and the interests of the Church generally. Up to this General Conference, there were 33 annual Conferences, besides Liberia,—17 in the old Eastern boundary, and 16 in the Western division. The 17 Eastern Conferences had a membership of 599,322; of travelling preachers, 2,400. The 16 Conferences in the Western division had of members, 550,462; of travelling preachers, 1,862. Total membership in the Methodist Episcopal Church, 1,171,356; total travelling preachers, 4,282; total increase in members in four years, 276,287; of travelling preachers in four years, 774.

It will be seen from the foregoing statistics, imperfect as they are, that the Methodist Episcopal Church, as one branch of the great Protestant family, prospered in these United States without a parallel in the history of the Church of Jesus Christ since the apostolic age. Only think of it : in despite of all the imperfections that attach to human institutions, the apostasy of some of our ministers, (and it is a mercy of God there were not more,) the backsliding of many of our members, the schisms created by O'Kelly, Hammett, Stillwell, and the self-styled Protestant Methodists, the True Wesleyans,—hush ! O, mercy, save the mark !—in about sixty years, more than a million of members had been raised up and united in Church fellowship in the Methodist Episcopal Church ; and this, too, by a body of uneducated ministers. Perhaps, among the thousands of travelling and local preachers employed and engaged in this glorious work of saving souls, and building up the Methodist Church, there were not fifty men that had anything more than a common English education, and scores of them not that ; and not one of them was ever trained in a theological school or Biblical Institute ; and yet hundreds of them preached the Gospel with more success, and had more seals to their ministry, than all the sapient, downy D.D.'s in modern times, who, instead of entering the great and wide-spread harvest-field of souls, sickle in hand, are seeking presidencies or professorships in colleges, editorships, or any agencies that have a fat salary, and are trying to create new-fangled institutions where good livings can be monopolized, while millions of poor, dying sinners are thronging the way to hell without God, without Gospel, and the Church putting up the piteous wail about the scarcity of preachers. And now, in the evening of life, at the dreadful risk (dreadful to some, not to me) of being called an *old fogy*, and pronounced fifty years behind the times, I enter my most solemn protest against the tendencies of the Methodist Episcopal Church to Congregationalism ; for it seems to me wrong that the ministers of God, divinely called to the holy work of saving souls, should leave that sacred work, and go and serve tables. Wherefore, let the Church look out competent and well-qualified lay teachers and officers for our literary institutions, who can build them up just as well as preachers, and make a " scourge of small cords," and drive these buyers and sellers out of the temples of learning, editorships, and agencies, into the glorious harvest-field of souls. No man, or set of men, in the same sacred sense, is called of God to these institutions and offices, as they are called of God (if called at all) to preach the everlasting Gospel to dying sinners that are so fearfully thronging the way to hell. Christ had no literary college or university, no theological school or Biblical Institute ; nor did He require

His first ministers to memorize His sayings or sermons, but simply to tarry at Jerusalem till they were endued with power from on high, when, under the baptismal power of the Holy Ghost, should be brought to their remembrance all things whatsoever He had commanded them.

I will not condescend to stop and say that I am a friend to learning, and an improved ministry; for it is the most convenient way to get rid of a stubborn truth, for these learned and gentlemanly ministers to turn about and say that all those ministers that are opposed to the present abuses of our high calling are advocates for ignorance, and that ignorance is the mother of devotion. What has a learned ministry done for the world, that have studied divinity as a science? Look, and examine ministerial history. It is an easy thing to engender pride in the human heart, and this educational pride has been the downfall and ruin of many pre-eminently educated ministers of the Gospel. But I will not render evil for evil, or railing for railing, but will thank God for education, and educated Gospel ministers who are of the right stamp, and of the right spirit. But how do these advocates for an educated ministry think the hundreds of commonly educated preachers must feel under the lectures we have from time to time on this subject? It is true, many of these advocates for an improved and educated ministry among us speak in rapturous and exalted strains concerning the old, illiterate pioneers that planted Methodism and Churches in early and frontier times; but I take no flattering unction to my soul from these extorted concessions from these velvet-mouthed and downy D.D.'s; for their real sentiments, if they clearly express them, are, that we were indebted to the ignorance of the people for our success.

CHAPTER XXVII.

THE GREAT SECESSION.

At the General Conference of 1844, a solemn dispensation came upon the Methodist Episcopal Church, then having more than a million of members in her communion. Up to this time no very destructive divisions had taken place among us. The small parties that had filed off, had rather been a help than a serious injury to the Church. No division in doctrines had ever taken place, and, as a large body of ministers and members, there was great unanimity on the Discipline of the Church; and now the division was narrowed

down to a single point, namely, slavery in the episcopacy. It is well
understood by those who have studied the government of the Methodist Episcopal Church, that she has adopted an itinerant or travelling
plan of ministerial operation, as the best and most scriptural mode of
successfully spreading the Gospel of Jesus Christ; and although we
believe there are but two ministerial orders, namely, deacons and
elders, and finding nothing in the Scriptures contrary thereto, the
Methodist Episcopal Church in her early organization saw proper to
create a separate office, not order, of superintendent, or bishop. By
the consent of all our travelling preachers, the bishop appoints from
year to year every travelling preacher to his field of labour. This saves
a vast amount of time and trouble in the ministry, in running about
and seeking to contract with congregations for a specified time and
stipulated amount of salary; moreover, it cuts off the temptation of
selling the Gospel to the highest bidder, and giving the Gospel exclusively to the rich, and leaving the poor to perish without the means of
salvation; and the poor under this arrangement find the fulfilment of
the promise of Jesus Christ, more fully than they can on any other
plan, namely, "Blessed are the poor: for they have the Gospel
preached unto them." Moreover, it is the disciplinary duty of our
bishops to ordain our deacons and elders, and to travel at large
throughout all our Conferences, and to have a general supervision of
the whole work; and in order to qualify them to act wisely and pru-
dently in changing and appointing the thousands of itinerant preachers
to their respective fields of labour, it is required of our bishops to be
constant itinerants themselves; and according to the provisions of the
Discipline of the Methodist Episcopal Church, if our bishops at any
time cease to travel at large throughout the Connexion, supervising
and superintending the general interests of the whole Church, they
shall forfeit the right to exercise the duties of their office.

And right here it may not be amiss to notice, in a few words, the
supremely ridiculous and slanderous statements that are constantly
emanating from the pulpits and presses of some of the prejudiced
denominations, against the absolute and despotic power of our bishops.
They state that our bishops give all the law of the Church, and that
our preachers and people are bound to bow to their *dictum*, under pain
of expulsion; and that all the Church property is deeded to the bishops
of the Methodist Episcopal Church. Now, so far from this charge
being true, I assert, without any fear of successful contradiction, that
a Methodist bishop has not even a vote in any of the rules or regulations of the Church, nor even a veto power on any rule passed by the
General Conference; and as for the charge of the bishops having all
the property of the Church deeded to them, this old, stale falsehood

R

has not now, nor ever had, the least foundation 'in truth to rest upon; for I will venture to say that if the whole United States and Territories were examined with a search-warrant by the entire marshalled hosts of the bigoted and malicious propagators of these falsehoods, not one solitary case can be found where the Church property is deeded to the bishops of the Methodist Episcopal Church. Why do our opponents so constantly and so recklessly persist in reiterating these false charges? Have they no sense of honour or of shame left them? But none are so blind as those that will not see; and I solemnly fear that those wretched editors and pamphlet-writers will have a very fearful account to render in the day of retributive justice. But they cannot meet us in the open field of manly and honourable debate, and therefore they resort to the pitiful fabrication of false statements in hope of gulling the ignorant part of mankind.

We have said, up to this time, 1844, no very serious division had taken place in the Methodist Episcopal Church. It is true that there were a few restless spirits, ministers, that had filed off and raised little trash-traps called Churches, such as O'Kelly, Stillwell, Hammett, the Radicals, or self-styled Protestant Methodist Church, and the Scottites, or, as they call themselves, the True Wesleyans. But in all these secessions, there never had been a difference of opinion on the cardinal doctrines of the Gospel propagated by Mr. Wesley, and unanswerably defended by the sainted Fletcher. So may it continue to the end of time!

The Methodist Episcopal Church, from its first organization, was opposed to slavery; and from 1784 to 1824, in her various rules and regulations on slavery, tried to legislate it out of the Church; and she succeeded in getting many of the slaves set free, and bettering the condition of thousands of this degraded race. But the legislatures of the different slave States greatly embarrassed the operations of the Church by narrowing the door of emancipation, and passing unjust and stringent laws to prevent manumission. At this course of legislation many of the citizens of the free States took umbrage, and commenced a dreadful tirade of abuse on the South, and threw the subject into the arena of politics. This unholy warfare of crimination and recrimination has been carried on with unjustifiable violence, until we are almost brought to a civil war, and the integrity of our happy Union is in imminent danger. How it will end, God only knows.

On the 1st of May, 1844, our General Conference met in New York. From 1824 to this time, our rules on slavery had remained the same. The Northern preachers of the Methodist Episcopal Church, some of them had taken the ultra ground that slaveholding, under all circumstances, was sinful, and therefore, law or no law, practicable or impracticable, all slaveholders, under all circumstances, should be expelled. However, the more prudent and far-seeing part of our ministers and members of the Church saw that this was totally wrong, and threw themselves into the breach, and prevented a fearful division of the Church ; and the fog and smoke of run-mad clerical abolitionism ended in a feeble secession under O. Scott and Co., and a few of the same cloth and kidney.

In the mean time, slavery in the South had been rapidly gaining strength by stringent legislative acts and ministerial advocacy. More and more did the legislatures of the South block up the way to practicable emancipation This threw the North into a fearful rage ; hence there was a mutual crimination and recrimination, and both ultra parties threw the subject into the political arena, and appealed to Cæsar instead of going to God in humble prayer, and asking Divine direction on this fearful question. There had at no time been a slaveholding preacher elected to the office of bishop in the Methodist Episcopal Church, nor was there ever a time within my remembrance when a slaveholder, as such, could have been elected bishop, without giving strong assurances that he would emancipate his slaves ; for the plain reason, to say nothing about the evil of slavery, he never could travel at large through the connexion, as the Discipline required, acceptably, as a slaveholder. There were many eminent and distinguished ministers in the Southern Conferences, some of whom would, no doubt, have been elected to the office of Bishop but for their being slaveholders. Bishop Andrew had been elected to that office in 1832 by the General Conference, but it was because we verily believed him free from the evil of slavery ; and but for the same cause of slavery, I have no doubt others of our Southern ministers would have been elected to that office. When we met in General Conference in New York, Bishop Andrew, by marriage and otherwise, had become connected with slavery. This fact came upon us with the darkness and terror of a fearful storm, and covered the whole General Conference with sorrow and mourning. Those of us who believed slavery an evil, though not sinful in all cases, saw at once that it was utterly impossible for Bishop Andrew to travel at large through the Methodist connexion, and discharge the important duties of that office with acceptability and usefulness, unless he would give the General Conference assurances that he would, as soon as practicable, free himself from this impediment. But this he absolutely refused to do Our Southern brethren took the strong ground that slavery was no impediment to the official relation of a bishop of the Methodist Episcopal Church. ·

The true course that the General Conference ought to have pursued toward Bishop Andrew, was to have arraigned him for improper con-

duct, as the Discipline provides for the trial of a bishop, and suspended him from all official acts; and then, if they of the South were
disposed to secede, let them secede and set up for themselves. Then
all the humbuggery about a division line, and of the Church property,
would have been saved. And if the division or secession of the
Church had been left to the vote of our Southern brethren, it would
have been a poor little thing; and I think that every unprejudiced
mind must see clearly, that the secession from our beloved Church
was brought about by a set of slaveholding Methodist preachers, and
not by slaveholding members, led on by a slaveholding bishop; and
every one acquainted with the circumstances of this dreadful rupture
in the Church, and with the actions and course of Bishop Soule, will
see that he was the leading spirit in the whole affair.

However I may forgive, I shall never forget the unjustifiable
course that Bishop Soule took in dividing the Methodist Episcopal
Church.

To talk about the General Conference having power to divide the
Church and to form a division line, that the ministers from either side
should not cross to bear the tidings of salvation to their dying fellow-
men, is certainly the climax of absurdity; and then to force the members on either side of this line, north or south, to hold their membership in a division that was not of their choice, is despotism in the
superlative degree. Could the pope of Rome more completely
demand passive obedience and non-resistance than did the General
Conference of 1844 in this monstrous act? And yet the very ministers composing the General Conference who, in conjunction with their
fellow-labourers in the ministry, had praised the Methodist Episcopal
Church as the best Church in the world, and had taken an active part
in taking into said Church the hundreds of thousands that composed
her membership, assumed to themselves the power to divide said
Church, and draw a line, and say to preachers and members, "Thus
far shalt thou come, and no further."

I sincerely thank God, upon every remembrance of the acts or
doings of the General Conference of 1844 on this matter, that my
little abilities were put forth to prevent this catastrophe, though I was
found greatly in the minority. Yet, I am glad to say, it was an
honourable minority, which, by the whining sycophancy of the South,
and uncalled-for sympathy of the North, were overwhelmed by the
vote of the majority.

I say here again, as I have elsewhere said in this narrative, that the
General Conference of 1844, and all the General Conferences that ever
existed, had no more power to divide the Church than I, as an individual, had; and it is my deliberate opinion, that the members of the

General Conference who concocted and completed this measure of so-called division of the Church, ought to refund the whole amount of money gained by the South in the Church suits, and let the poor, superannuated preachers, their wives and children, and the widows and orphans of our ministers that have been left nearly destitute of the means of living since the death of their faithful husbands and fathers, have it as a fund for their support.

It is as clear to me as a sunbeam, that the General Conference had no constitutional right to form this sham line of division that they did, and thereby force thousands of our pious and devoted members south of that line to take their membership in an openly avowed slaveholding Church, or remain for ever without Church privileges; and when the piteous wailings of these forsaken members, thus cut off from the Church of their early and only choice, came up for four years, is it any wonder that the General Conference of 1848, that sat in Pittsburgh, should virtually declare the action of the General Conference of 1844 unconstitutional, and declare that line null and void, to all intents and purposes, and once more authorize our preachers to go, without limitation or restriction, "into all the world, and preach the Gospel to every creature?" Now, although this is not to be wondered at, when we consider the sympathetic religious appeals made to that body from our lost members in the dreadful wilderness of slave territory, still there is a wonderful and marvellous thing that confounds all my sense of justice, truth, and righteousness, still existing in the Methodist Episcopal Church; that is, that there are to be found members, preachers, and editors of our Church papers, that, with run-mad violence, oppose the re-organization of Conferences in slave territory, and are unwilling to send, or support our preachers that are sent to preach, the Gospel of the Son of God to these misguided and blind slaveholders, or to the poor, degraded, ignorant thousands of slaves that have souls to be saved or lost for ever. I am fully aware that here I tread controverted, enchanted, and disputed ground; but, perhaps, as this may be the last opportunity that I may have this side the grave to be heard on this subject, I beseech my readers, whether they agree or disagree with me in my sentiments on this vexed question of slavery, to hear me for a few moments without "malice prepense" or aforethought, as to the history of the rupture in the Methodist Episcopal Church, at the General Conference of 1844. I beg leave to refer all concerned in this matter to the most excellent history of the great secession, published by Dr. C. Elliott; a book which, large as it is, ought to have a place in every library of the Methodist Episcopal Church. If they will get this book, and turn to chapters xx., xxi., pages 286–318, they will find all the facts concerning the acts and doings of the General Conference of 1844 detailed with an impartial and truthful particularity worthy of all commendation ; and, indeed, the book throughout is a valuable work, and should be in the hands of every preacher in the Methodist Episcopal Church.

I wish to say here, I was born and raised in a slave State, or States, and for more than sixty years have been acquainted with the sentiments of the Methodist Episcopal Church preachers and members on the subject of slavery. I have seen thousands of poor slaves converted to God ; I have, I verily believe, also seen thousands of slaveholders soundly converted to God, whose fruit in after-life gave ample evidence of the genuineness of their religion ; and since I have had a mature judgment on the subject of slavery, I have steadfastly believed it a great evil ; and, without boasting, I will say, I have been the agent or instrument of freeing scores of the poor slaves, and not only of their emancipation, but also of the colonization of many of them, returning them to their own country free and happy. But this all took place before the legislatures of the slave States blocked up the way, by stringent laws, to practical emancipation. These stringent laws of the legislatures of slave States were passed chiefly from two causes : first, their inherent love of oppression ; and, second, from the extreme and violent manner of intermeddling with the legal rights of the slaveholders in the South by the rabid abolitionists of the North. And now, I would soberly ask, What has all this violent hue and cry of proscriptive abolitionism done for the emancipation of the poor degraded slaves? Just nothing at all ; nay, infinitely worse than nothing. It has riveted the chains of slavery tighter than ever before ; it has blocked up the way to reasonable and practicable emancipation ; it has engendered prejudice ; it has thrown firebrands into legislative halls, both of the state and general governments ; millions are expended every year in angry debates ; laws for the good of the people are neglected ; time, talents, and money thrown away ; prejudice, strife, and wrath, and every evil passion stirred up until the integrity of the Union of our happy country is in imminent danger ; and what has it all amounted to ? Not one poor slave set free ; not one dollar expended to colonize them and send them home happy and free ; and such is the unchristian, excited prejudice, that mobs are fast becoming the order of the day. Presses demolished ; preachers of the Gospel, hailing from the free States, are hunted down by bloodhounds in human shape ; they are tarred and feathered, and threatened with the rope if they do not leave in a few hours ; and such is the prejudice produced by the angry and unchristian fulminating thunders of this one-eyed and one-ideaed, run-mad procedure, that the

Gospel is well-nigh totally denied in slave States to both owners and slaves in many places.

But I think I hear you say, "Let slaveholding preachers preach to these slaves and slaveholders." But if slavery is a sin in all circumstances, how can slaveholding preachers successfully preach the Gospel to these poor sinners? "Well," say you, "let the devil take them all." O no, God forbid! there surely must be a better way; these poor slaves surely are not to blame for their condition. Are there no bowels of mercy to yearn over them? Many of these slaveholders, from circumstances beyond their control, are not radically slaveholding sinners; above all men that dwell in the South, they are entitled to our pity and commiseration, and we should surely carry the Gospel to them, and our skirts will not be clear of their blood if we do not.

Do we reclaim drunkards by telling them that they steal their rum, and lie in the meanest way of all men to get their intoxicating beverages? No, verily; we pity them, reason with them, and, knowing the terrors of the Lord, we persuade men; and when all moral suasion fails, do we say, drunkenness is the open door to all sins, and therefore it is the sum of all villanies, and that they cannot be made Christians? No. When all moral suasion fails, we try by legal enactments to put the temptation out of their way, and urge them to become Christians. Do we induce sinners to reform, repent, and be converted, by abusing them, and telling them of all their dirty deeds, and saying it is impossible for persons guilty of such dirty crimes to become Christians? No, we warn them in a Christian spirit and temper, to flee the wrath to come; we assure them that the happy gates of Gospel grace stand open night and day, and that Christ will turn none away empty that will come unto Him; for whosoever shall call on the name of the Lord shall be saved. And we urge them to seek the Lord while He may be found, and call upon Him while He is near.

I blame no man for believing that slavery is wrong and a great evil, and every reasonable man must deprecate its existence; and I know that there are thousands of our Southern slaveholding citizens that not only believe, but know from daily experience, that it is a great evil, and would willingly make any reasonable sacrifice to rid themselves and their happy country of it. And I believe, from more than twenty years' experience as a travelling preacher in slave States, that the most successful way to ameliorate the condition of the slaves, and Christianize them, and finally secure their freedom, is to treat their owners kindly, and not to meddle politically with slavery. Let their owners see and know that your whole mission is the salvation of the slaves as well as their owners, and that you have not established any underground railroad, and that it is not your mission to abduct their slaves.

In this way more is to be done for the final extirpation of American slavery than all others put together; for these ultraists breathe nothing but death and slaughter.

. I will further state that it is my firm conviction that every Methodist preacher sent as a missionary herald to labour in slave territory, ought to be instructed by the ruling authorities of the Church not to meddle with slavery, but to attend strictly to his spiritual mission. This is the way the Wesleyan Mission Committee instructed their missionaries sent to labour in the West Indies, where slavery abounded in its worst forms; and if those missionaries were known to disobey those instructions, they were immediately recalled; and although these missionaries were tied up to the one grand object of Christianizing the people, yet finally the Gospel leaven so mightily worked, that slavery was abolished, and universal freedom triumphed and prevailed. Let us hope that this will be the case with American slavery; and after having expended all our wrath without availing anything worth talking about, let us now henceforth use Christian weapons, and Christian weapons alone, and the mighty monster will fall.

I do solemnly declare, that no circumstance ever occurred concerning the welfare of the Church, which afflicted me so sorely as the transactions of the General Conference of 1844. It seemed to me that I could not survive under the painful fact that the Methodist Church must be divided; and all the time of the protracted debates I knew, if the Southern preachers failed to carry the point they had fixed, namely, the tolerance of slaveholding in the episcopacy, that they would fly the track, and set up for themselves; and in that event many souls would be injured, and perhaps turn back to perdition; and that war and strife would prevail among brethren that once were united as a brotherly band, and that they must of necessity become a slavery Church. And I the more deeply regretted it because any abomination sanctified by the priesthood would take a firmer hold on the community, and that this very circumstance would the longer perpetuate the evil of slavery, and perhaps would be the entering wedge to the dissolution of our glorious Union, and perhaps the downfall of this great republic. And though I stood alone among the delegates, my colleagues, of my own beloved Illinois Conference, in my vote against all these revolutionary and divisive measures in the General Conference, it afforded me great pleasure to learn that my course in the General Conference was approved by an overwhelming majority of the preachers and members of our Conference. And it still affords me unspeakable pleasure to know that I shall not have to answer before my final Judge for the sin of dividing the Methodist Episcopal Church, a Church that, under God, I am indebted to for all

I have and am; a Church that I have spent a long life in trying to build up, and for the prosperity of which I have made sacrifices, and in the communion of which I have enjoyed so many unspeakable privileges, and all the comfort and pleasure, worth calling so, in this life

This Church I love, and want no other on earth; and in her fellowship I hope to live and die, and with her members, and all other fellow-Christians, I hope to spend a blissful eternity in adoring God the Father, God the Son, and God the Holy Ghost, in the enjoyment of redeeming grace and dying love.

CHAPTER XXVIII.

RESTRICTIVE RULE AND SLAVERY.

IN the fall of 1844, our Conference was held in the town of Nashville, Washington County, Illinois. Here the concurrence of the Conference was asked in the measures of the General Conference. Brother Stamper and Brother Berryman, who had voted with the South, took their stand for concurrence, and I took my stand for non-concurrence; and after we had debated the subject fully, the vote was taken, and there was a handsome majority in favour of non-concurrence. So the measure failed in our Conference, and it failed throughout all the annual Conferences of obtaining a three-fourths vote for concurrence, and the restrictive rule remained as it was, the recommendation of the General Conference to the contrary notwithstanding

Now, the plain state of fact was this: the main body of the members of the General Conference knew, and many of them openly said on the General Conference floor, both Northern and Southern members, that the General Conference had no power either to divide the Church, or the property or avails of the Book Concern, or the Chartered Fund; and the act of the General Conference to divide the property or funds of the Methodist Episcopal Church was only passed provisionally. They knew it was unconstitutional, and their design was to change the restrictive rule, or constitutional clause of the Discipline, so as to allow this division of the property, and proceeds of the Book Concern, and Chartered Fund of the Methodist Episcopal Church. But how was this change to be brought about in a constitutional way? Answer. See Discipline, part i., chap. ii, sec. ii., ans 6, thus. "They (the General Conference) shall not appropriate the produce of the Book Concern, nor of the Charter Fund, to any purpose other than for the benefit of the travelling, supernumerary, superannuated, and worn-out preachers, their wives, widows, and

children. Provided, nevertheless, that upon the concurrent recommendation of three-fourths of the members of the several annual
Conferences, who shall be present and vote on such recommendation,
then a majority of two-thirds of the General Conference succeeding
shall suffice to alter any of the above restrictions, excepting the first
article: and also, whenever such alteration or alterations shall have
been first recommended by two-thirds of the General Conference, so
soon as three-fourths of the members of all the annual Conferences
shall have concurred as aforesaid, such alteration or alterations shall
take effect."

The General Conference of 1844 recommended an alteration in this
sixth restrictive rule of the constitution of the Methodist Episcopal
Church, and sent round to all the annual Conferences for a three-
fourths vote of concurrence. Now, notwithstanding this was the
favourite measure of the South, and notwithstanding every member of
all the seceding slaveholding Conferences, save a solitary one, voted a
concurrence with this unreasonable recommendation, yet when the
votes of all the annual Conferences were counted, they fell far short of
a three-fourths vote of concurrence.

Does it not, therefore, shock all the honourable, high-minded feelings of mankind, to know that the public functionaries of justice could
be so corrupt as to decide against the Methodist Episcopal Church in
those Church suits in favour of the Southern seceders, the self-styled
and self-constituted Methodist Episcopal Church, South? I hope I
may be indulged in a few remarks on this vexed question of slavery.
I hold myself to be an unflinching conservative Methodist preacher. I
know that slavery is an evil, and a great evil; and although the South
denies this ground, and their interested cry is "Abolition! abolition!" that is, with many of them, this cry has never moved me one
inch. I can only pray, "Lord, forgive them; they know not what
they do."

Nine-tenths of them, members and preachers, came into the Methodist Episcopal Church with their eyes open, with our General Rules,
and other Rules, all open before them; if they did not like them, they
should not have joined the Church. If they joined, not knowing the
Rules, when they came to the knowledge of them, and then thought
them radically wrong, they should have peaceably retired, or withdrawn,
and not have rended the Church, and thrown her into violent commo-
tions; and turn round and abuse the Church that, under God, was the
means of their salvation. They always had tangible evidence that the
Methodist Episcopal Church would never tolerate slavery in one of her
bishops, and they had no just right to complain when the General
Conference arrested Bishop Andrew, and gave as the sense of that

respectable body, that he should desist from the exercise of his episcopal functions, until he rid himself of that impediment. As a prudent Christian bishop, he should have done this of his own accord.

On the other hand, the ultra-abolitionists of the North, or anywhere else, have no right to complain of me and others, and deny us the dignified privilege of being conservatives, and hurl their anathemas against us, and bring a railing accusation against us of "pro-slavery, pro-slavery!" And, indeed, they treat us with less decent respect than God permitted Michael the archangel to treat the devil, for he did not allow Michael to bring a railing accusation against his Satanic majesty; but permitted him only to say, "*The Lord rebuke thee.*" Mr. Wesley never made slaveholding a test of membership; and when, in 1784, the Methodist Episcopal Church was organized, slavery was not made a test of membership; it never has been a test of membership, from the apostolic day down to the present. I ask, then, what right have these Babel builders to introduce a new test of membership in the Methodist Episcopal Church? They, like the South, joined the Methodist Church under her present Rules on slavery, and did it with their eyes open. Why did they join her? And, if they were ignorant of our Rules on slavery when they joined, after they informed themselves, and did not, and could not, become reconciled to those Rules or the Church, why did they not peaceably withdraw or leave, and not keep the Church in an eternal agitation and confusion? thereby prejudicing the slaveholders in the South, and cutting off our access to them and their slaves, rending the Church, embroiling the whole nation, which threatens a rupture of our national union, and the destructive ravages of civil war. Before and at the time of the Southern secession, there were three of our Church papers, with three Methodist preachers as editors of those papers, in the South, paid for their services out of the funds of the Methodist Episcopal Church. They were elected and paid to spread religious knowledge, and defend the doctrines and the usages of the Methodist Episcopal Church; but how did they act, and discharge the highly responsible duties of their office? It is true, they wrote many good things, but it is also true, that they put into requisition all their tact and talent to abuse the Church which was giving them their bread, denouncing her as an ultra-abolition Church. Now, was this the course that honourable, high-minded Christian ministers should have taken? Surely not. Well, since this *glorious* inconsistency attached to the South, we have elected editors in the North and North-west, under precisely the same circumstances as the Southern editors who have lived on the pap of the Church; and they have opened their batteries, denouncing her as a pro-slavery Church. "O Consistency, thou art a jewel!" If these editors were conscience-stricken on these subjects, why did they not resign their editorial offices, and set up independent sheets, and vent their spleen against the Methodist Episcopal Church on their own responsibility, and support themselves?

The middle ground between these ultra extremes is what I call conservative ground; that is, we say, in the language of our most excellent Discipline, that slavery is a great evil; and the grand question is, What shall be done for its extirpation? Now, I suppose it will be admitted on all hands, that to do as the Southern preachers have done, that is, to plead that it is right, and justify it by the word of God, is not, and cannot be, the way to extirpate this evil.

On the other hand, if we inquire, "What has ultra abolition done to extirpate this great evil?" what must be the truthful answer? It is simply this: With the exception of a few Negroes that they have abducted, enticed to run away, or have been transported on their underground railroads to Canada, to starve, and to be degraded worse than with their lawful owners; and the very few runaway slaves that, by mob violence, and in contravention of law, they have kept from their legal owners; they have not secured the emancipation of a single slave, from Passamaquoddy to the Gulf of Mexico: nay, so far from it, they have greatly retarded the efforts of the colonization societies everywhere; they have poisoned the minds and inflamed the wrath of the slaveholders in the South, until a decent man, and especially a minister, hailing from a free State, can hardly pass, or repass, in a slave territory, without the risk of a suit of tar and feathers, and even pulling hemp by the neck occasionally. And this mighty mountain of the North, that for years, yea, many years, has been heaving, bellowing, and groaning, in mighty pain, to be delivered, has brought forth; and what is it? A poor little, insignificant m-o-u-s-e; while conservative Methodist preachers, in many instances, who have inherited slaves, have set them free, or colonized them in Africa. We have gone to slaveholders in Delaware, Maryland, Virginia, Tennessee, Kentucky, and Missouri, in a peaceful Christian way; and while we never ceased to bear an honest testimony against the moral evil of slavery, (but did not meddle with it politically,) we successfully persuaded many of these slaves and slaveholders to turn to God, and obtain religion; and we got hundreds and thousands of these poor slaves set free. Let the many emancipated slaves, and their former owners in the above-named States, bear witness to the truth of what I here record. This is the firm and impregnable ground for a true conservative to stand upon; and this ground will save the Church, the Union, the slave, and the slaveholder; and I would not exchange it for all the ultraisms of the North and South put together, and a thousand such.

In connexion with this subject I wish to say a few things concerning a meeting I accidentally fell in with in Cincinnati, I think in 1848. I do not think I heard the name of the meeting, if I did, I have forgotten it, but when I give a very feeble description of it, perhaps some of my readers may be able to christen the brat, for it was surely begotten in the regions or sprang from the soil of "Bigheadism," and the little thing's disease had turned to the "stiff complaint," or, in other words, I found the meeting to be composed of a heterogeneous mass of disaffected, censured, or expelled preachers; that is, the speakers were mostly from the Methodist, Presbyterian, and Baptist Churches. The house was filled with almost all sorts, sizes, and colours; black, white, and yellow, men, women, and children. They had called to the chair one of their number as moderator. If my memory is correct, the first speaker that rose and addressed the motley crowd, said he had been so many years a regular pastor of a Baptist Church in Kentucky, that he had used all his talents and influence to resist the damning influence of slavery, but was overruled in every attempt. He stated that the ministers and ruling members had often met, conversed, and debated the subject, but he was overruled every time. They would not turn slaveholders out of the Church, nor make slaveholding a test of membership, and after having his righteous soul vexed for years with their filthy conversation and conduct, he felt it was his duty to come out of the Baptist Church. He then warned the members of said Church, and all others, to come out of all slaveholding Churches: "Come out, come out; touch not, taste not, and handle not the unclean thing." This speech was received with applause by the listening crowd of many colours

Next arose a Mr. S——h. He said he was a Protestant Methodist, but had been a member and minister of the Methodist Episcopal Church, and travelled as such for years. He had also fought slavery for a long time to get it out of the Church, but always failed, for they loved the accursed thing; and that the Methodist Episcopal Church was, to all intents and purposes, a slaveholding and a slavery-approving Church. The crowd clapped him while he cried, "Come out, come out of her, my people;" and his speech was greatly applauded by the mixed multitude, coloured and all.

The third speaker was a Presbyterian preacher. He said he had experienced the same trials, conflicts, and debates with his brethren in the Church, that his two brethren who had spoken before had waded through, but all of no avail; his conscience would not let him remain a member or minister of a slaveholding Church any longer; he must come out; and exhorted all people to "come out, and be ye clean, and touch not the unclean thing; and I will receive you, saith the Lord; and I will be your God, and ye shall be My people, saith the Lord."

After this there arose on the floor a very respectable-looking man, and replied to most of the statements of these three come-outers, and he showed very clearly, and by irresistible arguments, that the ground they took was a false ground, and that they, or the principles they advocated, were clearly disorganizing and revolutionary in their nature, and in all their tendencies. There was a clerical gentleman sitting at my side, who said that from personal knowledge he could say that all three of these men who first addressed the audience, were under charges of immorality when they pretended to come out of their Churches on account of slavery.

I have seen a great many such preachers as above described. When their bad conduct could not be borne with in their respective Churches any longer, and the disciplinary excisions were about to be inflicted on them, they fled, picking some flaw, or alleging some dreadful wrong in the Church, as they ran and cried, "Come out, come out of her!" O, the infant Church of Christ, how it suffered in its very minority by the unfaithfulness of its ministers! In the very first little Conference of preachers that was organized, Judas turned traitor, and betrayed the blessed Saviour. Peter, perhaps the boldest of the twelve, denied Him with horrid oaths and bitter curses. What do you suppose the astonished ten thought under these appalling circumstances? Judas relented, and hung himself for the dreadful wrong he had done against the innocent Saviour. Peter felt compunction and wept bitterly; was mercifully reclaimed or converted from his apostasy, and, for many years of persecution and trial, strengthened his brethren. What a fearful account will unfaithful preachers, who have torn, rent, and divided the Church of God, have to give in the day of judgment, when the blighting curses of Heaven shall fall on their unfaithful and devoted heads! Lord, save us from unfaithfulness!

On my way to Conference at Nashville in the fall of 1844, I was suddenly taken ill with a real shaking ague in a large, extensive prairie, ten miles across, and shook so severely that I could not sit in my sulky. I got out and lay down on the grass, and really thought I should die for want of water. No house or water near, no human being approached me to aid me in any way; but after about two hours my shaking abated, and I travelled some ten or twelve miles to a camp-meeting which was in progress at Brother Gilham's camp-ground, where I lingered a day or two. There was a botanic doctor on the ground, who lived in Alton City. He kindly took me to his house, and, in a few days, checked my disease. The preachers all left me, being anxious to be at Conference, which was to commence on the

Wednesday following. They, as well as myself, were totally in despair of my reaching the Conference. I was very anxious to get there; for the great question, so far as our Conference was concerned, was to be settled of concurrence or non-concurrence with the recommendation of the General Conference.

I waited till Friday morning. I prayed for strength to go to Conference, and, while praying, a strong impression was made on my mind that I could get there; I rose from my knees and determined to try. The doctor remonstrated against my attempting to go, but I deliberately told him I was going, if I died in one mile. When he saw I was determined to try it, he put up some medicine, and I got a good brother to drive my horse for me, and started, and, strange as it may appear, I mended every mile, and on Sunday morning I reached the Conference, and was able to attend to business the balance of the session, and especially to take a part in the debates, and carry the vote in favour of non-concurrence. This circumstance I have always looked upon as a kind interposition of Providence; and, indeed, the defeat of this project by the annual Conferences was directed by God Himself; and could the Methodist Episcopal Church have gotten justice in the civil courts, according to the true merits of the case, the ill-gotten gains of the Southern secession would have been small; but I predict that it will not prosper with them.

My appointment this fall was to the Bloomington District, which was composed of the following appointments, namely, Bloomington, Mount Pleasant, Monticello, Clinton, Havana, Fancy Creek, Decatur, and Postville. This was a gloomy Conference year. We had very little revival influence in our District, or in the Conference, and, indeed, scarcely any throughout the Methodist Episcopal Church. The delegates of the General Conference from the Southern Conferences returned home, and appointed mass meetings in every direction, and poured out the vials of wrath upon the Methodist Episcopal Church, especially the majority of the members of the General Conference. They declared that we were all abolitionists, and drummed up a convention of the preachers from the slaveholding Conferences. Bishop Soule presided in it, sitting calmly on the ignited clouds, and directing the thunder-storm; and though that convention, by solemn vote, renounced the jurisdiction of the Methodist Episcopal Church, and formed themselves into a separate organization, and though Bishop Soule declared in the General Conference of 1844 that he would not be immolated on a Northern or Southern altar, but on the altar of the Methodist Episcopal Church, now, notwithstanding all this and a thousand times as much,, he had the very uncommon hardihood to come round and preside in our Conferences which had not seceded, and persisted in this course, lending all his aid and influence to the secession, until the Ohio Conference gave him a glorious ouster, and refused to let him preside over them. I had prepared this dose for his honour if he had attended the Rock River or Illinois Conferences; but after the rebuff the Ohio Conference gave him, prudence, with him, for once prevailed, and he did not attend our Conferences, but Bishop Morris attended and presided in them.

There never were more unfair and foul means resorted to by any set of ministers to divide and destroy a Church, than were resorted to by many of these slaveholding preachers in the South; and I cannot help blaming Bishop Soule more than all the rest. I shall always believe that the goodness of Bishop Andrew's heart was such that he would have voluntarily pledged himself to the General Conference that he would, as soon as practicable, remove the impediment; and if he had done this, it would have been hailed, and hailed with a shout, by the delegates from all the adhering Conferences, the few ultra-abolitionists not excepted If he had done so, how much better would it have been for himself, for the South, for the Methodist Episcopal Church, and, indeed, for our distracted country at large! and perhaps the blessedness of such a course in Bishop Andrew would have told with thrilling effect on the surrounding millions in other governments; and unborn millions, of future generations, would rise up and call him blessed. Though he might be dead, and gone to heaven, yet his noble, magnanimous, Christian example would have told in tones of thunder on an ungodly and oppressive world; and the lucid light of his Christian example would have shone with brilliant splendour, and the example thus set by a Methodist bishop would have said to all the world, " Follow me, as I have followed Christ."

The bishop in this case should have known no man, or set of men, after the flesh. I know the preachers friendly to slavery clung to him and his case as a forlorn hope, and as the last resort to carry their point with; namely, slavery in the episcopacy; and a fairer subject they never could have had; for although we think Bishop Andrew did wrong in this matter, and greatly erred, yet we love him, and think him a good man, and that he was every way worthy of the office of a bishop, slavery excepted.

My heart has bled at every opening pore, at the untold mischief this rupture in the Methodist Episcopal Church has and will produce, from the very nature of things, (I mean fallen nature). The Southern preachers will, in self-justification, throw the blame on the preachers of the Methodist Episcopal Church, and thereby poison the minds of a great majority of the slaveholding South; for they are as rabidly in favour of slavery as the extravagant abolitionists are against it. With the two extreme parties there is no middle ground ; for each of them, assuming that they are infallibly right, cry out, " They that are not for us are against us." I have contended with these two extremes for many years, as a preacher of the Methodist Episcopal Church ; and I have often been astounded beyond measure at the absurdities and inconsistencies of these extreme belligerent parties ; but why should I ? It is as certain for extremes to engender absurdities, inconsistencies, and self-evident contradictions, as for effects to follow causes, or for like to go to like philosophically. As one of these extremes has renounced the jurisdiction of the Methodist Episcopal Church, leaving the middle-ground ministers and members of it completely and altogether in the range and raking fire of the artillery of the Northern ultras, I have indulged in the fond hope that these Northern abstractionists would, if they cannot be reconciled to conservative, consistent Methodism, as it was from the beginning, go and set up for themselves, and let the old conservative Methodist Episcopal Church alone ; but no, they seem determined to agitate, and keep on agitating, till they drive us into another inglorious secession, and they remain in peaceable possession of the hard earnings of all the labours of conservative Methodist members and preachers from the beginning. But no, I can tell them for their comfort, if they are within the reach of comforting considerations, if this is their aim, they need not put any flattering unction to their souls on this ground ; for the Methodist Episcopal Church

> " Has fought through many a battle sore,"

and she

> " Expects to fight through many more,"

and will stand as she is, and as she has always been ; and while there is a splinter from a shattered plank of the old Methodist ship " Zion," I intend to hold on to her with a dying grasp, and, if necessity compels, with our dying breath cry to all around, " Don't give up the ship ! "

I am devoutly glad that there is an overruling Providence, where we may place our hope and confidence ; and though we cannot see through or comprehend the permissive providences of God, yet if we can, under all circumstances, trust God aright, we are assured that " all things shall work together for good to them that love Him." May not this slavery secession from the Methodist Episcopal Church be overruled by a Divine Providence, and re-act, and show that the wisdom of men is foolishness with God ? and, under the overruling interpositions of the Almighty, hasten in its time the total extinction of slavery, that has so long placed a foul blot upon the fair escutcheon of our country? Who knows, or can divine? Let us look to God, and constantly and ardently pray, "Thy kingdom come: Thy will be done in earth as it is in heaven;" use spiritual weapons, and leave all events to God.

It will be found, on an examination of our Minutes, that the year before the great Southern secession, the increase of membership in the Methodist Episcopal Church was over 100,000; that in the year of and after the secession there was a decrease of over 31,000 members. A great many of these were along what was called the line, in the border Conferences, who were not numbered in either division; and a great number, from the confusion and dissatisfaction that arose in the Church from this rupture, attached themselves to other Churches; and perhaps many went out that never returned to either division, nor did they seek membership in any other branch of the Christian Church, and perhaps were lost for ever. What an awful thought! These were the fearful, legitimate results of schism; and, indeed, this dreadful rupture in the Methodist Church spread terror over almost every other branch of the Church of Christ; and really, disguise it as we may, it shook the pillars of our American government to the centre, and many of our ablest statesmen were alarmed, and looked upon it as the entering wedge to political disunion, and a fearful step toward the downfall of our happy republic; and it is greatly to be feared that the constant agitation and unscrupulous anathemas indulged in by frenzied preachers and unprincipled demagogues, political demagogues, that seek more for the spoils of office than the freedom of the slave or the good of the country, will so burst the bonds of brotherly love and the real love of country, that all the horrors of civil war will break upon us shortly, and firebrands, arrows, and death be thrown broadcast over the land, and anarchy, mobs, and lawless desperadoes reign triumphant; and then the fair fabric of our happy republic will be tumbled into ruins, and the liberties that our fathers fought for, and that cost the blood and treasure of the best patriots that ever lived, will be lost for ever. I would beg imploringly all honest-hearted lovers of their country, and the liberties we enjoy, to unitedly stand up against every device, stratagem, and political combination, whether secretly or openly carried on, by dishonest intriguers, to ruin our country.

CHAPTER XXIX.

TRAVELLING PRAIRIE IN WINTER.

In the fall of 1845, our Illinois Conference was held in Springfield, September 3rd, Bishop Morris presiding. I was returned to the Bloomington District, which remained pretty near as before. This District lies in a vast, fertile prairie country, interspersed with delightful groves, and at this time was but sparsely populated; but since has rapidly filled up and improved. The District then extended from the mouth of the Sangamon River, where it empties into the Illinois River, and up said river to near the mouth of the Mackinaw River; thence east to Bloomington, and still east to the head of the Sangamon River; thence with said river to its mouth. There was also a part of the Decatur, and the entire of Monticello Circuits, south of this river, appended to the District. In the dead of winter, or in the spring floods, it was tolerably hazardous to go through and around this District, and very laborious to go round it four times in the year.

In the winter of 1845–46, my round of winter quarterly meetings commenced. There had fallen a deep snow, turned warm, and rained in torrents; then suddenly turned intensely cold; the streams mostly froze over, and nearly the whole face of the country was one continued sheet of ice. This storm came upon me at or near Bloomington, the north edge of my District. My next quarterly meeting was south of the Sangamon River, sixty or seventy miles distant. My friends dissuaded me from making even an attempt to go to it. I well knew it was hazardous in the extreme; but I, as a travelling preacher, had from the beginning of my itinerancy seldom ever made a disappointment, and had a very great aversion to these disappointments, having always made it a determined point, if possible, to fill my appointments; and if difficulties surrounded me, I never knew whether I could overcome them or not, till I tried: so to try was my motto; and if, after using due diligence in trying, my way was so insurmountably hedged up that I could not accomplish impossibilities, I in the main felt contented and happy; for, in my early career as a travelling preacher, I learned this happy lesson, not to fight against Providence. So, in despite of the importunities of my friends, I set out.

My way lay mostly through a dreary and uninhabited prairie, with a small blind path, which, in many places, was rendered invisible by the snow and ice; but, fortunately for me, my way led south, between two large branches, not far to my right and left; and these, being considerably swollen by the late rains, and then suddenly frozen over, I found to be a better guide than my blind path: for when I would

s 2

miss my path, and veer too much to the right, I would meet my branch frozen over, and wheel to the left again; and so it would be when I would get off the track to the left hand. Thus guided, I measured about twenty miles, and about one o'clock I hove up to a point where these two branches met and formed a large creek, which was overflowing its banks, and was swimming from bank to bank. For many miles back I had not passed a solitary house, but right here was a little, old, solitary, smoky cabin, and a poor, dirty, ragged family, hovering and shivering over a small fire. The man, the head of the family, was gone out hunting. I was hungry, and asked for food; but the good woman informed me she could not give me anything to eat, for the best of reasons, they had nothing for themselves. I looked around, and plainly saw I could not quarter there that night. But how to get on to the settlement about six miles ahead was the question. The woman informed me, if I could cross the branch which had guided me to the right as I came there, and then would take the timber along the margin of the large creek, into which my branches emptied, for my guide, in about seven miles I would come to houses. But how to get over this branch was the puzzle. It was at least one hundred yards across, being swollen with the last rains, and it was frozen over, but would not bear my horse. So I paused a minute, and thought over my condition. I plainly saw I must retrace my steps till I could cross this branch; and if I could not cross it at all, I must return to the settlement from whence I had started. So I got in my buggy, cracked my whip, and started back. In the course of a mile or two my branch narrowed considerably, which inspired me with cheering hopes.

I made several attempts to cross the branch, but my horse broke through, and with great difficulty I would retreat; and after retreating four or five miles, my branch spread out largely and became very shallow; so in I ventured. My horse broke through; but, from the shallowness of the water, I got safely across; and, leaving the branch to the left, and wheeling again south, took it for my guide, and presently came to the main creek, which leaving to my left, urged on my way for the settlement; and though I had to cross many ponds frozen over, and many branches in the same condition, my horse nearly worn down, and myself cold, hungry, and much fatigued, about dark I came up to a cabin, and it looked so much like the one I had left in the point that I passed on. The second cabin I came to looked better; and though a total stranger in this region of the country, when I hailed at the gate, who should come out but an old class-leader and exhorter in the Methodist Episcopal Church, whose acquaintance I had made some time before at a distant quarterly meeting? He

saluted me as one blessed of the Lord, bid me a cordial welcome, and
so did his fine sisterly wife and children. My horse was put up, and
well cared for; and soon a good backwoods supper, that abounded in
all the substantials of life, was on the table. We sat down, and I
partook with a relish only known to a weary, hungry man. We had
prayers, and the most of us got shouting-happy; and one of his
interesting sons, while we were all engaged in prayer, was solemnly
convicted; and, after praying in mighty agony for several hours, the
Lord blessed him with a powerful sense of the forgiveness of his sins.
For hours we sung, prayed, and shouted together; then I retired to
rest, and I slept as sweet and sound as if I had been bedded on
a divan of King Solomon's palace. This young man shouted and
praised God nearly all night.

This is the way God converts sinners in the backwoods, and a very
faint specimen of the way that Western pioneer Methodist preachers
planted Methodism in the valley of the Mississippi. This good old
brother remained a few years among us, and witnessed a good
confession; left the world with a triumphant shout, fell asleep in
Jesus, and went home to glory!

Next morning I started on to my quarterly meeting, and just as I
got to the bridge, on the main Sangamon River, the high water had
surrounded it, but not deep enough to swim my horse, who waded
through, and I passed over safely, and got to my quarterly meeting in
good time; and although the weather was disagreeable, yet the people
crowded out. The word of God took hold on sinners; many of them
wept, and cried for mercy, and found by happy experience that
Christ had power on earth to forgive sins. About twenty-eight were
soundly converted to God, the most of whom joined the Church, and
Methodism was planted here firmly, never to be destroyed, I humbly
trust. I have often thought of this scene, and many similar scenes
through which I have passed during my protracted ministry; and
when I look back on them, my heart grows warm, and swells with
gratitude to my heavenly Father for the sanction He has given to my
poor little ministry amid all the sacrifices and sufferings through which
I have passed, as a Methodist itinerant preacher; and to His holy
name be all the glory, both now and for ever!

In the Bloomington District I had many warm personal friends,
many members that I had received into the Church in Kentucky, and
some in whose houses I had preached in the days of my comparative
youth; and although it was a hard District for me to travel, my family
living entirely beyond its bounds, yet I was much attached to this
field of labour and the brethren, preachers and people. Some of these
old members had fought side by side with me in Kentucky and West-

ern Tennessee, where and when Methodism had many glorious triumphs over slavery, whiskey, and superfluous dressing. These were her internal foes ; but she not only triumphed over these enemies, but she triumphed over her combined hosts of inveterate and uncompromising sectarian enemies, and attained an elevated position in the affections of very many of the best citizens of those States. Now, many of those brethren who sung, prayed, and preached to and with us, have fallen asleep in Jesus, and sing and shout in heaven, while a few, and comparatively very few, of us old soldiers linger on the shores of time, still fighting under the banners of Christ; and our motto is, " Victory or death ! "

Our next annual Conference sat in Paris, Edgar County, Illinois, September 23rd, 1846, Bishop Hamline presiding. Our next, at Jacksonville, Morgan County, Illinois, September 22nd, 1847, Bishop Waugh presiding. During the three years I was on the Bloomington District we had general peace and some considerable prosperity. During the last Conference year that I was on this District, some incidents occurred, which I will relate.

My winter's round of quarterly meetings commenced at Bloomington ; Brother Samuel Elliott was preacher in charge, and it was his second year. There had fallen a very deep snow, which had greatly blocked up the roads; and by some strange forgetfulness in me, I started for my Bloomington quarterly meeting a week too soon, it was very cold, and I had an open bleak prairie to travel through. The first day I rode about forty miles, and late in the evening I arrived at a very friendly brother's house; but, behold ! when I went in, I found a large company, consisting of parts of several families, that had taken shelter under this friendly roof from the severe cold and pitiless storm of snow that had fallen ; but all was as pleasant as could be expected in a crowd, in very cold weather When we came to retire to rest, it was found that all the beds had to be put into requisition to accommodate the females : what was to be done with the five or six men of us that composed a part of the company ? Our accommodation was cared for in something like the following way : a large fire was made up, and plenty of wood brought in to keep it up all night. Large buffalo robes and quilts were spread down before the fire, and plenty of blankets and quilts for covering; and after praying together, we all retired to rest, and, though our bedding was hard, we slept soundly.

Rising early next morning, I mounted my horse, and started on my way to Waynesville, a little village which gave name to one of my Circuits. Brother John A. Brittenham was preacher in charge. He saluted me in good brotherly style, and inquired which way I was travelling. I informed him I was bound for the Bloomington quarterly meeting. He said, " That meeting is not till Saturday week; so Brother Elliott informs me."

I was surprised, and immediately turned to the District Book, and found it even so. Well, what was now to be done? Shall I retrace my steps, two days back home; and then travel over this dreary cold road here again? Or what shall I do? Said Brother Brittenham,—

" Stay with us, and let us have meeting every night till just time for you to reach your quarterly meeting in Bloomington."

" Agreed," said I.

This was a very wicked little village. The Church was feeble, and greatly needed a revival. We sent out, and gathered a small congregation, and tried to preach to them; and there were some signs of good. Next night our congregation was considerably larger, with increasing evidences of good. The third night our house was not sufficient to hold the congregation; and there were mighty displays of the power of God. Some shouted aloud the praise of God, some wept. Our altar was crowded with mourners, and several souls were converted; but, notwithstanding the place was made awful by reason of the power of God, some mocked and made sport. Among these were two very wicked young men, ringleaders in wickedness. After interrupting the congregation, and profanely cursing the religious exercises of the people of God, they mounted their horses, and started home. After or about the time of their starting home, they made up a race for a trifling sum, or a bottle of whiskey, and started off, under whip, at full speed; but had not run their horses far, till the horse of the most daring and presumptuous of those young men flew the track, and dashed his rider against a tree, knocked the breath out of him, and he never spoke again. Thus, unexpectedly, this young man, with all his blasphemous oaths still lingering on his lips, was suddenly hurried into eternity, totally unprepared to meet his God.

The tidings of this awful circumstance ran with lightning speed through the village and country round; an awful panic seized upon the multitude, and such weeping and wailing among his relatives and people at large I hardly ever beheld before There was no more persecution during the protracted meeting, which lasted for many days, and it seemed, at one time, after this calamity had fallen on this young man, that the whole country was in an agony for salvation. Many, very many, professed religion and joined the Church; but the exact number I do not now recollect.

Before our meeting closed here, Brother Elliott, who had kept up a series of meetings in Bloomington, preparatory to the quarterly meet-

ing,—which meetings had been greatly blessed,—met me in Waynesville, and we returned to the battle-field in Bloomington again. Our
meetings were recommenced, and, with constantly increasing interest,
were kept up night and day for a considerable length of time. Many
were convicted, reclaimed, converted, and built up in the most holy
faith. Of the number of conversions and accessions to the Church I
do not now remember, but it occurs to me that it was seventy or
eighty. Brother Elliott's labours were greatly blessed in this charge,
the last year of his pastoral labours there.

Another incident occurred, while I was on this District, which I
feel disposed to name. There were a good many settlements and
neighbourhoods in the bounds of the District where the people had
become, in opinion, Universalists, and, judging from their morality, or
rather their immorality, this doctrine suited them well; and it is
a little strange, but no stranger than true, I say, without any fear of
contradiction, the most of these Universalists had been members of
some Christian Church, and had backslidden and lost their religion, if
ever they had any. In the course of my peregrinations, I fell in with
one of their preachers, who really thought himself a mighty smart,
talented man, and was ready for debate, in public or private, on all
occasions. His assumed boldness gave him great consequence with
his hoodwinked disciples. He was very loquacious, and had some
clumsy play on words. After conversing with him a few minutes, I
took my line, common sense, and sounded him. He affected to
have great veneration for my gray hairs; but I soon found his veneration for my gray hairs arose more from a fear of my gray arguments
than otherwise. He was a man of slender constitution, and had
been, and was then, greatly afflicted with sore eyes, and was threatened with the total loss of sight. He, in the course of our conversation, said there could not be any such being as a personal devil, who
could be everywhere present at one and the same time, tempting mankind to evil; and as for a future place of punishment called hell, there
was no such place; that the temptations of man arose from his fallen
nature and not from the devil, and the punishment that man would
suffer for his evil doings he suffered in this life, and these sufferings
consisted in the compunctions of conscience for his moral delinquencies, and in his bodily afflictions.

"Well," said I, "my dear sir, if your argument is a sound one, I
must draw very unfavourable conclusions in reference to the magnitude
of your crimes."

"Why so?" responded he.

"Well, sir, for a very good reason   As to your moral delinquencies, and your compunctions of conscience, they are best known, per-

haps, to yourself; but as to your bodily afflictions, as a punishment, I think I can draw very fair inferences; for I cannot conceive of a greater bodily affliction than the loss of sight; and as your vision is almost gone, and you have expressed your firm belief that you will lose your sight altogether, I must, if your doctrine be true, number you among the greatest sinners on earth; for God is too wise to err, and too good to inflict undeserved punishment" I tell you his stars and stripes were not only dropped to half-mast, but trailed in the dust.

There were some evil reports about this preacher and a certain landlord's lady who kept public entertainment. Another Methodist minister and myself called to stay all night at this house, as we were on a journey. The landlord was from home. We were known to this lady, but she charged us tolerably high; and, Universalist as she was, I think her conscience smote her a little for charging preachers, and she began to make a kind of apology for doing so. She said, "Mr. Cartwright, I suppose you will think it a little strange that I charge Methodist preachers; but you need not, for I charge my own preacher, Mr. ——."

"O, no, madam," said I; "not at all, not at all. If reports about you and Mr. ——, your preacher, be true, such a course, perhaps, is right, and I have money enough to pay all Universalist bills, and they ought to have it; for all the happiness they will ever see is in this life; there is none for them in the life to come." You may depend upon it, apologies ceased, and a dumb dispensation came over our fair hostess.

Now, who does not see, from these rather desultory incidents, the legitimate fruits of a false foundation that proposes to save all mankind, irrespective of the moral temperament of the heart? or, in other words, who does not see the fatal error of the fallacious arguments that go to prove the final salvation of all mankind, without repentance toward God, and faith in our Lord Jesus Christ? How many poor, self-deluded souls are leaning on this broken staff, and will never be awakened to a sense of their true condition till they hear the dreadful communication!—"The great day of His wrath has come, and who shall be able to stand?"

In the fall of 1847, at our annual Conference in Jacksonville, our election of delegates to the General Conference that sat in Pittsburgh in 1848, came off, and, for the ninth time, it pleased the members of the Conference to return me one of its delegates. This General Conference was, on many accounts, a very interesting one, and especially on account of the state of things that had grown up under the late rupture in the Church. The Southern preachers had gone from the

General Conference of 1844 with predetermination to renounce the jurisdiction of the Methodist Episcopal Church, which was all planned and determined on before the delegates left New York. This is a fact clearly settled, and admits of no doubt. But how does this course of conduct agree with the solemn pledges publicly given to the General Conference by the Southern delegates, that, on their return home to their different fields of labour, they would, if possible, allay the agitation in the South? and if there was a rupture, it should be of imperious necessity, and not of choice? Did they do this? Was there a single Christian effort put forth to accomplish this? O, no! never, never! But a very different course was pursued. The tocsin of war was sounded; the Methodist Episcopal Church was denounced as an abolition Church, and the cry of self-defence was heard everywhere, from Virginia to Florida and Louisiana. To arms! to arms! ye great American people, or these abolitionists of the Methodist Episcopal Church will be down upon you, and come and steal all our Negroes!

The convention at Louisville was called, a convention of delegates from the slaveholding Conferences; and the delegates appeared in regular uniform, equipped and armed according to law. The yoke of the Methodist Episcopal Church, a rampant abolition Church, was thrown off; a separate organization was formed; their General Conference was appointed; Bishop Soule seceded from the Methodist Episcopal Church, went over and joined them, and acted as generalissimo. Bishop Andrew, unhurt by the dreadful extrajudicial act of the abolition General Conference of 1844, appears with all his pontifical robes, shining rather brighter by the abolition rubbing that he had gotten; two more slaveholding bishops elected; a jubilant song was sung to the tune and words of, "Farewell to abolitionists, Negro-stealers, and all the croakers of the North!" And, after heaping upon the Methodist Episcopal Church all kinds of abuse, and every opprobrious epithet that the fiery burning vocabulary of the South could afford, the Southern General Conference, in the plenitude of their goodness and wisdom, sent a delegate to the General Conference of the Methodist Episcopal Church, held in Pittsburgh, in 1848, asking a mutual and reciprocal fraternization between the Church, North, as they misnamed us, and the Church, South. Now, unprejudiced reader, what do you think of this? A better man and better Christian gentleman the whole South did not afford than Dr. Pierce, their messenger on this embassy; but the Methodist Episcopal Church was caricatured, abused, slandered, and in every sense maltreated by the South; and while they were wounded and bleeding at every pore, is it to be wondered at that this embassy failed, and that every single member of the

General Conference of the Methodist Episcopal Church of 1848 voted against fraternization? If they would undo the wrongs they had inflicted, and take back their hard speeches, and bind themselves to a Christian course in future, then, and not until then, could the Methodist Episcopal Church think of a Christian fraternization.

The constitutional vote having failed to be obtained from the annual Conferences, in order to render valid an alteration of the sixth restrictive feature of the constitution laid down in our Discipline, all the doings of the General Conference of 1844, with respect to a division of the Church, the property or funds of the Church, or a line of separation, were, to all intents, purposes, and constructions, null and void; but still the General Conference of the Methodist Episcopal Church of 1848 were unwilling that any act on their part should be wanting, to settle peaceably these Church difficulties; they, therefore, asked again the concurrent three-quarter vote, of all the annual Conferences, to a peace measure, to stop all, or prevent any, litigation on the property question; but before our bishops had time to submit this measure to the annual Conferences that remained firm in the union of the Methodist Episcopal Church, the Southern commissioners commenced a suit, thereby rendering all peaceful constitutional efforts on her part vain. The unjust decisions on these suits are well known, and will form part and parcel of the history of our country, and especially of the unjust judicial decisions of the court against the Church.

At the Conference held at Jacksonville, September 22d, 1847, my appointment was to the Springfield District, which was composed of the following appointments, namely, Springfield Station, Taylorsville, Sangamon, Petersburgh, Beardstown, Carlinville, Hillsborough, and Sharon Mission. During this Conference year, 1847–48, we had some splendid revivals, and an increase of over five hundred members in Springfield, under the faithful labours of Brother J. F. Jaquess. Great good was done, and many souls were converted, and added to the Church; and, although some of these promising youths, that joined the Church under hopeful prospects, through persecution and unfavourable causes fell back into their old habits, and made shipwreck of faith, a number stood firm, and ornamented their profession, and one of them is now an acceptable travelling preacher in the Illinois Conference. Taylorsville Mission shared, in a considerable degree, this year, in revival influence, under the labours of L. C. Pitner, preacher in charge. In Petersburgh there was also a good work, and a considerable number converted, and a very neat church erected, that does honour to the village, under the industrious efforts of Benjamin Newman, preacher in charge.

In the fall of 1848, our Conference was held in Belleville, St. Clair County, Illinois, Bishop Morris presiding. In the course of this year there was a good religious influence felt in the Sangamon Circuit, especially in several of the Southern appointments, that are now included in the Chatham Circuit. W. S. M'Murray was very successful here in winning over to Christ many precious souls. There were many conversions, and large additions to the Church; and though he has gone to his reward, he will long live in the affections of many in the bounds of the then Sangamon Circuit. He succeeded in erecting a decent church on Sugar Creek, and the Society honoured him in calling it "M'Murray chapel."

Brother M'Murray, his wife, and three of his children, were all violently attacked with the cholera, and in a few days of each other they fell victims to its violence; but he will long live in the affections and remembrance of many, especially of those whom he was the instrument, under God, of converting. Peace to his memory! and may the Lord take care of, and provide for, the three orphan children that Brother and Sister M'Murray left behind!

In the fall of 1849, our Conference was held in Quincy, Adams County, Illinois, Bishop Janes presiding. This year I was returned to the Springfield District. There were no great revivals in the bounds of the District this year, though the Church in the main was in a peaceful, healthy condition; some conversions, and some increase in the membership.

I beg leave here to devote a few lines in giving a small sketch of our German work. It is only a few years since it pleased God to awaken and convert Dr. Nast, now editor of the German "Apologist." He came to America a German rationalist, or infidel. He was awakened and converted under the labours of the ministry of the Methodists. He was soon licensed to preach, and was the first German missionary to thousands of our foreign German population. God soon gave him seals to his ministry; sent His awakening, convincing power, and powerfully converted some of his countrymen. He also raised up some of these new converts to preach the Gospel to the Germans; and with Dr. Nast and his co-labourers the German Mission started. Soon Circuits were formed, and the work of God spread through Ohio, Indiana, Missouri, and Illinois. God raised up faithful and able German preachers, to carry the tidings of salvation to their perishing countrymen that were here, or coming by the thousand to America. Many who were Catholics, Lutherans, rationalists, and infidels, were happily converted to God; the work spread and increased, till Stations, Circuits, and Districts were formed, and are still forming; and they come the nighest to old-fashioned or primitive Methodism of any people I ever saw.

I was once in conversation with Brother Jacoby, and advising him to Americanize his German Methodists, when he said to me, "There are three things that must be done to a German before you can get him right. He must first be converted in his head; for his head is wrong. Secondly, he must be converted in his heart; for his heart is wrong. Then, thirdly, he must be converted in his purse; for his undue love of money makes his purse wrong. If," said he, "we can convert him in all these respects, we can soon Americanize him and make a good Methodist of him, and then he will stick."

It will be remembered that these Germans in the West all belong to the Ohio, Indiana, Rock River, and Illinois Conferences. They are doing great good, and have been greatly prospered by the Lord. Thousands of the Germans can be reached by preachers of their own language, that can never be reached by English preachers. They need our aid and encouragement. Let us hold them up, and the good they are destined to do, and the hundreds of thousands that they may be, and will be, instrumental in bringing to the knowledge of the truth, are far beyond our most sanguine calculations. Many of them are poor, and many avaricious, and either cannot or will not support the Gospel till they are converted; then they will gladly and cheerfully give according to their ability; and by our aiding them now, and supporting missionaries to labour in those missionary fields till they are converted and able to become self-supporting, we shall do a good work.

What a blessing it is to have ministers to meet those foreigners when they land on our shores, and tender them salvation in their own language! I do not believe we can invest our missionary donations so as to do as much good anywhere else, as by applying it to the support of ministers to preach to all foreigners that are crowding to our happy country; and, by the bye, this is a much cheaper plan than to fit missionaries to go to foreign lands, and there undergo the tedious process of learning their languages, or of preaching to them through an interpreter; and our missionary appropriations will go further, and accomplish more good. And when I consider the good already done among the foreign population that are here in our midst from different nations, it gladdens my heart. I have been a close observer of the effect the Gospel has had upon these foreigners, so far as they have come under the influence of the usages of the Methodist Church. Their close attendance on, and attention to, class-meetings, prayer-meetings, lovefeasts, family prayer, and, in a word, all the means of grace, are worthy of all commendation; for I know close attention to these means of grace is the reason of the great success of the Methodist Church in other and former years; and the want of attention to these duties in our members now is the grand cause of the deadness and barrenness of the Church.

. In the fall of 1850, September 18th, our Conference was held in Bloomington, M'Lean County, Illinois; Bishop Hamline presiding. During this Conference year one of our old, well-tried, and faithful preachers, Charles Holliday, had fallen a victim to death. I had been long and intimately acquainted with him. We had long lived and laboured together, and nothing contrary to Christian love ever existed between us, that I know of. I was called upon to preach his funeral sermon before the Conference, and did so as best I could from the short and unexpected notice given me that I had it to do; and perhaps I cannot say anything about this good old brother better than to transcribe, substantially, what is said in his obituary, printed in our General Minutes, namely,—

"Rev. Charles Holliday died March 8th, 1850, in his seventy-ninth year. He was the son of James and Mary Holliday, and was born in the city of Baltimore, Maryland, November 23rd, 1771. His parents were members of the Presbyterian Church. They not only trained him up in its doctrines and moral discipline, but his education was conducted with special reference to his entering the ministry in that Church. His parents dying while he was in his minority, he abandoned the idea of entering the ministry, and turned his attention to secular pursuits. At what age he became pious we have no specific information. In the month of May, 1793, he was united in marriage to Miss Sarah Watkins, a lady of good understanding, sound and discreet judgment, who afterward became a devoted, pious, and faithful Christian. The day after they were married, they, in company, united with the Methodist Episcopal Church, and commenced family devotions the same evening. In 1797 he received licence as a local preacher. His licence was regularly renewed annually from that time until September 30th, 1809, at which time he was admitted on· trial in the travelling connexion in the Western Conference, and appointed to the Danville Circuit. In October of the same year he was ordained deacon by Bishop Asbury. In 1810 he was appointed to the Lexington Circuit, where he remained two years, and was ordained elder by Bishop M'Kendree, October 11th, 1811; in 1812 he was appointed to Shelby Circuit; in 1813 he was appointed presiding elder of Salt River District, where he remained three years; in July, 1816, being bereaved of his pious and faithful wife by death, who left him with nine children, he found it necessary to locate. The certificate of his location is dated September 7th, 1816, signed by Bishop M'Kendree. In the former part of the year 1817, he entered into a second marriage with Miss Elizabeth Spears.

This lady, who still lives, proved to be a devoted woman and wife, and a kind mother and faithful guardian to his children. His family being now provided for, he was re-admitted into the travelling work in 1817, and appointed to the Cumberland District, Tennessee Conference, where he remained four years. From 1821 to 1825, he laboured as presiding elder on Green River District, Kentucky Conference; in the fall of 1825 he took a transfer to the Illinois Conference, and was appointed to the Wabash District, where he continued to labour till the meeting of the General Conference of 1828, at which time he received the appointment of book agent at Cincinnati, in which he continued eight years. At the close of his term of service as book agent he was transferred to the Illinois Conference, and; in 1836, was appointed presiding elder of the Lebanon District, where he continued two years. He was appointed presiding elder on the Alton District in 1838, which was the last District on which he laboured. He continued in an effective relation to the Conference, filling such small appointments and doing such work as his declining strength would permit, until 1846, when he was granted a superannuation, and in this relation he remained until the close of his useful life. He attended the Conference in Quincy in September, 1849. On his way to that Conference he was attacked with disease of the kidneys, from which he never recovered. Although his sufferings in this his last illness were extreme, he frequently exulted in the grace of our Lord Jesus Christ, which enabled him to bear so much suffering without complaining. He retained his reason to the last It had been his practice, for thirty years, to pray three times a day in his family, and from his devotional spirit we wonder not that his sun of life set in great peace."

In summing up the character of our lamented Brother Holliday, we may say, that there are few traits of real excellence that he did not possess in an eminent degree. As a preacher, he was clear, sound, and practical. When he indulged in doctrinal controversy, although he was decided, and expressed his views in strong language, he was always kind and loving to his opponent; in all the relations of life, as a husband, a father, a pastor, a friend, a companion, he was a most lovely and interesting man; and in the sufferings and disappointments of life his conduct was characterized by that "charity that suffereth long and is kind." His end was peace, and many in the day of eternity will rise up and call him blessed Thus lived and thus died one of our old members of the Western Conference, the only Conference, at the time of our brother's commencing his itinerant life, that was in this natural as well as moral waste, or in the valley of the Mississippi. The death of Brother Holliday was a solemn dispen-

sation to me; and having to preach his funeral sermon to the whole
Conference, as well as many others, and having but a few minutes'
notice, and no time to prepare, it was a tremendous cross, and I have
always feared that I did not do justice to the life, labours, and Christian virtues of this man of God; but under the circumstances I did
the best I could, and ask a kind indulgence of the congregation for all
the defects of that performance. Let us unitedly join, and devoutly
pray, " Let me die the death of the righteous, and let my last end be
like his," as said the text on that occasion; and if this prayer is
answered, we shall soon reach the place where funeral dirges are never
sung, and death never enters.

In the fall of 1851, September 17th, our Conference sat in Jacksonville, Bishop Waugh presiding. Here we elected our delegates to
the General Conference which was to sit in Boston, May 1st, 1852;
and although the Indiana Conferences, Rock River, Iowa, and Wisconsin, had grown up, and were organized into separate Conferences
that once belonged to the Illinois Conference, yet, from the rapid increase of population in the State, and from the increase of members,
and especially the increase of preachers, both English and German, it
was found indispensable to divide again, and form a Southern Illinois
Conference; and the delegates were instructed accordingly. It pleased
the Conference to elect me as one of this delegation. This was the
tenth time I had been honoured with an election by the several
annual Conferences, of which I was an humble member, to represent
the interests of the Methodist Episcopal Church in the General
Conference.

Bishop Hedding, our honourable senior bishop, who died April 9th,
1852, was, at the date of our Conference, lingering, with no hope of
surviving but a few days Bishop Hamline's health also being extremely precarious, all the efficient work of superintending the interesting concerns of the whole Church devolved on Bishops Waugh, Morris,
and Janes. We 'all knew that several additional bishops must be
elected at our General Conference of 1852. From this view, together
with the infirmities of increasing years of Bishop Waugh, he delivered
us a very impressive address at the close of the Illinois Conference,
stating that it was probable this was the last time he should ever preside in our midst. This address greatly affected the whole Conference; for the bishop had presided among us with great acceptability,
and we honoured and loved him greatly. We all remembered that
our beloved Bishop Waugh had gone in and out among us blameless,
and that we had been greatly benefitted by his counsels, and the impartial manner in which he had presided among us; and we always
found him orthodox in the doctrines and discipline of the Church.

He was always accessible to the humblest preacher or member among us, and we found him to be what I believe constitutes an old-fashioned Methodist bishop : he raised no new standards in doctrine or discipline, but urged us to " mind the same things, and walk by the same good old Methodist rules." So may all our bishops do

In the fall of 1851, my four years having expired on the Springfield District, I was appointed to the Quincy District, where I had travelled fifteen years before · then my District extended from the mouth of the Illinois River to Galena, and, indeed, as far north as was inhabited by the whites ; and yet further still, into the Indian country, where I superintended the mission among the Pottawattomies. My District was then between four and five hundred miles from north to south, and I suppose would average one hundred miles from east to west. I then thought the District a small one ; for when I was first appointed to a District in the Illinois Conference, in the fall of 1826, my District commenced at the mouth of the Ohio River, and extended north hundreds of miles, and was not limited by the white settlements, but extended among the great, unbroken tribes of uncivilized and unchristianized Indians ; but now, in 1851, how changed was the whole face of the country ! The District was composed of the following appointments, namely, Quincy Station, Columbus, Warsaw Mission, Chili, Pulaski, Rushville Station, Rushville Circuit, Havana, and Beardstown Station, about one hundred miles from east to west, and I suppose would average from thirty to forty from north to south There was no District parsonage and accommodations near its centre. I lived entirely out of its bounds, and had the Illinois River to cross and recross five or six times each quarter, and the ravages of many years were upon me, so that I found it as hard to travel this small District as I did my first District in the Conference, which covered more than two-thirds of the geographical boundaries of the State. The country had not only greatly changed, in rising glory and strength, but I had greatly changed also ; my strength was failing, so that I dreaded a journey of one hundred miles more than I formerly did one thousand. I was well pleased with my appointment on many accounts. I was much gratified to see the growing improvements of the country ; the dense population ; the great increase in the membership of the Church ; the large, spacious churches that were built ; and in addition to all this, I met hundreds that I had taken into the Church in former years, when a new country tried men's souls. They gave me a cordial reception, and welcomed back their old presiding elder, and gave me unmistakable evidences of their friendship and brotherly love.

But, notwithstanding all this, and a thousand good things that I could say with truth and sincerity, I found that Methodism, in some

T

places, had gone to seed, and was dying out; and, to use our back-woods language, some of the prominent and leading members of the flock had become butting rams, or jumping ewes, or sullen oxen, or kicking mules. These things gave us trouble. One of my preachers, for some cause unknown to me, had become greatly prejudiced against me: he was appointed this year to the Warsaw Missionary Station. This young, flourishing little city of Warsaw stands on the eastern bank of the Mississippi, hard by the Fort Edward military post. We had a small though respectable little Society here, but no church to worship in. The brethren had rented a little, old, dilapidated frame, every way unsuitable, and in an out-of-the-way place. The Presby-terians had a small church; and when our quarterly meeting came on, they offered it for our use. The preacher in charge accepted the offer, but said perhaps we might protract the meeting. They replied we might have it as long as we pleased; we might go on and protract the meeting if we saw proper. The family of my preacher I was not acquainted with; and he, being prejudiced against me, had made a bad impression on the mind of his wife against me. However, she came to meeting, and the Lord blessed her; for she was a very good woman. The Lord also reached the heart of their interesting little daughter, and she joined the Church. After this, the preacher's wife expostulated with him, and told him to lay aside his prejudices against me, alleging that I must be a good man; for the Lord had blessed and was blessing my labours in a powerful degree. The old brother surrendered, and gave up his prejudices, and we became very friendly.

The power of God fell on the congregation almost every coming together; and we had crowded congregations by day and by night. Several were awakened and converted. We protracted the meeting, and intended to extend it over several Sabbaths; but were cut short by official information that the congregation who owned the church wanted to use it themselves after Friday night. We concluded our meeting, thankful for small favours; but did firmly believe that this unceremonious deprivation of the Presbyterian or Congregational church arose from jealousy, or fear of our success. If we judge wrong in this matter, we devoutly hope to be forgiven by the Lord.

The quarterly meeting which we have been speaking of was holden the first days of February, 1852. Our expulsion from the church, in the manner above stated, created considerable dissatisfaction, and pro-duced a determination, both in and out of our little society, to build a church that we could call our own, without the danger of being turned out of it at any time. Accordingly, a lot was selected, and a sub-scription opened to accomplish this desirable object; and from the amount subscribed by the citizens, together with several hundred dollars obtained abroad, we succeeded the next year in erecting a neat little brick church to worship in; and our quarterly meeting the next year was held in it, namely, the first Sabbath in February, 1853. This meeting was attended with great power. James I. Davidson was preacher in charge this year, whose labours were greatly blessed and owned of God. I tried to preach during our protracted quarterly meeting about ten times, to large and crowded congregations. Sinners were deeply convicted, and a great many, I verily believe, obtained religion. Over twenty joined the Church; among them some good, respectable citizens, whom we hope to meet in heaven, and unite in praising God for ever.

But right here I wish to say, that in most of our revivals many men and women of bad habits and ill fame become operated on, profess religion, and join the Church. This has long been, and now is, a great objection by many to these revivals, and it has been the cause of considerable persecution to the Church. But it should be remembered that the economy of the Church, in saving souls, is compared by Jesus Christ Himself to a fisherman casting his net into the sea, and enclosing a multitude of fish, both good and bad. But who ever condemned the fisherman, because his net gathered bad as well as good fish? or who ever drew the erroneous conclusion that the net was bad, because there were some bad fish enclosed in it? The net is to be thrown, the fish, bad and good, are to be enclosed, and then the net is to be drawn to shore, on dry land, and all alike, both good and bad, taken from their natural element Then, and not till then, the process of assorting them is to commence.

The Methodist Church, in our humble opinion, stands, in this respect, on pre-eminently scriptural ground. They give every sinner a chance, and take them on probation for six months, not as members, but under the care of the Church, on trial for membership; and surely, if they do not in that time give satisfactory evidence of their sincerity and fitness for membership, it is not likely they ever will. Well, if they do not in that time give satisfactory evidence that they are in good earnest in seeking their salvation, what then? Expel them? No; for they are not members to expel. What then? We simply drop them, and consider them no longer probationers for membership; leave them where we found them; we have at least tried to do them good, and have done them no harm. This is the safety-valve of the Methodist Episcopal Church,—six months on trial for membership. How dreadfully have other sister Churches been troubled in their mode of operation! They generally believe that a Christian can never fall away so as to be finally lost, and that it is wrong to receive any into the Church who are not Christians. Well, in order to get people into the Church, they are often found hurrying them into a profession of religion when they have none; and then, when such fall away, with what astonishing mortification they have to confess they were mistaken; that these souls were deceived; that they never had any religion! And yet they hurl their anathemas at Methodist preachers for taking persons as probationers for membership without religion, while they have actually done infinitely worse; for they have taken them into the Church as full members, and as Christians too, when they were not. Now, if our economy is wrong, what must theirs be?

God bless the citizens of Warsaw, and increase their mercies a hundredfold, for the many acts of kindness shown to me the two years I was labouring among them!

In the fall of 1851, Milo Butler, a transfer from the Michigan Conference, was appointed to the pastoral charge of the Quincy City Station. It was constituted a station under my former presidency in the Quincy District, and had existed as a station for more than fifteen years. The Church had ebbed and flowed, sometimes in prosperity and sometimes in adversity. There were some fine, substantial members here; but they at this time, 1851, were in a cold state, evidently on back ground. Brother Butler was greatly afflicted, and so were his family, this year. He laboured faithfully, according to his strength.

We had a small refreshing in the Church this winter, chiefly under the acceptable labours of Brother Wilson, brother-in-law to Doctor Butler. L. C. Pitner was appointed to Quincy Station in the fall of 1852; and during the months of December, 1852, and January, 1853, a glorious revival broke out, such as had never been in Quincy before. It really seemed as though it would at times overwhelm the whole city. High and low, rich and poor, old and young, bowed before the mighty power of God. Many of almost all kinds of education became the subjects of the converting grace of God, and joined the Church; and when our second quarterly meeting came off, in January, our church, though large, was filled at lovefeast to its utmost capacity. The city mission charge, under the pastoral care of James L. Crane, belonging to the Griggsville District, shared largely in this blessed revival, and our German Methodist Church caught the holy fire; and it was supposed that over one thousand were converted and added to the different charges and Protestant Churches in the city of Quincy during this happy year. Most of them have proved faithful, and are honouring the profession they have made; but some of them have fallen asleep in Jesus, and are numbered with the Church above.

During the two years I was on this District we had good times in Rushville Station and Rushville Circuit, Ripley Mission, Pulaski and Columbus Circuits; a number were converted and joined the Church in all these places. About the 20th of September, 1852, we had a camp-meeting at Sugar Grove, in the bounds of the then Columbus Circuit. Brothers J. I. Davidson, Butler, and Pitner came to our aid, and laboured like men of God; but what was better still, the Lord came and made one in our midst. The word was preached in demonstration of the Spirit and the power of God; the Church was greatly built up, and many sinners were convicted and soundly converted, and about sixty were added to the Church.

This Conference year was a great and prosperous one to the Church; and the two years I spent on the Quincy District, I number among the most pleasant of my life. Still we had some trials and disputes in the Church which gave us trouble; but the Lord, we trust, overruled all, and great good was done · the Church increased in numbers, in deep piety, in close attention to her peculiar institutions that God has so long blessed and prospered. My strength was failing from increasing years, and long and constant itinerant labours; I lived on the east end of the District, and I had to cross the Illinois River very often, which in winter was frequently frozen over for months, and in spring the banks were overflowed; and I had often to ferry five miles across the water extending from bluff to bluff; and when the winds were high, I have been detained for days together, causing me to risk my life, and to miss my appointments. Under these circumstances, I was impelled to ask the bishop to change the form of the District, and make the river the line.

Our Conference in the fall of 1852 was held in the town of Winchester, Scott County, Illinois; and in the fall of 1853, the 12th of October, at Beardstown, Cass County, Illinois. Bishop Scott was our presiding bishop, and a pleasant president he was. It was at this Conference the above alteration in the Quincy District was made, and the Pleasant Plains District formed. This District was composed of the following appointments, namely, Beardstown Station, Meredosia (now Concord) Circuit, Havana, Jacksonville Circuit, Sangamon, Virginia, and Island Grove; a very pleasant, convenient little District indeed.

I had now been a travelling preacher for more than forty-nine years, and was sixty-eight years of age. I had been appointed presiding elder by Bishop Asbury, at the first Tennessee Conference, held in Fountain Head, in the fall of 1812, which is now forty-three years since; and in all these forty-nine years of my life as a travelling preacher, I had never asked of the appointing power of the Church for any appointment, nor for any accommodation in an appointment; and although some of my brethren have thought that I was greatly favoured with accommodating appointments, I here call upon all the bishops that have given me my appointments for more than fifty years to bear me witness that the appointments given me by them were unasked for by me.

At this Conference at Beardstown, in the fall of 1853, for the first time in my life, I did ask to be appointed to the Pleasant Plains District, if appointed to a District at all, but at the same time said I would greatly prefer a small Circuit. Let Bishop Scott and his council bear witness in this matter. There was another strong reason, aside from my age and infirmities, that urged me to ask this accommodation, namely, that I might gain some time to write this sketch. But, alas! leisure time to write seems to be almost out of the question with me; I am appointed on so many Conference Committees, have to attend so many dedications of churches, to preach so many funeral sermons, besides all the important duties of the District, that leisure time with me is a very rare thing. And such have been my Church engagements, and such the length of time between the occasional hours or days devoted to this narrative, that when I have recommenced writing, I had entirely forgotten what I had written last, especially the connexion of subjects; and this has cost me a great deal of labour and loss of time. hence if there are some repetitions, unconnected incoherencies, I hope they will be regarded and inspected with this motto,—

"That mercy I to others show,
That mercy show to me."

I think it about time now to return and say a few things about our General Conference of 1852, which sat in Boston. When in Pittsburgh, at the General Conference of 1848, the New-England brethren pleaded hard for the General Conference of 1852 to be appointed in Boston, they alleged that New-England had never had a General Conference. I observed to Brother Crandall, and other New-Englanders, rather jocosely, that, judging from the Yankees that I had seen out in the West, I was a little afraid to venture myself in the General Conference among the Bostonians; for almost all that I had seen in the West had assumed such high ground, professed such mighty educational attainments, that we poor illiterate Western backwoods preachers could hardly hold an intelligible conversation with them; and that we were afraid to start any proposition whatever; and when we met them, we could only stand and look at them, and make ready to answer questions.

To this Brother Cran lall pleasantly replied, "Why, sir, you have never seen a genuine Yankee in the West; those you have seen are runaways, or pretenders, or impostors; they are an adulterated set of scape-gallows fellows; but come to Boston, and we will show you a real live, green Yankee."

"Very well," said I, "we'll go for Boston."

When a number of the delegates from different Conferences met in New York, on their way to Boston, we took the cars, a crowd of us together, and on our iron horse snorted toward the land of the Puritan metropolis, leaving the Empire City and State far behind.

Just about the time we entered the limits of the State of Massachusetts, our conductor proclaimed a halt of ten minutes. I dashed out without my hat; I wanted water, and as I had no relish for being left by the cars, I ran and watered, and with a quick step returned, and took my seat. I discovered that a good many of the preachers were indulging in a hearty laugh, and, as I thought, at my expense.

Said I, " Gentlemen, what are you laughing at ? "

One, somewhat composing his risibilities, answered,—

" How dare you enter the sacred, classic land of the Pilgrims bareheaded ? "

" My dear sir," said I, " God Almighty crowded me into the world bareheaded; and I think it no more harm to enter Massachusetts bareheaded, than for the Lord to bring me into the world without a hat."

There were several ladies sitting hard by, though I had not observed them; they pulled down their veils, and chuckled over my speech for miles. When we got to Boston, I expected to see no one that I had ever seen but a few of the Methodist preachers that I had become acquainted with at the General Conferences of former days; but I was very agreeably disappointed in this respect, and especially when I learned that Mr. Merrill, with whom I had formed a pleasant acquaintance at M'Kendree College, Illinois, some years past, was then living in Boston, and had petitioned for Dr Akers and myself to board with him during General Conference This Brother Merrill was the son of Rev. John A. Merrill, a fine old Methodist preacher of olden times, with whom I had been long acquainted, who had borne the glad tidings of the Gospel successfully to thousands; witnessed a good confession, lived faithful, died happy, and has gone safe home to heaven. I found myself very agreeably situated in this kind and generous family. Brother Merrill was intelligent, easy, and pleasant in conversation. His friendly little wife was kind, courteous, and easy in her manners; and her mother, a fine, intelligent old lady. All were easy, familiar, and agreeable. We were also favoured with the company of Brother J. F. Jaquess, who was collecting books for the female college in Jacksonville. My fear was, that I would get into a family that were cold, stiff, and distant in their manners. One of these formal, distant, ceremonious families was always a prison to me, and well calculated to make me feel unhappy, and far from home; but it was otherwise here.

The second Sabbath in Boston, I was appointed to preach at Church Street church at eleven o'clock. I took for the text Hebrews x. 22. We had a large congregation; several preachers present; and supposing that most of my congregation had hardly ever seen or heard of me, and that they were an educated people, and had been used to great preaching, I put on all the gravity that I well could command. I tried to preach one of my best sermons, in a plain, grave, sober manner; and, although I never thought myself a great preacher, yet I really thought I had done very near my best that time. Well, when I came down from the pulpit, a brother preacher introduced me to several of the prominent members of the congregation; and as I was introduced to them, they asked me very emphatically,—

"Is this Peter Cartwright from Illinois, the old Western pioneer?"

I answered them, "Yes, I am the very man."

"Well," said several of them, "brother, we are much disappointed; you have fallen very much under our expectations; we expected to hear a much greater sermon than that you preached to-day."

"Well, brethren," said I, "how can it be helped? I did as well as I could, and was nearly at the top of my speed."

I tell you this was cold encouragement; I felt great mortification; I hastened to my room and prayed over it a while. That night they had appointed me to preach at North Russell Street. There was a full congregation, and a good many preachers present. I read for the text Job xxii. 21. I had asked God for help; and when I took my text, I determined to do my very best, and did so; but failed, as in the forenoon, to meet the expectations of the people. And as I came down into the altar, I was again introduced to some of the brethren; and although they did seem to doubt that I was Peter Cartwright from the West, the old pioneer, yet they, in cold blood, informed me that I had fallen under their expectations, and as good as told me that my sermon was a failure. Now, was not this too bad? I tell you they roused me, and provoked what little religious patience I had, and I rather tartly replied to one, that I could give people ideas, but I could not give them capacity to receive those ideas, and left them abruptly; and in very gloomy mood retreated to my lodgings, but took but little rest in sleep that night. I constantly asked myself this question, "Is it so, that I cannot preach? or what is the matter?" I underwent a tremendous crucifixion in feeling.

The next day, I told Dr. Cummings not to give me any other appointment in Boston during the General Conference: "for," said I, "your people here have not got sense enough to know a good sermon when they hear it."

The Sabbath following I spent in Lynn, and had good meetings; then I went the next Sabbath to Fall River, and preached for Brothers Allyn and Upham, and had a pleasant time. Sometime in the following week, old Brother Taylor came to me and told me I must preach at his church the next Sabbath, at the Bethel Charge; and said, Dr. Akers and Brother J. F. Wright had both tried to preach in his church, and both failed; "and," said he, "you are the forlorn hope. If you flash, no other Western preacher shall preach in my church any more during the General Conference."

Said I, "Brother Taylor, you need not think that any of us Western men are anxious about preaching to you in Boston: your way of worship here is so different from ours in the West, that we are confused. There's your old wooden god, the organ, bellowing up in the gallery, and a few dandified singers lead in singing, and really do it all. The congregation won't sing; and when you pray, they sit down instead of kneeling. We don't worship God in the West by proxy or substitution. You need not give yourself any trouble about getting a Western man to preach in your church; we don't want to do it; and I do not think that I will try to preach in Boston any more, unless you would permit me to conduct the services after the Western manner."

Said Brother Taylor to me, "Brother, you must preach to us at the Bethel; and," said he, "roll up your sleeves, and unbutton your collar, and give us a real Western cut."

My reply was this: "If you will let me regulate your congregation, and preach as we do in the West, I have no objection to preaching to your congregation, or anywhere in Boston."

"Very well, at it you go," was his reply.

In the meantime, I had learned from different sources, that the grand reason of my falling under the expectations of the congregations that I had addressed was substantially this: almost all those curious incidents that had gained currency throughout the country concerning Methodist preachers, had been located on me; and that when the congregations came to hear me, they expected little else but a bundle of eccentricities and singularities; and when they did not realize according to their anticipations, they were disappointed, and that this was the reason they were disappointed. So on Sabbath, when I came to the Bethel, we had a good congregation; and after telling them that Brother Taylor had given me the liberty to preach to them after the Western fashion, I took my text, Matthew xi. 12; and

after a few commonplace remarks, I commenced giving them some
Western anecdotes, which had a thrilling effect on the congregation,
and excited them immoderately, I cannot say religiously; but I thought
if ever I saw animal excitement, it was then and there. This broke
the charm. During my stay after this, I could pass anywhere for
Peter Cartwright, the old pioneer of the West. I am not sure that
after this I fell under the expectations of my congregations among them.

I will say that a more generous, hospitable, and social people I never
found anywhere than in Boston. Their sociability and friendly greet-
ings reminded me more of our Western manners than anything I ever
found among total strangers, and many of them are sincere, devout
Christians; but their mode of worship I do most solemnly object to,
so far as their pews, promiscuous sittings, and instrumental music are
concerned. The salaries of their organists and choirs are expenses
unjustified by the word of God. I also take exceptions, in many
instances, to the moral character of the persons employed in these
departments. The evils that result from mixed sittings of male and
female, which are always attendant on the pew system, are neither few
nor small. The choir practice destroys congregational singing almost
entirely, and has introduced the awkward and irreverent practice
among congregations of turning their backs on the sacred desk, and
facing about to the choir; and this whole system has a tendency to
destroy the humble practice of kneeling in time of prayer, and con-
tributes largely to the Church-dishonouring practice of sitting while
the prayers of the Church are offered up to God. I shall not attempt
a laboured argument here against these evils; for I suppose, where
these practices have become the order of the day, it would be exceedingly hard to overcome the prejudice in favour of them, though I am
sure, from every observation that I have been able to make, that their
tendencies are to formality, and often engender pride, and destroy the
spirituality of Divine worship; it gives precedence to the rich, proud,
and fashionable part of our hearers, and unavoidably blocks up the
way of the poor; and no stumbling-block should be put in the way of
one of these little ones that believe in Christ.

I found the Bostonians to be a liberal people in their contributions
for benevolent purposes. It fell to my lot to be a solicitor for pecu-
niary aid to erect a church in Warsaw, Quincy District, Illinois Conference; and the members of the General Conference and citizens of
Boston gave me several hundred dollars for that object.

I will close this chapter by saying that the General Conference that
sat in Boston, in 1852, was the tenth General Conference which I
attended, or was elected to. These General Conferences had sat in
Cincinnati, Pittsburgh, Baltimore, Philadelphia, and New York; and

though we were treated very friendly in all these cities, yet the General Conference in Boston was more highly honoured by all classes of citizens than any that I ever attended; and, sure enough, to use the trite saying of Brother Crandall, I found live, green Yankees by the thousands, and some of them very talented, and most of them well educated; the poor among them are cared for, the children are gathered up in all directions and sent to school. But, after all, it would make a Western man laugh, in spite of his gravity, to hear a New-Englander talk of his great farm, containing all of two acres, and hear him tell how much it cost him to remove the stone off the farm, how much to manure it, how much to cultivate it; then the sowing of the products, the marketing of it, and the real product in cash. They will really talk scientifically about it. I could not but think of the contrast; for we have some farmers in Illinois that have from one to five thousand acres in their farms, in active, actual, productive, profitable cultivation. Hail, Boston! live for ever.

CHAPTER XXX.

GENERAL CONFERENCE IN BOSTON.

THE General Conference of 1852 was held in Boston. Our old beloved Bishop Hedding had just died and left us. From the precarious state of Bishop Hamline's health, and despairing of a recovery, he tendered to the General Conference his resignation of the office of bishop, to which we had elected him in 1844, and we accepted his resignation, and, as we have elsewhere said, we had but three bishops left. Brothers Waugh and Morris were getting pretty well advanced in life, and Bishop Janes, though in the prime of life, was failing from his excessive labours. Our Church was extending throughout this vast continent, and in Liberia, Germany, South America, and other different and distant nations; and as our Discipline very properly provides that our bishops should travel at large throughout the connexion, it was clearly seen that we must strengthen the episcopacy by electing a sufficient number to visit, personally, all parts of our widely-extending connexion. Accordingly, a resolution was adopted with great unanimity, that we elect four additional bishops; and, after exchanging and interchanging our opinions and views concerning the men proper to be set apart to this office, it was declared, with great unanimity, that Brothers Scott, Simpson, Baker, and Ames be elected.

A difficulty had taken place in the Ohio Conference concerning a pewed church. One of our good preachers, in aiding and defending those brethren that were in favour of the pew system, had been considered guilty of imprudence, and the Ohio Conference passed a vote of censure on this brother, and from this he appealed to the General Conference. The debates on this appeal brought on the controversy on the subject of pews. The General Conference cleared this brother from the censure. Then followed sundry motions to change the Discipline on the subject of pewed churches; and, finally, our old, well-tried rule was changed to what it is in our Discipline now. This was a real Yankee triumph. However, many of the members of the General Conference voted for this change, hoping to stop one source of Church litigation hereafter, and they may so far succeed as to prevent any future appeals to the General Conference; but they have, at the same time, opened a thousand doors for strife and contention, in all cases where there is any considerable division or difference of opinion on the subject in our societies. The pew system is inevitably at war with the best interests of the Church; for no honourable, high-minded man, who is poor, and unable to buy or rent a pew, but will feel himself degraded to intrude himself into a pewed church; and that form of worship adopted in any Church which goes to exclude the poor, contravenes the Divine law, and prevents the realization of that blessedness that God has provided for the poor. Fifty years ago there was not a member or preacher among the thousands in the Methodist Episcopal Church that thought of having a pewed church. But since the Church has risen in numerical strength, and become wealthy, this system of pewed churches is fast becoming the order of the day. The pew system must necessarily be extremely offensive to the Lord's poor, and we should all remember the words of Jesus Christ, that it were better that a millstone were hanged about our necks, and we drowned in the depth of the sea, than that we should offend one of those little ones that believe on Him. For my own part, I always feel embarrassed when, as a stranger, I enter a pewed church; and how mortifying it is to be directed by the sexton to some back, dirty, or dingy seat! and I involuntarily ask, "Are ye not partial?" Leaving the pew system for future adjudication of the Church, we sincerely hope that its evils will, with the pious, work its entire overthrow, and the restoration of free seats in all the churches, which so admirably agrees with a free Gospel.

I hope, if I make a few remarks right here on the speculations published not long since in the [American] "National Magazine," by its talented editor, on the qualifications of the bishops of the Methodist Episcopal Church, it will not be considered the unpardonable sin. Brother Stevens seems to think that our present bishops, at least some of them, have talents of too high a grade to be buried in the unimportant and comparatively small official duties of their office; and that it would be better to select men of less useful business talents to perform the small duties of a bishop, reserving those men of a high grade of talent for more important business matters or interests of the Church. I must confess that the position my respected brother takes took me rather by surprise; but my surprise was not so much at the talented editor of the " National " taking this position, as at the position itself, but then, why should I be surprised at any position taken in this educational, advanced age of the world, seeing that I am an old dispensationist, and fifty years behind the times? I have been acquainted personally with every bishop of the Methodist Episcopal Church (save Dr. Coke) from her commencement to the present; and though I have awarded to all of our bishops a high grade of talent, yet it never entered my mind for the first time that any of them had any talents to spare, or that were not necessary to be brought into requisition to superintend all the important interests of the Methodist Episcopal Church. When I consider the responsible duties of a bishop in our Church, to constantly travel at large throughout the entire bounds of our ministerial fields of labour, to oversee the temporal and spiritual interests of the whole Church, to assign, from year to year, the thousands of travelling preachers to their most appropriate fields of labour, and many other important duties too tedious to enumerate in this connexion, I must frankly say I have never had the first spasm or fear of getting men of too high a grade of talent, yea, of business talent, to perform the functions of their office with credit to themselves and promotion of the best interests of the Church of God. Moreover, though I may not admire the manner of these speculations of my beloved and talented editor, yet, should they tend to check the high aspirations of disappointed expectants, some good may result

It is a trite saying, that revolutions never go backward; but if the speculations of my brother are not driving things backward, then I must be very much in the dark. But the theory we have just noticed very forcibly reminds me of what is alleged to be the custom of the members of the Established Church of England, namely, If parents have a smart and promising son, or sons, he, or they, are selected for the bar, or for the medical department, or some other prominent position, and they are educated accordingly; but if they have a stupid boy, that promises very little usefulness to the world, or at least promises to shine not very brilliantly, he is immediately designated for the ministry; for then he can be supported by the state, and not by his acceptable and useful talents O, what a reproach to the Gospel of the Son of God, and what a withering curse to the Church!

At our Conference at Beardstown, October 12th, 1853, as I have already said, I was appointed to Pleasant Plains District, and bade an affectionate adieu to Quincy District. I do not know that I was ever appointed to any field of labour that I felt more attached to than I did to the Quincy District, and should have been glad to have spent at least two years more, but the best of friends in this life must part; we part, however, with a blessed hope of meeting in another and better world. I hardly ever left a field of ministerial labour but I felt sorrowful, and indulged in very gloomy reflections. Here are hundreds of my best earthly friends, whom I have lived and laboured with in great peace and harmony, we have preached and prayed together, often been happy and shouted the high praises of God together, many of whom are my spiritual children that God has given me. We have laboured and suffered together; but now, for the last time, we splice hands, and bid each other finally farewell, till we meet in the general resurrection. When l remember how swift time flies, and how soon God will call His suffering children home, then and there let us meet, where painful separations for ever cease.

Before I close this feeble sketch of my long life, I wish to give a very brief sketch of a few of my fellow-labourers who suffered long and endured much in spreading Methodism in these Western wilds, and thereby rescue from oblivion their names and worthy deeds, that generations to come may know their indebtedness to the early pioneer Methodist preachers, for the moral order in a great and good degree that prevails in the vast regions of the West. Whatever may be justly attributed to education and other instrumentalities, the present, as well as future generations, owe, and will owe, a debt of gratitude to the indomitable courage and pious labour of early suffering Methodist preachers, for the great and good order of this vast wilderness. When they entered it as preachers of the Gospel, very few ministers of any other denomination would brook the hardships and undergo the privations that must necessarily be endured in preaching the Gospel in these sparsely populated and frontier regions. But hardly had the early emigrant pitched his tent, raised his temporary camp, or log-cabin, when the early Methodist travelling preachers were there to preach to them the unsearchable riches of Christ; and how many thousands who had withstood the offers of life in the old settlements or States, have been followed into the wilderness by these early Methodist preachers, and won over to Christ! Many ministers of other Churches waited till flourishing towns, villages, and populous settlements had formed and improved the country, and could give them a good fat salary; and then they came and entered into the labours of these old pioneers. People unacquainted with frontier life, and especially frontier life fifty or sixty years ago, can form but a very imperfect idea of the sufferings nd hardships the early settlers of these Western States underwent at that day, when Methodist preachers went from fort to fort, from camp to camp, from tent to tent, from cabin to cabin, with or without road or path. We walked on dirt floors for carpets, sat on stools or benches for chairs, ate on puncheon tables, had forked sticks and pocket or butcher knives for knives and forks, slept on bear, deer, or buffalo skins before the fire, or sometimes on the ground in open air for downy beds, had our saddles or saddle-bags for pillows instead of pillows of feathers, and one new suit of clothes of homespun was ample clothing for one year for an early Methodist preacher in the West.

We crossed creeks and large rivers without bridges or ferry-boats, often swam them on horseback, or crossed on trees that had fallen over the streams, drove our horses over, and often waded out waist-deep; and if by chance we got a dug-out, or canoe, to cross in ourselves, and swim our horses by, it was quite a treat.

O, ye downy doctors and learned presidents and professors, heads of the Methodist literature of the present day, remember the above course of training was the colleges in which we early Methodist preachers graduated, and from which we took our diplomas! Here we solved our mathematical problems, declined our nouns and conjugated our verbs, parsed our sentences, and became proficient in the dead languages of the Indian and backwoods dialect.

Suppose these illiterate early Methodist preachers had held back, or waited for a better education, or for these educational times, where would the Methodist Church have been to-day in this vast valley of the Mississippi? Suppose the thousands of early settlers and scores of early Methodist preachers, by some providential intervention, had blundered on a Biblical Institute, or a theological factory, where they dress up little pedantic things they call "preachers;" suppose ye we should have known them from a ram's horn? Surely not.

JESSE WALKER, known to thousands in Illinois, Missouri, Indiana, Tennessee, and Kentucky, was a native of Virginia. His age has gone from my recollection. His commencement as a preacher was in the local order, and as such he moved to West Tennessee. This was about the time of the great Cumberland revival; and though he had a very limited education, and his preaching powers were not very profound, yet he could preach a plain, practical sermon; and he was a powerful exhorter.

In the fall of 1803 Brother Walker was received on trial into the travelling connexion, in the Western Conference, and appointed to travel the Red River Circuit, in Cumberland District; John Page was his presiding elder. He was this year blessed with glorious revivals, and received a great many into the Church. In 1804 he was appointed to the Livingston Circuit. This was a new field of labour which I had formed the year before under the elder. Here his family was greatly afflicted, and he lost by death two of his children; but Brother Walker's labours were greatly blessed, and many seals were added to his ministry.

In 1805 he remained on the same Circuit, with Hartford Circuit attached to it. His labours this year were greatly blessed. A great number were converted and joined the Church. In 1806 Brother Walker was appointed to Hartford Circuit; this was also a prosperous year in many additions to the Church. In 1807 he was appointed to the Illinois Circuit; for it will be seen, that the Illinois and Missouri States both belonged to Cumberland District. Here he entered the prairie wilderness, and spent a successful year on that Circuit. In 1808 he was appointed to Missouri, still further in the wilderness of the West; as usual, he had several revivals. In 1809 a new District was formed, called Indiana District, embracing Indiana, Illinois, and Missouri States, and J. Walker was appointed to Illinois Circuit. In 1810 and 1811 he was appointed to, and travelled with acceptability and usefulness, the Cape Girardeau Circuit, in Missouri. In the fall of 1811 the name of the Indiana was changed to Illinois District, S. Parker presiding elder; and in 1812 Brother Walker was appointed to the Illinois Circuit again.

It should be recollected, that in 1812 the General Conference sat in New York; this was the first delegated General Conference of the Methodist Episcopal Church. At this General Conference, the Western Conference was divided into two, called Ohio and Tennessee Conferences. In 1815 the Missouri District was formed; and in 1817 he was appointed to that District. Right here it should be remembered, that the General Conference which sat in Baltimore, May 1st, 1816, divided the Tennessee Conference, and formed a Missouri Conference. The Missouri Conference was composed of two presiding-elder Districts, namely, Illinois and Missouri; though it embraced four States, namely, Arkansas, Missouri, Illinois, and Indiana. The Missouri District covered two States west of the Mississippi,—Arkansas and Missouri. The Illinois District covered the States of Illinois and Indiana. These four States were all frontier ground; desperate, long, lonesome rides, and little or no support for preachers or presiding elders; and if our Districts were as large and hard to travel now as then, we should not have as many young aspiring expectants for that office as abound in our Conferences In 1818 and 1819, he carried successfully the Gospel to thousands of the scattered frontier settlers in Missouri and Arkansas, and many in the day of judgment from those poor frontier regions will rise up and call him blessed

I think it was in the fall of 1819 our beloved old Brother Walker, who had travelled all his life, or nearly so, came over to our Tennessee Confcrence, which sat in Nashville, to see us; but, O, how weather-beaten and war-worn was he; almost, if not altogether, without decent apparel to appear among us! We soon made a collection, and had him a decent suit of clothes to put on; and never shall I forget the blushing modesty and thankfulness with which he accepted that suit; and never did I and others have a stronger verification of our Lord's words, that "it is more blessed to give than to receive." In 1820 he was appointed Conference missionary, and sustained the relation of missionary to the Missouri Conference from 1821 to 1824.

He was instructed, in 1824, to pay attention to the Indians in the bounds of Missouri. During these years of extensive missionary travel, he visited St. Louis, which was almost wholly given to Romish idolatry. There was no Methodist society or church in the city, and perhaps no Protestant church in the place. It had been settled from an early day with French Catholics. In his visit to this place, he saw its deplorable moral condition, and resolved to seek a way to carry the Gospel to its perishing thousands. But how was he to do it? and how was he to be supported while doing it? Means of support he had none. He made it a matter of prayer, and asked aid of God. Accordingly, he made his stand in the city, and took up a day school of A, B, C scholars, by which he supported himself; and all he made over he applied to the erection of a small church, which, if my memory is not at fault, was the first Protestant house of worship in the city. God did not despise the day of small things, but crowned his efforts with signal success; so much so, that he not only succeeded in building a church, but gathered a congregation in it, and raised a Methodist society, which remains to this day, and Methodism has spread through the city, so that there are many charges, and a good many splendid churches erected, and several thousand members in the different branches of Methodism.

In 1824 the Missouri Conference was divided by the General Conference, which sat in Baltimore. The Illinois Conference was organized. Brother Walker was appointed missionary to the settlements between the Illinois and Mississippi Rivers, and to the Indians in the vicinity of Fort Clark, (now Peoria). He travelled extensively, and preached through this entire new country, raised several societies, one at Fort Clark, penetrated into the Indian country, visited their chiefs, made known his wishes to establish missions and schools among them, and met a friendly reception by their chief men, especially among the Pottawattomies; and in 1826 he was appointed missionary to that tribe of Indians. He was continued in this mission in 1827 and 1828, and, having obtained a grant from the Indians to a section of land, he built houses, opened a farm, preached to the Indians through an interpreter, established a school, and had some prosperity; and had it not been for the corrupting influences of white men, in selling whiskey to the Indians, and corrupt white men that cheated the Indians out of their annuities, there is no doubt but these Indians would have become civilized and Christianized. What a fearful account these unprincipled white men will have to render at the judgment for the demoralization and destruction of the Indians! I thank God, during my superintendence of this mission, while Brother Walker was missionary among them, we had the pleasure of seeing the hopeful conversion of several of them, and of baptizing them, and receiving them into the visible Church of Christ.

In 1828 Brother Walker was succeeded in the mission by Brother Isaac Scarritt, and was sent to the Peoria Circuit, where he laboured with his accustomed usefulness and acceptability. In 1829 he was returned to the mission among the Pottawattomies, which was located on Fox River, about twenty miles from Ottawa, where it empties into the Illinois River. In the mean time, the government had bought out the Indian claim; and although the Church had spent some thousands of dollars in its establishment, we lost it. The mission premises were reserved for one of the half-breeds, and Brother Walker was, in 1830, appointed to Chicago Mission, where he succeeded in planting Methodism in this then infant city. In 1831 he was appointed to the Des Plaines Mission, and organized many small societies in that young and rising country.

In 1832 there was a Chicago District formed, of mostly missionary ground. Brother Walker was superintendent of this missionary District, and missionary to Chicago town; and although he was well stricken in years, and well-nigh worn out, having spent a comparatively long life on the frontiers, yet the old man had the respect and confidence of the whole community, and in 1833 was continued in the Chicago missionary station. This year closed his active itinerant life. He had done effective and efficient service as a travelling preacher for more than thirty years, and had lived poor and suffered much; had won thousands of souls over to Christ, and built up and firmly planted Methodism for thousands of miles on our frontier border.

In 1834 he asked for and obtained a superannuated relation, in which relation he lived till the 5th of October, 1835; and then, being at peace with God and all mankind, and having fought a good fight, and finished his course, and kept the faith, he was ready for the messenger, and left the world in holy triumph; and his redeemed spirit rose triumphantly, and entered heaven, to be hailed and welcomed home by the thousands to whom, in the Divine economy, he had been the honoured instrument of salvation, and I hope to meet him in heaven before very long. He was the first minister who, by the authority of the Methodist Church, gave me my first permit to exhort. We have fought side by side for many years; we have suffered hunger and want together; we have often wept, and prayed, and preached together, I hope we shall sing and shout together in heaven. Peace to his memory!

SAMUEL H. THOMPSON was born in Westmoreland County, Pennsylvania, March 16th, 1786. He had a pious mother, who very diligently instructed young Samuel in the general principles of our holy religion, according to the Calvinistic views of the Presbyterian Church, for which Church through life he entertained a high regard, though he repudiated the Calvinistic doctrines. He received a good common English education for that early day, and was considered an honourable, high-minded young man. In his eighteenth year he joined the Methodist Episcopal Church, as a seeker of religion. For two years he sought an experimental knowledge of the forgiveness of his sins, and while engaged in secret prayer, a peaceful answer was granted to him, though not such an evidence of pardon as he desired; but shortly afterward, during family prayer, he obtained a clear evidence of the regeneration of his fallen nature, and immediately commenced exhorting his associates to seek God, and was licensed to preach. In the fall of 1810 he was received on trial as a travelling preacher, in the Western Conference, holden at Cincinnati, which was then the only Conference west of the mountains. He was appointed to the Whitewater Circuit, Indiana District, Ohio. Here young Thompson was received kindly, and preached successfully. In 1811 he was appointed to the Nolliechuckie Circuit, in East Tennessee; in 1812, to Clinch River Circuit. In both these Circuits he laboured zealously, and was useful. In the fall of 1812 he was ordained a deacon. At the division of the Western Conference, he fell into the Tennessee part, and in 1813 was appointed to the Knoxville Circuit, where his labours were greatly blessed. In 1814 he was appointed to Christian Circuit, and there were in this Circuit added to his ministry many seals.

In the fall of 1814 he was ordained an elder, and in 1815 he was appointed presiding elder of the Missouri District. He remained on this District in 1816. Vast was the frontier country that Brother Thompson explored on this District; and he successfully planted the standard of the Gospel and of Methodism in many log cabins and frontier settlements, and won many laurels for his Master in this

L 2

wilderness of the West, and the Lord gave him many souls for his hire.

At the General Conference of 1816, the Missouri Conference was stricken off from the Tennessee Conference; and in 1817 he was appointed to the Illinois District, which covered almost all the inhabited parts of the State of Illinois and Southern Indiana. He remained on this large District two years, and was aggressive in all his ministerial labours, organizing many societies in this new and rising country. In 1819 he was appointed to Shoal Creek and Illinois Circuits, joined together, where his labours were greatly blessed. Money was scarce through all this Western country; but Brother Thompson suffered on, through penury and want. In the mean time he had married, and had a young and growing family to provide for. In 1820 he remained on the Illinois Circuit, and was instrumental in greatly building up the Church. In 1821 Brother Thompson was again placed on the Missouri District as presiding elder, where he remained two years, still labouring and suffering for his Master, and planting Methodism in many new settlements, and many claimed him as the honoured instrument of their salvation; and many were the thrilling shouts of new-born souls brought into the liberty of the Gospel on the tented camp-ground, as well as from the log cabin. From 1823 to 1826 Brother Thompson was stationed on the Illinois District, Illinois Conference, which covered more than two-thirds of the geographical boundaries of the State; but with unfaltering steps he travelled night and day, seldom missing his appointments, through cold and heat, floods or snow-storms. His labours were greatly blessed, and there is very little doubt that he was the most popular and useful preacher in the State. Hundreds, if not thousands, from the Illinois District, in the great day of judgment will hail our beloved brother, and call him blessed.

From the hard fields of labour occupied by Brother Thompson, his poor fare, the privations he underwent, and his extraordinary zealous pulpit labours, the very many hardships and sufferings he endured incident to a new country, his fine constitution began to give way, and he found it necessary to relax his efforts in some degree. Accordingly, he asked for and obtained a supernumerary relation, and in that relation, in 1827, he was appointed to the Illinois Circuit, where his labours were fully equal to his strength. In 1828 he was continued on the same Circuit, and in 1829, having recovered his health a little, he was made effective, and appointed to the Shoal Creek Circuit. The Lord gave him a prosperous year, and made him a blessing to many souls. In 1830 there was a new District formed, called the Aska——a District, and Brother Thom———— was appointed presiding elder. He travelled this District in 1831 and 1832, abundant in labours and usefulness. In 1833 he was appointed travelling agent for the Lebanon Seminary, and acquitted himself honourably. In 1834 he was appointed to the Lebanon Circuit; and although he had preached for many years to the most of his congregations, yet the Church hailed him as a brother beloved, and his ministry was profitable, and he proved a blessing to many. In 1835 Brother Thompson sustained a superannuated relation to the Conference, and the rest from his energetic labours this year gave him some increase of strength, and he wanted to spend that strength in doing good; and his relation in 1836 was changed to supernumerary, and he was appointed to Alton Station. He was this year only partial in his labours, his constitution was fast giving way. Accordingly, in 1837 he sustained a superannuated relation again But his soul was restless when out of his field of ministerial work; accordingly, in 1838, he asked to be made effective; but the Conference gave him a supernumerary relation, and he was appointed to labour in the towns of Vandalia and Hillsborough. In 1839 he was again appointed to Alton City Station, as supernumerary. in 1840 he was appointed to labour in the Belleville Station, where he laboured but little. His physical powers evidently were fast giving way, and in 1841 he was placed in a superannuated relation, which relation he continued to sustain until his redeemed spirit returned to God who gave it, which happened on the 19th of March, 1842.

Brother Thompson laboured hard and suffered much for more than thirty years. His field of labour for those years embraced large portions of Ohio, Indiana, Tennessee, Kentucky, Illinois, Missouri, and Arkansas States, much of which was new and on the outskirts of civilization, destitute of means of comfortable support. In these respects, his zeal, like a quenchless fire, urged him on night and day, over desert wastes, towering mountains, rapid rivers. He often suffered hunger and almost nakedness in quest of lost and wandering sinners, to bring them back to God, and thousands now in heaven will praise God for ever that this self-sacrificing Methodist preacher taught them the way to life in their mud hovels and smoky cabins. The last year of his eventful life, his health almost entirely gave way; and while confined to his bed, from which he never rose, such was his ardent thirst for the salvation of souls, that he requested to call in the neighbours, and to be propped up in his bed, and to preach one more sermon to them before he left for heaven. His desire was granted; the room was crowded, and such a sermon hardly ever fell from the lips of mortal man. The power of God fell on the congregation; they wept aloud, and fell in every direction, and many will date their

start for heaven to that sermon. And now, having delivered his last
. message, he said, "My work is done, and I am ready to go at my
Master's bidding."

During the few lingering moments' that he remained he gave unmistakable evidence that he was at peace with God and all mankind,
and that he had a complete victory over the fear of death. He continued in this heavenly frame of mind until he sweetly fell asleep in
the arms of Jesus, and quietly breathed his last and went up to glory.
Brother Thompson was a gentleman as well as Christian. He was
faithful in the administration of the discipline of the Church; very
firm, but mild. He was courteous in manner, had a nice regard to
feelings, but remarkably faithful in reproving whatever he thought
wrong in saint and sinner. He had but few personal enemies; his
soul breathed the true spirit of Christian kindness and love. He has
left behind him thousands that claim him as the honoured instrument
in their conversion; and, if they are faithful, I have no doubt will
meet him in heaven with shouts of victory for ever and ever.

JOHN DEW was born on the 19th of July, 1789, in the State of
Virginia. In the days of his youth he embraced religion and joined
the Methodist Episcopal Church, of which he remained a worthy
member during life; and being deeply impressed that it was his duty
to preach the Gospel, he was recommended by his class, and obtained
licence to preach as a local preacher, and then joined the travelling
connexion in the Ohio Conference. In 1813 he was appointed to the
Salt River Circuit, in Kentucky, and was blessed with success. The
first year of his itinerancy, 1814, he was appointed to the Jefferson
Circuit, and laboured with acceptability and usefulness to the Church.
In 1815 he travelled the Madison Circuit: here he gave good proof of
his call to the ministry, and the Lord owned and blessed his labours.
In 1816 he travelled the Guyandotte Circuit, and had seals to his
ministry. This fall he located, and remained local for eight years, but
was an industrious and useful local preacher, and was the means of
doing much good in several parts that he visited. He preached with
great acceptability in the southern part of Kentucky and the Illinois
State.

In the fall of 1824, Brother Dew was re-admitted into the travelling
connexion in the Illinois Conference, and he was appointed to travel
the Illinois Circuit. Here he laboured faithfully, and did good. In
1825 he was continued on the same Circuit, and at the close of this
year was transferred to the Missouri Conference, and appointed presiding elder of the Missouri District. In 1827 he was stationed in
St. Louis City. In 1828 he was transferred back again to Illinois

Conference, and appointed superintendent and Conference collector for the Pottawattomie Mission on Fox River. He was active, vigilant, and useful in this field of labour. In 1829 Brother Dew was appointed to the Galena Station, in the extreme north-west corner of the Illinois State, at least four hundred miles from home; and such was the poverty of the country at that time,—for it was new and just in its forming state,—that he provided for his family where they were, and spent most of this year almost entirely from home. His labours were blessed in this new field of toil, and he was instrumental in planting Methodism firmly there.

In 1830 he was appointed to the Lebanon Circuit, and he acquitted himself as an able and useful minister of the Lord Jesus Christ; edified and built up the Church greatly. In 1831 he was appointed to Shoal Creek Circuit, with our beloved Bishop Ames; and long will he live in the recollection and Christian remembrance of the Methodists of Shoal Creek Circuit. In 1832 he was again appointed to the Lebanon Circuit; and though he had laboured long and preached much to that people, yet they received him as a messenger from God and a brother beloved, and he was useful.

In 1833 he was appointed to the Kaskaskia Circuit, where he was the instrument of great good, and souls were converted to God. Brother Dew was continued on this Circuit in 1834. From the hard fields of labour that he had occupied, and the little support he had received, with a young and growing family, in 1835 he located, to gather means of support, and to enable him to re-enter the itinerant field; for his soul was filled with holy fire, and he longed to spread the news of salvation from pole to pole.

In 1836 he was appointed president of M'Kendree College; and in 1837-38 he was re-admitted into the travelling connexion, and appointed to the Carlyle District as presiding elder. In 1839 he was appointed to the Lebanon District, where he finished his useful life, after an illness of about two weeks. On the 5th of September, 1840, he left these mortal shores for a better world, relying confidently on the goodness and mercy of God for his salvation He left an amiable wife and seven children, and an extensive acquaintance and circle of devoted friends, to lament their loss.

Brother Dew had a fine order of talent as a preacher, was a strong theological debater, had a clear and sound mind, and was well qualified to defend the doctrines of the Bible against infidelity, and the doctrines of Methodism against all sectarian assailants. He was popular and useful as a preacher, laboured hard, suffered much in spreading the Gospel, lived beloved, and died lamented by thousands; but his end was peace, and he has gone safe home to heaven, to reap his eternal reward.

.

CHAPTER XXXI.

GENERAL CONFERENCE IN INDIANAPOLIS.

In October, 1854, our Illinois annual Conference was held in Springfield, the seat of government, and I was re-appointed to the Pleasant Plains District. This was a year of general peace, and some prosperity to the Church. I think we numbered about four hundred conversions in the District this year; and nearly that number of accessions in the membership of the Church. In October, 1855, our annual Conference was held in Paris, on the eastern side of the State; and I was returned for the third year on the Pleasant Plains District, which was now enlarged from seven to ten Circuits and Stations. Our Districts in all the Western world are very different from down East and North-east. There they have from thirty to forty appointments in one presiding elder's District; most of their quarterly meetings are held on week-days or evenings, not embracing a Sabbath. The presiding elder goes round mostly to preside in trials of complaints or appeals, and as a kind of fiscal agent   Thus, no matter how talented he may be, his labours and usefulness as a preacher are thrown into the shade of comparative obscurity; and by the anti-Methodistic usages of these large Districts the presiding elder's office is not appreciated; nor can it be on this plan: hence the hue and cry against the office. In the vast West there is a Sabbath embraced in every quarterly-meeting appointment, and a presiding elder's services are properly appreciated, and if these Northern innovators would go back to the old land-marks of itinerancy, and not make so many little pop-gun, forty-dollar stations, the usefulness of presiding elders would now be as it was in the palmy, prosperous days of olden times.   No wonder preachers and people complain under the circumstances; the regular work is cut up into so many little and comparatively unimportant stations, and so poor withal, that the support of the ministry is fast becoming burdensome.   Go back to old Methodist preacher usage; let every quarterly meeting embrace a Sabbath, and then the old itinerant missionary will work well: but persist in cutting up the work, and making little stations, then appeal to the cupidity of these small fields of labour, and you may expect the table of the General Conference to groan under the petitions of the oppressed to change the office of presiding elder, till congregationalism is the order of the day.

This annual Conference was the fiftieth that I was entitled to a seat in; and during a half-century I had never missed attending but one of our annual sessions, and I missed this one by sickness. At this Conference we elected our delegates to attend the twelfth delegated General Conference, which sat in Indianapolis, May 1st, 1856. I was elected, among five other delegates, and this made the eleventh time I was elected to represent the interests of the Methodist Episcopal Church in that body

There were over two hundred and twenty delegates in this General Conference, from California and Oregon, and all parts of the United States and Territories. We had also delegates from the Wesleyan Methodists in England, and from Canada, also from Ireland; Brother Jacoby, from Germany, was also present.

From the unhappy political agitations of our country, we had anticipated troublous times in the General Conference, especially on the subject of American slavery. Many of our preachers who were strongly opposed to slavery, had suffered themselves to become too much excited by designing demagogues. Now it ought to be distinctly understood by all the people, and especially by Methodist preachers, that these demagogues care very little about human liberty, or the freedom of the poor down-trodden African. No; they are after the loaves and fishes, or the spoils of office; and while they are riveting the chains of the poor Negro ten times tighter than ever before, and threatening to rupture this Union, what do they care, if they can ride triumphantly into office and suck the public pap? Just nothing at all. But on this, and almost all other long-tried and prosperous regulations of our beloved rules and disciplinary regulations, there were found aboard the old ship ministers enough to keep the old, well-tried vessel well trimmed, and leaving in the distance these innovators and spoilers of ancient Methodism. So may it ever be.

Just so sure as a leaden ball tends to the earth in obedience to the laws of gravity, so sure the multiplying of our stations tends to locality and congregationalism. Better, far better, for the Methodist Church this day that we never had a station. Put all the work in Circuits, and put on as many preachers as the people need, and are able to support, and let the Church be blessed with the spice of variety and a constant interchange of preachers. There were several changes in the vital economy of the itinerant system of the Methodist Episcopal Church by which we have successfully spread the Gospel without a parallel in the history of any branch of the Christian Church since the apostolic day. I hope to be borne with while I make a few remarks on these matters.

At our late General Conference there were some of the preachers who wanted a change in the time a preacher might remain in a station or on a Circuit, namely, from two to three years They urged the

propriety of this change.   First. Because it would drive him to reading and study in order to keep up a variety for his hearers. Secondly.
That two years was too short a time to become acquainted with his
flock, so as to become a profitable pastor.   Thirdly. They urged that
the Canadian Methodist Church, our own child, or the daughter of
Episcopal Methodism in these United States, had lengthened out the
time that a preacher might remain in the same charge from one to five
years ; and that the Wesleyan Methodist Church in England, who is
the grandmother of the Canadian Methodist Church, had changed the
term of service, and that it worked well ; therefore it would work well
among us.

    To this I reply, First, That, from fifty years' experience, I find that
the return of a preacher, even the second year, to an appointment is
not as profitable as the first.   Secondly. If a preacher from sheer
necessity is to be driven to his books and study, in order to keep up
an interesting and profitable variety, there will be but little pastoral
duty performed, and but little spirituality in these forced sermons, and
a great deal of his preaching will be mere lecturing, and but little
real spiritual sermonizing.   Thirdly. The Canadian Methodist Church,
our child or daughter, when she requested to be set off as a separate
Church from us, on account of the civil disabilities under which she
laboured, instead of following the illustrious footsteps of her mother, the
Methodist Episcopal Church in these United States, in relation to the
time that her preachers might remain in a charge for consecutive years,
flung herself into the arms of her grandmother, the Wesleyan Methodist Church in England ; and as the grandmother is generally supposed to be somewhat in dotage, and seldom, if ever, qualified to raise
grandchildren aright, it is reasonable to suppose that these Canadians
borrowed this radical innovation on the itinerant plan of the Methodist
Episcopal Church from a dotard grandmother ; and however well it
may work in Canada or old England, it can have no other effect in
these United States but to localize our preachers, and finally destroy
our itinerant system ; and whenever this is done, farewell to the
triumphant success of the Methodist Episcopal Church.

    There was another regulation introduced into our late General Con-
ference on which I wish to remark ; I mean the admitting into membership and ordaining preachers who are appointed to presidencies and
professorships in our universities, colleges, and various institutions of
learning, without having travelled a single day, or having a pastoral
charge as a travelling preacher. These men, without undergoing any of
the privations or sacrifices of an itinerant life, are settled down with
large salaries.   Our colleges are rapidly multiplying, and I hope they
will continue to do so ; but who does not see that in a few years our

local agents, presidents, and professors may form even a majority of our annual Conferences, and then the itinerant system will be very much like a man riding a race with the reins of his horse's bridle tied to a stump. It is wrong, fundamentally wrong. The itinerant should be kept pure and unencumbered, and we should look out men to serve tables, or education if you please, but our itinerant men should give themselves wholly to the ministry of the word. These are politically and religiously perilous times, and there is a solemn crisis on the Church; but I hope God will guide the ship of State and Church. But surely this is no time to abandon old and long-tried usages for novel experiments.

CHAPTER XXXII.

CONVERSION OF AN INFIDEL DOCTOR.

Somewhere about thirty-five years ago, while I was travelling on the Cumberland District, in West Tennessee, there lived a Dr. ——, who was wealthy, and immensely popular as a practising physician. He had a large practice; he was gentlemanly in his manners, hospitable and kind. His family were very respectable; his wife was a devoted Christian and a faithful member of the Methodist Episcopal Church. They lived in affluence; they were benevolent and liberal in the support of the Gospel. I was introduced to the doctor and his amiable family at a camp-meeting which was held a few miles from his residence. Having a few days to rest between my camp-meetings, the doctor and family cordially invited me to spend those rest-days at his house, and I consented to do so. When our camp-meeting closed, in company with several other preachers, I repaired to the doctor's habitation. We were received cordially and treated princely There was everything earthly to make one comfortable. The family, black and white, were called in to family worship night and morning; and when we surrounded their bountiful table, we were invited to ask a blessing, and to return thanks. The next morning, after we had breakfasted, as we were seated in the parlour, the doctor informed me that he was a total unbeliever in the Christian religion; that he had read the Bible through and through again and again, and that he could not receive it as a revelation from God; that he liked the morals that the Christian system inculcated; he liked to encourage the Gospel, because of the good moral influence it had upon mankind; that he felt it not only a charity, but a positive duty, to support the Gospel; first, because it taught a pious reverence toward God; secondly, because it breathed peace and goodwill to all mankind;

thirdly, because it taught truth, virtue, honesty, and benevolence, in all
the civil, social, and moral relations of man, as he stood accountable to
his God, and as he stood connected with or related to all mankind.

Now, my gentle reader, you may well imagine that I felt a little
surprised, and that I felt greatly the need of right words, or rather
strong arguments and soft words; and, after pausing for a moment, I
looked the doctor full in the face and said,—

"Doctor, I hope you believe there is a God. Do you?"

"Certainly," was his reply

"Doctor, do you believe that God is too wise to err, and too good
to inflict pain or misery of any kind on his innocent and unoffending
creatures?"

"Certainly I do, sir."

"Well now, doctor, will you be good 'enough, laying the Bible
aside, to tell me how a wise and good God could push into existence
a race of human beings, subject to all kinds of mental, moral, and
physical wretchedness, misery, and woe? If He is wise, just, holy,
and supremely good, how could innocent man, coming immediately
from the plastic hand of his God, be filled with so many unholy and
impure passions as we see human nature heir to?"

"I must confess," said the doctor, "I cannot account for it; it is
wrapped in inexplicable mystery."

"Well, doctor, seeing God is supremely good and wise, and seeing
that man is limited in all his powers of mind and body, and subject to
so much misery and so many errors in judgment and practice, can we
not well imagine that God, who is the supreme source of all moral
excellence, and whose tender mercies are over all His works, would be
moved by the benignant laws of His own eternal nature,—after having
created man for His own pleasure, with all his liability to err and his
susceptibility to evil, would be prompted to give to this feeble race a
rule of faith and practice? And what else is the Bible? Nay, would
it not throw eternally into the shade all the perfections of God, at
whose almighty 'fiat teeming millions of erring human beings have
taken their existence in the world, and who have no power to control
or prevent their own existence, if that God should leave these millions
to wander in the mazes of animal passion without a well-defined
revealed rule of faith and practice?"

The doctor paused, and made a sorry reply. I saw I had made a
breach in his supposed impregnable wall, behind which he had in-
trenched himself, with all his boasted infidelity I saw there was not
a moment to be lost; and with haste I commenced re-adjusting my
battering-rams, that in my next onset I might widen the breach, and
enter the citadel, and take my infidel doctor prisoner, and silence all

his opposition to truth, when all of a sudden he said, "Mr. Cartwright, I know you are a man of reason and good sense ; and I think I can prove to you, beyond the power of successful contradiction, that there is no such thing as experimental religion, and that it is all imagination and delusion."

"Very well, doctor; try it."

"Well, sir," said he, "does not all knowledge, either human or Divine, depend upon sensible evidence?"

"Yes, sir."

"Does not faith, human or Divine, depend on credible evidence?"

"Yes, sir."

"Well," said he, "I will state a plain, unsophisticated case. Suppose you were called upon, as a judge or juror, to decide a case in litigation, and there were five witnesses introduced, all of them honourable, high-minded men, whose veracity was never called in question, and who stood unimpeached and unimpeachable everywhere, whose known integrity and intelligence were admitted on all sides ; and suppose a matter in controversy was brought before you, and these five witnesses were introduced as credible evidence ; and one of the witnesses deposed to the facts as stated by the plaintiff, A, and then the other four came forward, and with equal clearness deposed to the facts as claimed by the defendant, B. Now, sir," continued the doctor, "all things being equal, so far as the intelligence, truth, and veracity of the witnesses are concerned, how would you decide the case? Would you not instantly decide that all the probabilities and all the possibilities were in favour of the four who deposed to the facts stated by the defendant, and that the one lone witness who deposed to the facts claimed by the plaintiff must, to a certainty, be mistaken?"

I replied, "It is altogether likely I should give judgment for the defendant, B."

"Well, now, sir," said the doctor, "you contend that the Christian religion is an experimental fact, and that all Christians have sensible evidence of a change of heart, which you call 'religion.' Man has five senses, namely, seeing, hearing, tasting, smelling, and feeling. On the united and concurrent testimony of these five senses, or witnesses, all knowledge of experimental religion depends ; and all professions of the knowledge of facts that cannot be proved by these witnesses, must be fallacious, and, therefore, a deception. Now, sir," said the doctor, "permit me to ask you a few serious and solemn questions, and I demand honest and unequivocal answers, direct. Did you ever see religion?"

I answered, "No."

"Did you ever hear religion?"

"No."

"Did you ever smell religion?"

"No."

"Did you ever taste religion?"

"No."

"Did you ever feel religion?"

"Yes."

"Now, then," said the doctor, with apparent triumph, "I have proved, beyond a doubt, by four respectable witnesses, that religion is not seen, heard, smelled, or tasted; and but one lone, solitary witness, namely, feeling, has testified that it is an experimental fact. The weight of evidence is overpowering, sir, and you must give it up."

I paused, and seemed to be astonished and greatly perplexed, but recovering myself a little, I said, "Doctor, are you willing that your principles and professional practice shall be tested by the same array of testimony as you have adduced to overthrow revealed religion?"

"Yes, sir."

"Well, sir, you profess to understand the science of medicine. You have had, and now have, a large and lucrative practice. You profess to have cured various and complicated diseases, and to have relieved and removed many pains, in the complicated forms in which they have attacked the human system; and you have amassed a princely fortune by your successful practice."

"All true," said the doctor.

"Well, sir, do you not know that you have been playing the hypocrite, and practising a most wretched fraud on the gullibility of the people?"

"No, sir," he replied, very fiercely.

"Why, doctor," said I, "a man of your profound science and research must certainly know that there is no such thing as pain in the human system; and though ignorant people have thought so, yet you know better; and whenever you have visited poor dupes, that thought they were in great pain, and administered medicine to them, and thus persuaded them that you, by your medical skill, had removed their pains, and charged them large bills, you certainly knew you were practising a fraud on them, and getting their money under a false pretence; for you certainly knew that there was no such thing as pain."

Said the doctor, rather fiercely, "I certainly know no such thing, sir."

I replied, "Well, doctor, I will ask you a few questions, if you please, and I demand honest and prompt answers."

"Very well, sir," said the doctor.

"Well, sir, did you ever see a pain?"

"No, sir."

"Did you ever hear a pain?"

"No, sir."

"Did you ever smell a pain?"

"No, sir."

"Did you ever taste a pain?"

"No, sir."

"Did you ever feel a pain?"

"Certainly I did, sir."

By this time I had well-nigh taken the wind out of the doctor's sails, and his countenance betrayed confusion; but I rallied him, and said, "Do not be alarmed, doctor; four respectable witnesses have testified that there is no such thing as pain in the human system, and but one lone witness has deposed that there is; therefore, the idea of there being pain in the physical system of man is fallacious, and there is no reality in the thing; and you ought to go and restore the money you have taken from them, and acknowledge the fraud you have practised on them, and do so no more; and I charge you, as an honest man, to do it, and quit those fraudulent practices."

During almost all this conversation with the doctor, his wife and family sat around and listened with profound attention, and I frequently saw the tears coursing down the cheeks of the doctor's wife. The doctor became mute, and remained silent for a considerable time. I turned my conversation to the doctor's wife and children. Just at that moment the Lord, in a very powerful manner, blessed the pious wife of the doctor, and she shouted aloud and blessed God for revealed religion. She ran and threw her arms around her husband's neck, and exhorted him, with streaming eyes and words that burned, to be reconciled to God. I said, "Let us all kneel and pray." The doctor fell on his knees and wept like a child, and prayed fervently. The great deep of his heart was broken up, his infidelity gave way, and, for the first time in his life, he wept and prayed. All day after this he seemed to be melted into childlike simplicity. He fled to the woods, and earnestly sought salvation. That night, after prayer, he retired to bed, but not to sleep, for he prayed as in agony; and about midnight God spoke peace to his troubled soul, and we all awoke and got up, and joined in prayer and praise. Such thrilling shouts I seldom ever heard from the lips of mortal man. His conversion was the beginning of a glorious revival of religion in the settlement, and many were the souls saved by grace. Many of the doctor's slaves obtained religion, and many others of the slaves in the neighbourhood. The doctor fitted out and sent most of his slaves to Liberia. Thank God that I ever had the privilege of preaching the Gospel to slaves and slaveholders. Religion always makes better slaves and better masters, and will secure the freedom of more slaves than all the run-mad abolitionism in the world. The doctor shortly after was licensed to preach, and lived a pious, useful life. God gave him many seals to his ministry. He has long since fallen on sleep, and gone home to Abraham's bosom, while I am left to linger on the shores of time a little longer; but while I pen this little sketch, my heart grows warm with holy fire; and I hope soon to meet the doctor and his lovely family in heaven, with many, very many, of the spiritual children God has given me. Amen.

CHAPTER XXXIII.

METHODIST USAGES.

I WISH to say a few things in this chapter on the usages of the Methodist Episcopal Church. When I joined the Church, her ministers and members were a plain people; plain in dress and address. You could know a Methodist preacher by his plain dress as far as you could see him. The members were also plain, very plain in dress. They wore no jewellery, nor were they permitted to wear jewellery, or superfluous ornament, or extravagant dress of any kind; and this was the rule by which we walked, whether poor or rich, young or old; and although we knew then as well as we do now, that the religion of the Lord Jesus Christ did not consist in dress, or the cut of the garment, yet we then knew and know now that extravagant dress and superfluous ornaments engender pride, and lead to many hurtful lusts, directly at war with that humility and godly example that becomes our relation to Christ, that so pre-eminently becomes Christians. Moreover, when we look around us, and see the perishing millions of our fallen race dying in their sins for the want of a preached Gospel, and that this Gospel is not sent to them for want of means to support the missionary, may we not well question whether we are doing right in the sight of God in adorning our bodies with all this costly and extravagant dressing? Would it not be more godlike or Christianlike to give our money, laid out in these unnecessary ornaments, to send the Gospel to the poor, perishing millions that have souls to be saved or lost for ever? and will not God hold us accountable for the use of those means and moneys that He has given us? ... would not the simple fund that might be created by disposing of the ornaments of the members of the Methodist Church alone send the Gospel to hundreds of thousands, who must perish in all probability for the want of this little Christian sacrifice by the professed lovers of Christ? The Apostle James says, "Whether ye eat, or drink, or whatsoever ye do, do all to the glory of God." Now apply this rule to your consciences, and I have no doubt your piety will decide in favour of the sacrifice you ought to make, and the good example you ought to set.

The duty of family prayer is a very important one to the Christian. God has given the head of the family a very important and responsible position. It is a question very fairly settled, that from the early ages of the Christian religion, family prayer was required and expected of all who professed godliness. If we are to bring up our children in the nurture and admonition of the Lord, and if we and our household are professionally bound to serve the Lord, how can we be innocent before God and our families, and habitually neglect this duty? One of the great wants of the Church at this day is the want of more family religion; and has not God threatened to "pour out His wrath and fury upon the families that call not on His name?" How many happy thousands of children will bless God for ever for family prayer, or, in other words, for praying parents, who, morning and evening, called their little ones around them, and bowed down before God, and prayed with and for them! O, parents, think of the happy results of the discharge of this duty! Many of your children will thank you in heaven for ever for praying for them in your families.

And yet I am sorry to hear that many of the members of the Methodist Episcopal Church shamefully neglect this sacred duty of praying in their families. How shall we answer it to God? Is not this one among many other reasons, why so many of our members feel almost entirely unprepared to enter into the work of the Lord in times of revival, when God pours out His Spirit and convicts sinners among us? and perhaps, if we prayed more at home, we would be better prepared to hear the Gospel of our salvation when we attend church. Let no business, let no company that visits you, turn you away from, or cause you to neglect, this duty; have your family altar firmly fixed, and your sacrifice always on it, and then look up, and, in the very act of asking, expect God to send down the holy fire and consume your sacrifice, be it great or small. I long to see the time come when God shall abundantly revive family religion in the Church; then, and perhaps not till then, shall we see better and more glorious times of the work of God among us.

Prayer-meetings have accomplished great good, as practised in the Methodist Episcopal Church; but are they not growing into disuse among us? Some of my earliest recollections are those Methodist prayer-meetings, where men and women, young and old, prayed in public. We know there have been fashionable objections to females praying in public; but I am sure I do not exaggerate when I say, I have often seen our dull and stupid prayer-meetings suddenly changed from a dead clog to a heavenly enjoyment, when a sister has been called on to pray, who has reverently bowed and taken up the cross, and utterance was given her that was heavenly, and she prayed with words that burned, and the baptismal fire rolled all around, while the house and all the praying company were baptized from heaven, many sinners, tall and stout-hearted sinners, have been brought to quake and tremble before God, and have cried for mercy, and, while crying, have found peace with God through our Lord Jesus Christ. Many weeping mourners in those prayer-meetings have found the blessed pardon of all their sins; the members of the Church have also been greatly blessed, and have gone on their way rejoicing in the Lord.

One of the best revivals I ever knew was commenced and carried on by a prayer-meeting among the members of the Church without any preaching at all. The society felt that they were on back ground, and they covenanted to meet every evening for a week, and have public prayer, and pray for a revival. The first night God met them and blessed many of their souls; the second night the Lord very powerfully converted two souls; the meeting went on then for about twenty days and nights, and from one to twelve were converted at every coming together. The Saturday and Sunday on which their meeting closed, they sent for me to gather up the fragments, that nothing be lost. On Saturday I read our General Rules, and explained them, and showed the principles of the Methodist Episcopal Church. On Sunday I preached on baptism, and opened the doors, and received one hundred and nineteen into the Church, and baptized forty-seven adults and thirty children in the altar, and then marched off to the creek and immersed twenty-seven; making in all one hundred and nineteen accessions on trial, and one hundred and four baptized. This was the fruit of a prayer-meeting.

Class-meetings have been owned and blessed of God in the Methodist Episcopal Church; and, from more than fifty years' experience, I doubt whether any one means of grace has proved as successful in building up the Methodist Church as this blessed privilege. For many years we kept them with closed doors, and suffered none to remain in class-meeting more than twice or thrice, unless they signified a desire to join the Church. In these class-meetings the weak have been made strong; the bowed down have been raised up; the tempted have found delivering grace ; the doubting mind has had all its doubts and fears removed , and the whole class have found that this was "none other than the house of God, and the gate of heaven." Here the hard heart has been tendered, the cold heart warmed with holy fire, here the dark mind, beclouded with trial and temptation, has had every cloud rolled away, and the Sun of Righteousness has risen with resplendent glory, "with healing in His wings ; " and in these class-meetings many seekers of religion have found them the spiritual birth-place of their souls into the heavenly family, and their dead souls made alive to God.

Every Christian that enjoys religion, and that desires to feel its mighty comforts, if he understands the nature of them really, loves them and wishes to attend them. But how sadly are these class-meetings. neglected in the Methodist Episcopal Church! Are there not thousands of our members who habitually neglect to attend them? and is it any wonder that so many of our members grow cold and careless in religion, and finally backslide? Is it not for the want of enforcing our rules on class-meetings that their usefulness is destroyed? Are there not a great many worldly-minded, proud, fashionable members of our Church, who merely have the name of Methodist, that are constantly crying out and pleading that attendance on class-meetings should not be a test of membership in the Church? And now, before God, are not many of our preachers at fault in this matter? They neglect to meet the classes themselves, and they keep many class-leaders in office that will not attend to their duty; and is it not fearful to see our preachers so neglectful of their duty in dealing with the thousands of our delinquent members who stay away from class-meetings weeks, months, and for years? Just as sure as our preachers neglect their duty in enforcing the Rules on class-meetings on our leaders and members, just so sure the power of religion will be lost in the Methodist Episcopal Church O for faithful, holy preachers, and faithful, holy class-leaders ! Then we shall have faithful, holy members. May the time never come when class-meetings shall be laid aside in the Methodist Episcopal Church, or when these class-meetings, or an attendance on them, shall cease to be a test of membership among us ' I beg and beseech class-leaders to be punctual in attending their classes; and, if any of their members stay away from any cause, hunt them up, find out the cause of their absence, pray with them, and urge them to the all-important duty of regularly attending class-meeting. Much, very much, depends on faithful and religious class-leaders ; and how will the unfaithful class-leader stand in the judgment of the great day, when, by his neglect, many of his members will have backslidden, and will be finally lost?

CHAPTER XXXIV.

CONCLUSION.

In 1803, or fifty-three years since, next fall, I started to travel and preach the Gospel, being employed by a presiding elder, in my eighteenth year. I travelled five years as a single man. I then married, and have travelled forty-eight years as a married man. My wife has had nine children; seven daughters and two sons. We raised eight of those children; lost one lovely little daughter in her minority, but have lived to see all the rest married, though one has died since she married, but died in peace. We have now living thirty-eight grandchildren and eight great-grandchildren. All our children are in the Methodist Episcopal Church, and, we hope, are trying to be religious; several of our grandchildren are also in the Church, and trying to serve God and get to heaven. Forty-eight years ago I was appointed presiding elder by Bishop Asbury; and, with the exception of a few years, have been presiding elder up to this time, and am, perhaps, the oldest presiding elder in all the Western country. I have seen fifty-three sessions of annual Conferences, and never missed but one. I have been elected to eleven General Conferences, from 1816 to 1856.

When I started as a travelling preacher, a single preacher was allowed to receive eighty dollars *per annum* if his Circuit would give it to him; but single preachers in those days seldom received over thirty or forty dollars, and often much less; and had it not been for a few presents made us by the benevolent friends of the Church, and a few dollars we made as marriage fees, we must have suffered much more than we did. But the Lord provided; and, strange as it may appear to the present generation, we got along without starving or going naked.

I wish here to give a statement of my success, and loss and gain, as a Methodist travelling preacher, for fifty-three years, though I know it will be imperfect; but it shall be as perfect as my old musty and rusty account scraps will permit. And in the first place I have lacked, in the fifty-three years, of my disciplinary allowance, about 5,000 dollars; loss in horses to travel with, 1,000 dollars; loss in the sale of religious books, 200 dollars; loss in money, of which I was robbed, 150 dollars; loss in clothing stolen from me, 50 dollars. Total loss, 6,400 dollars.

I sold about 10,000 dollars' worth of books; my per-centage on these books would net me about 1,000 dollars; made in marriage fees, 500 dollars; presents in money, clothing, horses, &c, 500 dollars. Total, 2,000 dollars.

Given by me for the erection of churches and parsonages, 500 dollars; given to Missionary Society, Bible Society, Sunday-school Union, and other benevolent societies, 800 dollars; given to universities, colleges, &c., for education, 700 dollars; given to superannuated preachers, their widows and orphans, and other necessitous cases, 300 dollars; given unfortunate persons, burned out, 500 dollars. Total, 2,300 dollars.

I have travelled eleven Circuits, and twelve Districts, have received into the Methodist Episcopal Church, on probation and by 'letter, 10,000; have baptized, of children, 8,000; of adults, 4,000. I have preached the funerals of 500, and now, after all I have done or can do, and although I know well what a Methodist preacher's suffering life is, and have known what it is to suffer hunger and poverty, and also what it is, in some small sense, to abound, I feel that I have been a very unprofitable servant.

For fifty-three years, whenever appointed to a Circuit or District, I formed a plan, and named every place where and when I preached; and also the text of Scripture from which I preached; the number of conversions, of baptisms, and the number that joined the Church. From these old plans, though there are some imperfections, yet I can come very near stating the number of times that I have tried to preach. For twenty years of my early ministry, I often preached twice a day, and sometimes three times. We seldom ever had, in those days, more than one rest-day in a week; so that I feel very safe in saying that I preached four hundred times a year. This would make, in twenty years, eight thousand sermons. For the last thirty-three years, I think I am safe in saying I have averaged four sermons a week, or at least two hundred sermons a year, making, in thirty-three years, 6,600. Total, 14,600.

I was converted on a camp-ground, elsewhere described in this narrative; and for many years of my early ministry, after I was appointed presiding elder, lived in the tented grove from two to three months in the year.

I am sorry to say that the Methodist Episcopal Church of late years, since they have become numerous and wealthy, have almost let camp-meetings die out. I am very certain that the most successful part of my ministry has been on camp-ground. There the word of God has reached the hearts of thousands that otherwise, in all probability, never would have been reached by the ordinary means of grace. Their practicability and usefulness have, to some extent, been tested this year, 1856, in my District, Pleasant Plains; and I greatly desire to see a revival of camp-meetings in the Methodist Episcopal Church before I go hence and am no more, or before I leave the walls of Zion. Come, my Methodist brethren, you can well afford to spend one week in each year, in each Circuit, or station, on the tented field But there must be a general rally: it will be but a small burden if there is a general turn out; but if a few only tent, it will be burdensome, and will finally destroy camp-meetings altogether.

May the day be eternally distant, when camp-meetings, class-meetings, prayer-meetings, and lovefeasts shall be laid aside in the Methodist Episcopal Church!

And now I must draw this imperfect history of my life to a close. I am in the seventy-second year of my natural life. I have lived to see this vast Western wilderness rise and improve, and become wealthy without a parallel in the history of the world; I have outlived every member of my father's family; I have no father, no mother, no brother, no sister living; I have outlived every member of the class I joined in 1800; I have outlived every member of the Western Conference in 1804, save one or two; I have outlived every member of the first General Conference that I was elected to, in Baltimore, in 1816, save five or six; I have outlived all my early bishops; I have outlived every presiding elder that I ever had when on Circuits; and I have outlived hundreds and thousands of my cotemporary ministers and members, as well as juniors, and still linger on the mortal shores. Though all these have died, they shall live again, and by the grace of God I shall live with them in heaven for ever. Why I live, God only knows. I certainly have toiled and suffered enough to kill a thousand men, but I do not complain. Thank God for health, strength, and grace, that have borne me up, and borne me on! Thank God that during my long and exposed live as a Methodist preacher, I have never been overtaken with any scandalous sin, though my short-comings and imperfections have been without number!

And now, I ask of all who may read this imperfect sketch of my eventful life, while I linger on these mortal shores, to pray for me, that my sun may set without a cloud, and that I may be counted worthy to obtain a part in the first resurrection; and may, O may I meet you all in heaven! Farewell, till we meet at the judgment!

APPENDIX.

A.—*The Shakers*, page 10.

This sect, also known as the *United Society of Believers* and *Millennial Church*, had its origin in France, but is now confined exclusively to the United States. It is said to have sprung from the *Camisards* or *French Prophets*, who appeared first in Dauphiny, and *Vivarias* in France in 1688 More than five hundred persons of both sexes, who soon increased to thousands, at that period professed to be inspired by the Holy Ghost with the gift of prophecy, and while under this influence, their bodies became agitated,—they shook, staggered, fell down as though dead, and on recovering cried aloud for mercy, and proclaimed their mission in the streets and highways, their bodies undergoing the most frightful contortions. After a brief period their numbers gradually diminished, and in 1705 three of the most distinguished of the few remaining members repaired to England, where, prophesying the speedy coming of Christ and the near approach of the Millennium, they speedily obtained some two or three hundred adherents, all of whom exercised the gift of prophecy. Their most distinguished members seem to have originally belonged to the Society of Friends. In 1758, Ann Lee, afterwards known as "*Mother Ann*," and recognised by all the faithful members as their "*spiritual mother*," joined the Society She professed to have been favoured with a special revelation of God's will, and in a few years declared that it had been revealed to her that America was the chosen spot where the Church was to receive a speedy increase and permanent establishment. Accordingly, in 1774, accompanied by her husband and eight other persons,—probably the whole surviving church,—she left England; and, after some little wandering, finally settled down at Watervliet, near Albany. For some years the sect remained in retirement, making no attempt to add to its number. At length the moral and apparently blameless life of the members seems to have had attractions, for a gradual increase commenced, and settlements were established in the States of Indiana, Ohio, and Kentucky. In 1845, there were about fifteen of these settlements throughout the States, numbering from six to eight thousand souls. Their doctrines are peculiar They maintain that they are the only true Church, and have all the apostolical gifts, of prophecy, of speaking in unknown tongues, and of healing the sick, that baptism and the Lord's Supper, as sacraments, ceased with the apostolic age; that sin committed against God is committed against them, and can only be pardoned through them; that the wicked will be punished for a definite period only, except such as apostatize from the faith (of Shakerism), who will be punished for ever; that the Judgment and Millennium have commenced, and that Christ will not appear again in this life, except in the person of His followers (the Shakers). In their moral life they are exemplary, being strictly honest and straightforward in their dealings, abstaining from everything like sensuality, avoiding contentions, refraining from the politics of this world, and all questions likely to excite evil feeling,—exercising charity towards the afflicted, punishing idleness, and encouraging industry.

Their mode of worship is singular. "The people of this Society," says one of their advocates, "do not believe that any external performance whatever, without the sincere devotion of the heart with all the feelings of the soul, in devotion and praise to the Creator of all their powers and faculties, can be any acceptable worship to Him who looks at the heart. But in a united assembly a unity of exercise in acts of devotion to God is desirable, for harmony is beautiful, and appears like the order of heaven. It will be difficult to describe all the various modes of exercise given in the worship of God at different times because the operations of the Spirit are so various, that even the leaders are unable to tell beforehand what manner will be given by the Spirit in the next meeting. Yet *in a regular meeting, where nothing extraordinary appears, they sometimes exercise in a regular dance, while formed in straight lines, and sometimes in a regular march around the room, in harmony with regular songs sung on the occasion* Shouting and clapping of the hands, and many other operations, are frequently given, all of which have a tendency to keep the assembly alive, with their hearts and all their senses and feelings devoted to the service of God." These exercises they further justify by reference to the conduct of the Israelites on various occasions. The reader will observe that, with some of the peculiarities of both Mormons and Spiritualists, the Shakers have neither the grossness of the former nor the presumption of the latter, but, with both the sects we have named, they are wanting in that true spiritual life which faith and prayer can only realize.

B.—*Bishop M'Kendree*, page 12.

BISHOP M'KENDREE was one of the early Methodist preachers in America who endured and suffered much in extending the influence of that Church in the Western States. His memory is still cherished with respectful affection by those who owe so much to his labours. Born in 1757 of respectable parents, members of the American branch of the Church of England, in Virginia, he early felt the force of religious impressions; but it was not until his nineteenth year that he gave himself seriously to the consideration of religion, and joined the Methodist Episcopal Church. In 1787, a revival took place in the Circuit where he lived, and under the influence of the strong feelings which it excited, he determined to devote himself to the ministry. Nothing but ardent devotion to the cause of God could have led to this step It was a period when Methodist preachers had to endure every privation, to suffer persecution, to be ill fed, poorly clad, often in their journeys without a roof to shelter them. Yet, in face of these difficulties, he voluntarily took upon himself the duties of the office; for more than twelve years he laboured with great success in the West, following the emigrant into the far distant settlements, and ever bearing to him the word of life. In 1800, he was appointed by Bishop Asbury to superintend a District, comprising the States of Ohio, Kentucky, Texas, and part of Virginia and Illinois, and extending over some 1,500 miles Every three months he had to travel through it. The mere labour of travelling was much, but, added to this, he had to ford rivers, cross swamps, work his way through thick, tangled, and apparently impassable forests; to sleep night after night in the open air, far from human habitation Yet, with all this, his energy never flagged; wherever he could find hearers, he preached to them the Gospel, and no where, save in England, under the preaching of Wesley and Whitefield, was preaching so effective Careless men were aroused to a sense of danger, thoughtful men were led to find in the mystery of redemption more than sufficient to occupy every thought; strong, athletic men, whose mouths were one hour full of cursing and bitterness, the next lay like helpless children crying aloud to God for mercy; and the forests of the West often rang with sounds of prayer and praise, from the lips of those who had never before uttered the name of God, save with curses. In 1808, the General Conference was held at Baltimore, and here M'Kendree was made a bishop. Few incidents in his life are more remarkable For twenty years he had been a pioneer preacher, but his labours had been on districts having barely the elements of civilization, and his name was scarcely known to his fellow ministers. He was appointed to preach before the Conference. His tall, gaunt figure, clad in the most coarse and homely garments, and his awkward movements and hesitating utterance, led to expressions of wonder at such an appointment. Their wonder was increased when M'Kendree, having entered the pulpit, gave out a hymn and uttered a prayer with a faltering voice and listless manner. He selected as his text Jeremiah viii. 21, 22, " Is there no balm in Gilead?" &c. He dwelt on the spiritual disease of the Jewish Church and the human race, and analysed the feelings of God's faithful ambassadors at such a state of things in a commonplace and uninteresting manner ; but when he came to speak of the blessed effect upon the heart of the balm provided by God for the healing of nations, he seemed once more to feel the dignity of his office,—all tremor and listlessness left him, his eyes sparkled, his figure dilated, his voice became clear and musical, and with a hallowed eloquence he poured forth burning words and thoughts, which fell upon his audience, says a cotemporary, like a shower of Divine grace from the upper world. No longer were they apathetic, no longer seemed they indifferent to his words ; a spark of his own enthusiasm seemed to have fallen upon them ; in every direction sobs and groans and shouts of praise were heard ; eyes were suffused with tears, and hearts melted under the preacher's wonderful influence. As the preacher left the pulpit, but one feeling reigned,—" This is a man God delights to honour,—this is the man to make a bishop," and within a week he was appointed to that office For twenty-seven years M'Kendree held the office of bishop. During the first twelve years he was distinguished for the activity, zeal, and vigour with which he entered into every movement for extending the cause of God. The Missions to the Indians and general Missions owed much to his fostering care. The remaining fifteen years were to him years of affliction,—he was sorely tried by disease , relieved by the consideration of the General Conference from many of the laborious duties of his office, he yet continued at intervals to travel, though he had become so infirm as to be lifted into the carriage which conveyed him from place to place His last words to the Conference of 1832 were, " My brethren and children, love one another." Two years later, standing on the verge of another world, he cheered his sorrowing friends with the exclamation, " All, all is well !" and thus he passed from life, March 5th, 1835, beloved and honoured by all, a worthy soldier of Christ, who had well and truly fought the good fight

C.—*Bishop Asbury*, page 14.

No name in the history of the Methodist Episcopal Church of America stands out more prominently than that of Bishop Asbury. Its economy, discipline, and general arrangements, all bear the mark of his hand. For the first few years of its history, Asbury was its leading spirit, animating and exciting its ministers, bringing his calm judgment to bear upon their deliberations, or travelling from state to state, preaching the word of life, fostering infant Churches, forming new ones, encouraging the downcast, and spurring on to activity the lethargic. Yet, strange to say, of this man, of his self-denying labours, of his great exertions for the cause of God, his own Journal, extending from the 7th of August 1771 to December 7th, 1815, is the only authentic record. The full story of his life has yet to be told. From his Journal the reader cannot fail to form an opinion most favourable to the writer: he there opens out his heart fully; personal glorification there is none; personal joys and sorrows scarce have a place; but how his whole heart seems to rejoice! how full of praise and thanksgiving he seems to be when God's blessing is seen in the labours of the Methodist preachers! and how sorrowfully he grieves over the decay of God's work in some parts! How full of anguish he seems when narrating the story of some poor backslider, who, after living holily for a time, has stepped into the paths of sin, and is fast sinking into the very slough of corruption! With what a quiet humour, too, he tells of his occasional perplexities,—how the superintending bishop of the Methodist Episcopal Church is reduced to two dollars, and must needs ask some one for a replenishment of his purse! and with what a business-like conciseness, too, he here and there details his journeyings!

"Monday 31st, I rode down to Cambridge, and preached at eleven o'clock: my subject Psalm li. 9, 10. I felt assisted. Tuesday, April 1. We returned to Thomas Foster's; I saw Joseph Everett, feeble, but faithful, in patient waiting for his Lord." "*To move, move, seems to be my life,*" he says in one part, and every page testifies to the truth of the observation.

He was born at Handsworth, near Birmingham, August 20th, 1745 His parents were pious Methodists in very humble circumstances Their house was a preaching station. From his childhood he was seriously disposed, and his deportment at school acquired for him the nickname of *the parson* At thirteen years of age he was converted to God, and commenced holding meetings for reading and prayer with his companions In his sixteenth year he became a local preacher. Six years later, in 1767, in his twenty-second year, he became an itinerant Methodist preacher. He was appointed a Missionary to America, in 1771, by Mr. Wesley, who seems to have had a high opinion of his judgment. On reaching America, he found Messrs. Pilmoor and Boardman, who had preceded him as Missionaries, actively engaged; the former in Philadelphia, the latter in New York. During the two years they had been in America, they had confined their labours almost exclusively to the larger towns. Asbury at once directed his attention to the smaller towns, villages, and country places, and laboured so assiduously, that societies were soon formed in many districts, and ministers gradually increased. During the Revolution, Asbury alone, of all the English Missionaries, remained in America he continued preaching until his life was in danger, and then took refuge with a friend, who supported him until the season of danger had passed.

In 1784, Mr. Wesley ordained Messrs Coke, Whatcoat, and Vasey, and sent them to America with instructions to ordain Asbury as superintendent bishop of the American Methodist Church. Asbury, while looking upon Wesley as the founder of Methodism, felt that the ministry ought also to have a voice in his selection to that responsible office, and only accepted the appointment on condition that it should be ratified by a meeting of preachers. This was done, and Asbury was unanimously elected. As a bishop, he was dignified, yet affectionate, laborious himself, yet considerate to others, a strict maintainer of discipline, an active and zealous preacher Well or ill in health, he never allowed his duties to be neglected. From state to state, visiting every society, he travelled year after year, and though often, towards the close of his life, he wished for greater energy and more active physical powers, he discharged his duties to the satisfaction of all, and laid down his office with his life, March 31st, 1816 He was never married. His reasons for his celibacy we give in his own words:—

"I was called," he says. "in my fourteenth year. I began my public exercises between sixteen and seventeen. At twenty-one I travelled. At twenty-six I came to America. Thus far, I had reasons enough for a single life. It had been my intention to return to Europe at thirty years of age; but the war continued, and it was ten years before we had settled, lasting peace. This was no time to marry, or to be given in marriage. At thirty-nine I was ordained superintendent bishop in America. Among the duties imposed upon me by my office, was that of travelling extensively, and I could hardly expect to find a woman with grace to induce her willingly to live but one week out of fifty-two with her husband Besides, what right has any man to take advantage of the affections of a woman, make her his wife, and, by a voluntary absence, subvert the whole order and economy of the marriage state, by separating those whom neither God, nature, nor the requirements of civil society, permit long to be put asunder? It is neither just nor generous. I may add to this, that I had little money, and with this little I administered to the necessities of a beloved mother, till I was fifty-seven. If I have done wrong, I hope God and the sex will forgive me."

Some idea of his laborious life may be formed from the following estimate which has been made of his services and travels during the forty-five years of his ministry in America. 'He delivered not less than 16,425 sermons, besides lectures and addresses. He travelled over 270,000 miles. He presided at 224 Annual Conferences, and probably consecrated more than 4,000 persons to the sacred office.

D —*The Jerks and Revival Extravagancies*, page 21

THE extraordinary excitements narrated by Cartwright, as having occurred during the revivals, in which he took a prominent part, though seemingly extravagant, and in many cases almost beyond belief, are yet not without parallel in the religious history of this country. Mr Wesley's Journals abound with instances of wonderful excitement following or preceding conversions, instances, too, of opponents of religion, who, ridiculing these scenes, have suddenly been brought to their knees, and compelled to cry to God for mercy Dr. Gillies, in his *Historical Collections, relating to remarkable Periods of the Successes of the Gospel*, has many cases of a parallel character Indeed, scarce a revival of religion can be referred to, in which there have not been similar manifestations Into the physical causes of these excitements it would be vain to enter doubtless, there are cases which may be accounted for by the fact, that acute mental agony, such as the conviction of sin oft produces, acting upon a highly nervous temperament, will produce contortion of body, shrieks, and other symptoms of *hysteria*; but this does not meet one twentieth part of the cases which might be adduced. For instance : the reviler and opponent of religion is alike affected with the penitent mourner for sin the former is seized with convulsions in the very act of opposition, in direct antagonism to his mental leanings, his mind at the moment being affected only by contempt for the position of those around them ; no mere physical agency is at work in his case. As well might we account for St Paul's conversion by natural agency, as assume that any mere physical cause is at work in cases of this nature. We cannot but believe with Wesley and others, that the Almighty chooses these means "for the further manifestation of His work, to cause His power to be known, and to awaken the attention of a drowsy world."

E —*James Quinn*, page 41.

THE "Life of James Quinn," published in New York, is full of interesting facts connected with Methodist history, and gives the reader a very pleasing impression of his piety and zeal. The following graphic account of his eloquence and power in the pulpit, written by Bishop Morris will not be without interest :- -

"In the summer of 1812, when I was but a youth, and before I had any interest in Methodism, there was a Camp-meeting near where I resided in Western Virginia; and, attracted by the novelty of the occasion, in company with several associates, I repaired to it. The encampment was in a sequestered place, away from all public thoroughfares of travel, in a lonely wood, where nought but the voice of prayer, the song of praise, and the message of mercy, broke the impressive stillness of the forest The country was new and the population sparse, yet the people poured forth from farm and hamlet, hill and hollow, till a multitude had assembled, some to offer the sacrifice of the heart to God in the wilderness, but probably many more for mere recreation.   The general appearance of those present was what might have been expected,—that of rustic simplicity peculiar to new countries; yet they evidently felt, as I did myself, awed by the sacredness of the occasion, and conformed respectfully to the order of the public service.   The singing, though not scientific, was devotional and strictly congregational; so that the mingled voices of the many reverberated through the shady bowers like the roar of a mighty cataract, and were solemnly impressive.   After prayer and praise we heard a common-place discourse, of barely sufficient interest to secure respectful attention.   When the speaker had taken his seat, another of very different appearance rose up in the open stand, from whose remarks on the arrangements of the meeting we soon learned that he was the presiding officer of the District.   His features were comely, his form was symmetrical, and his movements were graceful.   He was in the vigour of life, of medium height, slightly corpulent, wore a loose, flowing robe; his countenance indicated heavenly serenity, and, taken altogether, made an appearance at once imposing and attractive.   Having finished his brief and well-timed announcements, he referred to the sermon summing up its parts in few words, like a wise master-builder, and explaining the use of each, he assumed the style of exhortation, earnestly persuading the people to embrace and practise what they had heard.   The slowly-measured but full-toned accents of his manly voice fell like heavenly music upon the ears and hearts of the enchained auditors, while the message of salvation, as borne by him, came to them as waters to a thirsty soul, and as good news from a far country.   As he progressed, he became inspired with his theme, and, rising from one point of interest to another, carried the whole assembly with him   Among the motives urged to leave off sinning and commence praying, was that of avoiding future misery and securing heavenly bliss.   Of the contrast between the final end of saint and sinner he furnished a scriptural example, which, though familiar to all, was so presented as to appear new; and fix a powerful impression.   Without circumlocution he recited the history of the rich man and Lazarus.   While portraying the sufferings of the beggar, his manner was plaintive and moving, but when introducing him by the ministry of angels to the society of redeemed and glorified spirits in the abodes of bliss, he became animating and inspiring, as if he saw the light of heaven, heard the music of angels, and felt the streams of consolation from the river of life.   But suddenly he recalled himself and hearers to attend to the case of the once wealthy and pompous, but now deceased and lost, sinner : 'The rich man also died, and was buried' Reciting these solemn words, the countenance and manner of the speaker were changed from joyful to sad, his trembling accents expressed the weight of anguish which pressed his heart; his eyes, which had just glowed with delight, now looked terrible things, as he saw the lost soul taking its downward plunge to endless perdition.   Then elevating his voice to its utmost extent, throwing his whole soul into his subject, and at the same time bringing his foot with all his might down upon the floor of the stand, he exclaimed, with fearful energy : 'And in hell he lifted up his eyes being in torment, and seeth Abraham afar off, and Lazarus in his bosom.' Cold chills ran all over us, the hair seemed to rise upon our heads, and the flesh to crawl upon our bones, while groans of pity and shrieks of horror commingled around us, like the startling tones of a sweeping tempest, attended with a shock of Divine power as sensibly felt as if it had been the tread of an earthquake. And, after all, his oratory was not the result of a studied art, but of nature inspired by grace, leaving a conviction that he was not only one of nature's noblemen, with a clear head and warm heart, but that he was an able minister of the New Testament, commissioned from Heaven as an ambassador of Christ, beseeching sinners to be reconciled to Him. Though I was but a youth when the scene transpired, all the changes of thirty-eight years have not been able to obliterate from my memory the impression which it produced. The name of that distinguished individual was James Quinn, of precious memory "

THE END.

LONDON: PRINTED BY WILLIAM NICHOLS 2 LONDON WALL

allen

Lightning Source UK Ltd.
Milton Keynes UK
UKHW022023200422
401802UK00006B/1310